COMPUTER SCIENCE
A Second Course
Using Modula-2

COMPUTER SCIENCE
A Second Course
Using Modula-2

Allen B. Tucker, Jr.
Colgate University

McGRAW-HILL BOOK COMPANY
NEW YORK ST. LOUIS SAN FRANCISCO AUCKLAND BOGOTÁ CARACAS
COLORADO SPRINGS HAMBURG LISBON LONDON MADRID MEXICO
MILAN MONTREAL NEW DELHI OKLAHOMA CITY PANAMA PARIS
SAN JUAN SÃO PAULO SINGAPORE SYDNEY TOKYO TORONTO

COMPUTER SCIENCE: A Second Course Using Modula-2
Copyright ©1988 by McGraw-Hill, Inc. All rights reserved. Printed in the United States of America. Except as permitted under the United States Copyright Act of 1976, no part of this publication may be reproduced or distributed in any form or by any means, or stored in a data base or retrieval system, without the prior written permission of the publisher.

1 2 3 4 5 6 7 8 9 0 HALHAL 8 9 2 1 0 9 8 7

ISBN 0-07-065444-1

This book was set in Bookman Light by Publication Services.
The editor was David M. Shapiro;
the cover was designed by John Hite;
the production supervisor was Diane Renda.
Project Supervision was done by Publication Services.
Arcata Graphics/Halliday was printer and binder.

Library of Congress Cataloging-in-Publication Data

Tucker, Allen B.
   Computer science.

   Bibliography: p.
   1. Modula-2 (Computer program language)   I. Title
QA76.73.M63T83   1988   005   87-26071
ISBN 0-07-065444-1

ABOUT THE AUTHOR

Allen B. Tucker, Jr., is the MacArthur Professor of Computer Science and Associate Dean of the Faculty of Colgate University. He served as Chair of the Computer Science Department at Colgate from 1983 to 1986, and at Georgetown University from 1976 to 1983. He received a B.A. in Mathematics from Wesleyan University in 1963, and an M.S. and Ph.D. in Computer Science from Northwestern University in 1970.

Professor Tucker has authored or co-authored numerous texts and research articles in the fields of programming languages, natural languages, and formal languages. His most recent research is in the area of artificial intelligence approaches to natural language understanding and translation, a project done in collaboration with Sergei Nirenburg and supported by the National Science Foundation. He has served often as an invited speaker and panelist at professional conferences and workshops.

Professor Tucker's professional interests also include the development of high quality undergraduate curriculum standards for computer science. He is currently a member of the ACM's Task Force on the Core of Computer Science and the Liberal Arts Computer Science Consortium. He serves as a reviewer for various conferences, journals, and publishers.

CONTENTS

Preface   xiii

1. COMPUTER SCIENCE AND PROGRAMMING METHODOLOGY   1

1-1	Rationale and Methodology: The Naive Instructor's Problem	3
1-2	A Modula-2 Overview	6
1-3	Organization for Team Programming: Abstraction	9
1-4	Program Verification	15
	1-4-1 Program Specifications for Verification	16
	1-4-2 Drivers	19
1-5	Computational Complexity	19
1-6	Problem 1: The Advanced Instructor's Problem	21
	Exercises	21

2. THE COMPUTING MACHINE   24

2-1	From Turing to von Neumann	24
2-2	Contemporary Machine Design	29
	2-2-1 Data Representation	30
	2-2-2 Addressing, Registers, and Instruction Sets	30
2-3	Low Level Facilities in Modula-2	32
2-4	Memory Representations of Elementary Types	35

	2-5	The Type BITSET and its Operators	38
		2-5-1 Bitwise Long Cardinal Sum	40
		2-5-2 Bitwise Long Cardinal Product	42
	2-6	Random Number Generation	43
		Exercises	47

3. LINEAR LISTS: AN ABSTRACT DATA TYPE — 50

3-1	Abstract Data Types: Linear List Definition	51
	3-1-1 The Constant Maxlist and the Global Variable Error	53
	3-1-2 Linear List Operator Definitions	53
	3-1-3 Notes on the Operator Definitions	56
	3-1-4 A Definition Module for Linear Lists	56
3-2	Controlling Memory Allocation in Modula-2: The Pointer	58
3-3	Contiguous Implementation of Linear Lists	61
	3-3-1 Type Implementation	62
	3-3-2 Operator Implementation	62
3-4	Verification and Complexity of the Contiguous Implementation	67
	3-4-1 A Driver for Verification of the List Operators	68
	3-4-2 Assertion-based Verification of the Insert Operator	69
	3-4-3 Complexity of the List Operators	71
3-5	Linking Memory Blocks Together in Modula-2: The Node	72
3-6	Linked Implementation of Linear Lists	74
3-7	Verification and Complexity of the Linked Implementation	81
3-8	Comparison of Implementation Strategies	83
3-9	Problem 1: The Advanced Instructor's Problem Revisited	84
	Exercises	89
	Team Project: Completion of the Less Naive Instructor's Problem	91

4. RECURSION, INDUCTION, AND VERIFICATION — 92

4-1	Recursive Functions and Modula-2	93
4-2	Recursion and Programming	97
	4-2-1 Recursive Definition of Mathematical Functions	97
	4-2-2 Recursion and Problem Solving: "Divide and Conquer" Algorithms	105
	4-2-3 Recursion and Linear List Operators	109
4-3	Recursion and the General Field of Computer Science	111
	4-3-1 Artificial Intelligence	111
	4-3-2 Formal Language Theory	112
	4-3-3 Programming Language Design	113
4-4	Inductive Verification: The List Search Operator	114
4-5	Recursion vs Iteration: Some Considerations on Efficiency	116

		Exercises	117
		Team Project	119

5. SORTING — 120

5-1	Selection and Insertion Sorts	121
	5-1-1 Analysis of Selection Sort: Best, Average, and Worst Case Assumptions	124
	5-1-2 Insertion Sort: An Improvement Under Best Case Assumptions	125
5-2	Shell Sort	126
5-3	Merge Sort	129
	5-3-1 Analysis of Merge Sort	134
5-4	Quicksort	135
	5-4-1 Analysis of Quicksort	138
5-5	HeapSort	139
	5-5-1 Analysis of HeapSort	142
5-6	Empirical Evaluation of Sorting Algorithms	142
5-7	Procedures as Parameters: A Useful Modula-2 Tool	144
	Exercises	145
	Team Project	147

6. STACKS AND QUEUES: HARDWARE AND OPERATING SYSTEMS — 149

6-1	Stack Definition and Operators	149
	6-1-1 Implementation of Stacks in Modula-2	151
	6-1-2 Verification and Complexity of the Stack Operators	155
	6-1-3 Computer Organization: Run-Time Stacks and Stack Machines	156
	6-1-4 Problem 2: Evaluation of Polish Expressions	159
6-2	Queue Definition and Operators	166
	6-2-1 Implementation of Queues in Modula-2	168
	6-2-2 Verification and Complexity of Queue Operators	171
	6-2-3 Operating Systems: An Overview	171
	6-2-4 Priority Queues	174
	6-2-5 Problem 3: Job Scheduling	178
	Exercises	179
	Team Project: Job Scheduling	180

7. STRINGS: TEXT PROCESSING AND INFORMATION RETRIEVAL — 181

7-1	String Definition and Operators	182
7-2	Implementation of Strings in Modula-2	189

	7-3	Verification and Complexity of the Search Operator	201
	7-4	Regular Expressions and Pattern Matching	204
	7-5	Information Systems: An Overview	207
	7-6	Problem 4: Text Search and Information Retrieval	208
	7-7	Generics, String Implementation, and Modula-2	212
		Exercises	213
		Team Project: A Simple Text Editor	216

8. TREES: COMPILERS AND ARTIFICIAL INTELLIGENCE — 217

8-1	Trees and their Properties	217
8-2	Binary Trees	222
	8-2-1 Binary Search Trees	222
	8-2-2 Binary Tree Balance and Search	224
	8-2-3 Binary Tree Traversal	227
	8-2-4 Binary Tree Operators	228
	8-2-5 Whole Tree Operators—Graft and Prune	236
	8-2-6 Additional Binary Tree Operators	237
8-3	Implementation of Binary Trees in Modula-2	238
	8-3-1 Basic Operator Implementations	241
	8-3-2 Tree Traversal, Inorder Search, and Binary Search	247
	8-3-3 Graft and Prune Operator Implementations	252
	8-3-4 Building a Balanced Binary Search Tree	253
	8-3-5 Verification and Complexity of Operator Implementations	258
8-4	An Overview of Compilers	260
	8-4-1 Problem 5: Parsing Arithmetic Expressions	263
8-5	Software Engineering and Object-Oriented Design	270
	8-5-1 Import-Export Trees	272
8-6	An Overview of Artificial Intelligence	272
	8-6-1 Trees and LISP Expressions	275
	Exercises	276
	Team Project: Parsing Regular Expressions	279

9. FILES AND HASHING: DATABASE MANAGEMENT SYSTEMS — 280

9-1	Secondary Storage Media and File Processing Principles	281
9-2	Modula-2 File Processing Facilities: The Module FileSystem	283
	9-2-1 Modula-2 File Characteristics	284
	9-2-2 Opening and Closing Files in Modula-2	284
	9-2-3 Reading, Writing, and Repositioning Within a Modula-2 File	285
	9-2-4 An Example of File Processing in Modula-2	287
9-3	Database Management Systems: Further Discussion	291
9-4	Random Access Files and Hashing	293
	9-4-1 Creating and Randomly Accessing a File in Modula-2	296

9-5	The Advanced Instructor's Problem Revisited	303
	Exercises	307
	Team Project: The Advanced Instructor's and Registrar's Problems Concluded	309
	Team Project: Bibliographic Information Retrieval Revisited	309

10. COMPUTER SCIENCE: THE DISCIPLINE IN PERSPECTIVE — 311

10-1	Defining Computer Science	311
	10-1-1 Tree Structure of the CR Categories	313
10-2	Algorithms, Data Structures, and Information Systems	319
	10-2-1 Graphs	319
	10-2-2 Complexity Classes and the Limits of Computability	320
10-3	Architecture and Concurrency	321
	10-3-1 Concurrency and Synchronization in Modula-2	322
	10-3-2 An Application: The Producer-Consumer Model	323
10-4	Operating Systems and the Human Interface	326
10-5	Programming Languages, Natural Languages, and their Processors	326
	10-5-1 Mice, Windows, and What About English?	327
	10-5-2 Language Processors: Compilers, Interpreters, and LISP Machines	329
	10-5-3 Fourth Generation Languages: The UNIX Environment	330
10-6	Mathematical Algorithms and Simulation	331
	10-6-1 Errors in Computer Arithmetic and Number Representation	331
	10-6-2 Mathematical Programming	332
10-7	Artificial Intelligence and Cognitive Science	333
10-8	Computer Science: The Discipline and the Profession	334
	Exercises	336
	A Short Annotated Bibliography of Selected Texts and References in Computer Science	338

APPENDIX A.	FROM PASCAL TO MODULA-2: AN INTRODUCTION	341
APPENDIX B.	ASCII CHARACTER SET	366
APPENDIX C.	MODULA-2 SYNTAX AND SEMANTICS	367
APPENDIX D.	MODULA-2 STANDARD LIBRARY DEFINITION MODULES	374
APPENDIX E.	ABSTRACT DATA TYPE DEFINITION MODULES	384
INDEX		395

PREFACE

OVERVIEW

This text is designed for use in a second course in computer science using Modula-2. Particular emphasis is placed on the principles of data abstraction, (informal) program verification, computational complexity, sorting, and certain abstract data types that occur throughout the study of computer science. These latter include linear lists, stacks, queues, strings, and trees. Additionally, the general field of computer science is introduced via a careful selection of examples, exercises, and team projects from the various core topics which collectively span the field. An overview of each topic, such as "operating systems," is placed strategically within the text. From this, the student not only learns about that topic as an application for the abstract data types but also gains an informed perspective that produces good answers for the question, "What is computer science?" We have chosen Modula-2 as the programming language for this course because of its strong support for the central concept of abstraction, its syntactic and semantic consistency with Pascal, and its widespread and efficient implementations on contemporary microcomputers, workstations, and timesharing systems.

MOTIVATION

The introductory curriculum in computer science has, over the last several years, undergone significant evolutionary changes. Because of these changes, the 1978 ACM standard[1] for the introductory courses, known as

CS1 and CS2, gave way in the early 1980's to the development of new standards for these two courses.[2,3] This text is designed to meet the newer ACM curriculum standard for CS2.[3]

This text also seeks to exceed that standard in significant ways, in an effort to broaden and upgrade the overall mission of the CS1-CS2 sequence. Our goals for CS2 extend beyond the traditional ones of teaching programming methodology and introducing data structures as the main subject matter. This point of view is strongly influenced by recent observations, perhaps most eloquently expressed by Peter Denning, which note that colleagues in other scientific disciplines are sometimes led by our current curriculum standards and our CS1-CS2 teaching style to the conclusion that computer science is nothing more than a lot of programming, and has little claim to calling itself a "science" in the usual sense. If computer science were really a science, these colleagues argue, then its core curriculum, beginning with CS1-CS2, would include theoretical and abstract principles (as well as implementation issues and applications which now appear), and a nontrivial overview of the field's major topics. To provide a constructive answer for these scientists, Denning outlines a broad definition of "computer science" as a science.[4] This definition promises to have significant impact on the content of future computer science curriculum standards.

Three concrete changes in the current CS1-CS2 sequence are suggested by this and other related work.[5,8] First, the introductory courses need to become more mathematical in style, requiring especially a discrete mathematics corequisite.[7] Second, a more rigorous treatment of the discipline of programming is needed. Students should become prepared to *analyze* the behavior and efficiency of a program, to *synthesize* programs from formal statements about their inputs and outputs, and to *reason* about the correctness of programs from these formal statements. In this regard, we are strongly influenced by the work of David Gries[6], which argues against the notion that programs are mere experiments that can be successively refined until they become "sufficiently bug-free." Instead, programming should be viewed as the development of algorithms which are provably correct, or *verifiable*, at the time they are written. Students who gain this ability to analyze and reason about program behavior tend to be ideally prepared to pursue further study in the "scientific" aspects of computer science at advanced undergraduate and graduate levels. Third, the introductory courses CS1-CS2 should contain significant discussions, examples, and exercises which collectively provide a broad overview of the major topic areas in the field of computer science. When students finish the CS1-CS2 sequence, they should be equipped to speak accurately to the question, "What is computer science?"

The incorporation of these three curricular changes affects, we believe, the CS2 course most significantly. These changes are reflected in a recent effort to define a model curriculum for a quality undergraduate major in computer science.[5] This model proposes that the CS2 curriculum be redesigned in the following way: "... CS2 should have the following principal themes:

- To consolidate the knowledge of algorithm design and programming that was gained in CS1, especially emphasizing the design and implementation of large programs.
- To begin a detailed study of data structures and data abstraction as exemplified by packages or modules.
- To introduce the uses of mathematical tools such as complexity (O-notation) and program verification.
- To provide an overview of computer science."

This text, together with the accompanying *Instructor's Guide* and diskette, is designed to meet these goals for CS2.

CONTENTS

The text begins by making a case for the systematic use of rigorous techniques for developing and verifying solutions to complex software problems. An introduction to the tools of program verification and computational complexity, and their use in solving such problems, is given in Chapter 1. There, we introduce the concepts of *assertions, preconditions, postconditions, invariants,* and *O-notation* that are used throughout the remaining chapters.

The second chapter continues to lay groundwork by exploring some essential underlying characteristics of *computer organization* that have immediate and continuing effect on problem solving and program design. Modula-2's "low-level facilities" are helpful here in exposing the ideas of memory addressing and number representation that are central to this level of study. For example, the mysteries of indirect addressing using the POINTER type and the origins of implementation-dependent maximum and minimum INTEGER values (-2^{15} through $2^{15}-1$) are exposed here.

The student's first thorough introduction to an *abstract data type*, the linear list, occurs next in Chapter 3. There, the distinction between the definition and the implementation of an abstract data type is explained, and the tools for large program design are presented and illustrated. The tools for informal program verification and complexity measurement are used here. As motivation, the choice between the contiguous and linked implementations for linear lists is exposed and evaluated.

Chapter 4 is devoted entirely to *recursion*. Its purpose is to help the student to understand the central role that recursion plays in computer science, and to become comfortable with the specification, implementation, and verification of recursive procedures. The strong intuitive connection between recursion as an execution-time phenomenon and induction as a verification tool is identified and illustrated here.

The next five chapters (Chapters 5-9) are devoted to covering essential concepts in sorting, stacks, queues, strings, trees, and files. Each chapter uses the same principles of data abstraction, verification, and complexity that were introduced in the first four chapters. Also, these chapters contain topical overviews of distinct areas in the field of computer science where such concepts are used. For example, Chapter 6 introduces the queue as an abstract data type, and then gives an overview of *operating systems* as a contextual vehicle for showing an application of the queue. Chapter 8 does the same, using the tree as an abstract data type and *compiler design* as a topical application domain. While none of these topics can be covered in an exhaustive way, these overviews nevertheless provide a reasonably representative impression about the broad substance of computer science as students work through these chapters.

Chapter 10 has two goals. The first is to introduce certain advanced topics in computer science that are not covered in the first nine chapters. In particular, we introduce the idea of *concurrency* and illustrate a simple example in Modula-2. The second goal of Chapter 10 is to review and summarize the broad discipline of computer science. It provides a well-focused and concise look at the field, and at the same time unifies the different concepts presented in the earlier chapters.

WHY MODULA-2?

In a nutshell, the subject of data abstraction is central in the CS2 curriculum, Modula-2 supports abstraction very well, Modula-2 has efficient implementations on microcomputers, workstations, and time-sharing computers. As our reference for the language, we use Niklaus Wirth's *Programming in Modula-2: Third, Corrected Edition*.[9] Instructors are cautioned that the second edition of this book varies slightly from the third, and some Modula-2 compilers may still not be updated to accommodate these variations. See Appendix C for more discussion of these variations.

Aside from its strong support for data abstraction and its efficient implementations, Modula-2 has another important advantage for CS2; it is a natural extension and refinement of Pascal (also designed by Niklaus Wirth). Students who have used Pascal in the CS1 course will find that the transition to Modula-2 is easy and natural. To facilitate this transition, Appendix A provides an introduction to Modula-2 for Pascal programmers. After completing one or two programming exercises, students should have little difficulty using Modula-2 for the remainder of this text.

Finally, Modula-2 is a robust language, designed to serve the needs of students in advanced computer science courses that will follow CS2 in the curriculum. For instance, Modula-2's support for concurrency is useful for advanced courses in operating systems and networking. Its support for data abstraction is useful for advanced courses in software engineering, compiler design, and database systems.

TEAM PROJECTS, LABORATORIES, AND SOFTWARE ENGINEERING

An important objective for the CS2 course, therefore, is to provide laboratory experiences that significantly enrich student views of the software development process. CS1, by contrast, usually contains an individualized laboratory experience; students work separately on problems, and individual creativity is encouraged in solving them. Problems are usually "small" in the sense that the resulting programs typically contain no more than a page or two of coding.

CS2, on the other hand, attempts to develop styles of interaction among students working in groups on somewhat larger laboratory assignments. Principles of software engineering tend to be introduced here, especially the idea of "top-down design" and "egoless programming." Concurrently, the programming problems tend to exceed, in their size, those which would normally be expected of a single student using normal working habits.

This text supports that style of laboratory activity by giving a "Team Programming Project" at the end of almost every chapter. Because these projects also require the use of abstract data types already implemented in the text, a diskette containing ASCII copies of all these implementations is provided along with an *Instructor's Guide*. Thus, the instructor can quickly bring the Modula-2 laboratory environment to a level of full support for the example programs and laboratory exercises that appear in this text. Students should be encouraged to *use* these implementations wherever possible, rather than "reinventing the wheel." The programming teams can therefore concentrate immediately upon the project at hand, exploiting the full functionality of this preexisting software library. Our experience shows that two- or three-student teams are most workable for handling the end-of-chapter team projects.

THE ABSTRACT DATA TYPES

The main abstract data types (data structures and related operators) that gain significant attention in this text are linear lists (Chapter 3), stacks and queues (Chapter 6), strings (Chapter 7), and trees (Chapter 8). Each one is defined abstractly in the initial part of its respective chapter, using precise specifications, or "preconditions" and "postconditions." Implementations of these operators in Modula-2 are then presented, discussed, and verified. Significant attention is also given to the *complexity* of those operator implementations in which efficiency is critical to performance. Finally, the applications of each abstract data type, both across the general field of computer science and in a particular problem selected from the field, are presented.

This order of presentation reinforces our principal aim of separating the *specification* of an operator from its *implementation*. With such separation, students can explore opportunities to reimplement a particular specification in two, three, or more different ways (on grounds of efficiency, verifiability, or readability). Students thus appreciate the preeminence of specification over program coding, and the importance of mathematically precise expressive styles in the design, implementation, and verification of algorithms.

INFORMAL PROGRAM VERIFICATION IN CS2

David Gries' excellent monograph *The Science of Programming* is written for use at the advanced undergraduate level in the computer science curriculum. It takes a strong position with respect to the proof of program correctness; namely that the proof of a program's correctness should ideally precede and motivate the implementation of the program itself. Thus, once the program is written it is necessarily correct; only minor syntactic errors could stand between the coding of the program and its correct functioning on the computer.

For the CS2 course, we take a somewhat more conservative approach to the relationship between a program's implementation and its verification. Like Gries and many others, we support the idea that programs should follow from precise specifications—in the form of explicit *preconditions* and *postconditions*. However, we rely upon fairly conventional and well-tested techniques to guide the program implementation itself, leaving its verification to follow the program's implementation rather than to lead it. Our verification techniques are nevertheless based directly upon the information provided in the preconditions and postconditions which compose the operator definitions themselves. We also draw heavily upon the natural parallels that exist among mathematical induction, recursion, and the specification of loop invariants. A careful discussion of these parallels appears in Chapter 4.

STRONG TYPING AND GENERICS IN MODULA-2 AND CS2

Modula-2 is a strongly-typed language; perhaps excruciatingly so in some instances. The advantage of strong typing, of course, is that more kinds of program errors are detectable at compile time, allowing students to establish better control of run-time behavior than they usually can with a weakly-typed language. Modula-2 is even more strongly typed than Pascal! For instance, Pascal's generic "Read" procedure is replaced in Modula-2 by the suite of procedures "ReadReal," "ReadInt," "ReadString," and so forth.

In this book, we consciously extend this strong typing philosophy wherever it makes sense, as we implement various abstract data types. For instance, the general operator "search" is implemented for different data types with different names; "SearchString," "SearchTree," and so forth. The advantage here, again, is improved program documentation and reliability.

However, this approach sometimes interferes with the competing idea of making procedures as generic as possible. Ada, for instance, allows its procedures to be generic, so that programmers need not reimplement the same function redundantly each time it is applied to arguments of a different data type. Modula-2, on the other hand, does not directly support generic procedures, although some work has recently been done to allow generic behavior to be simulated in Modula-2. We applaud these efforts, but we believe that the introduction of generic programming styles may not be in the best interests of the CS2 course. Later in the curriculum, additional programming techniques, including the selective use of generic procedures, will inevitably be taught.

COURSE ORGANIZATION

Most (if not all) of the material in this text can be covered in a one-semester course in CS2. Either of two different approaches can be followed. The first approach emphasizes the principles of abstract data types and team programming projects, while paying less thorough attention to verification and complexity issues. Such a course is heavily laboratory oriented, and requires students to work in groups to solve the "Team Programming Projects" at the end of various chapters. The second approach emphasizes the principles of abstract data types, verification, and complexity, while giving less emphasis to the team projects. This latter approach includes more written assignments and fewer programming assignments than the former.

Either approach should begin with the study of data abstraction, verification, complexity, and recursion that appears in chapters 1-4. Some instructors may wish to skip the low-level details of material in Chapter 2, and this is an acceptable choice. In any case, these chapters can be covered in the first five weeks of a 14-week semester. Chapters 5,6 and 8 are also essential chapters, requiring anywhere from five to seven weeks in total, depending on the amount of laboratory work that will be assigned. Chapter 7 should be covered before Chapter 8, but this coverage may be done lightly (i.e., the String abstract data type definition may be studied and its implementation details may be skipped) if the time remaining in the semester does not permit a careful treatment of strings. The study of trees (Chapter 8), however, should be covered carefully. The study of files (Chapter 9) deserves one week, and at least two lectures at the end of the semester should be reserved for Chapter 10. This provides an opportunity for students to crystallize their ideas about the field of computer science while, at the same time, they are completing the last Team Programming Project from Chapter 8 or Chapter 9.

An *Instructor's Guide* and accompanying diskette are also available for this text. The *Guide* contains answers to selected exercises, discussions of team projects, transparency masters, and some information about compiling and running Modula-2 programs on certain microcomputer, workstations, and timesharing systems. The diskette contains ASCII files for all of the Modula-2 data abstractions and sample programs in this text, so that no time needs to be spent tediously retyping program listings. In fact, the CS2 instructor should encourage students to freely copy these procedures and data type definitions as they work through the exercises and team projects.

ACKNOWLEDGMENTS

The development of a textbook is a synthesis of ideas from many persons, spread over a long period of time from start to finish. In writing this text, I am especially grateful to the following persons for their inspiration, guidance, and support during various stages of this textbook project.

To my friends and colleagues in the Liberal Arts Computer Science Consortium—Jim Bradley, Joyce Brennan, Kim Bruce, Jim Cameron, Bob Cupper, Scot Drysdale, Steve Fisk, Norm Gibbs, Jane Hill, Stu Hirschfield, Nancy Ide, Charles Kelemen, Bob Noonan, Jeff Parker, Rich Salter, Greg Scragg, Michael Schneider, Ted Sjoerdsma, and Henry Walker—whose intense curriculum efforts during our summer workshops (especially at Bowdoin in 1984 and Colgate in 1985) provided the original intellectual and pedagogical inspiration for developing this text. The Model Curriculum[5] cited above is the product of this Consortium's work.

To the reviewers—Mark Berger, Al Crawford, Peter Denning, Terry Gill, Brian Johnson, Deepak Kumar, Tom Myers, Rich Pattis, Lawrence Rose, David Saunders, and Ron Wallace—who helped guide the evolution of this manuscript in all of its stages. To my COSC420 students at Colgate, and to the CSCI136 students at Williams (led by David Levine), who have bravely and willingly class-tested this manuscript in advance of its publication.

To Colgate University, for its exceptionally strong support of computer science education and research, and to Dean Charles Trout at Colgate, who generously allowed me a work schedule that enabled this project to be completed expeditiously. To the MacArthur Foundation, whose generous support has allowed me to participate in professional activities that complement this project.

To Professors Michael Flynn, Albert Grau, and Gilbert Krulee, my graduate instructors and advisors at Northwestern University several years ago (and to whom this text is dedicated), for their early commitment to principles and theory in computer science education, and for their lifelong professional commitment as computer scientists and educators.

Finally, and most importantly, to my family—Meg, Jenny, Brian, Cleo, Tinker, Helen, Daryl, and Daryl—who have survived yet another of Dad's writing projects; they inspire my work and my life with their immeasurable love and fortitude.

REFERENCES

1. ACM Curriculum Committee on Computer Science, "Curriculum 78: Recommendations for the Undergraduate Program in Computer Science," *Communications of the ACM 22,3* (March, 1979) 147–166.
2. Koffman, E., P. Miller, and C. Wardle, "Recommended Curriculum for CS1, 1984," *Communications of the ACM 27,10* (October, 1984) 998–1001.

3. Koffman, E., D. Stemple, and C. Wardle, "Recommended Curriculum for CS2, 1984," *Communications of the ACM 28,8* (August, 1985) 815–818.
4. Denning, P., "The Science of Computing: What is Computer Science?" *American Scientist 73* (January, 1985).
5. Gibbs, N. and A. Tucker, "Model Curriculum for a Liberal Arts Degree in Computer Science," Communications of the ACM (March, 1986) 202–210.
6. Gries, D., *The Science of Programming*, Springer-Verlag, 1981.
7. Ralston, A., "The First Course in Computer Science Needs a Mathematics Corequisite," *Communications of the ACM* (October, 1984).
8. Shaw, M. (ed), *The Carnegie-Mellon Curriculum for Undergraduate Computer Science*, Springer-Verlag (1985).
9. Wirth, N., *Programming in Modula-2: Third, Corrected Edition*, Springer-Verlag, 1985.

COMPUTER SCIENCE
A Second Course
Using Modula-2

1
COMPUTER SCIENCE AND PROGRAMMING METHODOLOGY

A first computer science course is mainly a course in problem solving and programming. By its nature, though unintentionally, this course tends to leave the impression that the entire field of computer science is essentially programming. While the discipline of programming is an important step in one's initial encounters with computer science, it is really just the tip of the iceberg. Indeed, we would not be overstating the case to say that programming relates to the study of computer science as writing relates to the study of English literature. In this text, therefore, it is our purpose to broaden and enrich the study that was begun in the first computer science course, so that readers may gain an appreciation for the entire field of computer science: its principles as well as its applications, its theories as well as its experiments, its limitations as well as its fast and powerful machines and algorithms.

To begin, *computer science* can be broadly defined as the study of algorithms and data structures, including (1) their formal properties, (2) their linguistic and mechanical realizations, and (3) their applications. That is, the computer scientist studies and explores the principles that underlie algorithmic behavior, linguistic representations (programs and languages) of algorithms, and efficient mechanical realizations (actual computers and abstract machines) of algorithms. Formal properties of algorithms and data structures, including their theoretical foundations, are expressed in classical mathematical styles. Applications of the discipline include programming language design, compiler design, operating system design, natural language understanding, cognitive modeling, database design, computer networking, and many more. Thus, computer science is a far broader discipline than the reader may have assumed after completing the first course in the curriculum.

This second course is therefore designed to help develop this broader view of computer science. Here, we depart from the groundwork of the first course in four fundamentally new directions. First, we begin the systematic study of particular data structures, the operators that typify their manipulation, and some powerful alternatives (beyond the array) for implementing them. Second, we integrate the style and certain principles of discrete mathematics into the analysis and verification of algorithms (programs). Third, we begin to explore the characteristics of contemporary computers, where these data structures and their operators are implemented. Fourth, we give an historical and interdisciplinary survey of fundamental applications where these data structures and operators are widely used — including, information systems, artificial intelligence, compilers, and operating systems.

This chapter begins by reviewing basic principles of problem solving and program design and their realization in the Modula-2 programming language. Readers who are not already familiar with Modula-2 will be relieved to know that it is a straightforward extension of Pascal; the transition from Pascal to Modula-2 should be a relatively painless exercise. Appendix A, an introduction to Modula-2 for Pascal programmers, is provided to ease this transition; readers will be advised to read this appendix later in the chapter as it becomes necessary. Those facilities of Modula-2 that extend beyond Pascal will be fully introduced in later parts of this text as they are needed.

Perhaps the most important difference between Modula-2 and Pascal is Modula-2's extensive support for implementing an *abstract data type*. That is, a new data type may be defined (such as the "complex numbers"), together with its associated operators (such as "add" and "subtract"), as an addendum to those data types and operators that already exist in the language (such as "real" and the associated operators for real arithmetic). To implement such an extension in Modula-2, we may independently compile and save it in a permanent library for future use, just as if it were an ordinary member of Modula-2's own standard repertoire of types and operators.

Thus, an important goal of this course is to introduce, in a formal way, the major abstract data types and their associated operators, along with appropriate techniques for verifying them and analyzing the efficiency of their associated implementations. In support, the requisite principles of computer organization are introduced in Chapter 2, and the necessary mathematical tools of algorithm analysis and verification are developed in Chapters 1, 3, and 4. The notion of *abstract data type* is carefully introduced in Chapter 3 and illustrated with the linear list as an example. There, the linked and the array implementations are introduced separately, in order to draw further attention to the distinction between an abstract data type and its implementation(s).

1-1 RATIONALE AND METHODOLOGY: THE NAIVE INSTRUCTOR'S PROBLEM

To provide an immediate point of departure for the study of computer science in this course, let's take a look back at a problem that typifies the simpler ones that occurred in the first course. We call it the Naive Instructor's Problem. (By the way, it is the problem that is naive, not the instructor!) This problem might be informally described as follows:

> Given a list of student names, with three test scores for each name, develop a program that computes and displays the average of these scores for each student.

A sample of typical input and output for one run of this program is shown below.

Name	score 1	score 2	score 3	Average
backus	75	85	95	85.0
wirth	85	85	85	85.0
turing	90	85	80	85.0
gries	86	84	85	85.0
vonneumann	91	82	82	85.0
mccarthy	70	85	100	85.0
lovelace	55	100	100	85.0
church	80	80	95	85.0
markov	90	90	75	85.0
hopper	70	90	95	85.0
naur	84	84	87	85.0

Here, the input appears in the first four columns and the output appears in the last column. An interactive program for this problem should provide suitable prompts and headings so that the input is entered correctly and the output is well documented.

As we can see, this is not a particularly difficult problem, provided that we make the following assumptions (which are typical for a first-course treatment of this problem):

(1) Input is correct and complete.
(2) Input is presented student by student and all at one terminal session.
(3) Input for any number of students may be presented.
(4) All scores are presented on the same (100-point) numeric scale.
(5) Exactly three test scores appear for each student.
(6) No provision is made for changes in the class enrollment during the semester (i.e. "drop-add").
(7) Output appears in the same order as the input.

(8) All three test scores are equally weighted in the calculation of a student's average.

These assumptions tend to make the problem naive, in comparison with the requirements of "real" instructional and course management settings.

For example, in a real setting the collection of data during a semester usually occurs column by column, not row by row, as the grades are recorded for each individual exam. The list of names for the course (the first column) is established at the beginning of the semester, and each successive column is appended as the semester progresses. Some grades may, in fact, be on a 100-point scale, while others are on a different scale and may also, for that matter, contribute a different weight to the course average. During the semester, some students may drop the course, others may be missing a grade or two, and still others may be added to the initial class list. Such "real" considerations inevitably lead to a more circumspect approach to the problem's solution. We will return to a revised statement of this problem at the end of the chapter so that readers may begin to consider the additional design requirements that accompany a realistic solution.

For the moment, however, let us pause to review a Pascal program for the solution of this naive version of the problem.

```
program NaiveInstructor (input, output);
{ This program computes the average of three scores for
  each of an arbitrary number of students. }

type score = 0..100;
     array3 = array[1..3] of score;
var scores: array3;


procedure GetScores (var scores: array3);
{ This procedure obtains a student's name and three test
  scores from the terminal.  The name may not exceed 15
  characters.  The scores should be within the range
  0..100. }
var name: packed array[1..15] of char;
    i: integer;
begin
  i:=1;
  read(name[1]);
  while (i<15) and (name[i]<>' ') do
    begin
      i:=i+1;
      read(name[i])
    end;
  read(scores[1],scores[2],scores[3])
end;
```

```
procedure ShowAverage (scores: array3);
{ This procedure computes and displays the average of an
  individual student's three test scores. }
var average: real;
begin
   average:=(scores[1]+scores[2]+scores[3])/3;
   writeln(average:10:1)
end;


begin
   writeln('Enter a student name and three scores on ');
   writeln('each line.   End the last line with ctrl-z.');
   writeln;
   writeln('Name          score1   score2   score3    Average');
   writeln;
   repeat
      GetScores (scores);
      ShowAverage (scores)
   until eof(input)
end.
```

This program contains two procedures, GetScores and ShowAverage, whose purpose is self-evident. The simple logic of the main program appears as a single loop in which these two procedures are alternately invoked until end-of-file (ctrl-z in Turbo Pascal) is signaled at the terminal. Each iteration of the loop adds a new line of input and output to the run. The complete output occurs, therefore, as described earlier.

Some principles of program design are illustrated in this program, even though it is a very simple one. Indentation, comments, and line spacing conventions are used consistently, in order to improve program readability. A glimmering of top-down design is illustrated in the appearance of two separate procedures for input and output.

However, evidence of inflexibility is also apparent, in the sense of the assumptions under which this program is written. Some of that inflexibility can be quickly removed by making simple changes in the program. For instance, a slight change to procedures GetScores and ShowAverage, as well as the declaration of array "scores" itself, would permit the program to weaken assumption (5) so that it reads "There may be any number, up to a limit of (say) 15, of scores per student."

Other kinds of inflexibility, however, are not so easily removed. For example, what redesign would be required to alter assumptions (2), (6), and (7) so that they could read as follows?

(2)′ Input is presented one test at a time, using as many terminal sessions as there are tests during the semester.

(6)' Students may be dropped and/or added to the class list at any session.

(7)' Output is to appear, at the end of any session, in alphabetical order by student name.

These "weakened" assumptions (2)' and (6)' and "strengthened" assumption (7)' lead to a more serious kind of program revision. The overall size and complexity of the resulting program may grow substantially as each of these new assumptions is incorporated. It is a purpose of this text to introduce new program design tools and data abstractions that will make that task a reasonable one.

1-2 A MODULA-2 OVERVIEW

To some extent, certain limitations of the Pascal language itself tend to stand in the way of our solving "real" problems like the one suggested by revised assumptions (2)', (6)', and (7)'. For instance, we know that a Pascal array parameter must be declared with a fixed subscript range, which seriously restricts the generality of the procedure where it occurs. We also know that Pascal has no standard provisions for separate compilation of procedures or other parts of a program, which seriously inhibits efforts to develop and implement large programs.

Yet, we know that Pascal is a sound beginning language, and we are reluctant to "throw out the baby with the bath water" in abandoning it. Pascal's strong typing, clear syntax, widespread implementations, and other features combine to encourage good style and run-time reliability. These features should be retained as we choose a more robust language for more complex problem-solving tasks.

One such language, Modula-2,[1] was designed with exactly these ideas in mind. Its inventor, Niklaus Wirth, was also the inventor of Pascal.[2] In designing Modula-2, he was careful to retain the basic stylistic and semantic principles of Pascal. Yet, Modula-2 significantly exceeds Pascal because it strongly supports modular design and implementation methodologies that underlie contemporary principles of software engineering. Modula-2 also eliminates many of Pascal's troublesome limitations, such as the restricted use of array parameters noted above.

As a point of departure, we give below a simple Modula-2 program, which is an exact transliteration of the foregoing Pascal implementation of the Naive Instructor's Problem. So that we may initially show the syntactic and semantic similarities between the two languages, an effort was made to make the Modula-2 version conform stylistically to the Pascal version as much as possible. The one important divergence in our handling of array parameters that does occur here will be explained later.

[1] Wirth, N., *Programming in Modula-2:* 3rd edition, Springer-Verlag, 1985.

[2] Wirth, N. and K. Jensen, *Pascal User Manual and Report*, 2nd edition, Springer-Verlag, 1978.

```
MODULE NaiveInstructor;

FROM InOut IMPORT ReadString, ReadCard, termCH,
                  WriteLn, WriteString;
FROM RealInOut IMPORT WriteReal;

(*This program computes the average of three scores for
  each of an arbitrary number of students.*)

CONST EOF=32C;     (*ctrl-z is ASCII 32C, or end-of-input*)
TYPE score=[0..100];
VAR scores: ARRAY[1..3] OF score;

PROCEDURE GetScores (VAR scores: ARRAY OF score);
(*This procedure obtains a student's name and test scores
  from the terminal.  The name may not exceed 15 characters.
  The scores should be within the range [0..100].*)
VAR name: ARRAY[0..15] OF CHAR;
    i: CARDINAL;
BEGIN
  ReadString(name);
  WriteString ('    ');
  FOR i:=0 TO HIGH(scores) DO
    ReadCard(scores[i]); WriteString ('    ')
  END
END GetScores;

PROCEDURE ShowAverage (scores: ARRAY OF score);
(*This procedure computes and displays the average of an
  individual student's test scores.*)
VAR sum, i: CARDINAL;
BEGIN
  sum:=0;
  FOR i:=0 TO HIGH(scores) DO
    sum:=sum+scores[i]
  END;
  WriteReal(FLOAT(sum)/FLOAT(HIGH(scores)+1),10);
  WriteLn
END ShowAverage;

BEGIN
  WriteString('Enter a student name and three scores on');
  WriteLn;
  WriteString('each line.  End the last line with ctrl-z.');
  WriteLn;
  WriteString('Name         score1   score2   score3   ');
  WriteString('Average');
  WriteLn;
```

```
        REPEAT
            GetScores (scores);
            ShowAverage (scores)
        UNTIL termCH=EOF
    END NaiveInstructor.
```

In this listing, first notice the major similarities between Modula-2 and Pascal: similar type and variable declarations, similar procedure and parameter syntax and semantics, and similar syntax in general. Second, notice the following essential distinctions between the two languages at this elementary level:

- The program heading in Pascal is replaced by the heading "MODULE NaiveInstructor;" in Modula-2, which serves exactly the same purpose. The Modula-2 notion of "module" is thus comparable with the Pascal notion "program," in the sense that each is a complete unit of text to be compiled. Later, we shall see that individual procedures and groups of procedures may also be separately compiled as Modula-2 modules.
- In fact, the "IMPORT" statements, such as the two statements beginning "FROM InOut. . ." and "FROM RealInOut. . ." in this example, are needed at the beginning of any module that invokes procedures from other separately compiled modules. In this example, we import the input/output procedures ReadString, ReadCard, and so forth from the module InOut and the procedure WriteReal from the module RealInOut.
- Modula-2 subrange types are enclosed in brackets [ ], as shown in the type declaration for "score," whereas they are not so enclosed when declared in a Pascal program.
- The procedure ReadCard in Modula-2 reads a single CARDINAL value (which is similar to a Pascal integer value in the range 0..maxint). In general, each of Modula-2's standard input-output procedures transfers only a *single* value, rather than a list of values (as in Pascal's readln). Thus, we need to execute three ReadCards rather than just one, in this example program.
- The end of each procedure declaration in Modula-2 is always marked explicitly by the procedure's name. Thus, we see "END GetScores;", "END ShowAverage;", and "END NaiveInstructor." This convention serves to help document major boundaries within the text of the program.
- In the Modula-2 procedure ShowAverage, the calculation of the average is accomplished with the help of the built-in function FLOAT, which converts an INTEGER value to an equivalent REAL. (In general, the process of converting a value of one type to an equivalent value in another is called "coercion.") With respect to arithmetic expressions, Modula-2 is even more strongly typed than Pascal; mixed types are strictly forbidden, and a full complement of built-in functions is provided to assist the programmer to explicitly specify all necessary coercions.

The global CHARACTER variable "termCH" is exported by the Modula-2 InOut module as a device for marking the end of input. It always contains the last character value read from the terminal by the program. The expression "termCH = EOF," where EOF is a special character value that is used only to mark end-of-file (ctrl-z in our example), is thus equivalent to the Pascal expression "eof(input)."

The parameter named "scores" in each of the two procedures GetScores and ShowAverage is declared as an array without an explicit subscript range. This is an example of the so-called "open array parameter" in Modula-2, which is provided to relax Pascal's more severe restrictions on array passing. Specifically, any open array parameter, say AP, for the purposes of the body of the procedure where it is declared, is assumed to have subscript range [0..HIGH(AP)], where HIGH is a Modula-2 built-in function (just like FLOAT). All references to individual elements of AP, of the form AP[i], within the body of the procedure must assure that i is within that range. Now, when the procedure is invoked with a corresponding array argument, say A, it may have any subscript range [m..n]. At the time of invocation, the value of HIGH is dynamically computed as the difference $n-m$ (one less than the number of elements in the array A.

In our example, for instance, the argument is an array "scores" with subscript range [1..3]. At the time of the invocation of GetScores or ShowAverage, the individual entries of the argument and the corresponding parameter are matched with each other in the following way:

argument	scores[1]	scores[2]	scores[3]
parameter	scores[0]	scores[1]	scores[2]

Thus, the value of HIGH(scores) for this invocation is 2, and all references to individual entries of the array parameter, scores[i−1], affect the entries scores[i] in the corresponding actual array, which is the argument in the invocation.

A more systematic and complete introduction to Modula-2 for Pascal programmers is given in Appendix A. Readers who have only Pascal experience are encouraged at this point to read Appendix A and work its exercises before proceeding further in this chapter. The advanced features of Modula-2 that are extensions of Pascal will be introduced directly in later chapters of this text as they are needed.

1-3 ORGANIZATION FOR TEAM PROGRAMMING: ABSTRACTION

In making strong distinctions between "naive" and "advanced" versions of a problem, we require the immediate introduction of additional program design and implementation methodologies beyond those that accompany the first computer science course. These methodologies reflect the complex process of realistic software design, which cannot be circumscribed in a single sitting by a single person. Typically, the design and implementation of advanced software systems is accomplished by teams of persons, who collectively integrate entire suites of procedures, both prewritten and newly designed.

In this course, you will be encouraged to engage in this kind of activity. To support your work, Modula-2 contains facilities that support such team programming, and we shall exploit these facilities regularly. In particular, the team's creative energies are most effectively used when its members do *not* "reinvent the wheel" whenever the services of a fairly standard procedure are needed. Instead, the programming team will be encouraged to search the available procedure libraries to locate procedures that can participate in a problem solution. When such procedures are incorporated, documentary comments should be added to their headings to identify the source from which the procedure was obtained. This practice is thus equivalent to the time-honored practice of adding footnotes to document the use of borrowed ideas during the preparation of a scholarly paper.

As suggested in the solution to the Naive Instructor's Problem, Modula-2 provides library modules (such as InOut and RealInOut) that are separately compiled and contain generally useful procedures, types, and variables (such as ReadCard, termCH, and WriteReal). This facility is extended to the programmer; additional modules may be separately defined and then compiled independently of the program(s) that will ultimately use their embedded procedures, types, and variables.

To accomplish this, the programmer writes two distinct modules bearing the same name: a so-called DEFINITION MODULE and a companion IMPLEMENTATION MODULE. The DEFINITION MODULE serves simply to identify those procedures, types, and global variables that will be exported by the module. The IMPLEMENTATION MODULE contains, on the other hand, the complete code that defines the functioning of these procedures, types, and variables whenever they are exported to another program.

A most important aspect of this separation of a module into two distinct parts is that the DEFINITION MODULE may be compiled separately, before its companion IMPLEMENTATION MODULE is written. Moreover, any program that uses procedures from such a module may be compiled (but not executed) as soon as the DEFINITION MODULE is compiled, even though the corresponding IMPLEMENTATION MODULE is not yet written. This is an extremely useful device for top-down programming, since the general organization and key data structures and linkages may be established and verified without necessarily going to the bottom of the code for the most detailed procedures in the problem solution. This situation is shown graphically in Figure 1-1.

The second important concept supported by the separation of a module's definition from its implementation is related to the idea of developing independent and competing implementation strategies. That is, once

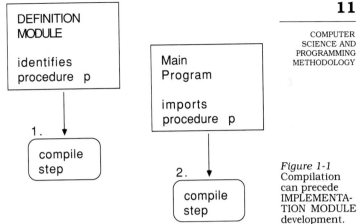

Figure 1-1
Compilation can precede IMPLEMENTATION MODULE development.

the DEFINITION MODULE is compiled, two or more alternative companion IMPLEMENTATION MODULEs may be written and evaluated, without either recompiling the DEFINITION MODULE or recompiling any of the programs that use the module's exported procedures. Second, the ability to develop an IMPLEMENTATION MODULE separately allows us to test its various procedures for correctness before any of them are actually imported by an application program. This separation, of course, allows a large task to be divided conveniently among several members of a team, and then the members of the team may work relatively independently in accomplishing their subtasks. This flexibility is displayed graphically in Figure 1-2.

In either of these "new" situations, however, it is important to stress that an addititonal step, called "linking," is needed before any actual execution of the main program module can take place. This is shown graphically in Figure 1-3. The purpose of linking is to draw together, into one executable unit, all the results of separately compiled modules as well as the

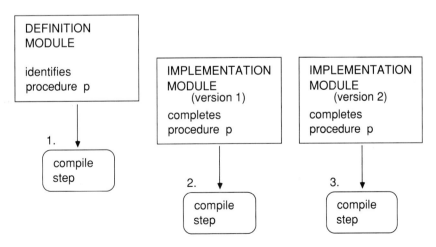

Figure 1-2
Compilation of alternative implementation versions.

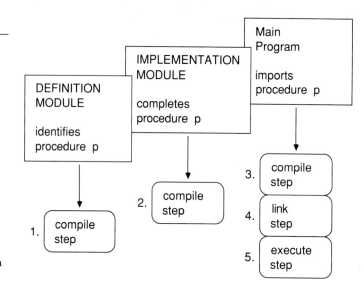

Figure 1-3
The link step must precede main program execution.

executable units for procedures imported from Modula-2's various standard libraries (especially the input-output procedures). The process of linking is unfamiliar to many Pascal programming environments, especially those that do not provide support for separate compilation of procedures.

To give a more concrete illustration of these ideas, suppose we reorganize the Modula-2 solution to the Naive Instructor's Problem and assign the type score and the procedures GetScores and ShowAverage to a separate library, say, NaiveLib. The definition module for NaiveLib follows.

```
DEFINITION MODULE NaiveLib;

EXPORT score, GetScores, ShowAverage;

(*This definition module identifies the opaque type score and
    the procedures GetScores and ShowAverage and their parameters.
    These three will be imported by the program NaiveInstructor. *)

TYPE score;

PROCEDURE GetScores (VAR scores: ARRAY OF score);
(*This procedure obtains a student's name and test scores
    from the terminal.  The name may not exceed 15 characters.
    The scores should be within the range [0..100].*)

PROCEDURE ShowAverage (scores: ARRAY OF score);

(*This procedure computes and displays the average of an
    individual student's test scores.*)

END NaiveLib.
```

Notice here that only the procedure headings for GetScores and ShowAverage are present, along with some explanatory comments and the acknowledgment that "scores" is a type. Neither the extended bodies of these procedures nor the completion of the type scores is needed in advance of the separate task of coding the IMPLEMENTATION MODULE for NaiveLib.

When we give such an abbreviated declaration of a new type in a DEFINITION MODULE, in which only the name of the type appears, this is called an "opaque type" declaration. The main implication of an opaque type is that any program using that type may make no assumptions about the details of that type—whether it is INTEGER or REAL, whether it is numeric or nonnumeric, and so forth. None of the program's statements that use variables of such an opaque type may therefore manipulate those variables explicitly! All such manipulation must be done by the procedures that accompany the identification of that type within the accompanying IMPLEMENTATION MODULE. In our example, for instance, "score" is an opaque type; the details of its declaration are left to the IMPLEMENTATION MODULE for NaiveLib, and so are the details of those procedures that manipulate variables of type "score" or GetScores and ShowAverage.

Continuing this example, the above DEFINITION MODULE gives all the information that is needed for the main program to be rewritten *and* recompiled. The program NaiveInstructor can thus be rewritten as follows.

```
MODULE NaiveInstructor;

FROM InOut IMPORT WriteString, WriteLn, termCH;
FROM NaiveLib IMPORT score, GetScores, ShowAverage;

(*This program computes the average of three scores for
   each of an arbitrary number of students.  It uses the type
   score and the procedures GetScores and ShowAverage which
   are separately defined and implemented in the module
   NaiveLib.*)

CONST EOF=32C;       (*ctrl-z is ASCII 32C, or end-of-input*)
VAR scores: ARRAY[1..3] OF score;

BEGIN
   WriteString('Enter a student name and three scores on');
   WriteLn;
   WriteString('each line.  End the last line with ctrl-z.');
   WriteLn;
   WriteString('Name         score1    score2    score3    ');
   WriteString('Average');
   WriteLn;
   REPEAT
     GetScores (scores);
     ShowAverage (scores)
   UNTIL termCH=EOF
END NaiveInstructor.
```

Here, we have made three important changes from the original version. First, an IMPORT statement has been added to indicate the separate module (NaiveLib) and the objects (score, GetScores, and ShowAverage) that will be imported by this program. Second, the IMPORT statements for InOut and RealInOut are changed from their original versions. This change reflects the fact that certain procedures are no longer explicitly used within the body of the main program and will instead be imported by the IMPLEMENTATION MODULE NaiveLib as they are needed. Third, the type declaration for score and the procedures GetScores and ShowAverage are now physically absent from the body of the main program (an IMPORT statement is in their place). Yet the main program may nevertheless be compiled separately.

Before we can execute this program, however, two additional steps are needed: the IMPLEMENTATION MODULE for NaiveLib must be written and compiled, and the main program must be linked with the compiled modules for all of the procedures that it imports. The IMPLEMENTATION MODULE for NaiveLib is shown below.

```
IMPLEMENTATION MODULE NaiveLib;

FROM InOut IMPORT ReadString, ReadCard, WriteLn,
                  WriteString, Done;
FROM RealInOut IMPORT WriteReal;

(*This module completes the implementations of the opaque
   type score and the procedures GetScores and ShowAverage.
   Its compilation must precede the linking and execution of
   the main program NaiveInstructor.*)

TYPE score = [0..100];

PROCEDURE GetScores (VAR scores: ARRAY OF score);
(*This procedure obtains a student's name and test scores
   from the terminal. The name may not exceed 15 characters.
   The scores should be within the range [0..100].*)
VAR name: ARRAY[0..15] OF CHAR;
    i: CARDINAL;
BEGIN
  ReadString(name);
  WriteString ('     ');
  FOR i:=0 TO HIGH(scores) DO
    ReadCard(scores[i]); WriteString ('    ')
  END
END GetScores;

PROCEDURE ShowAverage (scores: ARRAY OF score);
(*This procedure computes and displays the average of an
   individual student's test scores.*)
VAR sum, i: CARDINAL;
```

```
BEGIN
   sum:=0;
   FOR i:=0 TO HIGH(scores) DO
      sum:=sum+scores[i]
   END;
   WriteReal(FLOAT(sum)/FLOAT(HIGH(scores)+1),10);
   WriteLn
END ShowAverage;

END NaiveLib.
```

Here, we see finally the full declaration for the type score, together with the complete implementations of the two procedures GetScores and ShowAverage. The original program is thus reconstituted in its entirety, but now in a modular form with separate elements that can be managed independently.

The basic idea of *abstraction* reflects a conscious process of generalizing a type, procedure, or data structure in such a way that it can serve more purposes than the one for which it was originally designed. In redefining the solution of the Naive Instructor's Problem as we did, two important kinds of abstraction took place. First, the definition of the type "score" was separated from the main program and united with the two procedures that have particular interest in it. This allows for later refinements which, for example, might permit scores on the scale of 'A' through 'F' to be averaged as well as 0 through 100. Such refinements could be carried out entirely within the confines of NaiveLib's implementation, without any particular knowledge or alterations on the part of the program NaiveInstructor itself.

The second kind of abstraction that was exploited in the revision of this example involved the procedures GetScores and ShowAverage themselves. They were originally written so that they could process any number of scores, not just three. Their repackaging and export by a separate module makes these procedures more generally available as utility procedures for use in other programs beyond the NaiveInstructor program. For example, it is easy to envision some other program using the procedure ShowAverage to display an average of any collection of numbers, whether they represent test scores, ages, weights, times, or any other entities. Our preference for labeling the module where they are defined as a "library" kind of module (NaiveLib) tends to emphasize this conscious effort to promote wide utility through generalization. For instance, if the procedure ShowAverage were needed to display the average of an array of weights, it could be immediately IMPORTed from the module NaiveLib by the program that needs it. No further rewriting or recompiling of ShowAverage needs to be done.

1-4 PROGRAM VERIFICATION

We always try to develop programs that are correct. That is, we want them to give a predictable, well defined output for every reasonable set of input values that can occur. Unfortunately, our natural optimism causes us to overestimate our programs' tendencies to be correct; we often take too narrow a view of the diverse input combinations that may occur when our program goes into productive use. To offset these tendencies, some recent work in programming methodology has been aimed at helping programmers produce more reliable software. Certainly, the modular style that is explicitly supported by Modula-2's separate compilation contributes to improvements in this direction. In this book, we will use two specific methods for program verification. One is the use of a semiformal method of program specification and correctness proof. The other involves the detailed use of so-called "drivers," which allow us to vigorously exercise procedures separately as they are implemented and before they are incorporated for use by an application program. These are explained more fully in the following discussion.

Scientific principles for program verification are rapidly emerging. Students who will later read David Gries' excellent book, *The Science of Programming* (Springer-Verlag, 1981), will discover a mathematically based approach to program verification that may eventually provide substantially better verification methods than those now in use. In this course, we will take a first step toward this more advanced, yet ideal solution to the problem of program verification. Thus, in leaving the development of *formal* verification techniques to a more advanced course in the curriculum, we will concentrate here on laying appropriate groundwork—or *informal* verification methods—with which disciplined approaches to the vigorous study of program behavior may be introduced and exercised.

1-4-1 Program Specifications and Verification

Throughout this text, we will add *comments* to our programs in a very disciplined way. A comment will serve one of two purposes: (1) it will explain the general purpose of a procedure, variable, or other entity within the program; or (2) it will make a declarative statement, or *assertion* about the values of certain variables or other entities at the particular spot in the text of the program where the comment appears. Readers should be very familiar with the first kind of comment from prior experience in the first course. Examples of that kind appear at key points in the text of the foregoing example program NaiveInstructor.

The second kind of comment, or *assertion*, will be distinguished from the first in the text of a Modula-2 program by using the extended delimiters (** and **) for enclosure rather than the usual delimiters (* and *). The latter will continue to be used for type (1) comments. When placed within a particular point of a program, an assertion describes the possible range of values of all variables that are of interest when that particular point is reached during execution of the program. For example, suppose we see the following assertion and surrounding program statements:

```
k:=1;
(**0<=n<=10 and k=1**)
WHILE k<=n DO ...
```

This says that immediately after the assignment statement is executed and immediately before the WHILE statement is executed, the values of the variables k and n are guaranteed to be as described within the assertion, at exactly that point during program execution.

Further, three special classes of assertions play distinguished roles in the specification and verification of procedures and programs.

1. A *precondition* is an assertion that describes the possible values of all relevant variables and input immediately before a procedure or program segment begins execution. To denote that it is a precondition, this assertion is always placed just after the first BEGIN in the procedure or program it accompanies and is written in the following special way:

```
(**PRE: text of the assertion **)
```

2. Likewise, a *postcondition* is an assertion that describes the possible values of all relevant variables and output immediately after a procedure or program segment ends execution, assuming that the accompanying precondition is also satisfied. To denote that it is a postcondition, this assertion is always placed just before the last END within the procedure or program and is written in the following special way:

```
(**POST: text of the assertion **)
```

3. An *invariant* is an assertion that is used to describe the behavior of a loop within the body of a program or procedure. In particular, an assertion is a loop invariant if it is true before the first iteration of the loop and it remains true (i.e., it doesn't vary) after each successive iteration of the loop, including the last iteration. A loop's invariant is always placed just after the first statement of the loop itself and is written in the following special way:

```
(**INV: text of the assertion **)
```

To give an example of the use of preconditions, postconditions, and invariants in a procedure, the following rendition of the GetScores procedure is shown below with these three assertions added at the appropriate places.

```
PROCEDURE GetScores (VAR scores: ARRAY OF score);
(*This procedure obtains a student's name and test scores
   from the terminal.  The name may not exceed 15 characters.
   The scores should be within the range [0..100].*)
VAR name: ARRAY[0..15] OF CHAR;
    i: CARDINAL;
```

```
BEGIN
(**PRE: input is a 15-character string followed by a fixed
    number (say n) of integers.**)
        ReadString(name);
        WriteString ('    ');
        FOR i:=0 TO HIGH(scores) DO
(**INV: 0<=i<=n and scores[0..i-1] = the next i input
    integers.**)
            ReadCard(scores[i]); WriteString ('   ')
        END
(**POST: name = the input character string and
    scores[0..n-1] = the next n input integers.**)
END GetScores;
```

To a certain extent, the incorporation of these special assertions within the text of a procedure tends to replicate some of the function of the informal comments at the top of the program, which were there originally. Yet, the purpose of each is different. The informal comments, on the one hand, are placed so that the casual reader will obtain a fairly clear idea of the purpose of the procedure. The assertions, on the other, are more formal statements about the procedure's behavior and are necessary if we want to systematically verify the correctness of the procedure. What do we mean by "correctness" in this sense?

> A procedure is said to be *correct*, or *verified*, if all possible values for the input and variables that are defined by its precondition allow us to systematically infer (by hand-tracing an execution of the procedure's body) that the procedure satisfies its postcondition.

During this verification process, we will occasionally need to hand trace our way through a loop; at this point, the discovery and insertion of an appropriate loop invariant is essential. For instance, consider our invariant for the loop in the GetScores procedure. Before the first iteration of this loop, the invariant is certainly true, since i=0 and scores[0..-1]=the next 0 input integers (that is, none of the entries in scores and none of the input integers has yet been affected). Now, after each iteration of the loop, this assertion remains true since i is increased and the next input integer has been read and stored in scores[i-1]. Finally, after the *last* iteration, we see that this invariant resolves into an affirmation of the postcondition for the GetScores procedure.

Although these verification methods are quite disciplined, they are not fully formal in the sense of a mathematical proof of correctness. Yet, the systematic use of such informal methods, as we face the need to demonstrate the correctness of various procedures in this text, will help to develop the kind of skill in analyzing program behavior that is needed for developing formal mathematical proof techniques at a more advanced level in one's study of computer science.

Techniques for finding loop invariants and other relevant assertions during the process of program verification will be further developed as we proceed through this text.

1-4-2 Drivers

Another method for verifying a procedure or collection of procedures is to design a simple main program that vigorously exercises them, using a variety of different input values (in accordance with their respective preconditions). This allows the development of larger and more complex programs (in which the procedures will ultimately be embedded) to be delayed until the procedures themselves are verified. In this method, the simple main program is called a "driver," and its outputs are displayed in a form that allows quick sight-checking of each procedure's results (satisfaction of its postconditions).

Our example program for NaiveInstructor is so simple that to write a driver for checking the outputs of the procedures GetScores and ShowAverage would require more work than to implement the NaiveInstructor program itself. We therefore defer the development of an actual driver until the next chapter, in which more substantial requirements for manual program verification present themselves.

In summary, we shall use consistent program verification methods throughout this text in two complementary ways:

1. Documenting the program and each procedure with appropriate preconditions and postconditions, and (with the use of appropriate loop invariants) demonstrating by hand that the program or procedure satisfies its postconditions for any collection of values which satisfies its preconditions.
2. Using a driver to test a procedure independently, so that for any set of values that satisfy the preconditions, the procedure's outputs are displayed for manual sight-checking of postcondition satisfaction.

This methodology, if carefully followed, will provide tools to both develop reliable software and evaluate existing software for correctness.

1-5 COMPUTATIONAL COMPLEXITY

Evaluating efficiency is another principal issue in the development of large programs. That is, how well is the program designed with respect to the actual environment in which it will run? Answering this question is often a difficult and underestimated problem, and yet students should routinely expect to do so throughout their study of computer science.

More specifically, the field of computational complexity within computer science is a collection of exact methods for measuring the performance of an algorithm and then expressing these measures mathematically. Performance may be measured in either *time* or *space*, and usually as a function of the number n of input elements that will be processed by the algorithm. Time is expressed abstractly as the average number of *steps* executed during a run of the procedure that implements the algorithm; space is measured as the number of units of *storage* consumed by such a run.

As an example, consider the procedure ShowAverage in the revised version of the Modula-2 solution to the Naive Instructor's Problem, repeated below with comments removed and line numbers added, for later reference.

```
1   PROCEDURE ShowAverage (scores: ARRAY OF score);
2   VAR sum, i: CARDINAL;
3   BEGIN
4      sum:=0;
5      FOR i:=0 TO HIGH(scores) DO
6         sum:=sum+scores[i]
7      END;
8      WriteReal(FLOAT(sum)/FLOAT(HIGH(scores)+1),10);
9      WriteLn
10  END ShowAverage;
```

Lines numbered 1 through 3 and 10 are essentially declarative, and lines 4 through 9 contain the "executable" parts of the program. The analysis of a procedure's time complexity, therefore, can be based on counting the number of times that each of its statements is executed.

Except for the loop in lines 5 through 7, each of the statements in this procedure is executed exactly once, for a total of three steps. Within the loop itself, we count one step for the initial assignment of i, and n steps [n is the size of the array scores, given by HIGH(scores)+1] for each of the two "hidden" steps that test the value of i and increment the value of i, respectively. Finally, n additional steps are executed for line 6 itself. Thus, assuming each statement's step size (execution time) is the same, the following expression gives the total number of steps for executing the entire procedure ShowAverage. This is an expression of the *complexity* of ShowAverage.

$$\text{Number of steps} = 3n + 4$$

As shown, the complexity of this procedure varies linearly with the size of its input, n. If, say, n=3, then the number of steps for executing ShowAverage is 13. On the other hand, if the number of scores is 10000, the number of steps becomes 30004.

In general, the complexity of an algorithm may often be expressed as a polynomial with the variable in the expression denoting the size of the input to the algorithm. Since polynomials are expressions of the form:

$$\sum_{i=0}^{k} a_i n^i = a_0 + a_1 n + \ldots + a_k n^k$$

where n is the size of the input, the *degree* k of the polynomial (rather than the particular values of its coefficients a_i) tends to govern the magnitude of any calculation of the algorithm's complexity.

For that reason, we say that an algorithm is of order n^k in complexity when the polynomial representation of its step count is of degree k. The phrase "order n^k" is generally abbreviated by the expression $O(n^k)$ for notational convenience. Thus, the complexity of our ShowAverage procedure is order n, or $O(n)$ for short, since the polynomial representation of its step count is $3n+4$, which has degree $k=1$.

1-6 PROBLEM 1: THE ADVANCED INSTRUCTOR'S PROBLEM

In concluding this chapter, we pose a revision of the Naive Instructor's Problem as a subject for further study in later parts of the text.

> For an arbitrary course, and for an arbitrary moment during the grading period where a series of adds, drops, and test scores is to be entered, update the standing records for that course and, if requested, display the records for any or all students who are currently enrolled in it.

The solution for this problem may not be readily apparent after only a brief consideration of its design implications. Thus, we aim in this course to develop appropriate abstractions—data structures and algorithms—that will help make this kind of problem reasonably solvable. Such a solution should be sought with an eye to producing a program that is both mechanically verifiable (in the sense discussed in this chapter) and minimally complex. A solution to this kind of problem will generally result from a team effort, including the use of independently written library procedures, rather than a mammoth all-night effort by a single person. We shall return to consider a solution of this problem later in the text, after we have studied some of the data structures and algorithms which it requires.

EXERCISES

1-1. Do the exercises at the end of Appendix A; compile, link, and run the resulting Modula-2 programs.

1-2. For the procedure AMAX, which you wrote in exercise A-2 of Appendix A, add appropriate preconditions and postconditions to define its purpose.

1-3. Give an invariant for the loop that you wrote in the procedure AMAX in exercise A-2 of Appendix A.

1-4. Give a clear argument for the correctness of your procedure AMAX. Specifically, demonstrate that your loop invariant is satisfied upon entry to the loop, for any particular set of values that satisfy the preconditions, and that upon exit from the loop, the invariant is still satisfied. Finally, show that the procedure's postcondition is satisfied after exit from the loop and any remaining statements in the procedure are executed.

1-5. Compile, link, and run our second Modula-2 version of the Naive Instructor's Problem on your system. Note any system-dependent differences, especially in the input/output modules available, for future reference.

1-6. Rewrite the procedure GetScores in our second Modula-2 version of the Naive Instructor's Problem so that it will accept one or more missing grades for an individual student and record them as zeros. Recompile NaiveLib after making this change and relink the main program. Exercise the resulting program with the following data (-1 means "missing").

Name	score1	score2	score3
backus	75	85	95
wirth	-1	85	-1
turing	90	-1	80
gries	-1	-1	85
vonneumann	-1	-1	-1

In making this change, you need only to recompile the IMPLEMENTATION MODULE NaiveLib; no alterations or recompiling should be needed for the main program itself.

1-7. The following problem might be called the Naive Registrar's Problem. At the beginning of the semester, each student's name and course registration is given to the university registrar. The registrar, in turn, must determine the total number of students enrolled in every course. For example, the following input data should yield the resulting counts below it.

Student	courses				
backus	cosc101	hist200	engl101	chem101	math111
wirth	engl101	cosc101	phil320		
turing	math111				
gries	hist200	math410			
vonneumann	phil320	eeng200	engl101	cosc101	
mccarthy	eeng200	phil200	math111	chem101	cosc101
lovelace	cosc101	engl101			
church	cosc101	phil 320	engl101		
markov	math111	engl101	chem101		
hopper	chem101	cosc101			
naur	math410	phil320			

Course	Enrollment
cosc101	7
hist200	2
engl101	6
chem101	4
math111	4
phil320	5
math410	2
eeng200	2

Write a program to accomplish this task, assuming any number of students, but no more than 5 courses per student or 100 different courses altogether.

1-8. Make a complete list of the assumptions you made when designing a solution to the Naive Registrar's Problem.

1-9. Redefine the Naive Registrar's Problem so that the input assumptions identified above are weakened as much as possible (in the interest of making the problem more realistic) and the output assumptions are strengthened (to the same end).

1-10. Implement the slight generalization of the Naive Instructor's Problem that is suggested in the text. That is, write an Initialize procedure that obtains from the terminal the number of scores per student that are to be averaged (up to a maximum of, say, 15). Add this procedure to NaiveLib and then alter the main program accordingly. Appropriate changes should be made to those versions of GetScores and ShowAverage that already appear in NaiveLib.

1-11. Document your solution to the Naive Registrar's Problem by giving, for each procedure and the main program, its preconditions and its postconditions and, for each loop, its invariant.

1-12. Determine the complexity of the procedure you write for gathering the input in your solution to the Naive Registrar's Problem by counting the number of steps that will be executed for an arbitrary number, n, of students and writing a polynomial expressing that count. How many steps will be executed for a student body of 300, assuming 5 courses per student? How many for a student body of 30000? Is your procedure $O(n)$?

1-13. What is computer science? Be prepared to refine your answer to this question as you proceed through the text.

THE COMPUTING MACHINE

This chapter begins with a brief historical introduction to the concepts that led to the development of the modern computer. The Turing machine and the von Neumann machine model are especially distinguished in this introduction, which lays important conceptual groundwork for the study of computer organization and architecture in later courses. For our purposes, this material also sets the stage for studying the influence of computer organization on software design.

Here, we first identify Modula-2's elementary types and the details of their machine implementations. The notion of an *address* is also presented, along with the use of Modula-2's low-level facilities for displaying the contents of memory addresses for various types of values. Second, we examine the use of low-level facilities for extending Modula-2's elementary types, by defining the new type *long cardinal.* The utility of this is shown in the development of a random number generator, which is itself an important tool for many applications of computer science. In later chapters, we shall have use for the output of the random number generator, especially in the evaluation of various sorting strategies (Chapter 5). Third, the principles of abstraction and program verification that were introduced in Chapter 1 are also reinforced in this chapter.

2-1 FROM TURING TO VON NEUMANN

In the middle 1930s, the British mathematician Alan Turing published a paper[1] containing an abstract model of a very simple computing machine.

[1]Turing, Alan M., On Computable Numbers, with an Application to the Entscheidungsproblem, *Proc. London Math. Soc.*, Ser 2-42, 230-250.

That model was later dubbed the "Turing machine," and its operational principles strongly influenced the designs of the first computers during the close of that decade and the beginning of the next.

The Turing machine model is depicted in Figure 2-1, where we see four distinct parts. The *tape* is assumed to contain an arbitrarily long (yet finite) string of characters, initially the "input" to the machine. The *read-write head* is positioned to scan a single character at a time, to replace that character on the tape by a different character, and to reposition itself, or shift, one character to the left or right on the tape. The *state transition function* is a fixed sequence of instructions that direct the machine's activities (movements, scans, and replacements by the read-write head on the tape). Finally, the *control* is a mechanism that carries out the instructions given by the state transition function.

More precisely, the state transition function specifies in tabular form an action that the read-write head can take for each of the different possible scanned symbols and current states that can exist. At the beginning, a finite set of states $\{q_0, q_1, \ldots, q_n,$ and h (for "halt")$\}$ and a finite alphabet of tape symbols $\{0, 1,$ and b (for "blank")$\}$ are assumed. The possible single-step transitions that can be made for a particular "current state" and "current scanned symbol" are:

1. Move the read-write head one symbol to the left on the tape (designated by "L") and transfer to another state.
2. Move the head one symbol to the right (designated by "R") and transfer to another state.
3. Replace the current scanned symbol on the tape by another one in the alphabet and transfer to another state.

Initially, it is assumed that the read-write head is scanning the leftmost symbol on the tape, the tape has a finite sequence of 1s and 0s at its left end (which represent the machine's input) followed by an infinite sequence of b's, and the machine is in state q_0. The control then interpretively executes the steps specified by the transition function and thus transforms the "input" on the tape to an "output," stopping when state h is reached.

As an illustration, consider the following Turing machine designed to add two nonnegative integers together, leaving their sum on the tape. The integers are assumed to be stored initially as unary values (sequence

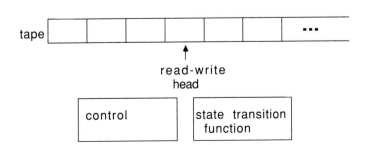

Figure 2-1 Organization of a Turing machine: functional elements.

of 1s), separated from each other by a single 0. Addition, in this context, is achieved by concatenation. That is, for example, the sum of 3 and 4 (given as 111 and 1111) is represented by 1111111. This Turing machine is shown below in Figure 2-2.

A trace of the execution for this input shows that the machine stays in state q0 as long as 1s are scanned; when 0 is reached it is replaced by 1 and state q1 is entered. Here, q1 scans right across the second sequence of 1s until it reaches blank (b). There, state q2 is entered, the 1 at the right end of the second string is erased, and the machine halts there. Thus, concatenation of two strings of 1s is achieved by inserting a 1 between them and deleting a 1 at their right end.

Although this is a very simple example, it does gives the reader a general feeling for the basic flavor and elementary nature of Turing machines. The spirit of programming is here, even though the operations are primitive. This fact should not, however, lead to hasty conclusions about the power of Turing machines in general. That is, the Turing machine model has been shown to be incredibly powerful in the following two ways:

1. There is an encoding scheme, and a very special Turing machine called the Universal Turing machine, that will simulate the behavior of any other (special-purpose) Turing machine when an encoding of the latter is placed on the Universal machine's tape.
2. Any procedure that can be effectively described in a programming language (or a sufficiently precise form of English) can equivalently be represented as a Turing machine.

The first finding, that of the existence of a Universal Turing machine, led to the realization of the notion of a "stored program" computer: one that, when finished executing one program, could execute an entirely different program by simply loading an encoding of that new program on its tape. The second finding, a conjecture posed by Alonzo Church and known widely as "Church's thesis," assures us that *any* programming language, from Pascal to machine language or Lisp or Modula-2, is equivalently adequate for expressing any algorithm and, moreover, none is intrinsically any more powerful than the basic Turing machine itself!

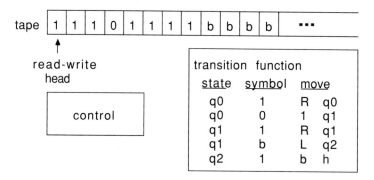

Figure 2-2
Turing machine that adds two integers.

Not only is this finding of great practical significance, it preserves the simplicity of the basic Turing machine model for theoretical studies in computer science. The use of Turing machines and other abstract computational models comprises a significant part of what we call the "theory of computation." These abstractions and their behavior have contributed not only to the design of actual computers and languages, but also to our understanding of the limits of computational models and processes in general.

By the early 1940s, several development projects had more-or-less independently arrived at the first practical realizations of the Turing machine model. Predominant among these are Eckert and Mauchly's ENIAC, Aiken's Mark I, Atanasoff's ABC, Wilks' EDSAC, and von Neumann's EDVAC. Although these models were conceptually similar, only the last two fully incorporated the stored program concept that was the hallmark of the Universal Turing machine. As computers have become refined over the years, they retained this basic characteristic, and thus most contemporary computers have come to be known collectively as "von Neumann machines." Most modern computers are still based, in their designs, upon the fundamental characteristics of the von Neumann model, which is pictured in Figure 2-3.

In this figure, we see that the storage medium of the Turing machine has now been subdivided into three parts; the *input tape*, which contains the input to the program: the *output tape*, which contains the program's output; and the *memory*, which contains an encoding of the program itself. Moreover, four special registers are added in order to allow the *control* to more accurately keep track of the state of program execution. First, the MAR, or memory address register, keeps track of the address (location in memory) where an operand of the currently executing instruction is stored. Second, the ACC, or accumulator, keeps track of the result of the most recent arithmetic calculation that has been executed. Third, the IR, or instruction register, contains a copy of the actual instruction that is currently being executed. Fourth, the PC, or program counter, keeps track of the address where the currently executing instruction itself is located.

To illustrate, let us briefly look at a program segment within the PDP-8 computer, a very popular version of the von Neumann model that was

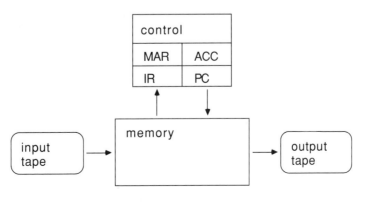

Figure 2-3
Organization of a von Neumann machine: functional elements.

developed by Digital Equipment Corporation in the 1960s. The memory of a PDP-8 consists of an array of 12-bit memory words whose addresses are represented in octal notation, as illustrated in Figure 2-4.

Notice here both the correspondences and the differences between the PDP-8 memory and the original Turing machine tape. The main differences are that the PDP-8 memory is *finite* in size and that the address assignments to all of the individual memory words allow the control to directly, or *randomly*, access any memory word. (This idea is the origin, by the way, of the term "random access memory," or RAM for short.) The Turing machine, recall, is an abstract model and therefore can postulate an infinitely long tape and a single read-write head, which in practice might take all day to reach a location on the tape, moving one symbol at a time.

The memory of the PDP-8 was designed to hold both program instructions and data, as a concrete realization of the concept originated in the Universal Turing machine. The excerpt in Figure 2-4 shows a sequence of *four* instructions at the addresses 0200-0203 and *three* data values at the addresses 0256-0260. The instructions that are available for writing machine language programs on the PDP-8 are more powerful than the elementary shift-left, shift-right, and rewrite instructions of the Turing machine, but not much. Each instruction is distinguished by a 3-bit *operation code*, so there are only eight different basic operations altogether on the PDP-8. For example, the binary operation code 001 (octal 1) designates "integer addition," and the operation code 100 (octal 4) designates transfer of control or "go to."

A complete PDP-8 instruction is given by its 3-bit operation code and a nine-bit *operand*, the latter specifying the memory address where a data value to be affected by the operation is stored. Indeed, the *address* of an operand in a machine language instruction plays the same role as the *identifier* of an ordinary variable in a Modula-2 statement. In the Figure 2-4 excerpt, we have the machine instruction 1256, which means literally to "perform integer addition [operation code 1] using as an operand the integer at the memory address 0256 [which is 0046]."

To facilitate execution of programs, the PDP-8 contains a small collection of special purpose 12-bit registers. These are called the program counter (PC), the accumulator (ACC), and the memory address (MAR). The PC keeps track of the address of the instruction currently being executed by the control unit. The MAR keeps track of the address of the operand of that

address	0	...	0200	0201	0202	0203	...
value		...	7600	1256	1257	3260	...

address	...	0256	0257	0260	...
value	...	0046	0037	0000	...

Figure 2-4 PDP-8 memory values and addressing.

instruction. Because each instruction allows only a single operand, those that perform two-operand functions, such as addition, use the accumulator (ACC) as an implicit second operand and result register. Thus, to add two integers in machine language, one integer must be previously moved into the ACC before the add instruction is executed.

Moreover, the result of each arithmetic instruction is left in the accumulator (ACC), so that if it is to be retained for subsequent use, it must be moved out of the ACC into a distinct memory location. To illustrate these points, let us return to the simple example of integer addition, which was simulated in the Turing machine model using unary notation and concatenation to accomplish the task. The instructions at locations 0200-0203 in Figure 2-4 simulate the Modula-2 statement z:=x+y (where x, y, and z are INTEGER variables), in which we associate the identifiers x, y, and z with the memory addresses 0256, 0257, and 0260, respectively.

Address	Instruction	Meaning
0200	7600	Clear the ACC (set ACC:=0).
0201	1256	Add x to ACC.
0202	1257	Add y to ACC.
0203	3260	Store this sum in z.

Thus, the effect of executing this sequence of machine instructions is conceptually the same as that of the foregoing Turing machine, except that now the addressing mechanism allows us to randomly access data stored anywhere within the memory, not just that currently scanned by the read-write head. The octal result, 0105, is thus left in location 0260 at the completion of these four instructions.

2-2 CONTEMPORARY MACHINE DESIGN

The PDP-8 was one of the first commercially successful realizations of the von Neumann machine, but there were many more. The decades of the 1960s, 1970s, and 1980s were marked by refinements and extensions of this basic model, in the interests of expanding its programming power and speed. Church's thesis notwithstanding, the realization of even the simplest of practical applications using an instruction set of only eight basic instructions and an address space of only 4096 words was a very tedious process.

In this section, we trace that evolution by examining the respective memory organizations, instruction set sizes, and programming considerations inherent in three contemporary species of computers: the Intel 8088, the Digital VAX, and the IBM 3081. The purpose of these illustrations is to complete the thread of von Neumann machine design that was begun in the last section and to lay a foundation for examining the machine representations of Modula-2 data types and addressing in the next section. Familiarity with this low level of representation will be also useful from time to time throughout this text, as various aspects of abstraction and computational complexity are discussed.

2-2-1 Data Representation

In machine designs since the PDP-8, the 12-bit word size has given way to the 8-bit *byte* as the elementary unit of storage. For one reason, the byte is the unit of representation for the nearly universal ASCII code (American Standard Code for Information Interchange) for the machine representation of characters. Because eight bits are an inconvenient basis for displaying binary values in octal, the *hexadecimal* representation ("hex" for short) for memory and addressing displays has come into widespread use. Since eight bits resolve exactly to two hexadecimal digits, the contents of each byte in memory is easily represented in this fashion. A brief look at Appendix B shows, for example, that the hex representation of the character 'A' is 41, the digit '0' is 30, and the symbol '+' is 2B.

Another prominent data representation scheme is the EBCDIC code (Extended Binary Coded Decimal Interchange Code), whose widespread use was popularized by the evolution of IBM's family of mainframe computers during the last two decades. Unfortunately, this scheme is fundamentally incompatible with the ASCII code, in the sense that the EBCDIC hex representation of each character is different from the ASCII hex representation of the same character.

2-2-2 Addressing, Registers, and Instruction Sets

In the PDP-8 the 12-bit word also was the unit of addressing, in the sense that each word had a memory address different from that of its immediate neighbors by a unit increment or decrement. In contemporary machines, this unit of addressing is the byte, and the notion of "word" now takes on a different meaning with each different machine species. For instance, the units of addressing for the Intel's 8088 (for the IBM PC), Digital's VAX, and IBM's mainframe are summarized in Figure 2-5.

Data representations for integers, reals, and other common data types also vary among the different machine species. We have already noted

	8088	VAX	IBM
unit of addressing	byte	byte	byte
2 bytes =	word	word	half word
4 bytes =		longword	word
8 bytes =		quadword	double word

Figure 2-5 Units of addressing in contemporary machines: the "word."

variations in representation for characters between the ASCII set and the EBCDIC set. These variations will be further explored in the next section.

Contemporary machines also extend the PDP-8's provision of a single accumulator to the provision of several so-called "registers." These are used for a variety of different operand addressing schemes beyond the simple, direct addressing scheme of the PDP-8. For example, the IBM mainframe provides sixteen "general purpose registers" and four "floating point registers" (the latter are reserved for REAL arithmetic operations). The VAX provides 16 general registers also, together with an additional memory area, called a "run-time stack," which helps control the structure of execution among procedures. In this sense, the run-time stack is an extension of the PDP-8's memory address register (MAR). The 8088, even though it is classed as a microcomputer, has an equally extensive collection of registers, addressing modes, and data representations.

The *instruction sets* of contemporary machines are also far more extensive than the PDP-8's 8-instruction repertoire. A single instruction consists, again, of an operation code (or "op code" for short) and 0, 1, 2, or 3 operands, each of which designates a memory or register address where a value is stored and will affect (be affected by) the outcome of the operation specified by the op code. The op code itself typically requires an entire 8-bit byte and therefore allows for potentially 256 different operations to be specified directly in machine language.

To illustrate these ideas, we again recast our simple addition program into three different forms: the machine languages of an 8088, a VAX, and an IBM mainframe. These are shown in Figure 2-6. Here, we assume that x, y, and z are stored in adjacent words in memory (these are denoted by the address expressions 0C124, 0C128, and 0C12C in the IBM version). The 8-bit op code 5A in this version denotes "add" and is equivalent to the PDP-8's op code 1. Here, however, the integers being added are 32-bit words rather than 12-bit words. The register (2 in this case) in which the addition takes place is now explicitly designated in the instruction; in contrast, ACC was an implicit operand in the corresponding

		Instruction	
	Address	**Op Opnd1 Opnd2**	**Meaning**
8088	A1A0	A1 0124 R	move x to AX
	A1A3	01 06 0126 R	add y to AX
	A1A7	A3 0128 R	move AX to z
VAX	A1A0	B0 CF0124 52	load x to r2
	A1A5	A0 CF0126 52	add y to r2
	A1AA	B0 52 CF0128	move r2 to z
IBM	0BA1A0	58 2 0C124	load x to r2
	0BA1A4	5A 2 0C128	add y to r2
	0BA1A8	50 2 0C12C	move r2 to z

Figure 2-6 Contemporary machine language versions of $z := x + y$.

PDP-8 instruction. Similar contrasts apply to the 8088 and VAX versions shown in the figure.

This brief example simultaneously suggests two different themes. First, the basic von Neumann model of stored program computers, instructions, and addressing has been preserved over the last three decades of machine design. Second, the power and flexibility of contemporary machine languages is greatly extended over the earlier (PDP-8 class) machines. More detailed studies of contemporary machine languages and computer organizations are reserved for later courses in the curriculum. This presentation is given mainly to trace the historical development of computer organization and its fundamental connections with the notion of Universal Turing machine, on the one hand, and Modula-2 programming, on the other.

2-3 LOW LEVEL FACILITIES IN MODULA-2

A most useful module, called SYSTEM, is provided with the Modula-2 language. This module includes Modula-2's so-called "low level facilities," which allow the programmer to investigate the memory representations that underlie various data types and structures. While these low level facilities should not be viewed as programming *tools* in the same sense as the other features of the language, their careful and selective use can provide some strategic insights into the interface between the program and the machine in which it is running. We shall use these facilities in this chapter to explore the machine representations of Modula-2's elementary types, using an 8088 microcomputer as our underlying machine. Readers are encouraged to do the same with their own machines and thus explore and compare low-level representations across different machine species.

The module SYSTEM contains the following types and procedures (among others).

```
DEFINITION MODULE SYSTEM;

TYPE WORD,    (*One word of memory — usually 2 or 4 bytes.*)
     ADDRESS; (*The memory address of one word.*)

PROCEDURE ADR(x: type): ADDRESS;    (*Returns the address of
                                        x.*)
PROCEDURE SIZE(x: type): CARDINAL;  (*Returns the number of
                                        bytes occupied by x.*)
PROCEDURE TSIZE(type): CARDINAL;    (*Returns the number of
                                        bytes occupied by
                                        'type'.*)
END SYSTEM.
```

The types ADDRESS and WORD are links to Modula-2's memory representations for all of its objects: REALs, INTEGERs, CHARs,

CARDINALs, BOOLEANs, BITSETs, ARRAYs, RECORDs, POINTERs, and so forth. Formally, the type ADDRESS is defined as a "POINTER TO WORD." This definition captures the tight connection between a memory word's address and its contents (value), as shown in the PDP-8 and other machine examples of the previous sections. Moreover, if "a" is a variable of type ADDRESS, the notation "a^" is used in Modula-2 to indicate the value, or contents, of the WORD whose address is 'a'.

To illustrate, and at the same time to elevate the example that shows the machine representation of the sum z:=x+y to the level of Modula-2, the following driver program is given.

```
MODULE LowLevelDriver;

FROM SYSTEM IMPORT ADR, SIZE;
FROM InOut IMPORT WriteString, WriteLn;
FROM MiscLib IMPORT ShowStorage;

(*This driver program exercises Modula-2's low level
  facilities to display the memory representations of the
  values of x,y, and z after the sum z:=x+y is calculated.
  The procedure ShowStorage is imported from the library
  MiscLib to display the address of each variable and its
  hexadecimal value.  An 8088 implementation of Modula-2
  is assumed here.*)

VAR x, y, z: INTEGER;

BEGIN
  x:=38;
  y:=31;
  z:=x+y;
  WriteString('The addresses and values of x, y, and z ');
  WriteString('are:');
  WriteLn;
  WriteString('x: '); ShowStorage(ADR(x),SIZE(x));
  WriteString('y: '); ShowStorage(ADR(y),SIZE(y));
  WriteString('z: '); ShowStorage(ADR(z),SIZE(z))
END LowLevelDriver.
```

This program uses the auxiliary procedures ADR and SIZE from the module SYSTEM, as well as the procedure ShowStorage, which was written and saved in our library of miscellaneous auxiliary procedures called "MiscLib." This library contains a small number of procedures useful in various places throughout the text; the details of its implementation are given elsewhere in the text. The particular procedure ShowStorage can be used to display the memory address and hexadecimal representation of any variable in any of our programs. It requires that the program supply the address (via ADR) and the length in bytes (via SIZE) of that variable in the invocation. Since our 8088 implementation of Modula-2 has 2-byte words, and since an INTEGER is stored in a single word, the following output appears when running this driver program.

```
The addresses and values of x, y, and z are:
x: Address: 0000   Value: 0026
y: Address: 0002   Value: 001F
z: Address: 0004   Value: 0045
```

Thus, we see that the sum of the hexadecimal integers 0026 (decimal 38) and 001F (decimal 31) is the hexadecimal integer 0045 (decimal 69), and the values of the three variables x, y, and z are stored, respectively, at the relative addresses 0000, 0002, and 0004.

We will have occasion to use the procedure ShowStorage in several chapters throughout this text. The other procedures of MiscLib will also have wide utility, and the complete DEFINITION MODULE for MiscLib is given below.

```
DEFINITION MODULE MiscLib;

FROM SYSTEM IMPORT ADDRESS;
EXPORT QUALIFIED Log2, MaxPower, Power, Random, ShowStorage;

PROCEDURE Log2 (i: CARDINAL): CARDINAL;
  (*Return the highest power of 2 that is less than
    or equal to i.*)

PROCEDURE MaxPower (i,j: CARDINAL): CARDINAL;
  (*Return the highest power of i that evenly divides j.*)

PROCEDURE Power (i,j: INTEGER): INTEGER;
  (*Return the result of raising i to the power j.*)

PROCEDURE Random (VAR randint: CARDINAL): CARDINAL;
  (*Generates an integer in the random sequence in the range
    0..65535 without repetitions. Each invocation should
    pass a CARDINAL variable randint, whose value must be
    that which was returned by Random from the previous
    invocation.*)

PROCEDURE ShowStorage (a: ADDRESS; length: CARDINAL);
  (*Display the contents of 'length' memory locations,
    beginning at address a.  All addresses and contents
    are shown in hexadecimal notation.*)

END MiscLib.
```

Appearing here, along with ShowStorage, are the procedures Log2, Power, MaxPower, and Random. The latter will be the subject of discussion in a later section of this chapter.

In order to provide a taste of system-level programming, the complete implementation of ShowStorage is given below.

```
PROCEDURE ShowStorage (a: ADDRESS; length: CARDINAL);

VAR i: ADDRESS;

BEGIN
  WriteString(' Address: '); WriteHex(a.OFFSET,4);
  WriteString(' Value:');
  i:=a;
  WHILE i.OFFSET <= a.OFFSET+length-1 DO
    WriteHex(CARDINAL(i^),4);
    INC(i,2)
  END;
  WriteLn
END ShowStorage;
```

Several Modula-2 features are used here in displaying the hexadecimal contents of a series of memory bytes. First, note that the procedure WriteHex is imported from the standard module InOut (see Appendix D). WriteHex displays the hexadecimal value of any CARDINAL type, and its second parameter specifies the number of output hex digits to display. Also note that the local variable i, of type ADDRESS, controls the loop that displays the value in memory, two bytes (4 hex digits) at a time. Recall that the notation i^ serves as a reference to the byte value at address i, and that value is displayed in two hexadecimal digits. As implied here, the arithmetic procedure INC may be used with ADDRESS variables, just as if they were CARDINALs. Third, note that the built-in "type transfer function" CARDINAL is applied to the value at address i. This function interprets that value as a CARDINAL integer, since that type is required by the procedure WriteHex.

In general, every Modula-2 elementary type (REAL, INTEGER, CARDINAL, CHAR, BITSET) has an associated type transfer function with the same name, that reinterprets its argument as a value of the designated type. These, of course, should not be used with abandon, since every interpretation that is syntactically legal is not reasonable in an arithmetic sense.

2-4 MEMORY REPRESENTATIONS OF ELEMENTARY TYPES

We continue in this section to investigate the memory representations for different Modula-2 types. Such an investigation gives insight into certain implementation-dependent constraints that accompany the range of values for these types, especially in the case of REALs, INTEGERs, and CARDINALs. Although the implementation used in this discussion is the 8088 processor, the principles that accompany this discussion apply equally to other computers and programming languages as well.

The type INTEGER is a set of values that can be represented in a single memory word, usually 16 or 32 bits, depending on the computer. INTEGER values are normally stored in "two's complement" notation, where nonnegative values appear in binary notation and negative values are obtained by computing the two's complement of the corresponding positive values. For instance, the INTEGERs 32, 1, -1, and -32 appear in 16-bit words as 0020, 0001, FFFF, and FFE0, respectively. Because of the 16-bit word length, the total number of distinct integers that can be represented is 2^{16}, and the range for INTEGER values is -2^{15} through $+2^{15}-1$ (assuming two's complement representation). Whenever an INTEGER arithmetic operation is performed yielding a result outside this range, an *overflow* error occurs, and program execution terminates with an appropriate error message.

The type CARDINAL has similar constraints in its range of values. The maximum CARDINAL value is $2^{16}-1$ (assuming a 16-bit word length), and overflow will occur if an arithmetic calculation results in a value larger than this or smaller than 0. CARDINALs are stored in the 8088 implementation simply as unsigned 16-bit binary integers: 0 is 0000, 15 is 000F, 32 is 0020, and so forth.

The type REAL in most of Modula-2's implementations is stored in 4 bytes (two words for the 8088). Here, the storage representation of a REAL has three parts, a 1-bit sign, a 6-bit exponent part, and a 25-bit mantissa part, as shown in Figure 2-7. The mantissa represents a hex fraction between 0 and 1, and the exponent represents a scale factor that is an appropriate power of 16 to be multiplied by the mantissa to obtain (an approximation to) the number being represented. In this manner, the REAL type permits a far greater magnitude of values to be represented (roughly $10^{\pm 38}$) than INTEGER or CARDINAL, but at the expense of *precision*. That is, no REAL value can exactly represent a number that has more than twenty-five significant binary digits (or, equivalently, about seven significant decimal digits), because of the fixed length of the mantissa in its internal memory representation.

Below are some examples of REAL values in Modula-2 and their internal 8088 memory representations. The last example in this list helps to explain why sometimes a REAL fraction does not have an exact representation when it is displayed. Here, the binary value stored is an approximation of the decimal value 0.1, since the latter does not have an exact 25-bit representation as a binary fraction.

Figure 2-7
Memory representation of a REAL value.

sign	exponent	mantissa
b	bbb bbb	b bbb bbb bbb bbb bbb bbb bbb bbb

Real Value	8088 Representation
1.5	40 C00000
2.0	41 000000
3.0	41 400000
−1.0	C0 800000
1000.0	45 7A0000
10000.0	47 1C4000
32768.0	48 000000
0.1	3E CCCCCC

There are two important functions built into Modula-2 that permit values to be converted between REAL and CARDINAL representation. These functions are TRUNC and FLOAT. When applied to a REAL value x, TRUNC(x) delivers the CARDINAL that results from truncating x (removing its fractional part without rounding). The reverse conversion is provided by FLOAT(c), which delivers the REAL value equivalent to the CARDINAL c.

The type CHAR, as already mentioned, denotes a single ASCII character. A full list of ASCII characters, and their 8-bit representations, is provided in Appendix B. Two important built-in functions are also provided for conversion between an ASCII character and its ASCII integer code; these are called ORD and CHR. ORD(c) delivers the ASCII integer code for the character c, while CHR(n) delivers the CHAR value whose ASCII code is n. Thus, for instance, CHR(65) = 'A' and ORD('A') = 65.

The types WORD, ADDRESS, and POINTER are tightly connected, as we have illustrated in earlier sections. To summarize, the type ADDRESS is always interpreted as a POINTER TO WORD. This conveys the low-level connectivity that occurs between a variable, the address where its value is stored, and the value itself in some specific machine implementation of Modula-2. Whenever we refer to an ordinary variable x we are calling on the machine to connect this reference to the corresponding memory address where its value is stored. Thus, the memory word at that address of x contains, at all times, the machine representation of the current value of x. Whenever we change the value of x by, say, an assignment statement in Modula-2, the corresponding machine instructions for that assignment are executed to accomplish that change by altering the actual memory contents at the address associated with the variable x. Consider, for example, the following declarations:

```
VAR x: INTEGER;
    a: ADDRESS;
    p: POINTER TO WORD;
```

If we write the following assignment statement in our program,

```
x := −1
```

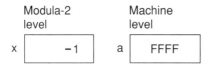

Figure 2-8
Modula-2 vs machine level representation of x := −1.

we are effectively calling for the storage of the hexadecimal value FFFF in the memory word whose address is x. That is, we could have done the same by either of the following two pairs of instructions:

```
a  :=ADR(x);                p := ADR(x);
a^:=0FFFFH                  p^:= WORD(-1)
```

Graphically, the correspondence between Modula-2 variables' values, on the one hand, and the values stored at machine-level addresses, on the other, is summarized in Figure 2-8 for the above instructions. On the left in the figure we see the value of x in its familiar decimal form, while on the right we see the 2-byte hex value that is stored in the memory address a. The latter is, thus, the actual hex implementation of the former on a specific machine (the 8088).

2-5 THE TYPE BITSET AND ITS OPERATORS

In some programming situations, certain constraints imposed by the implementation of the language prevent a problem from being solved in a straightforward manner. We shall see an example of such a situation in the next section. Sometimes these constraints can be overcome by exploiting one's knowledge of underlying machine representations, together with the Modula-2 type BITSET and its associated operators.

As introduced in Appendix A, the type BITSET denotes any set of integers in the range 0..W−1, where W is the word size of the machine. Usually, W is 16 or 32, so that BITSETs are relatively small collections of integers. In our discussions, we shall assume a word size of 16 bits. A BITSET value is written in Modula-2 as a series of such integers, separated by commas and surrounded by braces { and }. Below are some sample BITSET values.

```
{0,1,7}
{2}
{1..5,13,15}
{}
```

The third example shows how a contiguous sequence within a BITSET may be abbreviated, and the fourth example shows the empty set.

The operators +, −, *, and / may be applied to BITSETs to denote ordinary set union, difference, intersection, and symmetric difference, respectively. Recall that the union (+) of two sets, say s and t, is defined as the set of all values that are in either s or t. The difference, s−t, is the set of all values that are in s but not t. The intersection, s∗t, is the set of all values that are in both s and t. The symmetric difference, s/t, is the set of all values that are in either s or t but not both.

The set membership operator IN is applied to an integer argument i and a set argument s; we write the BOOLEAN expression "i IN s" to ask the question: "Is i a member of the set s?" The result delivered by this expression is TRUE or FALSE, depending on whether or not the current value of i is among the integers that comprise the current value of s.

The standard functions INCL and EXCL are used to add or delete, respectively, an individual integer from among the current members of a set. INCL(s,i) adds the value of integer i to the set s, while EXCL(s,i) deletes the value of i from the set s.

A further assumption about the implementation of sets can sometimes be made. That is, we can assume that the value of a set is stored as a series W bits (where W is the machine's word size) whose values correspond, from left to right, to the integers 0, 1, ..., W−1. A bit in this series has the value 0 or 1, respectively, as its corresponding integer is or is not a member of the set. (In fact, this is the case for the Modula Research Institute implementation of Modula-2 on the 8088, but not for the Logitech Modula-2 implementation on the same processor.) Under that assumption, for example, the BITSET value shown on the left below can be assumed to be stored as the 16-bit value shown on the right.

BITSET Value	Modula Research Institute's Machine Representation
{1..5,13,15}	01111100 00000101

However, other implementations represent BITSET's differently. For instance, the Logitech Modula-2 system for the 8088 *reverses* the bits in its machine representation, as seen below.

BITSET Value	Logitech's Machine Representation
{1..5,13,15}	10100000 00111110

Thus, any software development effort that depends upon the representation of values at this level must be sensitive to these differences among Modula-2 systems.

To provide a concrete application, consider those programming problems for which the implementation-dependent range for CARDINALs may be too limited for effective use. That is. suppose we want to extend the range for our implementation of CARDINALs from $[0..2^{16}-1]$ to $[0..2^{32}-1]$. We may accomplish this by defining a new type, say LONGCARD, as an array of two ordinary CARDINAL values and then defining appropriate arithmetic functions to accompany this new type. That is, we can define addition and multiplication with LONGCARD results, using procedures named Longsum and Longprod, under the assumption that a value of type LONGCARD is stored internally as a 32-bit binary integer. Below, for example, are the internal representations of some common CARDINAL and LONGCARD values.

CARDINAL Value	Memory (hex) Representation	LONGCARD Value	Memory (hex) Representation
1	0001	1	00000001
15	000F	15	0000000F
65535	FFFF	65535	0000FFFF
		65536	00010000
		65537	00010001
		$2^{32}-1$	FFFFFFFF

2-5-1 Bitwise Long Cardinal Sum

To continue this example, consider the design of a procedure Longsum, which computes the LONGCARD sum w of two LONGCARD integers u and v. This can be accomplished by using the following algorithm, which computes the 32-bit binary sum w by scanning the corresponding bit values of u and v from right to left, in a bit by bit fashion. Here, k denotes the carry out of bit j in word w. We denote each bit j of word w as w_j; w_0 thus signifies the leftmost bit of w, and w_{31} signifies the rightmost.

Step 1. Set w=0 and k=0.
Step 2. Repeat step 3 for each value of j from 31 down to 0.
Step 3. Compute $w_j = (u_j + v_j + k)$ mod 2.
Compute $k = (u_j + v_j + k)$ div 2.

This algorithm can be implemented in Modula-2 by reinterpreting the LONGCARDs u, v, and w as BITSETs, using the IN operator to examine the bit by bit contents of u and v, and using the INCL and EXCL functions to systematically reconstruct the LONGCARD sum w. The procedure Longsum is shown below.

```
PROCEDURE Longsum (u,v: LONGCARD; VAR w: LONGCARD);
(*This procedure computes the 32-bit sum w of two
   32-bit LONGCARD integers u and v, assuming that
   both u and v have 0 in their leftmost bit
   positions (i.e., no overflow can occur).  The sum
   is developed bit by bit in the array wb.  k is
```

the carry bit. The Logitech 8088 implementation of
Modula-2 is assumed here; all references to the
procedure Flip should be removed if the MRI implementation is used instead.*)

```
VAR uj,vj,wj,j,k: CARDINAL;
    ub,vb,wb: ARRAY[1..2] OF BITSET;

BEGIN
  ub[1]:=Flip(BITSET(u[1])); ub[2]:=Flip(BITSET(u[2]));
  vb[1]:=Flip(BITSET(v[1])); vb[2]:=Flip(BITSET(v[2]));
  wb[1]:={}; wb[2]:={};     (*Initial sum = 0.*)
  k:=0;                     (*Initial carry equals 0.*)
  FOR j:=31 TO 16 BY -1 DO (*Loop for bits 16 to 31.*)
    IF j-16 IN ub[2] THEN uj:=1 ELSE uj:=0 END;
    IF j-16 IN vb[2] THEN vj:=1 ELSE vj:=0 END;
    wj:=(uj+vj+k) MOD 2;
    k :=(uj+vj+k) DIV 2;
    IF wj=1 THEN
      INCL(wb[2],j-16)
    END
  END;
  FOR j:=15 TO 1 BY -1 DO  (*Loop for bits 1 to 15.*)
    IF j IN ub[1] THEN uj:=1 ELSE uj:=0 END;
    IF j IN vb[1] THEN vj:=1 ELSE vj:=0 END;
    wj:=(uj+vj+k) MOD 2;
    k:=(uj+vj+k) DIV 2;
    IF wj=1 THEN
      INCL(wb[1],j)
    END
  END;
  IF k>0 THEN
    INCL(wb[1],0)            (*Carry to bit 0 of wb.*)
  END;
  w[1]:=CARDINAL(Flip(wb[1]));
  w[2]:=CARDINAL(Flip(wb[2]))
END Longsum;
```

Note in the comments of this procedure that the auxiliary procedure Flip is used to reverse the order of the bit values within the 16-bit representation of a BITSET. This device permits portability between the Logitech and the Modula Research Institute implementations of BITSETs (as discussed previously). This procedure is straightforward and is left as an Exercise.

To illustrate the algorithm itself, we assume the original (Modula Research Institute's) representation for BITSETs and let ub, vb, and wb denote the BITSET values of u, v, and w, respectively. Now, suppose u and v are initially have the values 65535 and 1, respectively. Then ub, vb, and wb will appear as follows when the first FOR loop in Longsum is entered.

	[1]	[2]
ub:	00000000 00000000	11111111 11111111
vb:	00000000 00000000	00000000 00000001
wb:	00000000 00000000	00000000 00000000

The first iteration of this loop leaves the rightmost bit of wb equal to 0 and the carry bit k=1, since the rightmost bits of ub and vb are both 1. The carry subsequently propagates through all of the rightmost 16 bits of wb and has the value 1 as the second FOR loop is entered. This loop is identical to the first, except that it determines the bit values for bits 1 through 15 (rather than 16 through 31) of wb. Following this loop, the carry bit k is propagated into the leftmost bit of wb. The result is then (Flipped and is) finally assigned to the LONGCARD parameter w. The resulting value of wb, for our example, is shown as:

wb:	00000000 00000001	00000000 00000000

2-5-2 Bitwise Long Cardinal Product

Calculation of the LONGCARD product w of two CARDINAL integers u and v may be implemented in a similar fashion. We again denote the BITSET representations of these values as ub, vb, and wb. The following algorithm is adapted from Knuth.[2] The bits of the multiplier vb are scanned from right to left; for each bit $vb_j = 0$, a copy of ub is added to wb at an appropriate "shift" position. Here, again, k denotes a carry bit out of one of these additions. More formally, the algorithm is given below.

Step 1. Set wb=0 and k=0.
Step 2. Repeat steps 3 through 5 for each value of j from 15 down to 0.
Step 3. If $vb_j = 0$, then set $wb_j = 0$. Otherwise, set k=0 and repeat step 4 for each value of i from 15 down to 0.
Step 4. Compute $t = ub_i \times vb_j + wb_{(i+j)} + k$.
Compute $wb_{(i+j+1)} = t \bmod 2$.
Compute $k = t \operatorname{div} 2$.
Step 5. Set $wb_j = k$.

This algorithm can be implemented in Modula-2 by reinterpreting the LONGCARDs u, v, and w as BITSETs (ub, vb, and wb), using the IN operator to examine the bit by bit contents of ub and vb and using the INCL and EXCL functions to systematically reconstruct the LONGCARD product wb. Implementation of the procedure Longprod is left as an exercise.

[2]Knuth, D.E., *Seminumerical Algorithms*, 2nd edition, Addison-Wesley, 1981, p 253.

2-6 RANDOM NUMBER GENERATION

The utility and necessity of bit-level programming, such as that shown in the foregoing section, occurs when we are confronted with a problem that is not gracefully accommodated by Modula-2's standard data types. A familiar example of such a problem is the generation of random numbers. The need for a procedure that quickly and effectively generates long sequences of random numbers represents one of the most widespread uses of computers across the various scientific disciplines. Random number sequences are essential in the processes of statistical simulation, random sampling, numerical analysis, computer program testing and verification, executive decision making, and gambling. In later sections of this book, for example, we shall use sequences of random numbers both to help verify the correctness and to empirically measure the complexity of various sorting and searching algorithms.

The problem of random number generation is not, however, an easy one. What often seems intuitively to be an effective algorithm for generating random numbers can turn out to perform rather poorly. Ideally, a sequence of integers in a particular range, say 0..r, is said to be *random* if every possible value in that range is equally likely to occur at any place in the sequence. Thus, as the number, n, of values in the sequence grows large, the number of values in each of the n equal intervals of size r/n should become nearly equal. Many algorithms have been developed over the last several decades for using the digital computer to aid in the task of random number generation. Some have proven to be very effective, while others have turned out to be quite poor when their outputs are subjected to various tests for randomness.

One of the first scientists to suggest using the arithmetic of the computer to generate random numbers was John von Neumann in 1946. The method he suggested was called the "middle square method." This was an iterative process in which each new random number was derived mathematically from the previous one by squaring it and extracting the middle digits from the result. This method, however, turned out to be not so effective and was soon supplanted by the "linear congruential method," introduced by D. H. Lehman in 1949. In this method, a modulus m is chosen, together with a multiplier a, an increment c, and a starting value X_0 (called the "seed"). Each successive random number X_{n+1} is then computed from its predecessor in the sequence X_n by the following formula:

$$X_{(n+1)} = (a \times X_n + c) \bmod m$$

Now the problem is to find values for a, c, m, and X_0 which will result in a "good" sequence of random numbers.[3]

---

[3] The general problem of random number generation has been the subject of serious study by mathematicians and computer scientists for some time. Interested readers are referred, for example, to Knuth's *Seminumerical Algorithms*, which contains a detailed and contemporary survey of this problem.

What, then, makes a random number sequence "good"? Given a sequence of integers in the range 0..r, various tests for randomness can be applied. Two important characteristics of such a sequence are that it contain no "cycles" (that is, repetitions of the same sequence of integers), and that its integers are well distributed over the entire range of possible values (that is, they are not clustered in "bunches"). For example, if we pick $X_0 = a = c = 7$ and $m = 10$ in the above-mentioned linear congruential method, we generate the sequence 7, 6, 9, 0, 7, 6, 9 . . ., which has a cycle length of 4 and is not well-distributed over the range 0..9.

However, other choices for these critical parameters in the linear congruential method will yield very good random number sequences. For example, if we choose $a = 25173$, $b = 13849$, and $m = 65536$ (which is exactly the range of integers that can be stored in a 16-bit word size), then the linear congruential method is guaranteed to produce a sequence in which every integer in the range will occur exactly once before the first duplication occurs. Moreover, this property holds no matter what we choose as the initial seed value X_0.

This is an ideal situation for implementations of Modula-2 in which the entire range of 32-bit CARDINALs is supported. However, on machines with 16-bit word sizes, the multiplication and addition of 32-bit values must be simulated; otherwise, the linear congruential method will result in an overflow error as soon as the calculation of X_{i+1} is executed. The procedures Longsum and Longprod, developed in the foregoing section, are thus essential to the implementation of the random number generation procedure given below.

```
PROCEDURE Random (VAR randint: CARDINAL): CARDINAL;

VAR a,b,c: LONGCARD;

BEGIN
(*This procedure implements the random number generation
  algorithm given by the assignment statement

      randint:=(25173*randint+13849) MOD 65536

  under the constraint that the wordsize of the machine
  is 16 bits and the maximum CARDINAL value is 65535.
  To accommodate this constraint (and thus to prevent
  overflow), the special 32-bit cardinal type LONGCARD
  and the auxiliary procedures Longprod and Longsum are
  used.  Implementations that directly support 32-bit
  CARDINAL values can use the above assignment statement
  directly and ignore the type LONGCARD as well as the
  procedures Longprod and Longsum.*)

  Longprod(25173,randint,a);    (*a:=25173*randint*)
  b[1]:=0;
  b[2]:=13849;                   (*b:=13849*)
```

```
    Longsum(a,b,c);           (*c:=a+b*)
    randint:=c[2];            (*c[2] is sum MOD 65536*)
    RETURN randint
END Random;
```

To test this procedure, and to evaluate the randomness of the sequence it generates, we developed a driver program named RandomDriver. This program assumes that Random resides in the separate module MiscLib (along with LONGCARD, Longsum, and Longprod). RandomDriver uses the additional procedure TestRandom, which checks the n-integer sequence that was generated by Random to find both the shortest cycle and the number of integers from that sequence that fall into each of the r/n intervals in the range $0..r-1$. The development of TestRandom is left as an exercise, while RandomDriver is shown below.

```
MODULE RandomDriver;

FROM InOut IMPORT Read, WriteString, WriteLn, WriteCard,
                  ReadCard, OpenOutput, CloseOutput;
FROM MiscLib IMPORT Random;

(*This program generates and displays a series of n random
  integers in the range 0..r-1, given n and r from the
  terminal.  It uses the procedure Random, and tests the
  randomness of these integers by determining the number
  of repetitions and the length of the shortest cycle in
  the series.  The maximum value for r is implementation
  dependent; in the case of the 8088, it is 65535.*)

PROCEDURE TestRandom (a: ARRAY OF CARDINAL; n,r: CARDINAL);

(*This procedure tests the randomness of the n values
  in the array a, using the range 0..r-1.  It finds the
  length of the shortest cycle, as well as the
  number of values from a in each of the n intervals of
  size r/n.  Ideally, there should be no cycles (i.e.,
  no repeated values in a) and an equal number of values
  in each of the n intervals, which means that the values
  have a uniform random distribution over the interval
  0..r-1.  The maximum number of intervals is 1000.*)

VAR i,j,length,cyclebegin: CARDINAL;
    counts: ARRAY [0..999] OF CARDINAL;

BEGIN

  (*Implementation of this procedure is left as an
    exercise.*)

END TestRandom;
```

```
VAR i,n,r,c: CARDINAL;
    x: REAL;
    a: ARRAY[0..9999] OF CARDINAL;
    answer: CHAR;
    filename: ARRAY[0..11] OF CHAR;

BEGIN
  WriteString(' Begin random number generation driver.');
  WriteLn;
  LOOP
    WriteString(' Enter a count n (n=0 to quit) and a ');
    WriteString('range r:');
    ReadCard(n); WriteString('   '); ReadCard(r); WriteLn;
    IF n=0 THEN
      EXIT
    END;
    WriteLn;
    WriteString (' To save the numbers in a file, type y:');
    Read(answer);
    WriteLn;
    IF answer='y' THEN
      OpenOutput(filename)
    END;
    c:=0; (*Initialize the series with c=0.*)
    FOR i:=0 TO n-1 DO
      a[i]:=Random(c) MOD r; (*Compute and output next
                                      number.*)
      WriteCard(a[i],6);
      IF i MOD 12 = 11 THEN
        WriteLn
      END
    END;
    IF answer='y' THEN
      CloseOutput
    END;
    WriteLn;
    TestRandom(a,n,r)    (*Test randomness of the series.*)
  END;
  WriteString(' End random number generation.')
END RandomDriver.
```

The program, as seen, is set up to generate several sequences, choosing different values for n and r for each sequence. When r is less than 65535 (the ideal value for this particular generator), the program simply retains the remainder modulo r of Random(c). The variable c itself is initialized with the seed value of 0, which is arbitrary (and yet inconsequential).

For example, when n = 10 and r = 100 the following sequence of integers is given:

49   42   23   80   25   46   39   96   73   74

When n = 100 and r = 65535 we obtain the sequence below.

```
13849 48742 31223 17180 13925 61346 51939 31096 31473 18974
19983 57108 61373 10714 36731 61424 49353 10966 23335 26636
23061 10514 48403 17256 26529 16526   319 48644 54637 52554
45995 21472 53113 27462 41047 49404 49605 63106 54083   344
22609 35582 39023 20724 32541 33978 31707 11216 25129 32694
18823 19948 28021 22514  3443 45896 19713 10606  5023 38884
60621 20522 59403 30656 30937 26662 22199  3804 23845 19810
27555 22840 17841  7134 29391 37588  7805 12186 63547 14256
 5001  9366 51175   972 37077 54994 60883 62248 16993 25166
46591 16836  5165  8970 44139 27552 12857 46342 40215 11452
```

In this latter sequence, no cycles occur and the integers are fairly well spread among the 100 intervals in the range 0..65535. Moreover, as the number n of integers increases toward 65535, their distribution over this range becomes increasingly even.

Note, finally, that this driver allows the random number sequence to be stored as a separate file. This is a useful addition, since we will need to use a relatively large random number sequence when we exercise various algorithms in later sections of this text.

EXERCISES

2-1. Design a Turing machine that will compute the difference of two numbers, assuming that they are stored on the tape as unary integers. Assume also that the first number is the larger of the two. What is the importance of this assumption?

2-2. What is Church's thesis? What is its significance in the study of algorithms and computer science?

2-3. Design an algorithm U that will carry out the steps of an arbitrary Turing machine M, assuming that the machine is represented as an array of quadruples (q[j],s[j],t[j],r[j]). Here, q and r denote states, s denotes a scanned symbol, and t denotes a transition (L, R, 0, 1, or b). Assume also that the tape's contents are stored in a sufficiently large array, say T[1..1000], and that the current position of the read-write head is in the register i. The register j, as suggested above, is assumed to hold the subscript of the quadruple of M that is currently being executed.

2-4. Can you implement the algorithm of exercise 2-3 in Modula-2? If so, exercise it using as input a suitable encoding of the Turing machine that adds two integers, which was given at the beginning of the chapter.

2-5. Draw parallels between the algorithm U that you designed in exercise 2-3 and the components of the von Neumann machine model, as represented by the PDP-8 machine design. Specifically, identify U's parts that correspond to the registers MAR, IR, and PC; the input and output tapes; and the memory.

2-6. Using the procedure ShowStorage, write a Modula-2 program that will investigate the memory representations of the elementary types (INTEGER, CARDINAL, REAL, CHAR, BITSET) in your own machine implementations. Compare your findings with the ones shown in this chapter.

2-7. Implement the procedures Flip (required by Longsum) and Longprod, which computes the LONGCARD product w of two CARDINAL integers u and v. Test your implementations by recompiling MiscLib and running RandomDriver. Does your run produce the same random sequence shown in this chapter?

2-8. Define a new type LONGREAL. Discuss its internal memory representation in a series of four contiguous words (64 bits) and its implementation in Modula-2 by defining functions for the basic arithmetic operations +, −, *, and / and arguments of type LONGREAL, using existing BITSET, REAL, and CARDINAL arithmetic operations. Investigate also whether your machine already supports such a type directly.

2-9. The procedure Longsum works properly only if both arguments u and v have 0 in their leftmost bit. What will happen if that is not the case? What should happen if that is not the case? Discuss ways in which the procedure Longsum can be extended to properly accommodate the problem of overflow.

2-10. The procedure Longprod can be extended to handle arguments u and v of type LONGCARD, rather than just CARDINAL. Discuss this extension in terms of its impact on the algorithm itself and the problem of handling overflow (i.e., when the length of the product exceeds 32 significant digits).

2-11. The type LONGCARD is, at the moment, a "private type," since neither it nor either of the accompanying procedures Longsum and Longprod is exported by the module MiscLib. For our purposes, this is appropriate, since we would be bound to implement the remaining arithmetic operators (− and / at the least) if we exported this type for general use by other application programs beyond Random. Consider the implementation of these other operators as additional Modula-2 procedures and describe the particular extensions to MiscLib's

DEFINITION MODULE and IMPLEMENTATION MODULE that would be needed in order to make the type LONGCARD more widely available.

2-12. Exercise the random number generator Random, using $n = 1000$ and $n = 10000$. Exercise the driver again, this time generating 10000 integers in the range 0..65535 and saving them in the file named RANDOM.DAT. This file will be useful later in the course when we empirically test the complexity of different sorting, searching, and other algorithms.

2-13. When r is less than 65535, the program RandomDriver generates random numbers by simply taking the remainder modulo r of the value returned by Random(c). This particular technique, in general, has been shown not to generate "good" random number sequences. Test that conclusion by generating sequences with $r = 100$ and $r = 1000$. What is the shortest cycle length in these cases? Suggest other methods of extracting two- or three-digit integers from the result returned by Random(c) that lead to "better" sequences than the method used here, and then test your methods in the same way.

2-14. Complete the implementation of the procedure TestRandom in Modula-2.

3

LINEAR LISTS: AN ABSTRACT DATA TYPE

The ability to develop, use, and effectively share libraries of associated algorithms is a key ingredient in the repertoire of a computer scientist. Historically, some of these libraries have become so useful that their originators made them widely available for general use. As an early example in the field of mathematical programming, FORTRAN's Scientific Subroutine Package was developed to encapsulate a large and important collection of algebraic and statistical analysis algorithms for wide distribution among the scientific programming installations in academia, industry, and government. More recently, the proliferation of UNIX software development environments has brought with it a wide sharing of "software tools" for use by computer scientists who are developing contemporary compilers, operating systems, and related large pieces of software.

This ability is best developed early, so that it can be nurtured throughout one's experience with the intermediate and advanced courses that require significant laboratory work, such as the study of compilers, operating systems, information systems, and so forth. Without such an ability, students would be forced at every step to "reinvent the wheel" by spending valuable time rewriting software that others have already written and verified countless times before. That kind of rewriting is not without merit on a limited basis, for purely pedagogical reasons, but one should be able to avoid these details when the organization and implementation of larger software projects become the focus of attention.

In an effort to add a degree of coherence to the developing and archiving of software tools, the notion of an *abstract data type* has recently evolved. In this chapter, we introduce the process of defining and implementing abstract data types, which is known as *data abstraction*, using the "linear list" as our illustrative example. In the process, we shall see that the abstract data type linear list incorporates a somewhat more general notion than simply that of an ordinary one-dimensional array; in addition to containing a data structure, it has a small set of associated "operators" (insert, delete, and so forth) that are routinely used by the application programs that need the linear list abstract data type. Moreover, the definition of this type and its operators is completely *abstract*, or separate from any particular implementation—it is, in fact, stated in English and mathematical notation rather than in Modula-2. Thus, we may think about implementing the procedures that realize the operators of the data type as a separate exercise from that of understanding the meaning of the operators.

In the particular case of linear lists, we shall see that there are at least two different implementation strategies—one using contiguous arrays and the other using "dynamically linked structures"—that have merit. We shall examine the trade-offs, in time and space, between these two implementation choices, discussing their relative advantages and disadvantages after they are introduced. The "dynamically linked" alternative for implementing linear lists will also allow us to introduce Modula-2's facilities for dynamic storage management, which will be widely useful throughout the remainder of the text as we study other abstract data types. Principles of informal program verification are also expanded here, using our implementations of certain linear list operators in Modula-2 as a vehicle.

Finally, this chapter concludes by illustrating the value of the abstract data type concept in solving large problems. There, we develop an application of linear lists that solves a part of the Advanced Instructor's Problem that was introduced in Chapter 1.

3-1 ABSTRACT DATA TYPES: LINEAR LIST DEFINITION

An *abstract data type* is a *type*, a collection of associated *operators* that represent the different primitive transformations that may be performed on values of that type, and possibly a small collection of associated *global variables* and *constants*.

Some abstract data types are already implemented within the programming language. For instance, we have in Modula-2 the type INTEGER, which has its associated operators (+, −, *, /, DIV, MOD, ReadInt, WriteInt, <, =, >, SIZE, ABS, and so forth) and globals (the phenomenon *overflow;* the maximum INTEGER value; the global Done which is associated with the operator ReadInt; and so forth). Other abstract data types can be implemented separately by the programmer as "extensions" to the language, and different programming languages support this activity in different ways. Modula-2 supports the implementation of new abstract data types through a combination of its separate compilation features (introduced in Chapter 1) and its standard procedures. We shall exercise these facilities as we implement the abstract data type Linear List (to be defined below) in Modula-2.

An essential characteristic of an abstract data type is that its definition be made *separately* and *in advance of* its implementation. When we implement an abstract data type, we should do so in such a way that the details of that implementation are hidden from the view of application programs that use its facilities. For instance, consider the mathematical notion of "integer," with its associated operators $+$, $-$, and so forth. When we first consider the implementation of this type in Modula-2 (as INTEGER and its operators), we have a separate and intuitively complete notion of these objects and operators from our prior experience with mathematics. Further, when we use INTEGER variables and operators in our Modula-2 programs, we are generally spared the need to understand how these values are represented in the machine, how each of the associated operators is realized, and so forth. We only care that our prior intuition about the mathematical properties of integer arithmetic are well-preserved in the implementation, so that we may use INTEGERs with confidence in applications where they are needed.

The same principles apply as we proceed to extend the language by implementing new abstract data types of our own. In defining an abstract data type, we should use a programming language-free, mathematical style of expression to describe the type itself as well as the meanings of its associated operators and globals. Only after such a definition is complete should we consider the separate matter of implementation. The implementation should, however, provide Modula-2 code that permits its independent verification: that is, the application programmer who uses the type and its procedures should be confident that the original abstract definition has been faithfully represented.

To illustrate these principles, we first define a very important abstract data type known as the linear list. This definition is made below without the aid of any Modula-2 type or procedure declarations. Instead, the definition of each operator for an abstract data type relies principally on specifications given in a precise style using preconditions and postconditions. Later, we shall see that this method permits diverse implementation strategies to be developed separately for the same abstract data type.

Definition: A *linear list* is either empty, denoted by ( ), or a sequence of $n > 0$ elements that share the same type, denoted by:

$$(e_1\ e_2\ \ldots\ e_i\ \ldots\ e_n)$$

The associated operators for a linear list, which will each be defined in a later paragraph, are identified as follows: Create, Store, Retrieve, Insert, Delete, Search, Size, Display, and Dump. A linear list also has an associated global Error, whose Boolean value serves as a flag to indicate whether or not the the last-executed list operator was successfully completed.

The type that is shared in common by all the elements of a linear list may be scalar (such as INTEGER) or not (such as a character string or a record structure).

An important point to mention here is that linear lists are strictly linear. That is, they do not embody the more general data structures that would occur if each of the elements e_i were themselves allowed to be linear lists. In that case, we see that parentheses could be arbitrarily nested and a more general class (known as the *tree*) would emerge. This class is, for instance, the basis upon which expressions in the LISP programming language are built. We shall return to the very important topic of trees in Chapter 8.

Examples of linear lists (or just "lists," for short) abound in the field of computer science and its applications. Already in this text, we have seen two examples: a list of names in Chapter 1 and a list of random integers in Chapter 2. These are shown below in the notation of the foregoing definition:

```
(backus wirth turing gries vonneumann mccarthy lovelace
 church markov hopper naur)

(49  42  23  80  25  46  39  96  73  74)
```

The first list has eleven elements e_i, and each is a character string. The second has ten elements, and each is an integer.

3-1-1 The Constant Maxlist and the Global Variable Error

Associated with all linear lists L is an integer constant *Maxlist*, which identifies the maximum number n of elements e_i that L may have, and whose value is defined by the implementation. We shall later see that the value of Maxlist is much more constrained under one implementation strategy than it is under the other.

The global variable *Error* is also associated with all linear lists L. It becomes true under different circumstances, which are identified by the list operator definitions below. For instance, if we try to execute the Delete operator with a list containing no elements, the global Error will become true and the list will be unaffected. Any program that uses the abstract data type linear list can therefore rely upon this global as an indicator of effective operator utilization during its own execution. In this sense, the global Error for linear lists has the same utility to application programs as the global Done has for standard input/output operations in Modula-2.

3-1-2 Linear List Operator Definitions

In the following operator definitions, we denote by $L = (e_1 \ e_2 \ \ldots \ e_i \ \ldots \ e_n)$ an arbitrary linear list L, containing n elements, and by x an additional element of the same type as those of L. Moreover, the notation L' will denote the result of applying an operator to the list L, x' will denote the resulting value of x, and i' and n' will denote the resulting values of integer variables i and n, respectively, after the operator has been applied. The resulting value of the global variable Error is similarly indicated by Error'.

Definition: *Create*(L) brings into existence an empty list L' = ( ), sets n' = 0, and initializes the global Error' = false, provided that L does not previously exist. Otherwise, Create is undefined.

Preconditions: L does not exist.

Postconditions: L exists, with L' = (), n' = 0, and Error' = false.

Definition: *Retrieve*(L,i) returns the value of e_i in L.

Preconditions: L and i exist, and $0 < i \leq n$.

Postconditions: If $0 < i \leq n$, then Error' = false and e_i is returned. Otherwise, Error' = true. In either case, L is unchanged.

Example:
Let L = (backus wirth turing gries vonneumann mccarthy lovelace church markov hopper naur).
Then, Retrieve(L,3) returns turing, Error' = false, and L is unchanged.

Definition: *Store*(L,i,x) assigns the value of x to e_i in L.

Preconditions: L, i, and x exist, and $0 < i \leq n$.

Postconditions: If $0 < i \leq n$, then L' = (e_1 e_2 ... e_{i-1} x e_{i+1} ... e_n) and Error' = false. Otherwise, L is unchanged and Error' = true.

Example:
Let L = (49 42 23 80 25 46 39 96 73 74), and x = 17.
Then Store(L,3,x) leaves L' = (49 42 17 80 25 46 39 96 73 74), and Error' = false.

Definition: *Insert*(L,i,x) inserts the element x immediately after the ith element e_i in L.

Preconditions: L, i, and x exist, and $0 \leq i \leq n <$ Maxlist.

Postconditions: If $0 \leq i \leq n <$ Maxlist, then L' = (e_1 e_2 ... e_i x e_{i+1} ... e_n), n' = n + 1, and Error' = false. Otherwise, L is unchanged and Error' = true.

Example:
Let L = (backus wirth turing gries vonneumann mccarthy lovelace church markov hopper naur), and x = knuth.
Then, Insert(L,3,x) leaves L' = (backus wirth turing knuth gries vonneumann mccarthy lovelace church markov hopper naur), n' = 12, and Error' = false.

Definition: *Delete*(L,i,x) deletes the element immediately after e_i in L and assigns it to x.

Preconditions: L, i, and x exist, and $0 \leq i < n$.

Postconditions: If $0 \leq i < n$, then $L' = (e_1\ e_2 \ldots e_i\ e_{i+2} \ldots e_n)$, $x' = e_{i+1}$, $n' = n-1$, and $Error' = false$. Otherwise, $Error' = true$, and L and x are unchanged.

Example:
Let L = (49 42 23 80 25 46 39 96 73 74).
Then, Delete(L,4,x) leaves L' = (49 42 23 80 46 39 96 73 74), x' = 25, n' = 9, and $Error' = false$.

Definition: *Search*(L,i,x) searches the list L for an index j in which $e_j = x$ and assigns that index value to i. If there is no such index (i.e., x appears nowhere in L), then i is assigned the value 0 to designate this absence (of x in L).

Preconditions: L, i, and x exist.

Postconditions: If $n > 0$ and $e_j = x$ for some $j = 1,\ldots,n$ then $i' =$ the value of j. Otherwise, $i' = 0$.

Example:
Let L = (backus wirth turing gries vonneumann mccarthy lovelace church markov hopper naur), and x = gries.
Then, Search(L,i,x) leaves $i' = 4$.

Definition: *Size*(L) returns the current number of elements, n, in L.

Preconditions: L exists.

Postconditions: No change to L or n takes place.

Example:
Let L = (49 42 23 80 25 46 39 96 73 74).
Then, Size(L) returns the value 10.

Definition: *Display*(L) displays the list L.

Preconditions: L exists.

Postconditions: Output is of the form $(e_1\ e_2 \ldots e_n)$. No change to L or n takes place.

Definition: *Dump*(L) displays the list L, the value of n, and the current values of globals Maxlist and Error. Further, the memory addresses and hexadecimal representations of all the elements e_i in L are also shown.

Preconditions: L exists.

Postconditions: Output is as described above. No change to L, n, or Error takes place.

3-1-3 Notes on the Operator Definitions

Before we develop the implementations of these operators, it is worthwhile to observe several important characteristics which they bear. First, we have enlisted the idea of using preconditions and postconditions as sufficient formalisms for specifying the purpose of each operator. Now, however, they are not physically embedded within a Modula-2 procedure; they are instead part of a programming language-independent definition of the abstract data type. From this definition one should be able to implement linear lists in any programming language—Modula-2, Ada, C, FORTRAN, or Pascal. The important principle here, which shall be preserved throughout this text, is the *separation* of an abstract data type's definition from any particular implementation.

A second observation about these definitions is that they rely upon the existence of certain variables as a precondition for their satisfactory definition. By "existence," we mean that storage has been allocated to these variables. For instance, we read that the operator Insert requires the list L, the index i, and the variable x to exist as a precondition for it to meet its postconditions. However, when we implement such operators, there is no way in Modula-2 (or most programming languages, for that matter) to explicitly test for the existence of a variable. Instead, if we invoke a procedure, say Insert(L,i,x), and one of the arguments, say L, does not exist at the time, we will receive some kind of run-time error message and execution will halt. Thus, in our implementations of these operators, explicit tests for required existence of variables will be missing. Explicit tests for all other preconditions stated in these definitions, however, will be present.

The two operators Display and Dump are vehicles for showing a complete list on the terminal screen. The former is used for simply showing the list; the latter is intended for use during a more careful examination of the complete internal status of the list. For instance, we used Dump extensively during the development of our Modula-2 implementations of the linear list abstract data type and its associated driver program. These will be introduced and discussed in later sections.

3-1-4 A Definition Module for Linear Lists

Before proceeding to the implementation of linear lists, we give below a Modula-2 DEFINITION MODULE for the above abstract definitions.

```
DEFINITION MODULE Lists;

EXPORT QUALIFIED List, ListElement, ListIndex, ListError,
                 CreateList, Store, Retrieve, Insert, Delete,
                 SearchList, ListSize, DisplayList, DumpList;
```

```
TYPE List;
     ListElement = INTEGER;
     ListIndex = CARDINAL;

VAR ListError: BOOLEAN;

PROCEDURE CreateList (VAR L: List);

PROCEDURE Store (VAR L: List; i: ListIndex; x: ListElement);

PROCEDURE Retrieve (VAR L: List; i: ListIndex): ListElement;

PROCEDURE Insert (VAR L: List; i: ListIndex; x: ListElement);

PROCEDURE Delete (VAR L: List; i: ListIndex;
                  VAR x: ListElement);

PROCEDURE SearchList (VAR L: List; VAR i: ListIndex;
                      x: ListElement);

PROCEDURE ListSize (VAR L: List): CARDINAL;

PROCEDURE DisplayList (VAR L: List);

PROCEDURE DumpList (VAR L: List);

END Lists.
```

Here, note that the type List is opaque, while the types ListElement and ListIndex are not. This choice simultaneously reveals two principles which we shall preserve throughout the text. First, application programs have a "need to know" about the types for ListElement and ListIndex, so that they may reasonably deal with their own variables of that type (for instance, in choosing ReadInt rather than ReadString to input the value for an element). Yet, an application program that uses our implementation of this abstract data type should not operate directly upon any variable of type List without invoking one of the procedures given above. That is, our implementation of List contains all the procedures necessary for application programs to utilize this type effectively. Simultaneously, our making the type List opaque allows us to defer its complete declaration until we have chosen an implementation strategy for these operators and written a corresponding IMPLEMENTATION MODULE (see below) which embodies that strategy.

The second principle revealed here is that application programs using Lists should be able to know and exploit the fact that we are implementing only lists of INTEGERs (not lists of strings, lists of REALs, lists of CARDINALs, and so forth). That is, our implementation of lists is not generic. Concurrently, notice that we have appended the names of several list operators above with the prefix or suffix "List," in keeping with Modula-2's overall commitment to strong typing. For instance, the operator Create is implemented with the procedure "CreateList" rather than the procedure named "Create." That is because later chapters will define and implement other abstract data types—Strings, Stacks, Queues, and so forth—that will contain many of the same operators. This naming convention allows us to distinguish (say) the Create operator for Lists from the Create operator for Stacks, by writing CreateList in the one case and CreateStack in the other. Readers will note that this is a natural intuitive extension of Modula-2's naming conventions for standard input/output procedures. For instance, we use ReadInt to input an INTEGER, ReadCard to input a CARDINAL, ReadReal to input a REAL, and so forth.

Some programming languages explicitly support the use of generic procedures. For instance, we recall that Pascal contains a single Read procedure, which can be used to input values of any elementary type—real, integer, or char. Additionally, the language Ada contains explicit provisions for implementing generic procedures. That is, we could write the Create procedure once and use it in different places in our program to create objects of type List, String, Stack, and so forth. In the interests of programming ease, therefore, such a facility would seem to be quite attractive. However, the ability to define generic procedures comes not without its price. First, the language loses its commitment to strong typing, which, in many cases, appears to be an asset worth preserving. Second, the addition of generics to a language's features adds significant complexity to its implementation, as the implementors of Ada have discovered. The impact of this and other advanced features, therefore, is significant for persons using the language on contemporary microcomputers and time-sharing systems: compile speed worsens as the compiler becomes more complex. In any event, the provision and use of generic programming features remains at this writing one of the exciting research and development topics in the field of programming language design.

The remainder of this DEFINITION MODULE identifies the procedures (CreateList, Store, Retrieve, and so forth) that can be IMPORTed by an application program. As noted in Chapter 1, that program may be compiled as soon as this DEFINITION module itself is compiled. However, the program may not be executed until the IMPLEMENTATION MODULE is fully defined and compiled. The following sections develop and discuss two distinct implementation strategies for linear lists.

3-2 CONTROLLING MEMORY ALLOCATION IN MODULA-2: THE POINTER

In most cases, variables, arrays, and record structures in a Modula-2 program are activated (allocated memory) exactly when the procedures that declare them are activated (invoked). Moreover, the number of occurrences of such a variable, array, or record is constant and governed by the explicit number of variables that are declared with that type in the procedure. Often, we need to defer such memory activation until long after a procedure has begun execution, or else activate some number of occurrences of such a variable that cannot be determined until execution begins.

To accommodate these occasions, Modula-2 provides facilities by which a program or procedure may *dynamically* activate a variable, array, or record. These facilities are provided by the following two language elements:

1. The POINTER type is used to describe variables whose value is the address of a particular kind of memory block (which contains, in turn, a scalar, array, or record value in memory). A POINTER type can be declared in the following way:

```
TYPE identifier = POINTER TO type
```

Here, "identifier" names the type itself, and "type" specifies the type of scalar (CARDINAL, REAL, etc.), array, or record to which that variable points. In reality, a pointer is nothing more than an address, in the sense described in Chapter 2, and a pointer variable is thus a variable used for indirectly *addressing* the value of another variable in memory.

2. The NEW and DISPOSE procedures allocate and deallocate, respectively, such a memory block when they are invoked in a program. These procedures are, technically, abbreviations for the procedures ALLOCATE and DEALLOCATE, which are EXPORTed by the standard module "Storage."

To illustrate, the following declarations identify three new types, one addressing an integer value, another addressing an array, and the third addressing a record structure. These are followed by variable declarations for p, q, ap, and rp that possess these types, respectively.

```
TYPE Intptr = POINTER TO INTEGER;
     Arrptr = POINTER TO ARRAY[1..10] OF INTEGER;
     Recptr = POINTER TO RECORD
                          Name: ARRAY[1..15] OF CHAR;
                          Score: INTEGER
                        END;
VAR  p,q: Intptr;
     ap:  Arrptr;
     rp:  Recptr;
```

Now, whenever we want to allocate a new block of storage for one of these three types, during the execution of the program, we can write one of the following:

```
    NEW(p)              NEW(ap)              NEW(rp)
```

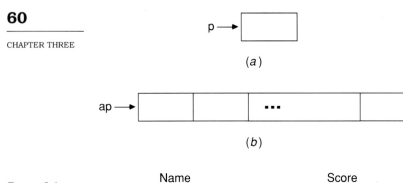

Figure 3-1 Dynamic allocation of INTEGER, ARRAY, and RECORD types.

Each of these, in effect, creates a new block of memory and assigns the address of that block its associated POINTER variable. This is shown in Figures 3-1a, b, and c, respectively. The arrow in each of these figures, and in all other figures throughout the text, denotes symbolically the notion that a pointer is an address, without explicitly writing a specific four-digit hexadecimal address's value as we did in Chapter 2.

To reference the value stored in each of these memory blocks, we must qualify it by identifying the pointer variable that currently contains its address. That is, at any time during the execution of a program, one or more instances of such a memory block may have been allocated. For instance, Figure 3-2 shows the effect of dynamically allocating two INTEGER blocks, one addressed by p and the other addressed by q.

In order to distinguish the block addressed by p from the block addressed by q, we use the qualifier pˆ or qˆ, respectively. Similarly, we may address the ith entry in the dynamically allocated array, using the notation apˆ[i]. Finally, to reference an individual field within a dynamically allocated record, we use the notation rpˆ.Name and rpˆ.Score. In this last example, since the Name is itself an array, we use the notation rpˆ.Name[i] to reference the ith character within the Name field of the record addressed by rp.

A variable that has the POINTER type may either have no value, have the value NIL (which means that it points nowhere), or have a value that points to (addresses) a memory block of its associated type. The distinction between the NIL value and a non-NIL address is conventionally depicted in

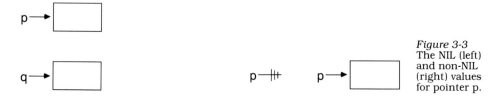

Figure 3-2 Two dynamically allocated INTEGER blocks.

Figure 3-3 The NIL (left) and non-NIL (right) values for pointer p.

Figure 3-4 Value assignment for a dynamic variable.

Figure 3-5 Reassignment of pointer values.

graphical form by a "Christmas tree" and an arrow, respectively, as shown in Figure 3-3.

Once the conventions for referencing dynamically allocated storage blocks are mastered, they may participate in Modula-2 programs in all the ways that a conventional variable may participate: appearing within arithmetic expressions, on the left of assignment statements, as arguments in procedure invocations, and so forth. For example, the statement p^:=49 assigns the value 49 to the INTEGER memory block currently addressed by p, as shown in Figure 3-4.

For another example, the POINTER variable itself may be assigned the value of another pointer variable, or else NIL, by the use of an assignment statement. For instance, if p is initially as shown in Figure 3-4, then the following pair of statements:

q := p ;
p := N I L

leaves p and q as shown in Figure 3-5. Figure 3-5 also illustrates our notational convention of showing a *change* to a pointer value by way of a dotted line. This convention will also be used throughout the text.

Finally, when a dynamically allocated memory block is of no further use to the program, it may be returned to the system by way of the DISPOSE statement. The statement DISPOSE(p), for instance, releases access to the memory block currently addressed by p (together with its current value) and leaves as "undefined" the value of the pointer p itself. No further access to that memory block or its value is thereafter possible after such a statement has been executed.

3-3 CONTIGUOUS IMPLEMENTATION OF LINEAR LISTS

With this introduction to pointers, we may proceed to consider an implementation strategy for the linear list abstract data type. A most straightforward strategy for linear lists L would be to allocate a contiguous block of storage, using an ARRAY[1..Maxlist], and then to store the element values $e_1, e_2, \ldots, e_n$ in the first n entries in that ARRAY. Offsetting this simplicity is the disadvantage that such a strategy is somewhat wasteful of storage, especially when Maxlist is large and n is much smaller than Maxlist. Additionally, the implementation of some list operators (notably Insert and Delete) under this strategy is inefficient, as we shall see. However, for small lists whose size doesn't grow or shrink dramatically during a program run, the contiguous implementation is both straightforward and effective.

3-3-1 Type Implementation

In the following declarations, we have chosen the constant value of 100 for Maxlist. The type List is a dynamically allocated record with two parts; an integer n, which reflects the current size of the list, and an array e, which contains in its first n entries the current values of the list itself. There may be many variables of type List simultaneously active during the run of an application program, each having a different size and collection of element values.

```
CONST Maxlist = 100;

TYPE List = POINTER TO ListRecord;
     ListRecord = RECORD
                    n: CARDINAL;
                    e: ARRAY[1..Maxlist] OF ListElement
                  END;
```

3-3-2 Operator Implementations

In this section, we show the implementation of each operator definition associated with the abstract data type List. All of these are based on the foregoing TYPE declaration and are realizations of the individual definitions given in a previous section. They are also based on the following procedures IMPORTed from various system and private libraries. In the implementation of the Dump operator, we take advantage of the procedure ShowStorage that was developed in Chapter 2. This is the first of numerous instances throughout the text where we avoid "reinventing the wheel" by judiciously archiving important procedures along the way.

```
FROM InOut IMPORT WriteInt, WriteCard, WriteString, WriteLn;
FROM SYSTEM IMPORT ADR, SIZE;
FROM Storage IMPORT ALLOCATE;
FROM MiscLib IMPORT ShowStorage, WriteBool;
```

The first three operator implementations for the abstract data type List are shown below.

```
PROCEDURE CreateList (VAR L: List);
   (*This procedure creates a list L using contiguous array
     storage.  Any program that uses the abstract data type
     List must first invoke this procedure in order to
     establish the array and initialize the global
     ListError.*)
```

```
BEGIN
  NEW(L);
  ListError:=FALSE;
  L^.n:=0
END CreateList;


PROCEDURE Store (VAR L: List; i: ListIndex; x: ListElement);
BEGIN
  WITH L^ DO
    IF (0<i) AND (i<=n)
    THEN e[i]:=x;
      ListError:=FALSE
    ELSE ListError:=TRUE
    END
  END
END Store;


PROCEDURE Retrieve (VAR L: List; i: ListIndex): ListElement;
BEGIN
  WITH L^ DO
    IF (0<i) AND (i<=n)
    THEN
      ListError:=FALSE;
      RETURN e[i]
    ELSE ListError:=TRUE
    END
  END
END Retrieve;
```

In implementing the procedures Store and Retrieve, we enclose the body of the text by "WITH L^ DO ... END" for notational convenience throughout the body of the procedure itself. We have also written these procedures in a style that exactly mirrors the preconditions given in the original definitions of these operators. Of course, the precondition of "existence" generally cannot be explicitly tested, but the others can and should. These routine conventions will be followed throughout all of our operator implementations. In addition to giving a strong stylistic resemblance to the original definitions, they also serve to facilitate the systematic verification of the operator implementations, as we shall see.

The implementation of the Insert operator is given below:

```
PROCEDURE Insert (VAR L: List; i: ListIndex;
                       x: ListElement);
VAR j: ListIndex;
```

```
BEGIN
  WITH L^ DO
    IF (0<=i) AND (i<=n) AND (n<Maxlist)
    THEN
      n:=n+1;
      j:=n-1;
      WHILE j>=i+1 DO
        e[j+1]:=e[j];
        j:=j-1
      END;
      e[i+1]:=x;
      ListError:=FALSE
    ELSE ListError:=TRUE
    END
  END
END Insert;
```

The procedure Insert works by first shifting the values of e[i+1] ... e[n] forward one position in the array, so that they occupy the entries e[i+2] ... e[n+1], respectively. This makes room for the new value x, which is stored in entry e[i+1] itself.

The procedure Delete works in the opposite fashion, shifting each of the values e[i+2] ... e[n] backward one position, so that they occupy entries e[i+1] ... e[n-1], respectively. Its implementation is left as an exercise.

Implementations of the list operators Size, Display, and Dump are given below.

```
PROCEDURE ListSize (VAR L: List): CARDINAL;
BEGIN
  RETURN L^.n
END ListSize;

PROCEDURE DisplayList (VAR L: List);
VAR i: ListIndex;
BEGIN
  WITH L^ DO
    WriteString('(');
    FOR i:=1 TO n DO
      WriteInt (e[i],6);
      IF i MOD 12 = 0 THEN WriteLn END
    END;
    WriteString(')'); WriteLn
  END
END DisplayList;

PROCEDURE DumpList (VAR L: List);
VAR i: ListIndex;
```

```
BEGIN
  WITH L^ DO
    DisplayList (L);
    WriteString('The list has the following addresses');
    WriteLn;
    WriteString('and hexadecimal element values:'); WriteLn;
    FOR i:=1 TO n DO
      ShowStorage(ADR(e[i]),SIZE(e[i]));
      WriteLn
    END;
    WriteString('Size=');    WriteCard (n,5);            WriteLn;
    WriteString('Maxlist='); WriteInt (Maxlist,5);       WriteLn;
    WriteString('Error=');   WriteBool(ListError);       WriteLn
  END
END DumpList;
```

Here, note that the Size operator is implemented in such a way that the number, n, of elements in list L is identified with the procedure invocation ListSize(L), from the point of view of the application program. Note also that the DumpList procedure makes use of the ShowStorage procedure, which was developed in Chapter 2, for displaying memory addresses and hexadecimal values of the list elements e_i. WriteBool is an auxiliary procedure that simply displays TRUE or FALSE, according to the Boolean value of its argument.

In implementing the Search operator for linear lists, we have at least two possible strategies; one is called the "serial search," and the other is called the "binary search." These two alternatives are shown and discussed in the paragraphs below.

3-3-2-1 Serial Search

The procedure SearchList, shown below, is an implementation of the familiar "serial search" strategy, which is sometimes called "linear search," or "sequential search." This strategy examines the list serially from its beginning, until either a matching element is found or the list is exhausted without a match.

```
PROCEDURE SearchList (VAR L: List; VAR i: ListIndex;
                                        x: ListElement);
BEGIN
  WITH L^ DO
    i:=1;
    WHILE (i<=n) AND (x<>e[i]) DO
      i:=i+1
    END;
    IF i>n THEN
      i:=0
    END
  END
END SearchList;
```

In the event that a match is found, i is left with the index of the first element e_i in L that matches x. Otherwise, i is set to 0 by the last IF statement in the procedure. Although this is a conceptually simple procedure, the serial search strategy has a serious disadvantage in its efficiency, especially as the size of the list L becomes large. That is, this procedure is O(n) in complexity, since each iteration of the WHILE loop eliminates only one element of the array as a candidate for a match.

One naturally asks, at this point, whether or not there are search strategies that will improve upon this complexity, at perhaps a slight loss in simplicity. The answer, as readers may well know, is in the affirmative—and one such strategy is called the "binary search."

3-3-2-2 Binary Search

In operation, the binary search procedure scans the list from the middle, each time aiming to eliminate fully half of its remaining elements from consideration in each successive loop iteration. In order for this procedure to be effective, the list elements must first be arranged in ascending sequence, or "ordered," in accordance with the following definition.

Definition: A linear list $L = (e_1 \; e_2 \ldots e_i \ldots e_n)$ is *ordered* if $e_i \leq e_{i+1}$ for all $i = 1, 2, \ldots, n-1$.

When the list is ordered, the argument x is first compared with the middle element e_i [i is initially computed as $(n+1)$ DIV 2]. If, on the one hand, $x < e_i$, the ordering of L guarantees that $x < e_j$ for all $j = i+1, \ldots n$ as well. Similarly, $x > e_i$ allows us to eliminate from further consideration not only e_i but also all of $e[1] \ldots e[i-1]$. This is an example of a large class of algorithms known as "divide and conquer" algorithms, since at every turn they divide the remaining problem to be solved to a much smaller problem than the one currently under consideration. Figure 3-6 shows the result of each step in a binary search of the ordered list (23 25 39 42 46 49 73 74 80 96) for the argument $x = 80$.

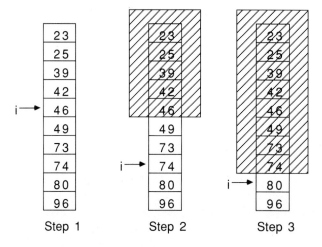

Figure 3-6 Steps in a binary search.

Below is our implementation of the binary search procedure.

```
PROCEDURE BinarySearchList (VAR L: List; VAR i: ListIndex;
                                         x: ListElement);
VAR low,high: ListIndex;
BEGIN
   WITH L^ DO
     low:=1;
     high:=n;
     IF n>0 THEN
        REPEAT
          i:=(low+high) DIV 2;
          IF x<e[i] THEN
             high:=i-1
          ELSE
             low:=i+1
          END
        UNTIL (x=e[i]) OR (low>high)
     END;
     IF (n=0) OR (x<>e[i]) THEN
        i:=0
     END
   END
END BinarySearchList;
```

Here, the condition for ending the search when x is nowhere in L is "low> high." That is, as we continue to cut the remaining list to be searched in half, there will eventually be a moment when low=i=high, x<>e[i], and one of the following two events occurs:

1. Low is assigned the value of i+1, and thus low>high is TRUE.
2. High is assigned the value of i−1, so low>high is again TRUE.

In either case, x is assured to be nowhere in the array, since the search closes in on its value systematically from either side (exploiting the fact that the list is ordered).

3-4 VERIFICATION AND COMPLEXITY OF THE CONTIGUOUS IMPLEMENTATION

In this section, two different methods are used for verifying this implementation of the Linear List abstract data type. The first method utilizes a driver, shown below, which builds a five-element linear list and then interactively allows each of the other operator implementations to be exercised at the terminal. The second method verifies an operator implementation by applying a systematic argument that associates its procedure implementation with the preconditions and postconditions in its corresponding operator definition. Finally, the complexity of our implementations of these operators is briefly discussed.

3-4-1 A Driver for Verification of the List Operators

Below is a driver for exercising the foregoing implementation of the Lists abstract data type.

```
MODULE ListDriver;

FROM InOut IMPORT Read, ReadInt, ReadCard, WriteLn,
                  WriteString, WriteInt, WriteCard;
FROM Lists IMPORT List, ListIndex, ListElement, ListError,
                  CreateList, Store, Retrieve, Insert, Delete,
                  SearchList, ListSize, DisplayList, DumpList;

VAR L: List;
    i: ListIndex;   (*ListIndex is assumed to be CARDINAL.*)
    x: ListElement; (*ListElement is assumed to be INTEGER.*)
    key: CHAR;

BEGIN
  WriteString ('Testing implementation of Lists data ');
  WriteString ('type:');
  WriteLn;
  WriteString ('Building a list of 5 integers:');
  WriteLn;
  CreateList(L);
  i:=0;
  FOR x:=1 TO 5 DO
    Insert(L,i,x);
    i:=i+1
  END;
  DumpList(L);
  REPEAT
    WriteString('Enter a letter to test a function:');
    WriteLn;
    WriteString('(s)tore, (r)etrieve, (i)nsert, (d)elete,');
    WriteLn;
    WriteString('s(e)arch, d(u)mp, or (q)uit:');
    Read(key);
    WriteLn;
    IF key<>'q' THEN
      CASE key OF
      's': WriteString('Enter an integer and an index:');
           ReadInt(x); WriteString('   '); ReadCard(i);
           WriteLn; Store(L,i,x);
           WriteString('The resulting list is:');
           DisplayList(L)
```

```
      'r': WriteString('Enter an index:');
           ReadCard(i); WriteLn;
           x:=Retrieve(L,i);
           WriteString('The value retrieved is:');
           WriteInt(x,5)                                |
      'i': WriteString('Enter an integer and an index:');
           ReadInt(x); WriteString('   '); ReadCard(i);
           WriteLn;
           Insert(L,i,x);
           WriteString('The resulting list is:');
           DisplayList(L)                               |
      'd': WriteString('Enter an index:');
           ReadCard(i); WriteLn;
           Delete(L,i,x);
           WriteString('The resulting list is:');
           DisplayList(L)                               |
      'e': WriteString('Enter an integer for the search:');
           ReadInt(x); WriteLn;
           SearchList(L,i,x);
           WriteString('The resulting index is:');
           WriteCard(i,5)                               |
      'u': WriteString('The current list is:');
           DumpList(L)
      ELSE
      END;
      WriteLn
    END
  UNTIL key='q';
  WriteLn;
  WriteString('End of Lists test.'); WriteLn
END ListDriver.
```

Here, we see that the terminal user has an opportunity to test every one of our operator implementations, especially trying cases where the Error global will be raised, ensuring that each one's execution delivers results consistent with its corresponding definition.

3-4-2 Assertion-based Verification of the Insert Operator

Another separate approach to the verification of these operator implementations begins by assuming that its preconditions are met and proceeds by systematically analyzing the individual steps in the procedure body to show that, under all possible execution paths, the corresponding postconditions are necessarily met. Central to this approach is the need to identify the invariant for each loop in the procedure body. For example, consider our implementation of the procedure Insert, and let us begin by assuming that the preconditions for Insert are met, namely:

L, i, and x exist, and $0 \leq i \leq n <$ Maxlist.

We then continue by hand-tracing through the body to deduce its satisfaction of the postconditions, namely:

```
If 0≤i≤n<Maxlist, then L'=(e₁e₂...e₁ x e₁₊₁...eₙ),
n'=n+1, and Error'=false.
Otherwise, L is unchanged and Error'=true.
```

Extracting the body of the procedure Insert; adding the preconditions, postconditions, and appropriate loop invariant; and numbering the lines (for cross-reference purposes), we have the following basis for systematically verifying this operator implementation.

```
       BEGIN
       (**PRE: 0<=i<=n<Maxlist **)
1        WITH L^ DO
2          IF (0<=i) AND (i<=n) AND (n<Maxlist) THEN
3            n:=n+1;
4            j:=n-1;
5            WHILE j>=i+1 DO
       (**INV: i<=j<=n, and L'=(e[1..i] e[i+1..j+1] e[j+1..n]) **)
6              e[j+1]:=e[j];
7              j:=j-1
8            END;
9            e[i+1]:=x;
10           ListError:=FALSE
11         ELSE
12           ListError:=TRUE
13         END
14     END
       (**POST: n'=n+1, L'=(e[1..i] x e[i+1..n]),
              and Error'=false**)
       END Insert;
```

Here, the postcondition inserted after line 14 reflects only the case in which the precondition is met; the other case, where i is outside the range [0..n], is uninteresting since the net effect is simply to set Error' = true.

Looking at the more interesting case, note first that line 2 essentially mirrors the precondition for Insert, except that it cannot explicitly test for the required existence of L, i, or x. Lines 3-10 are then executed whenever this precondition is met. Therein, line 3 itself guarantees that the postcondition $n' = n+1$ is met. The loop in lines 5-8 has as its invariant the following:

$$i \leq j \leq n \text{ and } L' = (e_1 \ldots e_i \ e_{i+1} \ldots e_{j+1} \ e_{j+1} \ldots e_n)$$

(In the Insert procedure above, this invariant is written in a slightly different style, since program coding does not permit us to shift below the line to record subscripts.) This is, in fact, an invariant because it is true before the first iteration of the loop and after each successive iteration as well. Preceding the first iteration, we have (line 4 sets j=n):

$i \leq j = n$ and $L' = (e_1 \ldots e_i\ e_{i+1} \ldots e_n)$.

That is, L is unchanged at this point. After each successive iteration of the loop, a copy of e_j is stored in the next adjacent element e_{j+1}, by line 6. Thus, the invariant partitions L into three parts: e[1..i], which never changes; e[i+1..j+1], which is decreasing by one element after each iteration; and e[j+1..n+1], which is increasing by one element after each iteration. Moreover, the last element e[j+1] of the second part is identical to the first element of the third part, by virtue of the copying activity that occurs in line 6. Thus, the invariant remains true after each iteration. The last iteration ends with the following assertion:

$j = i$ and $L' = (e_1 \ldots e_i\ e_{i+1}\ e_{i+1}\ e_{i+2} \ldots e_n)$.

The insertion of x in location i+1 is finally made in line 9 of the procedure, and line 10 routinely sets Error' = false. Thus, the postcondition for the Insert operator is fully satisfied, and our verification of this implementation is now complete.

Significant research has been done in the area of mathematical verification of programs, using more formal proof techniques than the ones used here. Our aim here is more modest: we wish to establish a rigorous framework for reasoning about program behavior and thus developing disciplined habits for systematic program verification. Often, the practice of looking at one's code with an analytic eye, rather than spinning through countless "debugging" runs to uncover errors, results in both a clearer understanding of the program's purpose and a longer night's sleep. Central to this practice is the development, for each new programming problem, of a complete set of preconditions and postconditions to specify the range of possible inputs and outputs for the program under consideration. Equally important is the development of a knack for finding loop invariants. This can be useful not only as an aid for program verification but also as an aid for writing the loops themselves.

3-4-3 Complexity of the List Operators

The complexity of the contiguous implementation of linear lists is O(c), or constant, for the operators Create, Store, Retrieve, and Size. That is, none of these procedures contains a loop, so that a fixed number of steps is executed in every invocation. For the operators Insert, Delete, Search, Display, and Dump the complexity is O(n), since each one does contain a loop that will be executed a number of times and that depends on n (the size of the list).

To illustrate, consider the serial search procedure SearchList, which was implemented in section 3-3-2-1. The number of times that the WHILE loop in that procedure is executed depends upon both the value of n and the position of x within the list. For instance, if x = e[1], then the loop will be repeated exactly one time. On the other hand, if x ≠ e[i] for any i = 1,...,n, then the loop will be executed n + 1 times. Assuming that each of the n + 1 possibilities for x's position in the list (including the possibility that x appears nowhere) is *equally likely* to occur, the *average* number of iterations for this loop is (n + 1)/2. Noting that this loop has two statements (the condition test and the assignment of i), and that there are two additional statements outside this loop that are executed exactly once, the average number of steps that will be executed in a typical invocation is 2(n + 1)/2 + 2, or n + 3 steps. This confirms the claim that the procedure SearchList is O(n) in complexity.

Central to this argument, and to many others later in the text, is our reliance on "typical expectations," or probabilistic behavior, for the input in an invocation of the procedure. This reliance requires, in turn, that the element values in the list at run time will occur according to our expectations, especially over a large number of invocations. In practice, of course, many applications do not always conform to such assumptions, and so we also construct "worst case" scenarios for the procedures in question as well as "average case" scenarios as we have done here. For the SearchList procedure, the reader can see that the worst case is one in which the argument x is *never* found in the list, forcing the WHILE loop to be executed n + 1 times at every invocation. Although that does not affect the O(n) *complexity* of SearchList, its actual execution time will increase (essentially double) when n is large.

3-5 LINKING MEMORY BLOCKS TOGETHER IN MODULA-2: THE NODE

Additional flexibility of dynamic storage allocation and pointers occurs when we define blocks of memory in such a way that an arbitrary number of them may be dynamically created and linked together in a chain, without the need to explicitly declare an arbitrarily large number of POINTER variables themselves. That is, we wish to avoid declaring more than two or three POINTER variables and simultaneously find a way for the memory block itself to be connected, or "linked," to another memory block of the same type. That process will be developed in this section and then used as a basis for an entirely different implementation of the linear list abstract data type in the next section.

> **Definition:** A *node* is a dynamically allocated record, which itself contains the information for a single list element, e_i, together with a linking pointer that is used to connect that element to its successor, e_{i+1}.

Schematically, we represent a node as shown in Figure 3-7, where "p" is a pointer to the node itself (since it is dynamically allocated) and "link" is a

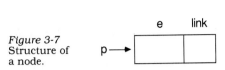

Figure 3-7
Structure of a node.

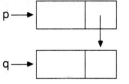

Figure 3-8
A pair of nodes linked together.

pointer embedded within the record that can connect the node to another node.

A node for implementing linked lists, and its associated variables, may be declared in Modula-2 as follows.

```
TYPE ptr = POINTER TO Node;
     Node = RECORD
              e: INTEGER;
              link: ptr
            END;
VAR p,q, head : ptr;
```

Here, the variables p and q are declared so that they may be used as auxiliary pointers for building and traversing these interconnected nodes in various ways (in the same spirit as i and j are generally used as auxiliary subscript variables when we work with arrays). The pointer variable "head" is specially designated for referencing the node for the first element, e_1, in the list.

Before examining the complete structure of a list implementation itself, we pause here to consider the dynamic creation and linking of a single pair of nodes, which will contain the element values e_i and e_{i+1}, to each other. The following sequence of Modula-2 statements accomplishes this.

```
NEW(p);
NEW(q);
p^.link:=q
```

These statements generate exactly the list fragment shown in Figure 3-8.

Note that these statements do not store the element values themselves in either node. For that to take place, an appropriate assignment must be made. For example, the assignments:

```
p^.e:=49;
q^.e:=42
```

leave the values 49 and 42, respectively, as the element values of nodes referenced by p and q.

3-6 LINKED IMPLEMENTATION OF LINEAR LISTS

We are now ready to develop the alternative "linked" implementation of linear lists. This implementation maintains a list in the general form depicted in Figure 3-9. Here, note the conventions that the node ListHead contains additional information beyond the current list size, n. The pointer "head" references the node containing the first element of the list, while the pointer "klink" references the so-called "current node" of the list. The value of klink is maintained dynamically by the list operators in such a way that the most recently executed operator leaves it pointing to the particular element that was affected by that operator. The value of k is maintained, in tandem with klink, with the corresponding ListIndex value of that element. Our purpose here is to provide means for adding efficiency to this implementation by avoiding a linear search of the list every time an operator is executed.

In Figure 3-9, each element's node is explicitly connected to the next by an explicit pointer "link," and the last node in the list is so designated by a NIL link value. Also by convention, an empty list can be recognized by the presence of a NIL head, which is always equivalent to the condition $n = 0$.

We begin this implementation by using the exact same definition module that was shown in section 3-1-4, prior to the contiguous implementation of linear lists. We intend to develop a suite of operator implementations that can be separately compiled and then automatically relinked with any application program that uses lists. That is, we are realizing the principles of data abstraction and separate compilation that were introduced in Figure 1-2 in Chapter 1. The following declarations are appropriate to

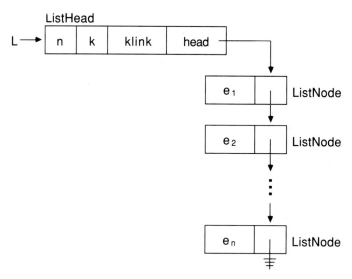

Figure 3-9
Linked implementation of linear lists.

maintaining lists in the form shown in Figure 3-9 and will be used by our subsequent operator implementations.

```
CONST Maxlist = 10000;

TYPE List = POINTER TO ListHead;
     ListLink = POINTER TO ListNode;
     ListHead = RECORD
                    n: CARDINAL;
                    k: ListIndex;     (*the "current" element*)
                    klink: ListLink;  (*and its corresp. link*)
                    head: ListLink
                END;
     ListNode = RECORD
                    e: ListElement;
                    link: ListLink
                END;
```

The constant Maxlist is now increased to a much larger value than it had in the contiguous implementation, in deference to the fact that we are now only allocating as many memory blocks as we need for the current list size. In the contiguous implemenation, recall, we had to allocate all Maxlist memory locations at the outset. Thus, the value of Maxlist itself had to be more conservatively chosen, especially in applications or machines where memory is at a premium.

One might further argue that there is no need to have Maxlist at all in this linked implementation, since memory will not be needlessly wasted in runs where the list size is small. However, this argument weakens in the face of the need to maintain the integrity of the procedures for verification purposes. We also need to acknowledge that memory is, in fact, finite under all circumstances (even though it often appears to be limitless!). In any event, we should pick the value for Maxlist in accordance with the maximum size of available storage for the machine we are using.

Thus, the linked implementation of any list L will always have exactly one record of the type ListHead, followed by n records of the type ListNode, chained together by the pointer "link." An example of this implementation is given in Figure 3-10, where the list L contains the five integers (49 42 23 80 25), and the current node is assumed to be that which contains e_2, or 42.

The individual operator implementations can now be redone using this strategy. Below is a reimplementation of the operator Create.

```
PROCEDURE CreateList (VAR L: List);
(*This procedure creates a list L using linked storage.
  Any program that uses the abstract data type List must
  first invoke this procedure in order to establish the
  list and initialize the global ListError. *)
```

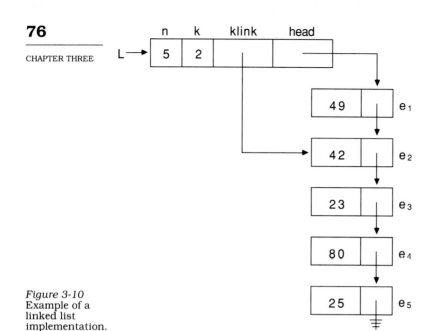

Figure 3-10
Example of a linked list implementation.

```
BEGIN
    NEW(L);
    ListError:=FALSE;
    WITH L^ DO
        n:=0;
        k:=0;
        klink:=NIL;
        head:=NIL
    END
END CreateList;
```

This is a straightforward procedure, in which the initialization of $n=0$ is now accompanied by an initialization of the current node index $k=0$ and its companion $klink = NIL$. The initialization of $head = NIL$ also signals the presence of an empty list.

The remaining procedures are slightly more difficult to implement because of the difference in roles between a list index value, say i, and its companion pointer value, say ilink, which references the corresponding node containing e_i. These procedures, when given an index value i as an argument from an application program, must translate that value into its corresponding pointer value "ilink," in order to reference the node where e_i is stored. (Recall that, in the contiguous implementation, this duality of usage was not a problem, because the index value i could serve directly as a subscript to reference the list element e[i].) Here, this translation is accomplished by the procedure FindLink, shown below, with the help of the index k for the current node and its companion klink.

```
PROCEDURE FindLink (VAR L: List; i: ListIndex): ListLink;
(*Find the link corresponding to the ListIndex i
   in List L.*)
VAR j: ListIndex;
    jlink: ListLink;
BEGIN
  WITH L^ DO
    IF i=k THEN       (*Is this the current element?*)
      RETURN klink
    ELSIF (i<=0) OR (i>n) THEN (*Index out of range?*)
      RETURN NIL
    ELSE j:=1;        (*Neither; search from the head*)
      jlink:=head;
      WHILE j<>i DO
        j:=j+1;
        jlink:=jlink^.link
      END;
      RETURN jlink
    END
  END
END FindLink;
```

By convention, this procedure returns NIL if the index i is out of range for the current size of the list L. Otherwise, it returns a link value corresponding to the value of i. Thus, if i=1, a link to the node containing e_1 is returned; if i=2, a link to the node containing e_2 is returned, and so forth. Note that a search for that link is necessary in cases where i is not identical with the index of the current node, k.

With the procedure FindLink available, the following implementations of Store and Retrieve can now be given.

```
PROCEDURE Store (VAR L: List; i: ListIndex; x: ListElement);
VAR ilink: ListLink;
BEGIN
  WITH L^ DO
    ilink:=FindLink(L,i);
    IF ilink<>NIL THEN
      ilink^.e:=x;
      ListError:=FALSE;
      klink:=ilink;
      k:=i                    (*Reset the current element.*)
    ELSE ListError:=TRUE
    END
  END
END Store;
```

```
PROCEDURE Retrieve (VAR L: List; i: ListIndex): ListElement;
VAR ilink: ListLink;
BEGIN
  WITH L^ DO
    ilink:=FindLink(L,i);
    IF ilink<>NIL THEN
      ListError:=FALSE;
      klink:=ilink;
      k:=i;                      (*Reset the current element. *)
      RETURN ilink^.e
    ELSE ListError:=TRUE
    END
  END
END Retrieve;
```

These procedures are simple variations of their counterparts in the contiguous implementation. In neither case is the structure of the list affected; only the value of e_i in the ith node is referenced. Note that each procedure begins its execution by finding the link corresponding to the index i and then performs its operation only in the event that the value of i is within the range [1..n] for the current values in L.

Below is the implementations of the operator Insert, which again uses the auxiliary procedure FindLink to associate an index value with its corresponding link.

```
PROCEDURE Insert (VAR L: List; i: ListIndex; x: ListElement);
VAR ilink,jlink: ListLink;
BEGIN
  WITH L^ DO
    ilink:=FindLink(L,i);
    IF (i>=0) AND (i<=n) AND (n+1<=Maxlist) THEN
      n:=n+1;
      NEW(jlink);
      jlink^.e:=x;
      IF i=0 THEN
        jlink^.link:=head; (*i=0 means insert at the head. *)
        head:=jlink
      ELSE jlink^.link:=ilink^.link; (*Otherwise, insert
                                                 after ith. *)
        ilink^.link:=jlink
      END;
      k:=i+1;                    (*Reset the current element. *)
      klink:=jlink;
      ListError:=FALSE
    ELSE ListError:=TRUE
    END
  END
END Insert;
```

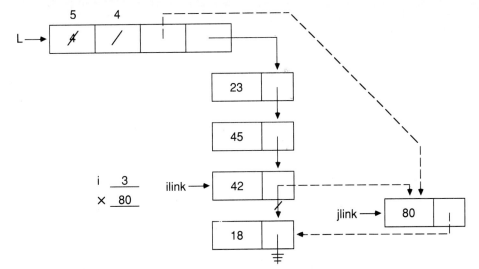

Figure 3-11
Insertion of an element in a linked list.

The important difference between this linked implementation and its contiguous counterpart is the absence of a "shift" loop. That is, if the *current* node k is identical with the index i, then the procedure FindLink itself does not need to loop in order to find the link "ilink" that corresponds to i. The act of insertion is thus accomplished in these cases by simply altering two pointer values. To illustrate, an insertion of the value 80 into the list L=(23 45 42 18), immediately after the element 42, is shown in Figure 3-11.

Deletion of the node following the ith should have similar considerations. For instance, Figure 3-12 shows how the element 80 can be deleted from the list (23 45 42 80 18). As we can see, the search is avoided if we assume that the current node k is identical with the index i. Otherwise, a search to find the corresponding link, ilink, must be carried out by the procedure FindLink itself. Implementation of the Delete operator for the linked implementation is also left as an exercise.

Implementations of the Search, Size, Display, and Dump operators for linked lists are shown below.

```
PROCEDURE SearchList (VAR L: List; VAR i: ListIndex;
                                        x: ListElement);
VAR ilink: ListLink;
BEGIN
  WITH L^ DO
    ilink:=FindLink(L,i);
    ilink:=head;
    i:=1;
    WHILE (ilink<>NIL) AND (x<>ilink^.e) DO
      ilink:=ilink^.link;
      i:=i+1
    END;
```

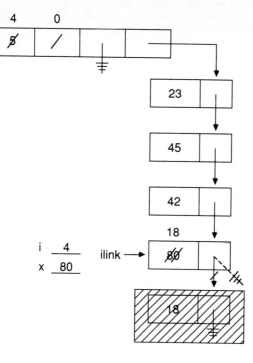

Figure 3-12
Deletion of an
element from a
linked list.

```
        IF ilink=NIL THEN
          i:=0
        ELSE
          k:=i;                    (*Reset the current element.*)
          klink:=ilink
        END
      END
  END SearchList;


  PROCEDURE ListSize (VAR L: List): CARDINAL;
  BEGIN
    RETURN L^.n
  END ListSize;


  PROCEDURE DisplayList (VAR L: List);
  VAR i: ListIndex;
      ilink: ListLink;
  BEGIN
    WITH L^ DO
      WriteString('(');
      ilink:=head;
      FOR i:=1 TO n DO
        WriteInt (ilink^.e,6);
        IF i MOD 12 = 0 THEN WriteLn END;
```

```
      ilink:=ilink^.link
    END;
    WriteString(')'); WriteLn
  END
END DisplayList;


PROCEDURE DumpList (VAR L: List);
VAR ilink: ListLink;
BEGIN
  WITH L^ DO
    DisplayList (L);
    WriteString('The list has the following addresses');
    WriteLn;
    WriteString('and hexadecimal element values:'); WriteLn;
    ilink:=head;
    WHILE ilink<>NIL DO
      ShowStorage(ADR(ilink^.e),SIZE(ilink^.e));
      WriteLn;
      ilink:=ilink^.link
    END;
    WriteString('Current=');    WriteCard(k,5);              WriteLn;
    WriteString('Size=');  WriteCard (ListSize(L),5); WriteLn;
    WriteString('Maxlist=');    WriteInt (Maxlist,5);   WriteLn;
    WriteString('Error=');      WriteBool(ListError);   WriteLn
  END
END DumpList;
```

Note that the procedure DumpList has been augmented to display the value of the current element index, k, along with the other information. In other respects, each of these procedures is a straightforward adaptation of its contiguous counterpart.

3-7 VERIFICATION AND COMPLEXITY OF THE LINKED IMPLEMENTATION

To verify the procedures for the linked implementation linear lists, one may either reuse the driver program ListDriver (introduced in section 3-4-1) or insert preconditions and postconditions within the body of the procedure and argue that the postconditions are satisfied by any particular input values that satisfy the preconditions. If the driver is used, it may be used without alteration or recompilation. Only a recompilation of the redesigned IMPLEMENTATION MODULE Lists is needed, followed by a link step that unites the previously compiled ListDriver main program with this newly compiled module Lists, and finally the execution step itself.

Alternatively, we may verify each of these operator implementations using preconditions and postconditions, as illustrated below for the Insert operator.

```
     BEGIN
     (**PRE: 0<=i<=n<Maxlist**)
 1       WITH L^ DO
 2         ilink:=FindLink(L,i);
 3         IF (i>=0) AND (i<=n) AND (n+1<=Maxlist) THEN
 4           n:=n+1;
 5           NEW(jlink);
 6           jlink^.e:=x;
 7           IF i=0 THEN
 8             jlink^.link:=head;   (*i=0 means insert at
                                       the head.*)
 9             head:=jlink
     (**i=0 and L'=(x e[1..n])**)
10           ELSE jlink^.link:=ilink^.link; (*Otherwise,
                                         insert after ith.*)
11             ilink^.link:=jlink
     (**i>0 and L'=(e[1..i] x e[i+1..n])**)
12           END;
13           k:=i+1;  (*Reset the current element.*)
14           klink:=jlink;
15           ListError:=FALSE
16         ELSE ListError:=TRUE
17         END
18     END
     (**POST: n'=n+1, L'=(e[1..i] x e[i+1..n]),
         and Error'=false**)
     END Insert;
```

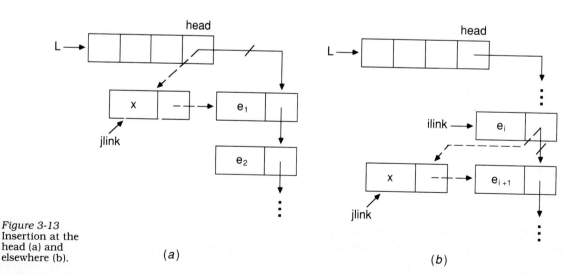

Figure 3-13
Insertion at the head (a) and elsewhere (b).

Here, there are no (explicit) loops in the procedure, so that the aid of an invariant is not needed. Instead, we have inserted two assertions that represent the two variations of the postcondition for the case i=0 and the case i>0, respectively, at appropriate places within the procedure. We also assume in this exercise that the FindLink procedure is correct; its verification should be done (see exercise 3-10) in advance. Note that the preconditions and postconditions shown here are identical with the ones used for the contiguous implementation of Insert.

To complete this verification, we now focus on these two cases separately, since each one leads independently to confirmation of the postcondition itself. The case i=0 leads to an insertion at the head, and lines 8-9 describe the appropriate actions which will realize this insertion. Specifically, the new node (referenced by jlink) is reconnected to the original head node, and the head pointer is reconnected to the new node. This is illustrated in Figure 3-13a (page 82). The case i>0 leads to an insertion after the ith node in the original list, and lines 10-11 accomplish this. That is, the new node is linked to the original i+1st node, and the ith node is linked to the new node. This is illustrated in Figure 3-13b. In either event, the prior execution of line 6 guarantees that the value of x is inserted in this new node, so that x assumes its proper place within the list. Also, line 4 guarantees in either event that the value of n is incremented to reflect the effect of the insertion on the list size.

3-8 COMPARISON OF IMPLEMENTATION STRATEGIES

It is clear that the linked implementation of linear lists improves upon the contiguous implementation with respect to storage utilization and flexibility. That is, the maximum size of the list is not so constrained as in the contiguous case, and all of the storage that is allocated in the linked implementation is actually used. In efficiency, however, each of the two implementations has advantages over the other, depending upon the operator in question and the status of the "current element" index in the linked implementation. These tradeoffs are summarized in the table below.

List Operator	Contiguous Complexity	Linked Complexity (i = current)	Linked Complexity (i ≠ current)
Store	O(c)	O(c)	O(n)
Retrieve	O(c)	O(c)	O(n)
Insert	O(n)	O(c)	O(n)
Delete	O(n)	O(c)	O(n)
Search	O(n)	O(n)	O(n)

In general, the contiguous implementation is ideally suited to applications in which the number of insertions and deletions is relatively small or about the same, and hence the overall list size is relatively stable and predictable in advance. As insertion activity grows, it makes more sense to consider the linked implementation. Even here, however, it is important to realize that *all five* of these operators have O(n) complexity in cases where their various invocations are not centered on a particular location in the list. That is, the more frequently the FindLink procedure must serially search the list to locate the node corresponding to index i, the fewer advantages in efficiency are realized for the linked implementation. The next to last column in the table above, however, portrays the most optimistic efficiency gains for the linked implementation over the contiguous one. When insertions and deletions occur at the current node, the linked implementation achieves O(c) complexity, whereas the contiguous implementation achieves only O(n) under all circumstances.

Thus, when choosing an implementation strategy for linear lists, one must examine the application with these considerations in mind. The choice of a strategy is not always the same; it will vary with the number and locality of list insertions and deletions. Moreover, if the list size n is relatively small, the choice of implementation strategy is really insignificant with respect to its overall impact on the efficiency of the application.

3-9 PROBLEM 1: THE ADVANCED INSTRUCTOR'S PROBLEM REVISITED

Recall the Advanced Instructor's Problem that was given at the end of Chapter 1:

> For an arbitrary course, and for an arbitrary moment during the grading period where a series of adds, drops, and test scores is to be entered, update the standing records for that course and, if requested, display the records for any or all students who are currently enrolled in it.

Now that we have some of the tools for dealing with that problem, let us put them to use by developing a partial solution. We call this solution the Less Naive Instructor's Problem. In particular, this solution allows the entry of student names for a class *first* (which reflects the registration process at the beginning of the semester) and then the entry of a series of test scores for the students in the class each time a test is given (which reflects the chronological series of events as the semester proceeds). Further, this solution allows any number of tests to be recorded for a class, not just three, and missing scores to be recorded in the event that a student misses a particular test. Although this is not a complete solution for the Advanced Instructor's Problem, it is a significant improvement over the naive version presented in Chapter 1. This exercise also serves as a good application for our implementation of the linear list abstract data type, illustrating the significant savings that can be derived from the conscious use of data abstraction in problem solving.

The input to this problem is assumed to be a sequence of student names, representing the registration list for this class, followed by several series of test scores—one series for each test. The list of student names is ended by <ctl-z> in order to it from the first series of test scores. Each series has an integer score for every student in the class (−1 means "missing") in the same order in which the original names were entered. The following sample terminal session illustrates these input conventions, including appropriate prompts.

```
Enter names, ending the last with ctl-z:
backus
wirth
turing
gries
vonneumann
mccarthy<ctl-z>
Enter a series of scores for each test, ending with ctl-z:
75
-1
90
86
91
70
85
-1
85
84
82
85
95
-1
-1
-1
82
100<ctl-z>
```

For output, this program is expected to process all of the data and then report the number of tests, current average, and test scores for each student in the class. A sample output for the foregoing input appears below.

STUDENT	# TESTS	AVERAGE	SCORES		
backus	3	85.0	75	85	95
wirth	0				
turing	2	87.5	90	85	
gries	2	85.0	86	84	
vonneumann	3	85.0	91	82	82
mccarthy	3	85.0	70	85	100

Most important to this example is our ability to use the linked implementation of the linear list to maintain the scores for each student. As indicated above, each such list can be a different size, depending on the number of tests that the student has taken. (Readers may also observe that the collection of student names is itself a list, but it is a list of character strings rather than a list of integers. We are not equipped to utilize our list implementation for that additional purpose, without first making our implementation generic. That task will not be addressed in the present exercise.)

The internal representation for a student's name and list of scores in this problem is suggested in Figure 3-14. For an entire class, we can declare an entire array of such records, one for each student. That suggests the following series of declarations, assuming that the maximum class size is 100 students.

```
CONST Maxclass = 100;

TYPE Student = RECORD
                  name: ARRAY[1..15] OF CHARACTER;
                  scores: List
               END;

VAR Students: ARRAY[1..Maxclass] OF Student;
    ClassSize: CARDINAL;
```

For example, the input shown above for student "backus" would be stored internally as shown in Figure 3-15.

Given access to the appropriate abstract data type for linear lists, the solution for this problem can be straightforward. The basic structure for this program is sketched below.

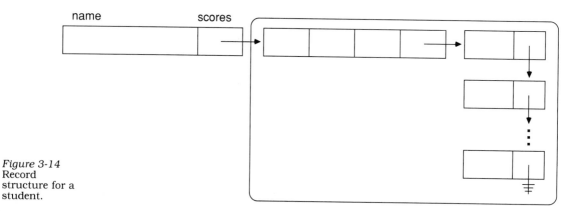

Figure 3-14
Record structure for a student.

Figure 3-15
Record
structure for
student
"backus."

```
MODULE LessNaiveInstructor;

FROM InOut      IMPORT ...
FROM RealInOut  IMPORT ...
FROM Lists      IMPORT ...


CONST EOF = 32C;            (*Keyboard ctl-z is EOF. *)
      Maxclass = 100;


TYPE Student = RECORD
                 name: ARRAY[1..15] OF CHAR;
                 scores: List
               END;

VAR Students: ARRAY[1..Maxclass] OF Student;
    ClassSize: CARDINAL;
    ...


PROCEDURE GetNames;
BEGIN
    WriteString('Enter names, ending the last with ctl-z:');
    WriteLn;
    ...
END GetNames;


PROCEDURE GetScores;
BEGIN
    WriteString('Enter a series of scores for each test,');
    WriteString('ending with ctl-z.');
    WriteLn;
    ...
END GetScores;
```

```
PROCEDURE ShowAverages;
BEGIN
    WriteString('STUDENT         # TESTS    AVERAGE    SCORES');
    WriteLn; WriteLn;
    ...
END ShowAverages;
BEGIN
    GetNames;
    GetScores;
    ShowAverages
END LessNaiveInstructor.
```

In this illustration, we have intentionally omitted the details of the program by inserting ellipses (...) in their place. Solution of this problem requires executing three separate procedures, which we call GetNames, GetScores, and ShowAverages. GetNames should input the class list and create an empty list of scores for each student in the class, finally establishing a value for the variable ClassSize. GetScores should input each series of scores and insert each nonmissing score at the end of the corresponding student's list. ShowAverages should produce the output in the format shown in our illustration. These procedures should therefore utilize most of the EXPORTed procedures from the module Lists. The details of this implementation are left as a Team Project at the end of the chapter.

Why do we suggest using the *linked* implementation of linear lists in preference to the *contiguous* one? The main reason is that the former is much more efficient and flexible in its utilization of memory than the latter. Consider an extreme case, in which the number of tests is extremely large, say over 100 (not likely, but not impossible either). The variable Maxlist for the contiguous implementation would need to be adjusted and the Lists IMPLEMENTATION MODULE recompiled in order to handle this case. Consider another extreme case, in which the number of tests is not large, say ten tests for the class. Here, avoidance of recompiling the Lists IMPLEMENTATION MODULE results in wasting 90 percent of the allocated space for each student's test scores. The limitations of a small memory size might, in fact, prevent execution of the program from successful completion without recompiling with either a smaller value of Maxlist (in the Lists IMPLEMENTATION MODULE) or a smaller value of Maxclass (in the application program itself). Neither of these extreme cases requires special consideration when we use the linked implementation of lists instead.

The main principle displayed by this application of linear lists is that, once defined, the basic functions of the abstract data type play the role of a language extension; the overall organization of the resulting program can thus become less cluttered, and the solution can be more clearly laid out and can have only a modest need for elaborate documentary comments. The well-definedness of the operators that comprise the linear list abstract data type encourages application programs to be written straightforwardly and clearly.

In conclusion, this chapter illustrates the importance of separating the implementation of an abstract data type from its definition, on the one hand, and from the application programs that use it, on the other. Once enforced, that principle allows different, competing implementations to be developed independently. It also allows an implementation to be reused by different applications, thus conserving significant amounts of software development effort as a result. Much of this conservation also results from the high level of reliability that arises out of our relatively rigorous standards for procedure verification: the use of a comprehensive driver program and the use of analytic verification methods.

History tells us that when these principles are not systematically followed, software developers must essentially start every new application with an empty software library, thus redeveloping and reverifying common procedures (such as the ones that implement the linear list operators). Later chapters will identify and implement other abstract data types that have similarly widespread utility as linear lists.

EXERCISES

3-1. Implement the Delete operator for the linked and contiguous versions of linear lists. Then, thoroughly test the contiguous and linked versions, using the driver given and providing extensive test input data.

3-2. Our definition of the linear list abstract data type might arguably have the additional operator *Destroy*, which would serve a role opposite to the Create operator. That is, for an existing list L, the operator Destroy(L) should take L out of existence. Define and implement this new operator, being sure in your implementation to free all storage areas that had been allocated for the existing elements of L.

3-3. Extend the ListDriver program and test the Destroy operator that you implemented in exercise 3-2.

3-4. Using the same techniques as shown for Insert, verify the correctness of your contiguous implementation for Delete. That is, show that its postconditions are necessarily satisfied by the Delete procedure's body whenever the preconditions are met. In the process, discover its loop invariant.

3-5. Illustrate how the binary search procedure works by tracing the values of low, high, and i for $x = 45$ and the following list:

L = (23 28 31 38 43 46 55 57 62 69 70 71 88 94 96 97)

How many steps (comparisons) are made? How many comparisons would be made if a serial search had been done instead?

3-6. Verify the correctness of the linked implementation for Delete, showing how the values of pointers change as each step in the procedure's body is executed, and demonstrating thereby that the postconditions in the original definition are necessarily met.

3-7. In the same way, verify the correctness of the linked implementation for Search. Can the binary search method be applied to the linked implementation for linear lists? If so, what additional requirements must be met? If not, why not?

3-8. A "circular linked list" is an alternative implementation method for linear lists in which the *last* node is linked directly to the first node, rather than having the value NIL, as shown in Figure 3-16. Discuss how each of the operator implementations for linked lists given in the text needs to be altered in order to support this circular implementation method.

3-9. A "double linked list" is an implementation method for linear lists in which each node is linked directly to its predecessor, as well as its successor, as shown in Figure 3-17. Give a revised declaration for a node in such a list. Show how the implementation of operators Create, Insert, and Delete would be altered in order to support the double linked implementation. Are the other operator implementations affected? Explain.

3-10. Verify the FindLink procedure that is defined for the linked implementation of the Linear List abstract data type, in section 3-6.

3-11. Show that the complexity of the FindLink procedure in the linked implementation of linear lists has O(c) complexity in one case and O(n) complexity in the other, by counting the number of steps executed in each case.

3-12. Experimentally corroborate the differences in complexity for linked vs contiguous implementations of the Insert and Delete procedures, by establishing a fairly large list (perhaps using the output of the

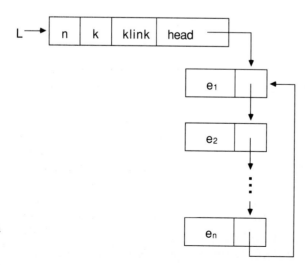

Figure 3-16
Implementation of circular linked lists.

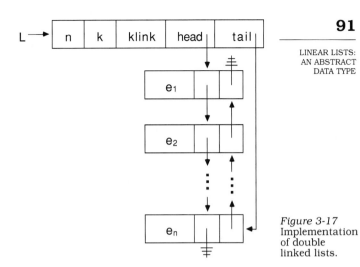

Figure 3-17 Implementation of double linked lists.

random number generator of Chapter 2), performing a large number of insertions and deletions (say 1000), and measuring the actual run times under each of the two implementations. Does the run time of the contiguous implementation actually grow with n? Does the run time of the linked implementation actually remain constant, regardless of the growth of n, in instances where the insertions and deletions occur at the current node? How about the instances where insertions and deletions are not at the current node? Tabulate the results of this experiment and compare them with the abstract complexity comparisons given in section 3-8.

TEAM PROJECT: COMPLETION OF THE LESS NAIVE INSTRUCTOR'S PROBLEM

Complete the solution of the Less Naive Instructor's Problem, as sketched in the last section of the chapter. If the class is divided into three-person teams, each person may implement one of the three procedures GetNames, GetScores, and ShowAverages. Collectively, the team should then determine the individual procedures that need to be IMPORTed from InOut, RealInOut, and Lists, in order to complete the solution. Different teams should alternately choose the linked and contiguous implementations of linear lists and, as time permits, investigate the influence of that choice on the flexibility of the application program itself. Each team should turn in a completed version of LessNaiveInstructor, documenting authorship of each procedure, together with the output of its execution using the sample input shown in this chapter, and the output of its execution using additional input that explores the limitations of the implementation.

4

RECURSION, INDUCTION, AND VERIFICATION

A most widely-used methodology in the definition and implementation of computer algorithms is the use of *recursion*. In this chapter, we shall examine the origins of recursion and its many uses in computer science. We shall also describe methods for tracing the execution of recursively defined procedures and systematically verifying them by the method of mathematical induction.

The use of recursion to define functions originated in mathematics many centuries ago. Its central role in computer science emerged in the 1930s, when it was discovered that the formal notion of "recursive function" is equivalent in expressive power to the formal notion of "Turing computability." Recall from Chapter 2 that the Turing machine is the conceptual progenitor of the von Neumann machine, which in turn is the underlying model for iterative algorithm execution. Thus we have a profound connection, that says that any algorithm which can be expressed with an iterative procedure can equivalently be expressed with a recursive procedure, and vice versa. Recalling also the principle of Church's Thesis from Chapter 2, which says that we can represent any well conceived algorithm as a Turing machine, the same expressive power is thus inherited immediately by the recursive functions as well.

These discoveries have had continuing and profound impacts on the field of computer science. During the 1950s and 1960s, as the Turing machine was serving as a conceptual foundation stone for the design of von Neumann machines and the predecessors of Modula-2 were being developed, the recursive function simultaneously became a conceptual foundation from which an entirely different style of computer (the stack machine) and programming language (LISP) were evolving. Today, we therefore have widespread use of this latter mode of computation throughout many fields of computer science, especially in the field of artificial intelligence. The formal equivalence between Turing machines and recursive functions (or, effectively, between Modula-2 and LISP as media for describing algorithms) assures us that neither mode of expression is intrinsically "more powerful" than the other; instead, our choice can be decided by the nature of the problem and its efficient implementation.

Although LISP has, throughout the last three decades, served as the premier language for expressing algorithms recursively, Modula-2 also supports recursion (as do most other programming languages). It is the purpose of this chapter to take a rather comprehensive look at recursion, exposing the breadth of its applications in computer science. We also wish to explore the mechanical aspects of executing recursively defined procedures in Modula-2, paying special attention to their verification and complexity.

4-1 RECURSIVE FUNCTIONS AND MODULA-2

Informally, a recursively defined function is one that uses itself in its own definition. For example, consider the following definition of the ordinary product of two positive integers:

Definition: The *product* of two positive integers i and j, denoted i*j, is either:

    (i) i   if $j=1$, or
    (ii) $i+i*(j-1)$ if $j>1$.

Part (ii) of this definition says "the product i*j is computed by adding i and the product $i*(j-1)$, in the event that $j > 1$." Operationally, in order to use this definition for computing a particular product, say 4*3, we must first compute the product 4*2, thus repeatedly applying part (ii) of the definition until part (i) can be applied. This leads to the following series of events:

$$\begin{aligned} 4*3 &= \\ 4 + (4*2) &= \\ 4 + (4 + (4*1)) &= \\ 4 + (4 + 4) &= \\ 4 + 8 &= \\ 12 & \end{aligned}$$

Here, we have added parentheses to distinguish each successive recursive, or repeated, application of the definition. Thus, the second line above calls for applying the function to the arguments 4 and 2, while the third calls for the same with the arguments 4 and 1. At this point, part (i) of the definition takes over, and the product 4*1 emerges as simply 4. Thereafter, the (predefined) notion of "sum" is used to carry out each of the remaining steps.

Several general characteristics of recursive functions are revealed in this simple example. First, a recursive function may call for the repeated application of its own definition when it is actually evaluated with a specific set of arguments. Second, a recursive function must be defined in such a way that this repetition will always have a "stopping point," regardless of the particular arguments to which the function is applied. Typically, the provision of such a stopping point leads to the separate specification of a "part (i)" in a recursive function definition. Third, recursively defined functions form a hierarchy, in which each function's effective realization depends upon the preexisting definitions of certain other, more "primitive," functions. In this example, the effective realization of the product function depends upon the fact that the sum function has previously been defined. At the bottom of the hierarchy, a small number of "most primitive functions" are assumed to exist; these are the so-called "constant functions" (which return constants as results), "the successor function" (which adds 1 to an integer), and the "predecessor function" (which subtracts 1 from an integer). More formally, the notion of recursive function can be defined in the following way:

Definition: A *recursive function*[1] f(x,n), where x denotes any (list of) argument(s) and n is a positive integer, is either a "primitive function" or defined in the following way:

(i) g(x)   if n = 1
(ii) h(x,f(x,n−1))   if n > 1.

Here, g and h may be any other recursive functions. The "primitive functions" are the constant functions, the successor function, and the predecessor function. The constant functions define a constant value, while the successor and predecessor functions are defined as x+1 and x−1, for any positive integer x. These are directly implemented in Modula-2 as INC(x) and DEC(x), respectively.

How does the example definition of the product fit this more general definition scheme for recursion? To see that, we identify x as the single integer i and n as the single integer j. The function g is the identity function, and the function h is the the sum (assumed to be previously defined) of the product and identity functions.

To implement a recursive function definition in Modula-2, a procedure is written that contains, in its body, an invocation of itself. This style of presentation parallels that which occurs in the text of the function definition. To illustrate, consider the following recursive statement of the Modula-2 procedure Product, which implements the definition given above.

---

[1]Strictly speaking, the above definition identifies a class known as the "primitive recursive functions" which, although extensive, does not cover the complete range of recursion in the sense of Turing computability.

```
PROCEDURE Product(i,j: CARDINAL): CARDINAL;
BEGIN
   IF (i=0) OR (j=0) THEN
      RETURN 0
   ELSIF j=1 THEN
      RETURN i
   ELSE
      RETURN i + Product(i,j-1)
   END
END Product;
```

The procedure Product has in its definition three parts, the first part serving as a "guard" against either argument being 0, and the other two mirroring exactly the two parts to the abstract recursive definition of the product given above. We shall see that most recursive procedures can be directly encoded in this way; once the abstract definition is discovered, its encoding into a Modula-2 procedure is straightforward.

To trace the execution of a recursive procedure when it is invoked, we may employ a simple tabular technique to keep track of each level of activation when the procedure invokes itself, as well as the arguments passed at each invocation. To illustrate, suppose the procedure Product were invoked to compute the product of 4 and 3, via the statement:

```
Product(4,3)
```

The table shown below gives all the information needed to understand how this procedure is recursively activated, and what information is passed to and from each activation.

Activation in Control:	Activated by	i	j	Result Returned
1. Product(4,3)		4	3	4+Product(4,2)
2. Product(4,2)	1.	4	2	4+Product(4,1)
3. Product(4,1)	2.	4	1	4
2. Product(4,2)	1.			4+4=8
1. Product(4,3)				4+8=12

The table is read from top to bottom, reflecting a chronological sequence of procedure activation, suspension, and reactivation. When we arrive at the third line, for instance, we see that three different activations of Product have been initiated: one with the arguments (4,3), one with (4,2), and one with (4,1). At that point, both the first and the second activations are in suspension, awaiting a result to be returned by the third. After completion of the third activation, the second activation receives the result (4), subsequently completes its computation, and returns its own result (8) to the first activation. Finally, this activation completes its own computation and returns the final result (12) to the original invoking statement.

Another equivalent way of looking at the structure of recursive activations of a procedure is by using a graphical display. The example above is shown in this form in Figure 4-1. There, the different activations are numbered as nodes on the graph, the arguments passed to an activation are attached to a downward pointing arrow, and the results returned by an activation are attached to an upward pointing arrow.

Our definition of the product depended upon the preexistence of a definition for the sum. That is, recursive functions are usually hierarchically arranged, so that the more complex ones are written to take advantage of other functions that have already been defined. At the risk of belaboring this point, as well as to expose the "bottom end" of the hierarchy of recursive function definitions, we define the sum function as follows:

Definition: The *sum* of two positive integers i and j, denoted i+j, is either:
    (i) INC(i)   if j=1, or
    (ii) INC(i)+DEC(j)   if j>1.

Here, we see that the definition depends upon the existence of no other recursive functions beyond the successor and predecessor functions INC and DEC, together with the sum function itself. Thus, the "bottom" of the hierarchy has been reached for positive integer arithmetic, and other arithmetic functions may be defined in a way that assumes the existence of the sum and the product.

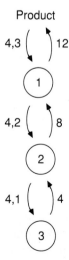

Figure 4-1 Graphical display of recursion: Product (4,3).

4-2 RECURSION AND PROGRAMMING

In practice, we are not tempted to implement such simple functions as the sum or the product using a recursive Modula-2 procedure. In cases where the function is more complex than these, we can generally choose between using recursion, using a WHILE loop (because of the formal equivalence between loops and recursion), or expressing the calculation in "closed form."[2] In the following sections, we present a variety of recursively defined functions and their implementations in Modula-2. In doing so, we expose the existence of choices between recursion, iteration, and closed form implementations for functions.

4-2-1 Recursive Definition of Mathematical Functions

Recursion originated in the field of mathematics. Some of the more common recursively defined mathematical functions are given in this section, together with their Modula-2 implementations.

4-2-1-1 The Factorial: Recursion and Induction

The *factorial* of a cardinal integer n, denoted n!, is defined iteratively as the product of the first n positive integers, or $n*(n-1)*(n-2)*\ldots*2*1$. Its implementation is thus usually realized in the form of a loop repeated $n-1$ times to multiply the first n integers together. Below is an equivalent recursive definition of n!:

Definition: The *factorial* of n, denoted n!, is defined as:
    (i) 1   if $n = 1$
    (ii) $n*(n-1)!$ if $n > 1$

Note that this definition relies on the preexistence of the product function (*) and is equivalent to the original iterative definition given above. The Modula-2 procedure for this recursive definition is straightforward, and we leave it as an exercise.

As this example shows, the identification of an equivalent iterative definition of a recursively defined function is often straightforward. However, there are many functions whose iterative definitions do not submit easily to straightforward recursive definitions, and vice versa.

We can usually prove mathematically that the recursive and the iterative definitions of the same function are, indeed, equivalent. In doing this,

---

[2]The notion of "closed form" for a function definition denotes a form in which the function is defined without the help of recursion or iteration. The presence of a closed form definition allows its Modula-2 implementation to avoid both recursion and the use of a loop, using instead a simple arithmetic expression.

we rely on the method of mathematical induction, which is illustrated below for the factorial example. This is an extremely important part of the algorithm discovery process. That is, if we have a correct algorithm that implements a particular function recursively, we may search for an iterative or closed form version of the same function and then prove by induction that this version is equivalent to the original recursive version.

Recall from mathematics that an inductive proof of a claim proceeds in two steps. The first step shows the truth of the claim for the special case n = 1. The second step requires that we show, for any other value of n > 1, that the truth of the claim for the case of n directly implies the truth of the claim for the case of n + 1.

We can apply this technique to show that the recursive definition of the factorial is equivalent to its iterative definition. As a first step, we note that the two definitions of factorial for n = 1 both give 1! = 1. As a second step, assume for some particular value of n > 1 that:

$$n! = n*(n-1)*...*2*1 = n*(n-1)!$$

That is, assume that the iterative definition (in the center) gives the same result as the recursive definition (on the right). This assumption gives us the following, for the case of n + 1:

$$(n+1)! = (n+1)*n*(n-1)*...*2*1$$
$$= (n+1)*n!$$

in which the first line follows directly from the iterative definition and the second line follows from the assumption itself. Thus, we have shown that the closed form and recursive definitions of factorial are equivalent for the case n + 1, under the assumption that they are equivalent for some particular n > 1. This completes the inductive proof.

4-2-1-2 Fibonacci Sequence

The so-called "Fibonacci numbers" (Leonardo Fibonacci, c. 1200 AD) are a sequence of positive integers with many useful applications in mathematics and statistics. Each number in the sequence is defined simply as the sum of the previous two numbers, and the first two numbers in the sequence are 1 and 1. More formally, the definition may be given recursively as follows:

Definition: The Fibonacci numbers *Fib(n)* are defined as:
        Fib(0) = 1
        Fib(1) = 1
        Fib(n) = Fib(n−1) + Fib(n−2)   for n>1

Thus, the first few numbers in the Fibonacci sequence are as follows: 1 1 2 3 5 8 13 21 34 . . . . This is an example of a function whose equivalent iterative definition is not straightforwardly obtained. A complicated derivation, however, would show that a closed form definition of Fib(n) can be defined by rounding the following expression to an integer:

$$\frac{1}{\sqrt{5}}(\Phi^{n+1})$$

where Φ is approximately 1.618034 and is known as the "golden ratio" (for reasons related to the history of geometry). Interested readers are referred to Knuth's *Seminumerical Algorithms* for a full discussion. It is beyond the scope of this text to further explore the equivalence of this definition with the recursive definition. Note, however, that the closed form gives a far more efficient method of computing Fib(n) than its recursive counterpart, if we were to implement them both in Modula-2.

Below is a Modula-2 implementation of the recursive definition for the Fib function. Notice again how closely its text mirrors the text of the definition itself.

```
PROCEDURE Fib (n: CARDINAL): CARDINAL;
BEGIN
   IF (n=0) OR (n=1) THEN
     RETURN 1
   ELSE
     RETURN Fib(n-1) + Fib(n-2)
   END
END Fib;
```

An execution trace of this procedure, for n = 4, yields the graphical display shown in Figure 4-2. Here, we see that the original invocation spawns two

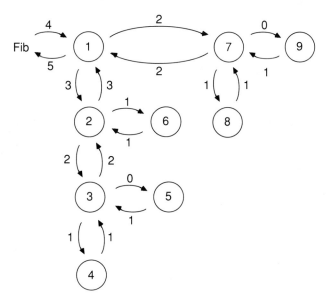

Figure 4-2
Graphical display of recursion: Fib(4).

invocations (one for n = 3 and the other for n = 2), each of these spawns two more, and so forth.

This display reveals some of the inherent inefficiency of Fib's recursive implementation. Note, for example, that Fib(2) is computed *twice*, once for calculating Fib(4) and again for calculating Fib(3). Such is the case for *every* computation of Fib(i), where $i < n - 1$. Worse yet, an application program using the procedure Fib is unaware that its implementation contains so much redundancy. Such a program cannot take advantage of that redundancy by saving, for instance, all the intermediate calculations of Fib(i), for $0 \leq i < n$, in a separate array during the process of computing Fib(n). If this were possible, the application program could invoke Fib just once, and thereafter access values of Fib(i) directly out of the array rather than recalculate them by invoking the Fib procedure again. One would not, therefore, use this particular implementation of Fib in any substantial practical programming application.

4-2-1-3 Polynomial Evaluation

Many different mathematical applications require the evaluation of a polynomial, whose definition usually appears in the following familiar form:

$$P(a, x, n) = \sum_{i=0}^{n} a_i x^i = a_0 + a_1 x^1 + \ldots + a_n x^n$$

Yet, a straightforward implementation of this expression will also yield some inefficiency, since its recalculation of the different powers of x contains significant redundancy. In general, the computation of products, quotients, and powers is much more costly in execution time than the computation of sums and differences. Thus, when implementing an algebraic expression like this one we want to see if we can rewrite it using a minimal number of products, quotients, and powers. Such is the case for the following recursive redefinition of P(a,x,n):

$$P(a, x, i) = a_n \qquad \text{for } i = 0$$
$$= a_{n-i} + xP(a, x, i - 1) \quad \text{for } 0 < i \leq n$$

This recursive definition suggests an algorithm that requires only $n-1$ multiplications and $n-1$ additions. In contrast, the original iterative definition required $n-1$ multiplications, $n-1$ exponentiations, and n additions. Thus, we have made some important efficiency gains in redefining the function.

A further improvement in efficiency can be gained if we can rewrite this definition in such a way that recursion is also eliminated. The following "nested" iterative definition of P(a,x,n) accomplishes that goal:

$$P(a, x, n) = a_0 + x(a_1 + x(\ldots(a_{n-1} + xa_n)\ldots))$$

The equivalence of this definition and the recursive one can be seen if we "unravel" the second part of the recursive definition beginning with $i = n$. The following results from this process, for instance, when $n = 4$:

$$P(a, x, 4) = a_0 + xP(a, x, 3)$$
$$= a_0 + x(a_1 + xP(a, x, 2))$$
$$= a_0 + x(a_1 + x(a_2 + xP(a, x, 1)))$$
$$= a_0 + x(a_1 + x(a_2 + x(a_3 + xP(a, x, 0))))$$
$$= a_0 + x(a_1 + x(a_2 + x(a_3 + xa_4)))$$

Notice also that if we multiply out this last expression, we regain the form of the original definition of $P(a,x,4)$.

The procedure Poly, given below, implements the latter definition. Also, for convenience and reliability, we have imported the List type from Chapter 3, along with the implementations for operators Size and Retrieve.

```
PROCEDURE Poly (a0: ListElement; a: List; x: REAL): REAL;
VAR i,n: ListIndex; P: REAL;
BEGIN
  n:=ListSize(a);
  P:=FLOAT(Retrieve(a,n));
  i:=n-1;
  WHILE i>0 DO
    P:=P*x+FLOAT(Retrieve(a,i));
    i:=i-1
  END;
  RETURN P*x+a0
END Poly;
```

In using the List type, we are required to retrieve the coefficients a_i with an index range of [1..n] rather than [0..n] as given in the definition of $P(a,x,n)$ above. Thus, we have added the parameter a0, which corresponds to the coefficient a_0 in the definition. Notice that the loop in the procedure Poly computes the following partial result (for n = 4):

$$a_1 + x(a_2 + x(a_3 + xa_4))$$

The RETURN statement completes the computation by performing the final multiplication by x and addition of a0.

4-2-1-4 Binomial Coefficients

The *binomial coefficients* are a special series of coefficients $a_{n,i}$ (i = 0,...,n) for a polynomial $P(a,x,n)$, that allow the polynomial to be rewritten simply as:

$$P(a, x, n) = (x + 1)^n$$

For n = 5, for instance, we have

$$(x + 1)^5 = x^5 + 5x^4 + 10x^3 + 10x^2 + 5x + 1$$

and the binomial coefficients $a_{5,i}$ are 1, 5, 10, 10, 5, and 1, for $i = 0,...,5$ respectively.

Calculation of these coefficients a_i may be defined either in closed form or recursively. The closed form definition is as follows:

$$a_{n,i} = \frac{n!}{i!(n-i)!} \quad \text{for } i = 0,\ldots,n$$

The equivalent recursive definition is:

$$a_{n,i} = \begin{cases} 1 & \text{for } i = 0 \text{ or } i = n \\ a_{n-1,i-1} + a_{n-1,i} & \text{for } 0 < i < n \end{cases}$$

We leave as an exercise the inductive proof that these two definitions are equivalent. Below is a Modula-2 implementation of the recursive version of this definition.

```
PROCEDURE Binomial (n,i: CARDINAL): CARDINAL;
BEGIN
   IF (i=0) OR (i=n) THEN
      RETURN 1
   ELSE
      RETURN Binomial(n-1,i-1) + Binomial(n-1,i)
   END
END Binomial;
```

The graphical display given in Figure 4-3 illustrates the development of the binomial coefficient Binomial(4,3) using this procedure.

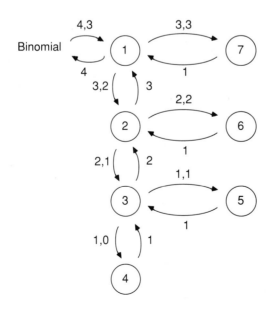

Figure 4-3
Graphical display of recursion: Binomial(4,3).

This display illustrates an inherent inefficiency here, since many additional coefficents $a_{m,j}$ with $m < n$ and $j < i$ must be computed in order to arrive at the value of $a_{n,i}$ itself. An application program that uses the binomial coefficients, therefore, should plan its strategy so that the required coefficients $a_{n,i}$ are computed just once, and then saved in a two-dimensional array for later retrieval during the program run itself. Readers may recall that such an array is familiarly known as "Pascal's triangle."

4-2-1-5 Greatest Common Divisor

One of the oldest mathematical algorithms to be expressed recursively is that of computing the greatest common divisor (GCD) of two nonnegative integers. It was first described by Euclid in about 700 B.C. Simply stated, the greatest common integer divisor of two integers, say i and j (assuming $i \geq j > 0$), is the largest integer that divides both i and j evenly. To find GCD(i,j), we note that it is identical to the GCD of j and remainder of i/j. When j reaches 0 in this recursive process, we have reached a stopping point, and the greatest common divisor is the resulting value of i itself. To illustrate, consider the following sequence of calculations to compute the greatest common divisor, GCD, of 330 and 21.

i	j	GCD(i,j)
		GCD(330,21)
330	21	GCD(21,MOD(330,21)) = GCD(21,15)
21	15	GCD(15,6)
15	6	GCD(6,3)
6	3	GCD(3,0)
3	0	3

This particular example of recursion is also interesting because it does not converge to a final result in a manner proportional to j. Rather, the complexity of GCD has been shown to be $O(\log_\Phi j)$, where Φ is the "golden ratio" mentioned in a preceding section. Again, interested readers are referred to Knuth's *Seminumerical Algorithms* for a full discussion. A Modula-2 implementation of GCD is given below.

```
PROCEDURE GCD(i,j: CARDINAL): CARDINAL;
BEGIN
   IF i<j THEN
     RETURN GCD(j,i)
   ELSIF j=0 THEN
     RETURN i
   ELSE
     RETURN GCD(j,i MOD j)
   END
END GCD;
```

Note that the first IF statement is included in GCD to trap cases in which the two arguments are given in reverse order from that specified by the preconditions of the recursive definition. That is, in cases where i < j, we can find GCD(i,j) by recursively computing GCD(j,i) instead and obtaining the same result. For example, GCD(21,330) = GCD(330,21) = 3.

4-2-1-6 Prime Numbers

A number is *prime* if its only integer divisors are itself and 1. For instance, 37 is prime (since its only divisors are 1 and 37), but 24 is not (since its divisors are 1, 2, 3, 4, 6, 8, 12, and 24). A simple iterative algorithm to determine the primeness of n is given in the procedure below.

```
PROCEDURE Prime (n: CARDINAL): BOOLEAN;
VAR a: CARDINAL;
BEGIN
   FOR a:=2 TO TRUNC(sqrt(FLOAT(n))) DO
      IF n MOD a = 0 THEN
         RETURN FALSE
      END
   END;
   RETURN TRUE
END Prime;
```

This algorithm says, in effect, that if we can find any integer, a, between 2 and $\sqrt{n}$ that evenly divides n, then n is not prime. Otherwise (we cannot find any such integer), n is prime. The discovery of a recursive algorithm to determine whether or not n is prime is left as an exercise.

4-2-1-7 Summing a Sequence: Recursion, Iteration, and Closed Form

As we have discovered already, some algorithms that are recursively or iteratively defined have more efficient realizations in closed form. Such was the case in our investigation of the Fibonacci numbers, for instance. It is important that readers become sensitive to the idea of discovering alternative equivalent realizations of algorithms. When given a recursive algorithm, we should always ask, "Is there an equivalent iterative definition?" When given a recursive or iterative algorithm, we should also ask, "Is there an equivalent closed form definition?" When these questions are answered positively, large efficiency gains can often be made in the resulting implementation.

In these cases, the use of either a recursive procedure or a loop is inferior to the straightforward evaluation of the equivalent closed form expression. For example, the following iterative expressions on the left have the equivalent closed form expressions shown on the right:

$$\sum_{i=1}^{n} i = \frac{n(n+1)}{2}$$

$$\sum_{i=1}^{n} i^2 = \frac{n(n+1)(2n+1)}{6}$$

$$\sum_{i=0}^{n} 2^i = 2^{n+1} - 1$$

$$\sum_{i=0}^{n} x^i = \frac{x^{n+1} - 1}{x - 1}$$

On the other hand, some don't. For instance, the sum:

$$\sum_{i=1}^{n} \frac{1}{i} = 1 + \frac{1}{2} + \frac{1}{3} + \cdots + \frac{1}{n}$$

can be fairly well approximated by the expression $\ln(n) + 0.7$ and, for large n, the constant term may be dropped. An exact sum, however, must be explicitly computed using an iterative loop.

4-2-2 Recursion and Problem Solving: "Divide and Conquer" Algorithms

The philosophy behind a "divide and conquer" algorithm is that we first divide the problem into two or more simpler ones and then express the original problem's solution in terms of the combined solutions to the simpler problems.

All recursive solutions to problems are of this "divide and conquer" style, since each invocation decrements by 1 the value of the controlling parameter n until the case n = 1 is finally reached. The following two problems are also good illustrations of the divide and conquer approach, and they deal with relatively intuitive and informal problem solving situations.

4-2-2-1 Counting Change

Suppose we want to change a predetermined amount of money, say M dollars and cents, into a particular array of coins—say halves, quarters, dimes, and nickels—generally n different kinds in all. Then, the number of ways of making change using all n kinds of coins is:

the number of ways of changing M (using all but the first kind)
+   the number of ways of changing M − d (where d is the denomination of the first kind)

For instance, the number of ways of changing 1.35 is the sum of:

> the number of ways of changing 1.35 (using all but halves)
> + the number of ways of changing 0.85

Now, we have two (simpler) problems, the first using one less denomination and the second using a reduced amount to be changed. Eventually the solution converges, as suggested in the following table for the first few steps in the counting of change for 1.35:

Invocation	Amount(M)	Use	Invoke
1	1.35	halves,quarters,dimes,nickels	2
			3
2	1.35	quarters,dimes,nickels	4
			5
3	0.85	halves,quarters,dimes,nickels	6
			7
4	1.35	dimes,nickels	8
			9
5	1.10	quarters,dimes,nickels	10
			11
6	0.85	quarters,dimes,nickels	12
			13
7	0.35	halves,quarters,dimes,nickels	14
8	1.35	nickels	
9	1.25	dimes,nickels	⋮
⋮	⋮	⋮	

4-2-2-2 Towers of Hanoi

The problem known as the Towers of Hanoi is an interesting one for two reasons. First, it is another good example of the divide and conquer approach to problem solving. Second, its recursive solution is far more straightforward and intuitive than its nonrecursive solution. The problem involves a pile of n concentric disks, initially stacked on the leftmost of three available posts. Each disk is a different diameter, and they are stacked in such a way that no disk sits on top of a smaller one. This initial situation is illustrated in Figure 4-4 (for n = 4). The object of the problem is to specify a sequence of moves in which the pile finally ends up in the same arrangement on the second (post B in the figure) of the three posts, under the constraint that no move in the sequence leaves a disk stacked above a smaller one on the same post.

To arrive at a solution to this problem, we may develop the solution to each of a series of increasingly larger problems, starting with the simple

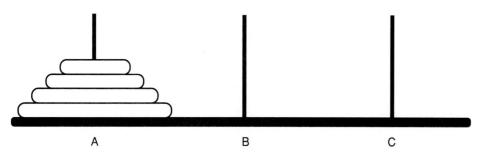

Figure 4-4
Initial setup for Towers of Hanoi (n = 4 disks).

case of n = 1 disk. In that case, the solution (assuming Source = A and Target = B) is:

> Move 1 disk from Source to Target.

A solution to the problem for n = 2 (where Source = A, Target = B, and Intermediary = C) is not much more difficult:

> Solve the 1-disk problem for Source and Intermediary.
> Move 1 disk from Source to Target.
> Solve the 1-disk problem for Intermediary and Target.

However, note how this solution is cast; the original solution to the 1-disk problem is used twice, once from post A to post C, and once from post C to post B. The 3-disk problem's solution is cast in a similar way:

> Solve the 2-disk problem for Source and Intermediary.
> Move 1 disk from Source to Target.
> Solve the 2-disk problem for Intermediary and Target.

That is, we can state the solution to the 3-disk problem in a way that relies on the preexistence of the 2-disk solution. In this manner, we have solved the problem by "dividing" it into a simpler problem and "conquering" the solution by expressing it in terms of the solutions for the simpler problems. Now, we may generalize this approach and solve the n-disk problem, for any n, giving its solution in terms of the solution to the (n-1)-disk problem:

> Solve the (n-1)-disk problem for Source and Intermediary.
> Move 1 disk from Source to Target.
> Solve the (n-1)-disk problem for Intermediary and Target.

A complete trace of the solution to the 4-disk problem exposes the recursive application of this set of three rules in a more explicit fashion:
   Here, the levels of indentation suggest the hierarchy of recursive calls that take place as the solution is reapplied with different numbers (n) of disks and different identifications for the Source, Target, and Intermediary posts. For instance, the first seven moves in the last column in the table

Problem (n)	Source	Target	Intermediary	Move (from..to)
4	A	B	C	
3	A	C	B	
2	A	B	C	
1	A	C		A to C
				A to B
1	C	B		C to B
				A to C
2	B	C	A	
1	B	A		B to A
				B to C
1	A	C		A to C
				A to B
3	C	B	A	
2	C	A	B	
1	C	B		C to B
				C to A
1	B	A		B to A
				C to B
2	A	B	C	
1	A	C		A to C
				A to B
1	C	B		C to B

above represent the solution of a 3-disk problem from post A to post C, and the last seven steps represent the same for posts C and B.

Below is a Modula-2 procedure for solving the Towers of Hanoi problem.

```
PROCEDURE Hanoi (n: CARDINAL;
                Source,Target,Intermediary: CHAR);
(*This procedure solves the Towers of Hanoi problem for
  n disks, given n>0 together with Source, Target, and
  Intermediary posts. *)
BEGIN
  IF n=1 THEN
    WriteString ('Move from '); Write(Source);
    WriteString (' to '); Write(Target); WriteLn
  ELSE
    Hanoi(n-1,Source,Intermediary,Target);
    WriteString ('Move from '); Write(Source);
    WriteString (' to '); Write(Target); WriteLn;
    Hanoi(n-1,Intermediary,Target,Source)
  END
END Hanoi;
```

A trace of this procedure, for n = 4, gives the output sequence shown in the foregoing table.

4-2-3 Recursion and Linear List Operators

Recursion is a frequently used tool in the implementation of various operators on data structures. We shall see in later chapters that recursive implementations of various stack, queue, and tree operators are often more straightforward and efficient, compared with their iterative counterparts. To illustrate the utility of recursion with data structures, this section gives recursive implementations for the serial and binary search operators that initially appeared in Chapter 3. Readers should compare these implementations with the original iterative versions.

4-2-3-1 Serial Search

Recall the Search operator that was defined for linear lists in Chapter 3. The invocation SearchList(L,i,x) denoted a serial search of the list L for an instance of x, and a return of the index i for an element e_i for which $e_i = x$. A slight redefinition of this operator in the following way allows a recursive implementation to be developed:

Definition: *Search(L,m,i,x)* searches the sublist L[m..n] of L, whose size is n, for an occurrence of an element e_j that satisfies $e_j = x$ and assigns the value of the index j to i accordingly. If there is no such element e_j, then x occurs nowhere in L and i is assigned the value 0 accordingly.
Preconditions: L, m, i, and x exist, and either n = 0 or $0 < m \leq n$.
Postconditions: If n = 0 or m > n, then i' = 0. Otherwise, if x occurs in L[m..n] and j is an index in the range [m..n] for which $x = e_j$, then i' = j. Otherwise, x does not occur in L[m..n] and i' = 0.

A recursive implementation of this definition, using a serial search strategy and contiguous storage allocation for L, follows immediately from a divide and conquer approach. That is, if Size(L) = 0, then x cannot be in L. If Size(L) > 0, then x is in L[m..n] if either of the following two conditions is met:

```
(i)    e_m=x
(ii)   m<n and x is in L[m+1..n]
```

Otherwise, x is not in L. All of this argument is embodied in the following implementation of Search.

```
PROCEDURE SearchList(VAR L: List; m: ListIndex;
                 VAR i: ListIndex; x: ListElement);
```

```
BEGIN
   IF ListSize(L)=0 THEN
      i:=0
   ELSIF (0<m) AND (m<=ListSize(L)) THEN
      IF x=Retrieve(L,m) THEN
         i:=m
      ELSIF m<ListSize(L) THEN
         Search(L,m+1,i,x)
      ELSE
         i:=0
      END;
      ListError:=FALSE
   ELSE
      ListError:=TRUE
   END
END SearchList;
```

4-2-3-2 Binary Search

A binary search strategy can also be implemented recursively using this definition, if we assume also that L is *ordered*.

```
PROCEDURE BinarySearchList (VAR L: List; m,n: ListIndex;
                            VAR i: ListIndex; x: ListElement);
VAR mid: ListIndex;   (*mid is the midpoint of L[m..n]*)
BEGIN
   IF ListSize(L)=0 THEN
      i:=0
   ELSIF (0<m) AND (m<=n) AND (n<=ListSize(L)) THEN
      mid:=(m+n) DIV 2;
      IF x<Retrieve(L,mid) THEN
         BinarySearchList(L,m,mid-1,i,x)
      ELSIF x>RetrieveList(L,mid) THEN
         BinarySearch(L,mid+1,n,i,x)
      ELSE
         i:=mid
      END;
      ListError:=FALSE
   ELSE
      ListError:=TRUE
   END
END BinarySearchList;
```

Note here that we have introduced an additional parameter, n, to designate the *high* end of the sublist L[m..n] that can change with any invocation. In the serial search we did not need this parameter, since the high end of the sublist was always fixed at Size(L).

To illustrate this recursive implementation of BinarySearch, consider the list L=(23 25 39 42 46 49 73 74 80 96) and the argument x=80. The procedure invokes itself once for every step shown in Figure 3-6 (see Chapter 3). Specifically, the series of sublists L[m..n], and values for m, n, and mid for each invocation in this example, are shown below.

Invocation	m	n	L[m..n]	mid
1	1	10	(23 25 39 42 46 49 73 74 80 96)	5
2	6	10	(49 73 74 80 96)	8
3	9	10	(80 96)	9

4-3 RECURSION AND THE GENERAL FIELD OF COMPUTER SCIENCE

These illustrations provide only a brief glimpse of the widespread uses of recursion throughout the field of computer science. Students who continue in this field of study will soon become experts at recognizing situations where recursion is used creatively, at understanding recursively defined algorithms, and at implementing correct recursive solutions to problems when such solutions are appropriate and preferable to iterative or closed form solutions. In this section, we survey an even broader spectrum of subjects in the field of computer science for which recursion plays an important role.

4-3-1 Artificial Intelligence

The field of artificial intelligence (AI) attempts to model, in potentially useful ways, intelligent behavior of all sorts. Conventionally, this field includes the simulation of game-playing strategies, human perception and vision, human language usage and understanding, and various other motor skills and senses that contribute to intelligent behavior. Although this field originated in the 1950s, AI is in many ways still in its infancy. The techniques of artificial intelligence research rely largely upon the development of prototypical models: models of human understanding, models of game-playing strategies, models of natural language usage, and so forth.

Typically, these models use symbols (rather than numbers) as their primary elements of computation, and their basic dynamic qualities rely upon the manipulation of symbols and structures of symbols. The area of symbolic theorem proving, for instance, is concerned initially with the representation of mathematical axioms and then with the characterization and effective application of systems of axioms and theorems to draw conclusions about other mathematical expressions.

Like mathematics itself, artificial intelligence research therefore relies heavily upon recursion as a tool for expressing the axioms that underly its models of mechanical "understanding" systems. LISP, the predominant

AI programming language, has at its heart the ability to define functions recursively rather than iteratively. The basic element of data in a LISP program is not the number, but the symbol. Thus, LISP programs are eminently able to express the dynamic relationships among the functional parts of machine models of intelligence, whether it be linguistic, perceptual, visual, robotic, or some other aspect of human behavior.

4-3-2 Formal Language Theory

Within this general domain, the problem of abstractly describing natural language syntax and semantics has challenged scholars for centuries. In the middle 1950s, Noam Chomsky[3] developed a landmark theory of language that has guided linguists and computer scientists over the last three decades. This theory uses recursion as a basic expressive tool for describing the functional relationships among various abstract notions in natural language description. To illustrate, consider the following statement about the syntactic structure of an ordinary English language "noun phrase."

> A *noun phrase* may be constructed either as a simple noun, as a noun phrase preceded by an adjective, or as a noun phrase preceded by an article.

This definition is recursive in its second part, since any number of adjectives or articles can precede the "simple noun" that is at its head. For instance, the following are noun phrases under this definition:

    fox
    brown fox
    quick brown fox
    the quick brown fox

Observant readers will see that some counterintuitive noun phrases can follow from this definition as well, such as "the quick the fox." In any event, the use of recursion in this setting is useful and powerful. Our example can be more tersely expressed with the following simple formalism:

```
nounphrase ::= noun |
               adjective nounphrase |
               article nounphrase
```

Here, the symbol ::= denotes "is defined as," the vertical bar (|) denotes "or," and the juxtaposition of terms like "adjective" and "nounphrase" denotes syntactic ordering. It is understood that juxtaposition has higher precedence than the vertical bar (in the same sense that * has higher precedence

---

[3]Chomsky, N., *Syntactic Structures*, The Hague, 1956.

than + in a Modula-2 arithmetic expression). Thus, we have a formalistic way of stating the same definition that appeared in prose above.

Additional defining power can be gained if we add the following symbols to our repertoire: enclosure within brackets [ ] denotes "the enclosed entities are optional," and enclosure within braces { } denotes "the enclosed entities may occur 0 or more times." It is also understood that brackets and braces have highest precedence in these definitions (in the same sense that parentheses have highest precedence in Modula-2 arithmetic expressions). With these additional tools, we can restate the above definition in the following simplified, yet equivalent, way:

```
nounphrase ::= {adjective | article} noun
```

That is, "a noun phrase is a series of 0 or more adjectives and/or articles, terminated by a single noun." This definition may be argued to be conceptually clearer than the original one, and it also does not use recursion. That is, the arbitrary number of adjectives and articles preceding the noun in a noun phrase is described by a kind of "iterative" definition scheme rather than a recursive one.

To become a bit more precise, this added formalism also allows us to conveniently restrict the definition so that phrases like "the quick the fox" are disallowed:

```
nounphrase ::= [article] {adjective} noun
```

That is, a noun phrase is now understood to be "an optional article, followed by 0 or more adjectives, and terminated by a single noun."

4-3-3 Programming Language Design

Chomsky's discoveries about the description of natural language syntax were quickly adapted for use in the formal description of programming languages. In the early 1960s, the first formalism shown above was used directly in the syntax definition for the programming language Algol 60. This adaptation became widely known as BNF, short for "Backus-Naur Form." Further refinements to this style led to the last formalism shown above, and this has become a standard mechanism for the syntactic description of contemporary programming languages. The syntactic definition of Modula-2 itself[4] uses this style, and this is replicated in its entirety in Appendix C of this text.

To illustrate, consider the following definition of Modula-2's "simple expression," adapted from Appendix C to include only the arithmetic operators +, −, *, and / (with their usual meanings) and only the operand types ident and number. Suppose further that we assume the preexistence of

---

[4]Wirth, Niklaus, *Programming in Modula-2* (third, corrected edition), Springer-Verlag, 1985.

definitions for ident and number. That is, idents—short for "identifiers"—are variable names (such as Sum, L, and i) and numbers are integers and reals (such as 33, −1.5, and 0). The following are examples of simple expressions:

```
33
Sum
Sum+33
i*(Sum+33)
(Sum+33)*i/j-2
```

The following definition of SimpleExpression characterizes this syntactic classification.

```
SimpleExpression ::= term {+ term | - term }
term ::= factor {* factor | / factor }
factor ::= number | ident |
          ( SimpleExpression )
```

This definition is clearly recursive, since its last line includes the notion of "SimpleExpression" itself. To see how this definition operates, suppose we want to convince ourselves that the fourth example above is a SimpleExpression. We apply the four lines of the definition in the following steps:

```
  SimpleExpression = term                      (from line 1)
                   = factor * factor            (from line 2)
                   = ident * factor             (from line 3)
                   = ident * ( SimpleExpression ) (from line 4)
                   = ident * ( term + term )    (from line 1)
                   = ident * ( factor + term )  (from line 2)
                   = ident * ( factor + factor ) (from line 2)
                   = ident * ( ident + factor ) (from line 3)
                   = ident * ( ident + number ) (from line 3)
                   = i * ( Sum + 33 )           (assumed)
```

This simple example helps to reveal the essential role of recursion in the area of programming language design and compiler construction. Students who continue with such courses will further appreciate the central role of recursion in these areas. A careful reading of Appendix C at this point will help to provide additional familiarity with these notions and notations of recursive syntax description.

4-4 INDUCTIVE VERIFICATION: THE LIST SEARCH OPERATOR

Early in the chapter, we showed by mathematical induction that the recursive version of the factorial function definition was equivalent to the nonrecursive version. Here, we verify by induction the recursive version of the serial search operator, in order to provide another example of the close relationship between recursive definition and verification by induction.

For this, we first extract and number the lines in the body of the procedure SearchList, as follows.

```
(**PRE: Either n=0 or 0<m<=n**)
1     IF ListSize(L)=0 THEN
2         i:=0
3     ELSIF (0<m) AND (m<=ListSize(L)) THEN
4         IF x=Retrieve(L,m) THEN
5             i:=m
(**x=e[m] and i'=m**)
6         ELSIF m<ListSize(L) THEN
7             Search(L,m+1,i,x)
(**x<>e[m], m<n and i'=Search(L[m+1..n],i,x)**)
8         ELSE
9             i:=0
(**x<>e[m], m=n, and i'=0**)
10        END;
11        ListError:=FALSE
12    ELSE
13        ListError:=TRUE
14    END
(**POST: Either n=0 and i'=0, x is in L and i'
         is an index j for which
         e[j]=x, or x is not in L and i'=0. **)
```

As an aid in the proof, we have not only followed the usual custom of restating the preconditions and postconditions as assertions at the beginning and end of the procedure body, we have also added three more assertions at key points within the body of the procedure for additional clarification during the verification process.

For the verification itself, consider first the special case where n is 0. In this case, the postcondition requires that $i' = 0$, and that is exactly what occurs in lines 1-2 above.

For the case $n > 0$, we use an inductive method as follows. The initial case is that in which $m = n$ (the sublist L[m..n] has length 1). Here, we see that either line 5 is executed or line 9 is executed, and thus either $i' = m$ (when $x = e_m$) or $i' = 0$ (when $x \neq e_m$), respectively. Note the assertions that follow lines 5 and 9 indicate the state of affairs at each of those points during the computation. Thus, the postcondition for Search is satisfied for this initial case.

For the induction step, assume that $m < n$ and Search(L,m + 1,i,x) is correct. That is, for the sublist L[m + 1..n], which is shorter by 1 than the sublist L[m..n], assume that i' will either be 0 (if x is not in L[m + 1..n]) or be equal to some index for which $e_{i'} = x$. The recursive invocation in line 7 will cause that assignment for i' to take place, as indicated in the assertion that immediately follows line 7. Now consider the entire sublist L[m..n], where m < n. If, on the one hand, x = e_m, then i' = m (because of line 5), and the recursive invocation in line 7 will not be reached. If, on the other hand, x <> e_m, then x is in L[m..n] only if x is in L[m + 1..n] and lines 6 and 7 are guaranteed to be executed in this case (remembering that m < n). But our assumption for this induction step guarantees a proper assignment of i' in this case. We have thereby shown by induction that, if Search(L,m + 1,i,x) is correct, then Search(L,m,i,x) is guaranteed to be correct also, for any m and n that satisfy 0 < m < n = Size(L).

4-5 RECURSION VS ITERATION: SOME CONSIDERATIONS ON EFFICIENCY

Some programmers follow the dictum: "Don't use recursion in place of iteration, because recursion is less efficient." We have seen in this chapter a fairly wide collection of recursion examples. In some cases, an iterative counterpart was easily found. In other cases, a closed form counterpart was identified. In still other cases, the iterative form was found first and its recursive counterpart was not readily apparent.

We have also illustrated that computer science owes much to recursion for its contribution as a syntactic descriptive tool in the definition of programming languages, in addition to its traditional uses in mathematics. Generally, recursion makes irreplacable contributions to the wealth of algorithms that has developed across the theoretical and applied areas of the field of computer science.

So, indeed, there are three basic ways of implementing a function: using recursion, using iteration, or using a closed form expression. In terms of machine efficiency alone, the closed form expression is always preferable to either recursion or iteration. The machine efficiency of iteration is also superior to that of recursion, if we limit our "machine" model to the traditional von Neumann architectures introduced in Chapter 2. However, the rapid evolution of non-von Neumann machine architectures (especially those designed specifically for the direct execution of LISP programs) is beginning to render the efficiency of recursion at least as good as iteration.

In any case, the question of "human efficiency" must also be considered when choosing between recursion and iteration. That is, in a typical large programming project, where the implementation details may change several times over the life of the project, programs must be organized and presented in such a way that they can be quickly read and their underlying logic assimilated by different programmers. In that setting, an iterative (or recursive) implementation of an operator will be preferred over its recursive (or iterative) counterpart in grounds of clarity or straightforwardness.

Thus, computer scientists remain prepared to examine all of these fundamental choices—recursion, iteration, and closed form—in a variety of algorithmic domains. Any sweeping generalization such as the dictum cited above should be avoided, especially during one's initial experiences within the field of computer science.

EXERCISES

4-1. Implement in Modula-2 the recursive definitions of the sum and factorial functions that were given at the beginning of this chapter.

4-2. Give a recursive definition of the "Power" function, assuming the preexistence of the sum and product functions. That is, given positive integers i and j, define recursively i^j. Implement this definition as a Modula-2 procedure.

4-3. Evaluate the efficiency of the recursive implementation of the Fib procedure given in the text, by running it for each value of n from 10 to 20 and measuring the elapsed time for this run. Implement the same procedure using the closed form calculation given in the text and evaluate the efficiency of that implementation by the same method. (Note: the Power function in the library MiscLib should be used in preference to the power function that you implemented in exercise 4-2.) What is the outcome of your experiment? By what other means could the process of computing Fibonacci numbers have been implemented so that it would be more efficient than the recursive version?

4-4. Give a recursive definition of the formula for calculating interest B_n, given the yearly interest rate r and the number of years n (where $n \geq 0$), which is expressed as:

$$B_n = 100(1 + r)^n$$

Implement your definition as a Modula-2 procedure.

4-5. Using the closed form expression $\frac{1}{\sqrt{5}}\Phi^n$, write a procedure to compute the first n Fibonacci numbers. Are they identical with those that are computed using the recursive definition? Let your program do the comparisons and see how large a value of n can be used to exercise each of these two different implementations.

4-6. Show by induction that the nonrecursive and recursive definitions of the binomial coefficients are equivalent.

4-7. Give an alternative iterative implementation of the GCD function in Modula-2 (using a WHILE or REPEAT loop rather than recursion).

4-8. Implement the change-counting algorithm in Modula-2 and exercise it to display the number of ways of making change from 1.35.

4-9. Implement the procedure Prime using recursion rather than iteration.

4-10. Show by induction that $\sum_{i=1}^{n} i = \frac{n(n+1)}{2}$.

4-11. Exercise the Towers of Hanoi program to convince yourself that it gives the correct sequence of moves for the 4-disk problem. Repeat the exercise with n = 7 and n = 10. How many moves are required for each of these values of n? How many moves are required for an arbitrary value of n? How many recursive invocations of Hanoi are needed for arbitrary n?

4-12. Many sports and games, like tennis and bridge, have round robin tournaments. In such a tournament, each team plays one match with every other team entered in the tournament. The tournament spans a series of time intervals (hours or days) in which each team plays either 0 or 1 match. The goal is to schedule all the matches in the tournament in such a way that the total number of time intervals (days) is minimized. The simplest situation is one in which the number of teams, n, is a power of 2, say 2^k. Then the number of days for the tournament is n−1, and there are exactly n/2 different matches scheduled for each day. The problem is, of course, to devise a method for scheduling such a tournament for an arbitrary number of teams. The following table shows a sample scheduling for a four-team round robin tennis tournament, with one match per team per day.

Opponent	Day 1	Day 2	Day 3
Team 1	2	3	4
Team 2	1	4	3
Team 3	4	1	2
Team 4	3	2	1

Using a divide and conquer approach, devise a recursive algorithm that will schedule a round robin tournament with an arbitrary number, $n = 2^k$, of teams. Implement your algorithm as a Modula-2 procedure and then exercise it with a driver that displays the scheduling for each of a variety of values of n. What if, in addition, we drop the restriction that n be a power of 2? How can the scheduling algorithm be adjusted to accommodate this change?

4-13. Using the BNF syntax in Appendix C for Modula-2 SimpleExpression, show that "a − b − c" and "a OR b AND c" are each syntactically correct SimpleExpressions.

4-14. Trace execution of the BinarySearch procedure by showing the values of m, n, and i for each invocation, assuming x = 80 and L = (23

25 39 42 46 49 73 74 80 96). How many invocations of BinarySearch are needed, for this particular L, in the worst case (i.e., assuming that x is not found)? What about for a list L of an arbitrary size, n? How does this finding compare with the complexity of the *nonrecursive* version of binary search that was given in Chapter 3?

4-15. Adapt the driver program from Chapter 3 so that it exercises both the nonrecursive and the recursive versions of the binary search, given a reasonably large list L (say, the odd integers from 1 to 1001, which is easy to generate algorithmically) and an even value of x (say, x = 2), so that x will not be found. Obtain thereby an empirical measure of execution time for the recursive and the nonrecursive versions. How do your results compare with your answers to the previous exercise?

4-16. Show by induction that the recursive implementation of the binary search is equivalent to the iterative implementation given in Chapter 3.

TEAM PROJECT

Reimplement all of the linear list operators from Chapter 3 using recursion. Use these new versions for your team project solution to the Less Naive Instructor's Problem at the end of Chapter 3. Obtain an empirical measure of the differences in efficiency between the two implementations by running each one independently against the same data. Are the differences in execution speed significant? Are the differences in storage requirements significant?

5
SORTING

As our binary search example has shown, the need to create an ordered linear list out of an unordered one is fundamental to many applications in computer science. The operator that satisfies this need is called *Sort*, and we shall devote this entire chapter to the study of sorting linear lists. Because of its central role in various applications, from data processing to artificial intelligence to mathematics, the development of efficient sorting algorithms has been widely studied by computer scientists. Although it is provably not possible to derive a Sort operator with complexity $O(n)$—that is, whose efficiency is directly proportional to the size (n) of the list being sorted—we shall see that some clever and intricate approaches to sorting algorithm design have made significant improvements upon the more straightforward methods, which have complexity $O(n^2)$.

We begin this chapter with a review of sorting using two methods known as "selection sort" and "insertion sort." These methods are conceptually straightforward, and yet they are relatively inefficient for lists that are not reasonably small. Following this, we study four additional sorting methods that are conceptually more intricate than the first two but that yield significant gains in efficiency. These are, in turn, the "Shell sort," the "merge sort," the "quicksort," and the "heapsort." Each of these methods is illustrated with an example, implemented in Modula-2 as a variation of the abstract operator Sort, and evaluated for complexity in terms of *average case* performance. That is, we assume that the list to be sorted initially appears in random order, so that an average number of comparisons (e_i vs e_j) will occur during the sort process.

To supplement this development, the different sorting methods are exercised using a list of random numbers generated by the procedure Random from Chapter 2. To unify the presentation of the sorting algorithms themselves, their implementations also import the list abstract data type and its operators, as defined and implemented in Chapter 3. This practice also helps to reinforce the principles of data abstraction, operator verification, and software reliability that are emphasized throughout the text.

In practice, the "average case" assumption is often not valid. That is, many applications encounter lists that are partially ordered, and thus the performance of the sorting algorithm can be (adversely or favorably) affected by such additional preconditions. We thus draw additional distinctions among "worst case," "best case," and "average case" assumptions and their effects upon the performance of the various sorting algorithms.

Many more sorting algorithms are in use, beyond the six that are studied in this chapter. For a complete treatment of the field of sorting, the reader is referred to Knuth's classic work, *Sorting and Searching* (Addison-Wesley, 1975). This chapter will, however, leave the reader with an appreciation of the importance of the Sort operator in computer science, as well as a basis for studying additional strategies and implementations for this operator in the future.

As a working basis for studying the sorting algorithms discussed in this chapter, we will assume the following definition of the Sort operator throughout:

Definition: *Sort(L)* rearranges the elements in the list L so that the resulting list L' is ordered (recall the definition of *ordered* from Chapter 3).
Preconditions: $L=(e_1\ e_2\ ...\ e_n)$ exists, and $n \geq 0$.
Postconditions: If $n \leq 1$, then $L' = L$. Otherwise, $L' = (e_{j_1}\ e_{j_2}\ ...\ e_{j_n})$ where the indexes $j_1, j_2, ..., j_n$ are a rearrangement of the indexes $1, 2, ..., n$ in such a way that L' is ordered.

Example:
Let L = (49 42 23 80 25 46 39 96 73 74), with n = 10. Then Sort(L) leaves L' = (23 25 39 42 46 49 73 74 80 96). Here, the required rearrangement $j_1, j_2, ..., j_{10}$ of the original indices is 3,5,7,2,6,1,9,10,4,8.

Other examples of the Sort operator can be given using character strings rather than numbers, but this particular example will be used throughout the chapter, so that we may focus attention on the details of the different algorithms themselves.

5-1 SELECTION AND INSERTION SORTS

The *selection sort* (sometimes called the "interchange sort" or the "exchange sort") is an example of the divide and conquer strategy in algorithm design. It begins with a list $L=(e_1\ e_2\ ...\ e_n)$ of n elements, selects the smallest element, and then exchanges that element with the first element, e_1. Thereby, two goals are satisfied: the smallest element is in its final position for the duration of the sort, and the remainder of the list to be sorted is of length $n-1$ (rather than n). If, at this point, the same procedure is repeated with the sublist L[2..n], then the next smallest element is interchanged with e_2 and the problem will be reduced to an $(n-2)$-element sort. Repeating this procedure exactly $n-1$ times thus leaves the list ordered, and the postconditions for Sort are satisfied.

As an example, consider the list L = (49 42 23 80 25 46 39 96 73 74) of size n = 10. In the first phase of the algorithm described above, we fix our attention on the position of the first element, 49, and mark that index with the variable i = 1. We then search L to select the index, say j, of the smallest element in the sublist L[i..n]: in this example, j = 3. Thus, we exchange e_3 with e_1, leaving L′ = (23 42 49 80 25 46 39 96 73 74). We now identify the sublist L[2..n] by incrementing i and searching that sublist to find the index j of the smallest element in it. The entire sequence of selections and interchanges is summarized in Figure 5-1, for this particular list.

The selection sort is implemented in three parts: a main procedure SelectionSort and two auxiliary procedures called Min and Swap. Min finds

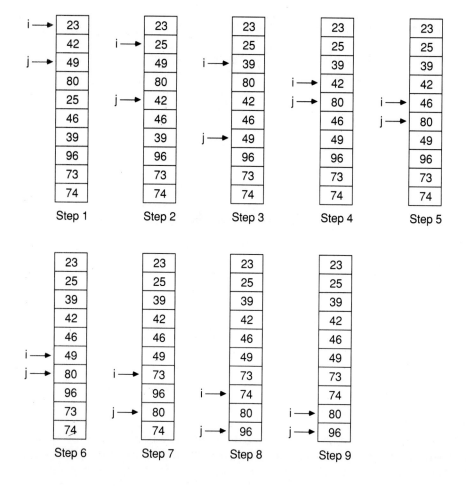

Figure 5-1
Example illustration of the selection sort.

the index j of the smallest element e_j in the sublist L[i..n], while Swap performs a single exchange of element e_j with element e_i. This implementation uses the type List and its associated operators from Chapter 3 and therefore makes no particular assumptions about whether Lists are represented in contiguous or linked storage.

The main procedure controls the index i as described above, invokes the procedure Min to set the index j of the smallest element in the sublist L[i..n], and invokes the procedure Swap to exchange e_i and e_j. This procedure is given below.

```
PROCEDURE SelectionSort (VAR L: List);
VAR i,j: ListIndex;
BEGIN
   FOR i:=1 TO ListSize(L)-1 DO
      j:=Min(L,i);         (*e[j] = smallest in L[i..n]. *)
      Swap(L,i,j)          (*Interchange e[i] and e[j]. *)
   END
END SelectionSort;
```

The implementations of Min and Swap are simple and appear below. Note the general usefulness of the List operators Retrieve and Store, as well as the types ListIndex and ListElement, within these two procedures.

```
PROCEDURE Min (VAR L: List; i: ListIndex): ListIndex;
   (*Search the sublist L[i..n] and return the index of the
     smallest element in that sublist. *)
   VAR j,k: ListIndex;
BEGIN
   j:=i;
   FOR k:=i+1 TO ListSize(L) DO
      IF Retrieve(L,k)<Retrieve(L,j) THEN
         j:=k
      END
   END;
   RETURN j
END Min;

PROCEDURE Swap (VAR L: List; i,j: ListIndex);
(*Exchange the elements e[i] and e[j] in list L. *)
VAR Temporary: ListElement;
BEGIN
   Temporary:=Retrieve(L,i);     (*Save a copy of e[i]. *)
   Store(L,i,Retrieve(L,j));     (*Move e[j] into e[i]. *)
   Store(L,j,Temporary)          (*Move copy into e[j]. *)
END Swap;
```

For documentation, note that the bodies of these procedures include precise statements of their respective purposes. The local variable Temporary is needed in the procedure Swap, of course, because the first Store invocation destroys the value of e[i] when it makes a copy of e[j] in its place.

5-1-1 Analysis of Selection Sort: Best, Average, and Worst Case Assumptions

To evaluate the complexity of this selection sort implementation, we first look at the main procedure itself and note that the number of iterations of the FOR loop therein is n−1 (where n is the size of list L). There are two statements embedded within that loop: one invoking the procedure Min, and the other invoking the procedure Swap. Thus, the complexity of the main procedure is (n−1)(M+S), where M and S represent the average number of steps in a single invocation of Min and Swap, respectively.

For the procedure Swap, the same number of steps (S=3) is executed whenever it is invoked. For the procedure Min, the number of steps varies with the length of the sublist L[i..n] being searched. For the ith invocation (i=1,...,n−1), that length is n−i+1. The IF statement in Min's FOR loop is thus repeated n−i times in the ith invocation. In addition, two extra steps are executed during the ith invocation of Min: one for the assignment j:=i, and one for the RETURN statement. Therefore, the *average* number of steps for an invocation of the Min procedure is given by the following:

$$M = \sum_{i=1}^{n-1} \frac{(n-i+3)}{n-1}$$

Combining these, we arrive at the following step count for a selection sort with a list L of size n:

$$(n-1)\left(\frac{\sum_{i=1}^{n-1}(n-i+3)}{n-1} + 3 \right)$$

$$= \sum_{i=1}^{n-1}(n-i+3) + 3(n-1)$$

$$= (n-1)(3+n) - \frac{n(n-1)}{2} + 3(n-1)$$

$$= \frac{1}{2}n^2 + \frac{11}{2}n - 6$$

(Readers should notice here that we used some of the information from Chapter 4 in order to replace an iterative expression by an equivalent closed form expression in the next to last line of this derivation.) The last line here shows that the selection sort procedure is $O(n^2)$ in complexity. For increasing values of n, the value of n^2 grows rapidly, as shown in the following table:

n value	n^2 value
1	1
10	100
100	10,000
1,000	1,000,000
10,000	100,000,000
100,000	10,000,000,000

We should also note that the selection sort's step count does not vary with respect to different assumptions about the degree to which the initial list L is already in order.

Other sort strategies, as we shall see, do vary in their step counts with different assumptions about the initial ordering of L. Such assumptions fall into three major categories: called "best case," "average case," and "worst case" assumptions. In the best case, we assume that the list L is initially ordered (or nearly ordered) before the sort procedure begins, potentially allowing a *minimum* number of steps to be executed in the sort. In the worst case, we assume the opposite: that the list is so prearranged that a *maximum* number of steps will be executed in the sort. Average case assumptions presumably cover the most likely situation: that the list L is so prearranged that an average number of steps will be executed by the sort. For the remaining sort algorithms in this chapter, we use average case assumptions unless otherwise indicated.

5-1-2 Insertion Sort: An Improvement Under Best Case Assumptions

In the case of the selection sort, the total number of steps does not vary if we move from the average case to either the best case or the worst case. Its step count is always the same, as given by the quadratic polynomial in the foregoing section. The *insertion sort* is another simple sorting algorithm that, although $O(n^2)$ in complexity in the average and worst cases, approaches $O(n)$ complexity under best case assumptions.

The insertion sort searches the list L serially until an element e_i is found that is out of order with respect to its predecessor, e_{i-1}. When such an element is found, it is removed from L and saved in a temporary location, and a search is made backward in the list until the first occurrence of an element e_{j-1} is found in which $e_{j-1} \leq e_i$. The saved value of e_i is then reinserted into L immediately after e_j. All of this is embodied in the following implementation.

```
PROCEDURE InsertionSort (VAR L: List);
VAR i,j: ListIndex;
    Temporary: ListElement;
BEGIN
   FOR i:=2 TO ListSize(L) DO
      IF Retrieve(L,i)<Retrieve(L,i-1) THEN
         Delete(L,i-1,Temporary);
         j:=i;
         REPEAT
            j:=j-1
         UNTIL (j=1) OR (Retrieve(L,j-1)<=Temporary);
         Insert(L,j-1,Temporary)
      END
   END
END InsertionSort;
```

The interesting characteristic of insertion sort is its variation in complexity with respect to differing assumptions about the initial ordering of list L. In the average case, it is not difficult to show that this procedure is $O(n^2)$ in complexity. In the best case, however, the initial ordering of the list L allows all n−1 steps of the FOR loop to be executed without a single execution of the embedded REPEAT loop. That is, the fact that the list L is ordered guarantees that $e_i \geq e_{i-1}$ for every value of i from 2 to n. The extraction and reinsertion of an element e_i into its proper position, therefore, never needs to take place. Thus, the complexity of the insertion sort is $O(n)$ in this best case.

5-2 SHELL SORT

Returning to the average case, we note a serious operative handicap in the performance of the selection and insertion sorts. That is, an element can be swapped several times before it finally reaches its destination in the ordered list. Looking back at the example in Figure 5-1, we see that the integer 80 drifts in this manner; it appears in positions 4, 5, 6, and 7 before it is eventually swapped into position 9, which is its final destination.

The *Shell sort,* invented by Donald Shell in 1959, attempts to eliminate most of these intermediate movements by stretching the minimum distance a swapped number must travel in a single move. Thereby, the number will be moved closer to its final destination in the list upon its *first* movement, rather than taking only a single short step at a time (as does the number 80 in the selection sort).

To accomplish this, we initially define this minimum distance, or "gap," arbitrarily as $\lfloor \frac{n}{3} \rfloor + 1$ and then design a specialized (selection or other) sort procedure that will sort each group of elements in the list separated from each other by this fixed distance. The effect of this initial step, using our example 10-element list and a gap size of 4, is shown in Figure 5-2. Here, the index k is used to identify the starting index for each such

[Figure 5-2 diagram showing initial setup for Shell sort]

Figure 5-2
Initial setup for the Shell sort.

group, and the asterisk (*) is used to mark the elements of the group that are to be sorted. As readers can see, the swap of the numbers 25 and 49 places them both nearer to their final destination, while the number 80 is not frivolously swapped at this step.

Next, the gap size is reduced by a factor of 3, and this step is repeated. This is done as many times as necessary until the gap size becomes 1. Thus, for a list of size 10, the initial four sorts of groups separated by 4 is followed by two sorts of groups separated by 2, and finally one sort of the group of elements separated by 1 (i.e., the entire list). The effect of these three additional sorts is shown in Figure 5-3. Note here that the number 80, when finally moved, is left immediately adjacent to its final destination at the end of the sort. In this way, the total number of intermediate swaps is reduced, compared with the selection sort, and the efficiency of the Shell sort is expected to be improved.

Implementation of the Shell sort is done in two parts. The first part, called GapSort, is a variation of the insertion sort, except that it sorts only those elements in list L that begin with index k and are separated by gap g.

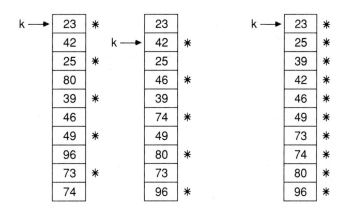

Figure 5-3
Last two steps in the Shell sort.

```
PROCEDURE GapSort (VAR L: List; k,g: ListIndex);
(*This procedure is an InsertionSort, except that
   only the sublist of elements e[k], e[k+g], e[k+2g],
   e[k+3g], ... are sorted.  That is, the invocation
   GapSort(L,1,1) is an InsertionSort for all of L. *)
VAR i,j: ListIndex;
    Temporary: ListElement;
BEGIN
  i:=k+g;
  WHILE i<=ListSize(L) DO
    IF Retrieve(L,i)<Retrieve(L,i-g) THEN
      Temporary:=Retrieve(L,i);
      j:=i;
      REPEAT
        Store(L,j,Retrieve(L,j-g));
        j:=j-g
      UNTIL (j=k) OR (Retrieve(L,j-g)<=Temporary);
      Store(L,j,Temporary)
    END;
    i:=i+g
  END
END GapSort;
```

Reader should note that the Procedure GapSort is similar to the original Procedure InsertionSort, except that the list operators Insert and Delete are replaced by list operators Store and Retrieve. However, the original effect of InsertionSort is preserved in spite of these changes.

The second part of the Shell sort controls the overall process and is given below.

```
PROCEDURE ShellSort (VAR L: List);
VAR k,g: ListIndex;
BEGIN
  g:=ListSize(L) DIV 3 + 1;
  WHILE g>1 DO
    FOR k:=1 TO g DO
      GapSort(L,k,g)
    END;
    g:=g DIV 3 + 1
  END;
  GapSort(L,1,1)
END ShellSort;
```

Analysis of the Shell sort is a very difficult matter. Interested readers may wish to scan appropriate pages 85-95 of Knuth's *Sorting and Searching* to gain a feeling for this difficulty. Although the average number of moves for the Shell sort is not straightforwardly derived, empirical studies show that it is in the vicinity of $O(n^{1.25})$ whenever the list size n is in the range between 100 and 60000. For large values of n, this is a significant improvement over selection and insertion sorts, as the following table indicates.

n value	n^2 value	$n^{1.25}$ value
1	1	1
10	100	17.8
100	10,000	316
1,000	1,000,000	5,623
10,000	100,000,000	100,000

Later in the chapter, we shall return to the question of empirical evaluation of sorting efficiency—once from our own experience and again in the context of a team programming project at the end of the chapter.

5-3 MERGE SORT

The divide and conquer strategy is useful in other sorting algorithms beyond the selection sort. The *merge sort*, for example, splits the original list L into two lists, say L1 and L2, which are individually sorted and then merged together to yield the result. For example, consider our ten-element list:

$$L = (49\ 42\ 23\ 80\ 25\ 46\ 39\ 96\ 73\ 74)$$

We first split it into two lists, say L1 and L2:

$$L1 = (49\ 42\ 23\ 80\ 25) \text{ and}$$
$$L2 = (46\ 39\ 96\ 73\ 74)$$

Now, we sort L1 and L2 individually, so they appear as follows:

$$L1 = (23\ 25\ 42\ 49\ 80) \text{ and}$$
$$L2 = (39\ 46\ 73\ 74\ 96)$$

Finally, the two lists are recombined, or merged, into a single ordered list L as follows:

$$L = (23\ 25\ 39\ 42\ 46\ 49\ 73\ 74\ 80\ 96)$$

These steps form, as the reader can see, a naturally recursive algorithm, since the sorting of the smaller lists L1 and L2 can be handled by invoking the same procedure twice more. The stopping point for recursive invocation occurs when the size of L1 or the size of L2 is reduced to one in the course of a split. A complete outline of the merge sort is shown in Figure 5-4, for our example list.

To implement the merge sort, we must be careful not to waste storage. That is, if we use the strategy of making a complete copy of the elements from list L in order to form the two smaller lists L1 and L2, the storage requirements immediately double. In fact, they double at *each* level of recursion where this copying is done.

An alternative strategy avoids most of this redundancy. That is, each time we move an element from list L to list L1 or L2, we simultaneously delete it from list L. Further, when all elements of list L are so copied, we take list L (which is at this point empty) out of existence, using the operator

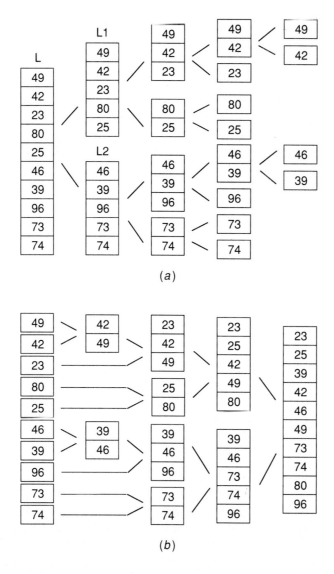

Figure 5-4 Outline of the merge sort.

Destroy. Recall that this operator was suggested at the end of Chapter 3 as a useful addition to the list of standard operators for the List abstract data type. The amount of actual storage savings that takes place under this strategy depends, of course, upon the implementation strategy that is chosen for the List abstract data type itself. At the level of implementing the merge sort, of course, we have no control or knowledge of this choice. If we did, we would naturally encourage the linked strategy to be used, since it permits immediate storage recovery upon execution of each Delete operation for a single list element. The contiguous strategy does not recover storage with each Delete; that occurs only when an entire list is destroyed.

With these considerations in mind, the following procedure Split copies the first half of the elements in L into the new list L1 and the second half into the new list L2. These elements are systematically deleted from the list L at the same time, using the operator Delete, so that L is empty at the end of the second copying loop. L is then destroyed.

```
PROCEDURE Split (VAR L, L1, L2: List);
VAR i, n, middle: ListIndex;
    x: ListElement;
BEGIN
  n:=ListSize(L);
  middle:=n DIV 2;
  CreateList(L1);
  CreateList(L2);
  FOR i:=1 TO middle DO
    Delete(L,0,x);
    Insert(L1,i-1,x)
  END;
  FOR i:=middle+1 TO n DO
    Delete(L,0,x);
    Insert(L2,i-(middle+1),x)
  END;
  DestroyList(L)
END Split;
```

Here, we see that the index i is used to count the number of elements that are copied, "middle" marks the break from L1 to L2, and n gives the total number of elements in L at the outset. The result of this step, for our sample ten-element list, is shown in Figure 5-5.

The second fundamental step in the merge sort merges two lists L1 and L2 into a single list L, assuming that L1 and L2 are each ordered. Here, the same storage recovery strategy is used again, with each element

L = ( )   L1 = (49 42 23 80 25)

                   L2 = (46 39 96 73 74)

Figure 5-5
Initial split step for the merge sort.

immediately deleted from L1 or L2 as soon as it is transferred to L. Lists L1 and L2 may thus be destroyed at the end of this process, since they have become empty.

In the following procedure Merge, indexes n1 and n2 define the original sizes of the lists L1 and L2, before any elements are deleted. Indexes i and j keep track of the number of elements that have been deleted from L1 and L2, respectively, while index k keeps track of the number of elements that have been added to L. Elements are deleted always from the beginning of L1 or L2 and inserted at the end of L as the first WHILE loop in the procedure Merge is executed.

```
PROCEDURE Merge (VAR L, L1, L2: List);
VAR i,j,k,n1,n2: ListIndex;
    x: ListElement;
BEGIN
  CreateList(L);
  n1:=ListSize(L1);
  n2:=ListSize(L2);
  i:=1;
  j:=1;
  k:=0;
  WHILE (i<=n1) AND (j<=n2) DO
    IF Retrieve(L1,1)<=Retrieve(L2,1) THEN
      Delete(L1,0,x);
      Insert(L,k,x);
      i:=i+1
    ELSE
      Delete(L2,0,x);
      Insert(L,k,x);
      j:=j+1
    END;
    k:=k+1
  END;
  WHILE i<=n1 DO
    Delete(L1,0,x);
    Insert(L,k,x);
    i:=i+1;
    k:=k+1
  END;
  WHILE j<=n2 DO
    Delete(L2,0,x);
    Insert(L,k,x);
    j:=j+1;
    k:=k+1
  END;
  DestroyList(L1);
  DestroyList(L2)
END Merge;
```

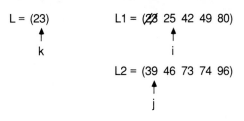

Figure 5-6
First loop iteration for the merge step.

It is important to illustrate carefully the behavior of this step Merge. Suppose L1 and L2 are the ordered sublists of length 5, shown in Figure 5-6. Initially, i and j index the first elements in these two lists, respectively. The index k indexes the position in the merged list after which the first insertion will be made, whether it comes from L1 or L2 (whichever has the smaller first element). Thus, the first iteration of the WHILE loop leaves i, j, and k as shown in Figure 5-6, and the second iteration leaves i, j, and k as shown in Figure 5-7.

Subsequent steps in the loop add one element (from either one or the other of the lists L1 or L2) to the merged list at a time, until one of the two lists becomes exhausted. Since we cannot predict which one that will be, the final two WHILE loops cover both cases. In our example, L1 becomes exhausted first, leaving j indexing the tail end of L2 (the element 96). Thus, the second of these two WHILE loops completes the merge process by simply copying the remainder of list L2 over to the merged list L, deleting the elements as they are copied.

Now, the main procedure MergeSort can be written using Split and Merge, in the following way.

```
PROCEDURE MergeSort (VAR L: List);
VAR L1,L2: List;
BEGIN
   IF ListSize(L)>1
   THEN
      Split(L,L1,L2);       (*Split L in half.*)
      MergeSort(L1);        (*Sort left half of L.*)
      MergeSort(L2);        (*Sort right half of L.*)
      Merge(L,L1,L2)        (*Merge the two halves.*)
   END
END MergeSort;
```

As shown, the MergeSort procedure is recursive in the way that was initially described. It uses the auxiliary lists L1 and L2 at each level of recursion.

Figure 5-7
Second loop iteration for the merge step.

However, L1 and L2 are not actually *Create*d until such time that they are needed by the Split procedure, at which time L is simultaneously *Destroy*ed. On the other hand, L is not *recreated* at the same level of recursion until such time that L1 and L2 can be destroyed—at the time of the Merge. Thus, at any stage of this process, only one copy of each element in the original list actually exists in storage.

5-3-1 Analysis of the Merge Sort

Analysis of the procedure MergeSort is not difficult, remembering that each invocation of Split divides the remaining list in half. The number of Split invocations, for an initial list L of size n, is therefore $\lfloor \log_2 n \rfloor$. It should be clear that the same number of invocations occurs for the procedure Merge as for the procedure Split. Now, for a single invocation of the procedure Split, with a list of size r, the number of steps is $O(r)$, or exactly $2r+5$. That is because the two FOR loops within Split combine to total r iterations (at 2 steps per iteration) and the remainder of the procedure contains a constant number (5) of steps. For the procedure Merge, with two lists L1 and L2 of combined length r, the number of steps is also $O(r)$, or exactly $4r+8$. That is because a single iteration within each of the three WHILE loops adds exactly one element to the merged list L and contains exactly 4 steps, and there are 8 additional steps in the procedure outside of these three loops. Assuming for convenience that the list size n is an exact power of 2, the following table gives us a lead toward discovering the overall complexity of MergeSort.

Sublist Size (r)	Number of Split's	Number of Merge's
n	1	1
n/2	2	2
n/4	4	4
:	:	:
$n/2^k$	2^k	2^k
:	:	:
2	n/2	n/2

That is, for each of the sublist sizes $n/2^k$, there are 2^k invocations of Split and Merge. Setting $r=n/2^k$ in the individual step counts for Split and Merge, and summing these columns, gives us a complexity for MergeSort as follows:

$$\sum_{k=0}^{\log_2 n - 1} 2^k[(2(n/2^k) + 5) + (4(n/2^k) + 8)]$$

$$= \sum_{k=0}^{\log_2 n - 1} 2^k[6n/2^k + 13]$$

$$= 6n(\log_2 n - 1) + 13 \sum_{k=0}^{\log_2 n - 1} 2^k$$

$$= 6n(\log_2 n - 1) + 13(2^{\log_2 n - 1} - 1)$$

$$= 6n(\log_2 n - 1) + 13(n/2 - 1)$$

The dominant term in this last expression, as n grows large, is $n\log_2 n$. We can conclude, therefore, that the complexity of MergeSort is $O(n\log_2 n)$, which represents a substantial gain over the selection and insertion sorts. The following table summarizes that gain for a few key values of n.

n value	n^2 value	$n\log_2 n$ value
1	1	0
10	100	33.2
100	10,000	664
1,000	1,000,000	9,965
10,000	100,000,000	132,880

5-4 QUICKSORT

Another approach to sorting, *quicksort*, was discovered by C.A.R. Hoare in 1962. Unlike the merge sort, which makes several copies of sublists during the process, the quicksort operates directly on a single copy of the list, and still maintains a complexity of $O(n\log_2 n)$. Thus, the significant waste of storage, which is caused by copying many sublists, can be avoided without sacrificing sorting efficiency.

The quicksort uses a divide and conquer strategy in the following way. Suppose again that we have the list:

$$L = (49\ 42\ 23\ 80\ 25\ 46\ 39\ 96\ 73\ 74)$$

We begin by setting indexes i and j at the first and last elements of L, respectively, and the "pivot" index k at the middle element of L, or 25 in our example. Now we move i and j successively toward each other, until we find an element $e_i >= e_k$ and another element $e_j <= e_k$. If such a pair is found, they are, respectively, on the "wrong" sides of the pivot element (with respect to the desired ordering of L); so we swap them. This is shown in Figure 5-8, where the elements $e_1 = 49$ and $e_3 = 23$ are swapped.

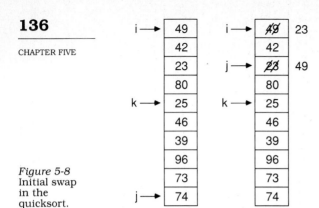

Figure 5-8
Initial swap in the quicksort.

Thereafter, i and j continue their movement toward the pivot, swapping all other pairs that are on the wrong side of each other, until they meet (i.e., until i≥j). At that moment, all elements that precede e_j are no greater than the pivot, and all elements that follow e_i are no less than the pivot. For our example, this situation is shown in Figure 5-9.

Now, we divide the list into two sublists $L1 = L[1..i]$ and $L2 = L[i+1..n]$ and recursively invoke the quicksort for each of these sublists in turn. The stopping point for recursion in each case is exactly the point when the length of L1 or L2 is reduced to 1. For our example list, the result at each of these stages is summarized in Figure 5-10.

The quicksort algorithm is implemented below, in two procedures. The principal procedure is called SublistQuickSort and sorts any sublist of list L defined by the beginning and ending indexes i and j. The main procedure QuickSort simply invokes this procedure for the *entire* list L, setting parameters i and j, respectively, to reference L's first and last elements. In the procedure SublistQuickSort, the local variables ileft, iright, jleft, and jright are used to mark the left and right ends of the partition of L into sublists L1 and L2, respectively. The local variable k is used to index the pivot element, and the auxiliary procedure Swap is assumed to be as previously defined for the selection sort (at the beginning of the chapter).

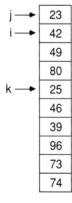

Figure 5-9
End of first stage in the quicksort.

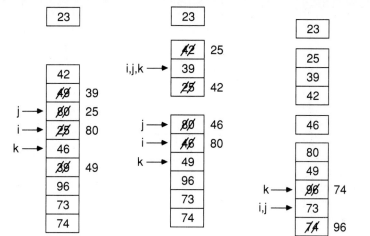

Figure 5-10 Summary of next three stages in the quicksort.

```
PROCEDURE QuickSort (VAR L: List);
VAR i,j: ListIndex;
BEGIN
  i:=1;
  j:=ListSize(L);
  SublistQuickSort(L,i,j)
END QuickSort;

PROCEDURE SublistQuickSort (VAR L: List;
                            VAR i, j: ListIndex);
VAR ileft, iright, jleft, jright, k: ListIndex;
    pivot: ListElement;
BEGIN
  k:=(i+j) DIV 2;      (*Choose pivot element.*)
  ileft:=i;            (*Save left boundary for sublist L1*)
  jright:=j;           (*and right boundary for sublist L2.*)
  pivot:=Retrieve(L,k);
  i:=i-1;
  j:=j+1;
  REPEAT
    REPEAT
      i:=i+1
    UNTIL Retrieve(L,i) >= pivot;
    REPEAT
      j:=j-1
    UNTIL Retrieve(L,j) <= pivot;
    IF i<j THEN
      Swap(L,i,j)
    END
  UNTIL i>=j;
```

```
    IF i>j THEN
      iright:=j;          (*Save right boundary for L1*)
      jleft:=i            (*and left boundary for L2.*)
    ELSE
      iright:=j-1;
      jleft:=i+1
    END;
                          (*Continue for sublist sizes > 1.*)
    IF ileft<iright THEN
      SublistQuickSort(L,ileft,iright)
    END;
    IF jleft<jright THEN
      SublistQuickSort(L,jleft,jright)
    END
END SublistQuickSort;
```

This division of the quicksort into two procedures enables the recursive activation of the algorithm for successively smaller sublists, as indicated at the end of the procedure SublistQuickSort.

5-4-1 Analysis of Quicksort

The efficiency of quicksort depends upon the initial ordering of the list L. That is, the arbitrary identification of the pivot e_k as the middle element of L assumes that approximately half of all the elements will be less than e_k and half will be greater. If that is the case, then the boundary for the partition of L into sublists L1 and L2 will be close to k, and the recursive calls to QuickSort will be each working on lists of approximately half the size of the original list.

If we use this particular best case assumption for *every* level of recursion, $2[\log_2 n] + 1$ invocations of SublistQuickSort will occur for a list of size n. Assuming, for simplicity, that n is a power of 2, there will be 2^s invocations of SublistQuickSort for each sublist size $n/2^s$, for $s=0,1,...,\log_2 n-1$. Each such invocation (with sublist size $n/2^s$) will require at most $n/2^{s+1}$ iterations of its major REPEAT loop. This limit is reached in the event that *every* pair of elements in the sublist must be swapped in order to place them on the proper side of the pivot element e_k. A single iteration of that loop executes five steps for that event, two for each embedded REPEAT loop and one for the Swap itself. Adding the ten fixed steps outside the loops of the procedure SublistQuickSort, we have a grand total of $10 + 5 \times n/2^{s+1}$ steps in a single invocation. Summing over all values of s from 0 to $\log_2 n - 1$, and adding two additional fixed steps for the initial invocation of QuickSort before it invokes SublistQuickSort for the first time, we have the following total step count for QuickSort under these assumptions.

$$2 + \sum_{s=0}^{\log_2 n - 1} 2^s (10 + 5 \times \frac{n}{2^{s+1}})$$

$$2 + \sum_{s=0}^{\log_2 n - 1} (10 \times 2^s + \frac{5n}{2})$$

$$2 + 10(n-1) + \frac{5n}{2} \times (\log_2 n - 1)$$

Thus, quicksort is $O(n\log_2 n)$ in complexity, as shown by the third term in the last line of the above derivation. This result is subject to our best case assumption that the pivot element in each sublist will also be a median, in the sense it will divide the sublist into two equal halves in preparation for the next level of invocation.

However, this best case is not always guaranteed by the initial ordering of the list L. For instance, the initial ordering of our example ten-integer list L caused a first partition into two-element and eight-element sublists. In the worst possible case, one can construct a list in which the first partitioning will yield sublists of sizes 1 and $n-1$, the second will yield sublists of sizes 1 and $n-2$, and so forth. In this case, the total number of recursive invocations of QuickSort will be $n-1$, rather than $\log_2 n$, and its complexity will become, therefore, $O(n^2)$. This performance is, therefore, no better than that of the interchange sort presented at the beginning of the chapter.

In between these two extremes, however, experience has shown that the quicksort performs quite well for lists of reasonably large size and randomness. Furthermore, refinements can be made to the pivot selection procedure so that the worst case $O(n^2)$ complexity can be eliminated. We shall view some empirical evidence of quicksort's performance at the end of the chapter.

5-5 HEAPSORT

The final sort algorithm to be presented in this chapter is the *heapsort*. It was discovered in 1964 by J.W.J. Williams, has complexity $O(n\log_2 n)$, and avoids not only the extra storage requirements of merge sort but also the best case ordering assumptions underlying the quicksort's optimal performance. To understand the heapsort, we first define the notion of a "heap:"

Definition: A *heap* is a linear list $L = (e_1\ e_2\ \ldots\ e_n)$ in which each element e_i is not less than either of the elements e_{2i} and e_{2i+1} if they exist, for all $i = 1,\ldots,n/2$.

Thus, L is a heap if $e_1 \geq e_2$ and $e_1 \geq e_3$, $e_2 \geq e_4$ and $e_2 \geq e_5$, and so forth. The following three reorderings of our original list L are all heaps:

(96 80 74 73 46 42 49 25 39 23)
(96 74 80 73 46 42 49 25 39 23)
(96 80 74 73 49 46 42 39 25 23)

We see that a heap does not necessarily reflect a reverse ordering for a list, although it can. We see also that the very largest element in any heap must appear first, even though we have some flexibility in arranging the remaining elements.

The heapsort algorithm has two major loops, beginning with an initial list L. The first loop rearranges the elements of L so that they form a heap. The second loop begins by exchanging e_1 and e_n in the heap (thus placing the largest element in its final position for the sort) and then remaking a heap out of the remaining sublist L[1..n−1]. This second step is then repeated n−1 times to complete the sort.

The main logic of the heapsort is reflected in the following procedure HeapSort.

```
PROCEDURE HeapSort (VAR L: List);
VAR left, right: ListIndex;
BEGIN
   IF ListSize(L)>1 THEN
(*Build the initial heap from e[1] to e[n]. *)
      left:=ListSize(L) DIV 2 + 1;
      right:=ListSize(L);
      WHILE left>1 DO
         left:=left-1;
         SiftUp(L,left,right)
      END;
(*Exchange e[1] and e[right] and remake heap
   L[1..right-1].  Note: left=1 throughout. *)
      WHILE right>1 DO
         Swap(L,left,right);
         right:=right-1;
         SiftUp(L,left,right)
      END
   END
END HeapSort;
```

Essential to both the initial loop (which builds the heap) and the final loop (which maintains the heap) is the procedure SiftUp. This procedure maintains the heap's integrity with respect to the elements e[left], e[2*left], e[2*left+1], and all subsequent pairs of elements in the sublist L[left..right] whose indexes are displaced by a multiple of 2 from the largest of these three elements. Specifically, the SiftUp procedure is as follows.

```
PROCEDURE SiftUp (VAR L: List; left, right: ListIndex);
   VAR i,j: ListIndex;
BEGIN
   i:=left;
   j:=2*i;
```

```
    WHILE j<=right DO
      IF j<right THEN
        IF Retrieve(L,j)<Retrieve(L,j+1) THEN
          j:=j+1                (*Locate the larger of e[2*i]*)
        END                     (*and e[2*i+1]. *)
      END;
      IF Retrieve(L,i)<Retrieve(L,j) THEN
        Swap(L,i,j);            (*Exchange that with e[i] if*)
        i:=j;                   (*it is larger than e[i],*)
        j:=2*j                  (*and continue the sifting.*)
      ELSE
        j:=right+1              (*Otherwise, force an end to*)
      END                       (*the sifting.*)
    END
END SiftUp;
```

To illustrate this process, consider our example list once again, where HeapSort initially invokes SiftUp with the sublist e[6..10], as shown within braces {} on the first line of Figure 5-11.

Left	Right	e[1]	e[2]	e[3]	e[4]	e[5]	e[6]	e[7]	e[8]	e[9]	e[10]
6	10	49	42	23	80	25	{46	39	96	73	74}
5	10	49	42	23	80	{25	46	39	96	73	74}
4	10	49	42	23	{80	74	46	39	96	73	25}
3	10	49	42	{23	96	74	46	39	80	73	25}
2	10	49	{42	46	96	74	23	39	80	73	25}
1	10	{49	96	46	80	74	23	39	42	73	25}
		{96	80	46	73	74	23	39	42	49	25}

Figure 5-11 Initial heap build for the heap sort.

Each of the next five lines shows the effect of adding one more element to the sublist and subsequently invoking the SiftUp procedure to incorporate that element at its proper position in the heap. For instance, after the first invocation of SiftUp, the elements 25 and 74 are swapped, so that $e_5 = 74$ and $e_{10} = 25$. After the second invocation, the larger of e_8 and e_9, or 96, is swapped with $e_4 = 80$, since e_4 is not the larger of the three. Similarly, the third invocation leaves $e_3 = 23$ swapped with the larger of e_6 and e_7. Note, in the next invocation of SiftUp, that $e_2 = 42$ is first swapped with the larger of 96 and 74, and then the process is not finished; that is, since placing 46 in location e_4 leaves it not the largest among e_8 and e_9, it is further swapped with e_8, leaving 42 finally in e_8 and 80 in e_4. Readers should carefully review these steps to become convinced that a heap is indeed created at the point where left finally becomes reduced to 1.

The final loop in the HeapSort procedure removes element e[1] from the heap and swaps it with e[right]; since e[1] is the largest element in the heap, it ultimately belongs in the rightmost position. Thereafter, the list is reduced by 1 at its right end, the procedure SiftUp is recalled to reinstate this shorter list as a heap, and the next-largest element is thus extracted. One by one, the elements of L are thus placed in their final position, as summarized in Figure 5-12.

Left	Right	e[1]	e[2]	e[3]	e[4]	e[5]	e[6]	e[7]	e[8]	e[9]	e[10]
1	10	{96	80	46	73	74	23	39	42	49	25}
1	9	{80	74	46	73	25	23	39	42	49}	96
1	8	{74	73	46	49	25	23	39	42}	80	96
1	7	{73	49	46	42	25	23	39}	74	80	96
1	6	{49	42	46	39	25	23}	73	74	80	96
1	5	{46	42	23	39	25}	49	73	74	80	96
1	4	{42	25	23	39}	46	49	73	74	80	96
1	3	{39	25	23}	42	46	49	73	74	80	96
1	2	{25	23}	35	42	46	49	73	74	80	96
1	1	{23}	25	35	42	46	49	73	74	80	96

Figure 5-12 Completion of the heap sort.

Note here that, at any stage, the only element in the sublist L[1..right] that is swapped out is e[1], and therefore only *one* pass through the list by SiftUp (beginning at e[1]) is needed in order to restore the integrity of the heap.

5-5-1 Analysis of Heapsort

Complexity of the heapsort can be determined by observing first that the SiftUp procedure, for a sublist of size k, requires at most $\log_2 k$ iterations of its WHILE loop. In the first loop within HeapSort itself, $\frac{n}{2} + 1$ invocations of SiftUp are executed, with sublists of size increasing by 1 at each invocation. In its second loop, HeapSort invokes SiftUp $n-1$ times, with sublists of size k decreasing by 1 at each invocation. Combining these observations, we have the following estimate for the complexity of HeapSort:

$$[(n/2 + 1) + (n - 1)]\log_2 n$$
$$= O(n\log_2 n)$$

This estimate should be viewed as conservative, since most of the actual invocations of HeapSort are for sublists of a size k that is far smaller than the list size n. A more exact calculation of this complexity is difficult and will not be developed here.

5-6 EMPIRICAL EVALUATION OF SORTING ALGORITHMS

As suggested in some of the above presentations, the performance of a particular sorting algorithm can depend upon the initial ordering of the list L. For instance, we noted that the quicksort is particularly poor in the worst case that the partitioning of L does not yield relatively equal-sized sublists. Our complexity analyses of the different sorting algorithms in this chapter are each based on average case, best case, or even worst case assumptions about the initial ordering of elements in the list L. When we assume that the list L is randomly ordered at the outset of the sort, we create a setting for "on the average" kinds of argumentation in estimating an algorithm's complexity.

In practice, however, this assumption may be inappropriate. That is, some applications require a sort for data that is already partially in order; sorting algorithms can sometimes be "tuned" to perform more optimally under this reality than any of the standard sorting algorithms presented here. For this reason, it is sometimes useful to obtain empirical measures of the performance of different sorting algorithms, starting with a list L of "live" data that typefies the actual application to which the sorting algorithm will be applied.

For instance, we wanted to obtain measures of the relative performance of the six different sorting algorithms in this chapter, in order to corroborate the derived measures that were obtained by computing step counts. For this, we took a list L of 100 random integers (generated by the procedure Random from Chapter 2) and exercised each of the sorting algorithms with those integers. Furthermore, we exercised the six sorting algorithms again using a 100-element list L that was originally ordered (i.e., the integers from 1 to 100 inclusive) and, finally, using a 100-element list L that was originally in reverse order (i.e., the integers from 100 to 1 inclusive). All of these runs were made on a PC-compatible microcomputer. The resulting execution times are shown in Figure 5-13.

Sort Algorithm	Speed (sec) Random Order	Increasing Order	Reverse Order
Selection	33.2	31.7	32.6
Insertion	14.8	0.5	22.8
Shell	5.6	2.6	5.3
Merge	11.0	10.7	10.8
Quick	4.3	2.0	2.6
Heap	6.4	7.5	5.6

Figure 5-13 Sorting 100 integers: linked implementation.

These results are interesting. Insertion sort, as predicted, performs dramatically better when the list is already ordered. However, in the general case, the Shell sort, quicksort, and heapsort are substantially better. The merge sort didn't perform quite as efficiently as these three, probably due to the significant amount of sublist copying that it requires.

Another significant question surrounds the impact of different linear list implementation strategies on the performance of list sorting algorithms in general. The results given in Figure 5-13 are based on the linked implementation strategy. For a comparison, we reran this experiment using the contiguous implementation of linear lists, and the results are shown in Figure 5-14.

Sort Algorithm	Speed (sec) Random Order	Increasing Order	Reverse Order
Selection	3.0	3.1	3.1
Insertion	2.4	0.0	4.4
Shell	0.8	0.4	0.7
Merge	4.0	3.9	4.5
Quick	0.6	0.3	0.3
Heap	1.4	1.6	1.3

Figure 5-14 Sorting 100 integers: Contiguous implementation.

As shown, the use of contiguous storage for implementing linear lists yields significant performance gains, even though this practice sacrifices a certain amount of flexibility and efficiency in storage utilization.

5-7 PROCEDURES AS PARAMETERS: A USEFUL MODULA-2 TOOL

Modula-2 has a feature that is particularly useful when, at run time, we wish to allow one from among several different alternative implementations of an operator to be chosen, depending upon some external information (such as a choice by the terminal user or the discovery of a particular characteristic of the data that would favor one alternative over the other). This feature permits the procedure type itself to be specified with a formal parameter, thus allowing procedure names themselves to be passed as arguments to other procedures.

To accomplish this, the procedure type is provided in Modula-2. Its general form is one of the following:

```
TYPE proceduretype = PROCEDURE(parametertypes);
TYPE proceduretype = PROCEDURE(parametertypes): resulttype;
```

The first form is used when the procedure type is being declared for a group of implementations of an operator that is not a function, while the second is used for an operator that is a function procedure.

For example, the following characterizes a group of function procedures that take a single INTEGER argument and return an INTEGER result:

```
TYPE IntegerFunction = PROCEDURE (INTEGER): INTEGER;
```

Having this, we may declare other procedures that themselves take an IntegerFunction f and a List x as arguments, such as:

```
PROCEDURE Plot (f: IntegerFunction; x: List);
PROCEDURE Display (f: IntegerFunction; x: List);
```

The procedure Plot can thus be written to take the name of any Integer Function and, using the list of values x, can plot a two-dimensional graph of x and f(x). Similarly, the procedure Display can take the name f of any such function and simply display two columns: one with the values of x and the other with the computed values of f(x). For example, here are some appropriate invocations for the procedure Plot.

```
Plot (Factorial, x); (*Plot x! for the given values of x. *)
Plot (Square, x);    (*Plot x squared for the given x. *)
Plot (Div10, x)      (*Plot x DIV 10 for the given x. *)
```

An important restriction to be remembered when using procedure types is that the name of a *standard* procedure (such as ODD or INC) cannot be used as an argument in such an invocation.

This particular facility has special usefulness in the implementation of different sorting algorithms. That is, we can think of Sort as a single operator to be implemented within the module Lists, along with the other operators Insert, Delete, and so forth. In this way, the user is shielded from needing to choose one from among several different alternative algorithms for sorting; he or she might simply want to be able to say "Sort(L)" to accomplish a sort of L, leaving the details of choosing the best sorting algorithm to the implementation.

However, there is one important restriction when we use a procedure type as a parameter to the single procedure Sort; that is, all invocations of Sort must pass an argument of exactly that same type. For our six sort implementations, this restriction presents no problem; all six are procedures of the following type:

```
PROCEDURE (List)
```

Readers who are interested in developing such a unification are encouraged to do exercise 5-12 at the end of the chapter.

EXERCISES

5-1. Give a loop invariant that will aid in the verification of the SelectionSort procedure. Verify this procedure, by showing that the postconditions for Sort are satisfied for any list L that satisfies the preconditions.

5-2. Alter the SelectionSort procedure so that it invokes the procedure Swap to interchange e_i and e_j *only* whenever i and j point to *different* elements (it's useless to swap an element with itself). What impact, if any, does this refinement have on the complexity of this sort? Explain.

5-3. Write a procedure Ordered that, given list L, determines whether or not L is ordered and returns the BOOLEAN value TRUE or FALSE accordingly.

5-4. The *bubble sort* is a straightforward sorting procedure, which readers may recall from an earlier course. Here, a series of complete passes is made over the entire list until the list is ordered. For a single pass, every adjacent pair of elements e_i and e_{i+1} is examined, and if the elements are out of order with respect to each other, they are swapped. Otherwise, they are left alone. When an entire pass is made over the list (say, for i = 1 to n−1) in which *no* such swaps are needed, the list is known to be ordered. Illustrate the bubble sort for our example list L given in this chapter. Implement a procedure BubbleSort that embodies this strategy, using the auxiliary procedure Swap as well. Show that the average case complexity of BubbleSort is $O(n^2)$, but that its best case complexity is $O(n)$.

5-5. Exercise the insertion sort procedure given in the text by showing the resulting element sequence in L after each successive iteration of the FOR loop. Use as an example list L the same list that is given for illustrating the selection sort.

5-6. Show that the procedure InsertionSort is equivalent to the procedure GapSort in the special case where the gap size is 1. Verify the GapSort by giving preconditions and postconditions, and arguing systematically that GapSort's postconditions are satisfied for any sublist of L defined by beginning element k and gap size g.

5-7. Exercise the MergeSort algorithm by showing the value of the index k as the final merge invocation is executed, using the example list of numbers given in that section.

5-8. Considering again the Merge procedure used by MergeSort, give a systematic argument to show that the postcondition $L' = (e_1'\ e_2'\ \ldots\ e_n')$, L' is ordered, and L' consists of exactly the elements of L1 and L2 is satisfied, given the precondition $L1 = (e_{11}\ \ldots\ e_{n1})$, $L2 = (e_{12}\ \ldots\ e_{n2})$, and L1 and L2 are ordered.

5-9. Trace execution of the QuickSort procedure for a list that is already ordered, such as L = (1 2 3 4 5). How many steps are executed? Do the same for a list that is in reverse order, such as L = (5 4 3 2 1).

5-10. Show by an example that for the procedure SiftUp used by HeapSort, the order in which the original list L is converted into a heap is crucial. That is, if SiftUp were invoked in a loop that varied the index left from 1 to $\frac{n}{2} + 1$, rather than from $\frac{n}{2} + 1$ down to 1, the result would not necessarily be a heap.

5-11. Implement the procedure Display, which is described in the last section of the chapter. Test it using each of the following invocations, together with the example list L that is used throughout the chapter.

> Display (Square, L);
> Display (Div10, L)

Of course, the procedures Square and Div10 must also be separately defined.

5-12. Assume that all six of the sort algorithms in this chapter are implemented using linked allocation for linear lists. Describe what changes must be made to each of the six implementations of these algorithms in order that a single procedure type:

```
TYPE SortProcedure = PROCEDURE (List);
```

and a single procedure

```
PROCEDURE Sort (Algorithm: SortProcedure; L: List);
```

can be implemented. This would have the advantage of allowing the user access to any of our six sort algorithms, but with the same interface for each one. For example, an invocation of the interchange sort for the list L would look like:

> Sort (Interchange, L)

while an invocation of the Shell sort algorithm for the same list would be written as:

> Sort (Shell, L)

As an additional exercise, consider allowing the user an option to let the procedure Sort select the algorithm, by saying:

> Sort (AnyAlgorithm, L)

and adding provisions to the Sort interface procedure for choosing intelligently among the six alternatives (considering their relative performance, the size of L, and other reasonable assumptions).

TEAM PROJECT

Using the six sorting algorithms presented in this chapter, develop a project that will conduct an empirical analysis of their performance, using an internal timer and lists of 10, 100, 500, and 1000 (and, perhaps, 5000 and 10000 depending upon the internal speeds of the computer that you use) random integers. The analysis should collect execution times for each of the algorithms and each of the given list sizes. Each programming team in this project should gather and plot the resulting execution times for one of the six algorithms. The team should then compare its plot with the theoretical complexity given for that algorithm in the chapter. Worst case and best case assumptions may also be made, as time permits, along the lines suggested in the last section of the chapter. Such common system utilities, such as the measurement of elapsed time and the procedure Ordered (exercise 5-3 above), should be shared among the teams so that unnecessary duplication of effort is avoided and reliability of results will be assured. The same common utility should be made of an implementation (linked or contiguous) for the List abstract data type, so that the timing results obtained by different teams will be comparable.

STACKS AND QUEUES: HARDWARE AND OPERATING SYSTEMS

The linked implementation of linear lists allows maximum flexibility, in terms of its efficient adaptation of storage size to the size of the input for the problem, as we saw in Chapter 3. However, a genuine handicap of the linked implementation, in comparison with the contiguous (array) implementation, is its relatively inefficient performance for the Retrieve and Store operators for linear lists. That is, the contiguous implementation of list L permits immediate access to any of its constituent elements e_i, while the linked implementation usually requires a loop in order to reach the same element.

There are, however, some circumstances in which such loops can be completely avoided; those circumstances arise in programming problems where *all* of the insertions and deletions are at the head (or at the end) of the list. Many significant applications, as we shall show in this chapter, occur in which such constraints are realistic. In these applications, we thus gain both the storage flexibility of the linked implementation and a level of retrieval efficiency comparable to that of the contiguous implementation.

That special class of linear lists where insertions and deletions are made only at the head is called a *stack*. That class in which all insertions are made at the end (after e_n) and all deletions are made from the head is called a *queue*. The study of stacks, queues, and their applications is the subject of this chapter.

6-1 STACK DEFINITION AND OPERATORS

Informally, a stack can be visualized as a kind of pile, in which elements are added by placing them on top of the pile and elements are removed by taking them off the top of the pile. A pile of trays in a cafeteria is a good vehicle for this visualization. For this reason, stacks are often called "push-down" lists, or "last-in-first-out" (LIFO, for short) lists. A more exact definition of stacks follows:

Definition: A *stack* is a linear list $S = (e_1 \; e_2 \; \ldots \; e_n)$, with $n \geq 0$, in which insertions and deletions can be made only at the head. Such insertions are called *Push* operations, and such deletions are called *Pop* operations. The associated operators for a stack, which will be defined below, are: Create, Push, Pop, Size, Display, and Dump. A stack also has an associated global Error, whose Boolean value serves as a flag to indicate whether or not the last-executed stack operator was successfully completed.

In the following operator definitions, we denote by $S = (e_1 \; e_2 \; \ldots \; e_n)$ an arbitrary stack of n elements, and by x an additional element of the same type as those of L. S', x', and n' will denote the results of applying an operator to the stack S, with initial size n and additional element x. Maxstack is an implementation-dependent constant that provides an upper limit for the number of elements that a stack can contain. The global variable Error is used in the same way that it is used for linear lists (Chapter 3), and its resulting value after an operation is designated by Error'.

Definition: *Create*(S) brings into existence an empty stack $S' = (\,)$, sets $n' = 0$, and initializes the global Error' = false, provided that S does not already exist. Otherwise, the operator Create is undefined.
 Preconditions: S does not exist.
 Postconditions: $S' = (\,)$, $n' = 0$, and Error' = false.

Definition: *Push*(S,x) inserts the element x immediately ahead of the first element e_1 in S.
 Preconditions: S and x exist, and $0 \leq n < \text{Maxstack}$.
 Postconditions: If $0 \leq n < \text{Maxstack}$, then $S' = (x \; e_1 \; e_2 \; \ldots \; e_n)$, Error' = false, and $n' = n + 1$. On the other hand, if $n \geq \text{Maxstack}$, then Error' = true and $S' = S$.
 Example:
  Let $S = (42\;23\;80\;25\;46\;39\;96\;73\;74)$ and $x = 49$.
  Then Push(S,x) leaves $S' = (49\;42\;23\;80\;25\;46\;39\;96\;73\;74)$, and $n' = 10$.

Definition: *Pop*(S) deletes the element e_1 from S, and returns it.
 Preconditions: S exists, and $0 < n \leq \text{Maxstack}$.
 Postconditions: If $0 < n$ then $S' = (e_2 \; e_3 \; \ldots \; e_n)$, Error' = false, $n' = n - 1$, and e_1 is returned. On the other hand, if $n = 0$, then Error' = true and $S' = S$.

Example:
    Let S = (49 42 23 80 25 46 39 96 73 74).
    Then Pop(S) leaves S' = (42 23 80 25 46 39 96 73 74) and n' = 9, and returns 49.

The operators Size, Display, and Dump are defined for stacks in the same way that they are defined for linear lists (Chapter 3). Their definitions appear here for completeness, and their implementations are left as an exercise. As in the case for linear lists, Display provides a convenient tool for systematically displaying the elements of a stack on a terminal screen, while Dump adds address information and internal representations as an aid in program verification.

Definition: *Size*(S) returns the current number of elements, n, in S.

Definition: *Display*(S) displays the individual elements e_i of stack S, for each i = 1,...n.

Definition: *Dump*(S) displays the elements of stack S, the value of n, and the current values of global variables Maxstack and Error. Moreover, the memory addresses of the elements e_i and their hex representations are also shown.

6-1-1 Implementation of Stacks in Modula-2

The linked implementation of stacks is far more straightforward than that of linear lists, since the operators Push and Pop are dealing with the topmost element e_1 only. This allows us to retain the storage flexibility of linked allocation without sacrificing efficiency, since these stack operators are necessarily O(c) in complexity rather than O(n). Below is a Modula-2 DEFINITION MODULE for the Stack abstract data type.

```
DEFINITION MODULE Stacks;

EXPORT QUALIFIED Stack, StackElement, StackIndex, StackError,
            CreateStack, Push, Pop, StackSize,
            DisplayStack, DumpStack;

TYPE Stack;
     StackElement=INTEGER;
     StackIndex=CARDINAL;

VAR StackError: BOOLEAN;

PROCEDURE CreateStack (VAR S: Stack);

PROCEDURE Push (VAR S: Stack; x: StackElement);
```

```
PROCEDURE Pop (VAR S: Stack): StackElement;

PROCEDURE StackSize (VAR S: Stack): StackIndex;

PROCEDURE DisplayStack (VAR S: Stack);

PROCEDURE DumpStack (VAR S: Stack);

END Stacks.
```

Here, as in linear lists, we have extended the nonunique operator names with the affix "Stack," in deference to Modula-2's strong typing and lack of direct support for generic procedures. For the same reasons, as well as for simplicity, we have also assumed here that stacks contain elements of type INTEGER.

To implement the stack operators, the following declarations are assumed.

```
CONST Maxstack = 10000;   (*This limit is arbitrary and can be
                           reset to reflect the actual amount
                           of storage available.*)

TYPE Stack=POINTER TO StackHead;
     StackLink=POINTER TO StackNode;
     StackHead=RECORD
                 n: CARDINAL;
                 head: StackLink
               END;
     StackNode=RECORD
                 e: StackElement;
                 link: StackLink
               END;
```

Here, we see a pattern reminiscent of the linked implementation for linear lists. The constant Maxstack is set arbitrarily at a rather large number, which ought in practice to reflect the actual amount of storage available. The node StackHead contains the current value of n, the number of elements in the stack, and a pointer to the first such element, e_1. StackNode contains space for an individual element, e_i, and a link to the next stack element's node.

The operator Push is implemented in the procedure shown below. Since the head node always denotes the location for inserting the new element, no parameter of type StackIndex needs to be passed by the invoking program. Instead, the local variable ilink is used to temporarily mark the new node while it is being properly linked at the head of the list. Thereafter, the need for retaining ilink disappears.

```
PROCEDURE Push (VAR S: Stack; x: StackElement);
VAR ilink: StackLink;
BEGIN
  WITH S^ DO
    IF n< Maxstack THEN
      n:=n+1;
      NEW(ilink);
      ilink^.e:=x;
      ilink^.link:=head;
      head:=ilink;
      StackError:=FALSE
    ELSE
      StackError:=TRUE
    END
  END
END Push;
```

The dynamics of the Push operator are straightforward and are illustrated in Figure 6-1 for our example stack with x=49.

As shown, a new node is created and ilink is used to reference it. The value (49) of x is then stored in the element ilink^.e, the new node is linked to the former head node (by ilink^.link:=head), and the head of the stack is adjusted to point to the new node (by head:=ilink). The global StackError is set appropriately.

The procedure Pop is similarly straightforward, since the StackIndex of the node to be removed is always identified by the value of S^.head. Note also that special actions are taken in the marginal event that the stack is empty (n=0) upon invocation. That is, the StackError global is set to warn the invoking program, and an artificial result is returned in that event.

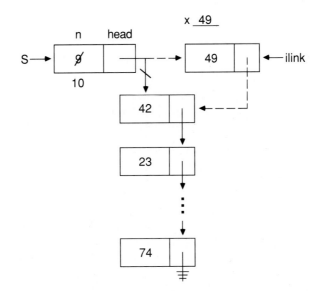

Figure 6-1
The Push (S,x) operator implementation for x=49.

```
PROCEDURE Pop (VAR S: Stack): StackElement;
VAR ilink: StackLink;
    x: StackElement;
BEGIN
  WITH S^ DO
    IF n>0 THEN
      n:=n-1;
      x:=head^.e;
      ilink:=head;
      head:=head^.link;
      DISPOSE(ilink);         (*Get rid of the deleted node.*)
      StackError:=FALSE;
      RETURN x
    ELSE
      StackError:=TRUE;
      RETURN 0
    END
  END
END Pop;
```

The Pop operator, therefore, is effective only in the normal case where the stack is not empty. Such a case is portrayed in Figure 6-2, using our familiar example. Here, we see that the value 49 at the head of the stack is first assigned to x, and the local POINTER ilink temporarily holds

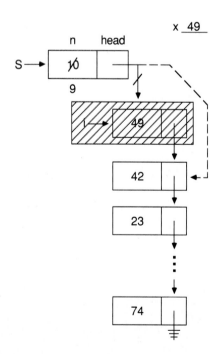

Figure 6-2
The Pop (S) operator implementation.

onto the address of the first node while we move the head POINTER forward to the second node (by the statement head: = head^.link). Finally, we dispose of the original first node since the POINTER ilink still references it. The procedure is completed upon an appropriate setting for StackError and an appropriate RETURN statement.

Implementation of the stack operators Create, Size, Display, and Dump are left as an exercise. These are straightforward and should closely mirror their counterparts in the linked implementation of linear lists.

6-1-2 Verification and Complexity of the Stack Operators

Correctness of our implementations of the operators Push and Pop can be determined either by employing a driver and exercising them or by standard analytic techniques. Here, we informally verify the Push procedure analytically, by first numbering the lines and adding pre- and postconditions to the body of the procedure as follows.

```
        BEGIN
        (**PRE: 0<=n< Maxstack, S=(e[1] e[2] ... e[n]).**)
1           WITH S^ DO
2             IF n< Maxstack THEN
3               n:=n+1;
4               NEW(ilink);
5               ilink^.e:=x;
6               ilink^.link:=head;
7               head:=ilink;
8               StackError:=FALSE
9             ELSE
10              StackError:=TRUE
11            END
12        END
        (**POST: n' =n+1, S' =(x e[1] e[2] ... e[n]).**)
        END Push;
```

Here, we have added only the postcondition that reflects a normal (nonerror) outcome. Note also that explicit testing for existence of S is not possible in Modula-2; instead, its nonexistence will raise a run-time error.

For verification of this Push implementation, we observe that line 3 guarantees the postcondition $n' = n+1$. Lines 4-7 effectively add x as the new head element for the stack S, thus satisfying the postcondition $S' = (x\ e_1\ e_2\ ...\ e_n)$. The steps represented by these lines were already discussed in conjunction with the example of Figure 6-1.

Complexity of this implementation is $O(c)$, since exactly six steps are executed (lines 3-8) in the normal case where the precondition for Push is satisfied.

6-1-3 Computer Organization: Run-Time Stacks and Stack Machines

In the introduction to computer organization in Chapter 2, our simple model of a von Neumann machine omits several embellishments that have evolved over the last two decades of computer architecture. One such embellishment is the so-called "run-time stack," which is used to maintain a running record of active procedure calls during execution of a program. To illustrate, suppose we have the following skeletal Modula-2 program.

```
Statement                       Address

MODULE MainProgram;

  PROCEDURE P;
    ...Q...                     0100
  END P;

  PROCEDURE Q;
    ...                         0200
  END Q;

  PROCEDURE R;
    ...P...                     0300
    ...Q...                     0400
  END R;

BEGIN
  ...R...                       0500
END MainProgram.
```

Here, we have internal procedures P, Q, and R, and the MainProgram invoking procedure R. Moreover, the procedures P and R invoke Q, and the procedure R invokes both P and Q. The addresses in the righthand column designate arbitrary machine addresses where the code corresponding to each of these invocations might be located in the machine language implementation of this program.

Now, it is clear that, as execution of the MainProgram begins, an invocation of R must be activated. Moreover, the system at that point must *save* the return address (0500) in MainProgram, so that completion of R's activation may return control to the next instruction following that invocation. Now, R's execution invokes procedure P, in which that return address (0300) must similarly be saved. Finally, P's activation invokes Q, so that the return address within P must also be saved. Thus, at the time when Q is finally activated, three different return addresses have been saved. Moreover, the *order* in which they are saved is critical; that is, the *last* one saved is necessarily the *first* one to be retrieved. Thus, when Q finishes it must return control to that address (0100) within P from which it was originally invoked. Looking further into the execution of this program, we can see that Q will be invoked again, this time from within procedure R (address 0400), and that address must be effectively maintained as the return address for Q when that later point in the process is reached.

Because of this "last-in-first-out" structure of storing return addresses during procedure invocation, contemporary computer organizations often include a run-time stack for keeping track of the active return addresses. A Push operator, in this setting, is synonymous with the invocation of a procedure; the return address placed on top of the stack is thus maintained in last-in-first-out fashion. A Pop operator is synonymous with the return of control at the completion of a procedure invocation, and the address thus retrieved tells the system where to resume execution in the calling program.

Thus, for our example, the run-time stack appears as shown in Figure 6-3 as each of the procedures P, Q, and R are invoked during its execution. (This pattern also assumes that no additional invocations of P, Q, and R appear in the program and that none of the invocations shown appears within a loop.) Here, we see that the run-time stack and its associated Push and Pop operations play a central role in the control of instruction addressing during procedure activations. For this reason, an address stack and the operators Push and Pop are directly implemented as part of the instruction set in many contemporary machines.

The second direct impact that stacks have had in the area of computer organization is in the realization of so-called "stack machines." Here, the contents of the run-time stack are arithmetic operands (in addition to addresses), and the machine instruction set contains arithmetic operators (addition, subtraction, and so forth) that take their operands off the top of the stack and return their results back onto the top of the stack. By contrast, a conventional von Neumann machine instruction for adding two integers (as shown in Figure 2-5) performs addition by specifying the two memory addresses where the integers to be added currently reside. The result of that instruction's execution is then placed in one of those operand addresses.

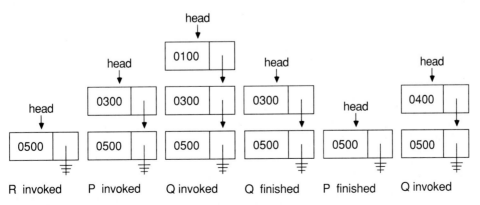

Figure 6-3 Run-time stack operations for the example program.

For example, suppose we have three numbers, say 35, 17, and 40, and we want to add the first to the product of the second and the third. In Modula-2 (or ordinary mathematics, for that matter) we would specify this calculation as follows:

```
35+17*40
```

With our prior schooling about the precedence of multiplication over addition, we know that this expression captures what we want to accomplish. An ordinary von Neumann machine would require the following sequence of instructions to accomplish this calculation:

```
LOAD      17 into a register
MULTIPLY  register by 40
ADD       register and 35
```

Here, we make the reasonable assumption that a register is used as a temporary location where arithmetic operations can be performed, and the results of MULTIPLY and ADD are inividually left in the same register. Thus, the final result, 715, of evaluating the expression $35+17*40$ is left in that register after these three machine instructions are executed.

Now, if a stack machine were to carry out this same calculation, the run-time stack would first need to be loaded with the operands in the order that the respective operations (* and +) would be applied to them. That is, at the time the multiplication instruction is executed, the stack must contain all three operands, in the order shown in Figure 6-4. In a stack machine there are PUSH, POP, ADD, and MULTIPLY instructions, along with the run-time stack itself. ADD and MULTIPLY, moreover, are specified without operands, since they implicitly take their operands from the top two entries in the stack and place their result on top of the stack. Thus, the following sequence of instructions in a stack machine will realize the desired calculation.

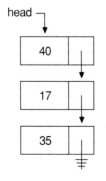

Figure 6-4
Contents of the stack during execution of $35+17*40$.

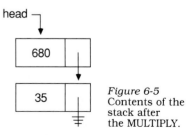

Figure 6-5
Contents of the stack after the MULTIPLY.

```
PUSH 35
PUSH 17
PUSH 40
MULTIPLY
ADD
```

Completion of the third PUSH instruction in this sequence leaves the stack as shown in Figure 6-4. Completion of the fourth instruction leaves the stack as shown in Figure 6-5. Completion of the fifth instruction leaves the single result, 715, at the top of the stack.

6-1-4 Problem 2:
Evaluation of Polish Expressions

The development of an algorithm that evaluates ordinary arithmetic expressions is not a simple matter. The rules for precedence of multiplication over addition, for left-to-right evaluation, and for the use of parentheses to dictate a different order of evaluation add complexity to a mechanical process that, intuitively, has become second-nature for humans to assimilate. If we had to develop an algorithm that would evaluate the following expression, for example,

```
35+17*(40−9)−7
```

the algorithm would have to understand and interpretively apply the precedence rules, the left-to-right rules, and the parenthesization rules in order to reveal the fact that the subtraction 40−9 occurs first, the multiplication by 17 occurs second, the addition of 35 occurs third, and the subtraction of 7 occurs fourth.

One asks, therefore, whether there is any simpler convention for writing expressions that can allow these "counterintuitive" rules about parenthesization and precedence to be dropped, while not compromising the general level of expressive power in the process. Fortunately, the answer to this question is "yes." Such an alternative method of writing expressions was invented by the Polish mathematician Lukasiewicz, long before the development of the computer. For that reason, this style of expression writing is called "Polish notation," and expressions written in this style are called "Polish expressions."[1]

---

[1] In fact, there are four different variations of "Polish expressions." Here, we use only one variation, in which the expression is scanned from left to right and the operators are placed to the right of their respective operands. Therefore, this particular variation is often known as "postfix notation." The other three variations are achieved by changing the direction of the scan (right to left) and/or placing each operator before (rather than after) its respective pair of operands. This latter variation, therefore, is often called "prefix notation." The conventional form, to which we are normally accustomed, is familiarly known as "infix notation," since the operator is placed between its two operands rather than before or after them.

Definition: A *Polish expression* is a series of arithmetic operands x, y, ... (numbers) and binary arithmetic operators ("op": typically +, −, *, /, and ^), formed by the following rules:
  (i) x is a Polish expression.
  (ii) If p_1 and p_2 are Polish expressions, so is p_1 p_2 op.

Because it is recursive, this definition allows Polish expressions of arbitrary length to be defined. In particular, the following are all examples of Polish expressions (their infix equivalents are shown on the right).

Polish Expression	Infix Equivalent
17 40 *	17*40
35 17 40 * I	35+17*40
35 17 40 9 − *7 − +	35+(17*(40−9)−7)

The interpretation of a Polish expression, for the purpose of calculating a final result, is governed by the following pair of rules, which are continuously applied until the expression contains a single number. The scan in step (i) begins at the leftmost symbol of the expression. Each time this scan is repeated, it begins where it left off, rather than at the beginning of the expression.

  (i) Scan the expression to the right, until the first operator, "op," is reached.
  (ii) Apply that operator to the two operands, p_1 and p_2, immediately on its left, obtaining the result p, and then replace the triple "p_1 p_2 op" in the expression by p.

To illustrate, suppose we wish to evaluate the third expression above, applying this pair of rules four successive times (once for each operator). The result is summarized in Figure 6-6. In each line of this figure we see an underlined part that indicates the next operation to be applied. The

```
35 17 40 9  − * 7 − +

35 17    31   * 7 − +

35       527     7 − +

35            520    +

              555
```

Figure 6-6 Evaluating the expression 35 17 40 9 − *7 − +.

subsequent line shows the expression after that operation is complete. For example, the second line shows the result (31) of applying the operator — to the operands 40 and 9. This new expression thus yields to the application of the operator * to the operands 17 and 31, whose result is shown in the next line, and so forth.

It is not difficult to see how the Polish form can be used for *any* arithmetic expression, thus making parentheses and precedence rules unnecessary. Whenever parentheses would be used to force one operator to be applied before another in an ordinary expression, the equivalent Polish expression simply has that operator placed to the left of the other. In general, if we look at an ordinary arithmetic expression and its equivalent Polish counterpart, we see that the operands occur in the same order, from left to right. But in the Polish counterpart, the operators are placed, from left to right, in exactly the order in which they will be evaluated.

The case for using a stack in the evaluation of these expressions may now be evident. If we look at an arbitrary Polish expression and have a mechanism for scanning it from left to right, we see that at any point in the scan the two most recently scanned operands are the ones that will be needed at the time the first operator is encountered. Moreover, the result of applying that operator will replace these operands in the expression as the scan is resumed. That is, the operands in the expression are treated in a last-in-first-out manner as the expression is scanned from left to right. An informal algorithm that captures this process can therefore be designed around an "operand stack" as follows:

(i) Scan the expression from left to right. As each operand is reached, perform step (ii). As each operator is reached, perform step (iii).
(ii) *Push* the operand onto the operand stack.
(iii) *Pop* the topmost two operands from the stack, apply this operator to them, and *Push* the result onto the stack.

This very simple algorithm will, when the scan is completed, leave on the stack the final value of the Polish expression. Its action is illustrated in Figure 6-7, for the example expression 35 17 40 9 − *7 − + . Here, we see in the first four steps that the stack increases in size, until the first operator (−) is reached. After that step, the stack has three operands in it, the topmost being the result of applying the operator − to the two operands 40 and 9.

To implement this algorithm, we present a Modula-2 program named EvaluatePolish, which evaluates an arbitrary Polish expression entered at the terminal and displays the stack contents as each operator or operand is scanned within the expression. The final stack contents displayed, therefore, is the final value of the expression itself. The program also protects itself against improper input by displaying a message and allowing the user to retype the invalid operand or operator before proceeding.

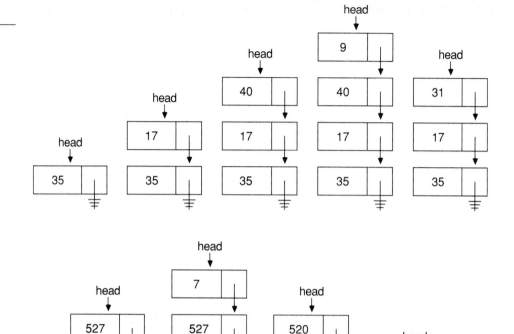

Figure 6-7
Stack contents during expression evaluation.

The EvaluatePolish program uses our implementation of the *Stack* abstract data type, together with two additional string-scanning procedures that allow us to lexically classify different types of strings as they are encountered in the input. These procedures, called ReadLex and ClassifyLex, are part of the *Strings* abstract data type, which will be fully presented and implemented in Chapter 7. Here, we give only an informal description of these two string operators as they apply to the evaluation of Polish expressions. Recall that a Modula-2 string is stored as a sequence of ASCII characters, in an array whose subscript range begins with 0 and whose last character is followed in the array by the delimiter NUL (ASCII 00). The array may be declared of any length, say n, appropriate to the application; that length serves as an upper bound for the length of any string value stored in the array. Thus, the following hypothetical string variable declaration is assumed.

```
VAR s = ARRAY [0..n] OF CHAR;
```

Now, the purpose of the procedure ReadLex is to read a sequence of nonblank input characters—skipping over initial blank, end-of-line, and carriage-return characters—and store them in s[0], s[1],..., until the next blank, end-of-line, or carriage-return is reached. At that time, ReadLex fills the remainder of the array s with NUL characters.

The procedure ClassifyLex serves to classify any such string read by ReadLex as either a "number," an "identifier," an "operator", or an "other"— using the following definitions as a basis:

- A *number* is any sequence of decimal digits (0-9), possibly preceded by a sign (+ or −), and possibly containing an embedded decimal point (.).
- An *identifier* is any sequence of letters (A-Z, a-z) and digits (0-9), the leftmost of which must be a letter.
- An *operator* is any of the symbols +, −, *, /, or ^.
- An *other* is any sequence of ASCII characters that doesn't fall into one of the above three classes.

These classes are exported as the type LexClass by the Strings module.

Given these definitions, we assume that the Strings module therefore exports the procedures ReadLex, ClassifyLex, and StrInt (which will be described below), as well as the type LexClass. ReadLex and ClassifyLex are invoked in the following way:

```
ReadLex(s)
ClassifyLex(s)
```

ReadLex is an ordinary procedure, while ClassifyLex is a function procedure that returns a LexClass value as a result. To illustrate, suppose we have the following input:

```
35 17 40 9 − * 7 − + <CR>
```

where <CR> denotes the carriage-return character. A sequence of invocations of ReadLex(s) and ClassifyLex(s) will leave s and its corresponding lexical class as shown in Figure 6-8. The procedure StrInt is invoked with two arguments, s and i, of types String and INTEGER, respectively. Its purpose is simply to convert the value of s to an equivalent INTEGER value i, assuming that the lexical class of s is numeric. In the event that s contains a decimal fraction, its corresponding INTEGER value is obtained by truncation.

The following development therefore assumes the availability of ReadLex, ClassifyLex, and StrInt. The beauty of separate compilation and data abstraction in Modula-2 is that the development of implementation details for these auxiliary procedures, which is not a trivial task, can be temporarily removed from the present task of illustrating the behavior of stacks in evaluating Polish expressions. The complete program EvaluatePolish is thus given below.

164

CHAPTER SIX

Figure 6-8
Behavior of
ReadLex(s) for
example input.

s	Lexical Class
35	number
17	number
40	number
9	number
—	operator
*	operator
7	number
—	operator
+	operator

```
MODULE EvaluatePolish;

FROM Stacks    IMPORT Stack, StackIndex, StackElement,
                      StackError, CreateStack, Push, Pop,
                      DisplayStack;
FROM Strings   IMPORT LexClass, StringError, DumpString,
                      ReadLex, ClassifyLex, Eof, StrInt;
FROM MiscLib   IMPORT Power;
FROM InOut     IMPORT WriteString, WriteLn;
FROM MathLib0  IMPORT entier;

PROCEDURE WriteError;
BEGIN
  WriteString('Error: improper token skipped');
  WriteLn
END WriteError;

VAR operands: Stack;
    token: ARRAY[0..20] OF CHAR;   (* String type *)
    tokenclass: LexClass;
    operand1, operand2: INTEGER;

BEGIN
  CreateStack(operands);
  WriteString ('Enter a Polish Expression:'); WriteLn;
  ReadLex(token);
  tokenclass:=ClassifyLex(token);
  WHILE NOT Eof DO
    IF tokenclass = number
      THEN StrInt (token, operand1);
        Push (operands, operand1);
        DisplayStack (operands);
```

```
      ELSIF tokenclass = operator THEN
         operand2:=Pop(operands);
         operand1:=Pop(operands);
         CASE token[0] OF
            '+': Push (operands, operand1+operand2)    |
            '-': Push (operands, operand1-operand2)    |
            '*': Push (operands, operand1*operand2)    |
            '/': Push (operands, operand1 DIV operand2) |
            '^': Push (operands,
                       entier(Power(FLOAT(operand1),operand2)))
         ELSE
            WriteError
         END;
         DisplayStack (operands)
      ELSE
         WriteError
      END;
      ReadLex(token);
      tokenclass:=ClassifyLex(token)
   END
END EvaluatePolish.
```

Here, we see that the presence of powerful data abstractions, Stacks and Strings, allows us to greatly simplify the presentation of the main program itself. The implementation details of their respective operators are hidden from view, as we concentrate on the application at hand.

In this program, we have also used another procedure, from the module MiscLib, which contains a collection of useful procedures that appear nowhere else in the Modula-2 standard libraries. This procedure, called Power, takes a REAL and an INTEGER argument, x and i, and computes the result x^i. Implementation of this function is left as an exercise.

Note that the program EvaluatePolish issues a gentle error message when the token it encounters is neither a number nor one of the operators +, −, *, /, or ^. In that event, the token is simply skipped and processing of the expression continues with the next token. The reader should exercise this program with various (valid and invalid) Polish expressions to corroborate this behavior. A sample of the output is displayed in Figure 6-9 for the expression 35 17 40 hi there 9 − *7 − +, which contains a couple of embedded invalid tokens.

However, our program does not guard against *all* errors. That is, there are many sequences of operators and numbers that do not form a valid Polish expression. For instance, every Polish expression must contain exactly one less operator than it does operands. Furthermore, the ith operator from the left end of a Polish expression must not appear before at least $i+1$ operands have appeared, when scanning the expression from left to right. In the erroneous event that the number of operands exceeds the number of

s	Lexical Class	Output
35	number	(35)
17	number	(17 35)
40	number	(40 17 35)
hi	identifier	Error: improper token skipped
there	identifier	Error: improper token skipped
9	number	(9 40 17 35)
−	operator	(31 17 35)
*	operator	(527 35)
7	number	(7 527 35)
−	operator	(520 35)
+	operator	(555)

Figure 6-9 Output of EvaluatePolish for example input.

operators by more than one, the stack will contain more than one entry upon termination of the program. In the erroneous event that the ith operator appears to the left of the i + 1st operand, the program will attempt to Pop more operands from the OperandStack than are there, thus causing the global StackError to become TRUE. The task of modifying the program to accommodate these additional error situations is left as an exercise.

6-2 QUEUE DEFINITION AND OPERATORS

Informally, a queue can be visualized as a kind of waiting line, in which persons enter by placing themselves at the end, or tail, of the line and persons leave from the head of the line (at the time they are served). A waiting line of persons at the teller's window at the bank, or airplanes at the takeoff runway at the airport, provide good examples for this visualization. Because of their behavior, queues are often called "first-in-first-out" (or FIFO) lists. A more precise definition of queues follows:

Definition: A *queue* is a linear list $Q = (e_1\ e_2\ \ldots\ e_n)$, with $n \geq 0$, in which insertions can be made only at the tail and deletions can be made only at the head. These operators are called *Enter* and *Leave*, respectively. The associated operators for a queue, which will be defined below, are: Create, Enter, Leave, Size, Display, and Dump. A queue also has an associated global Error, whose Boolean value serves as a flag to indicate whether or not the last-executed queue operator was successfully completed. The implementation-dependent variable Maxqueue is assumed to indicate the overall limit, usually quite large, on the size of a queue for the particular implementation.

In the following operator definitions, we denote by $Q = (e_1\ e_2\ \ldots\ e_{n-1}\ e_n)$ an arbitrary queue of $n \geq 0$ elements and by x an additional element of the same type as those of Q. Q', x', and n' will denote the result of applying an operator to the queue Q with size n, using the additional element x. The value of the global variable Error after an operator application is given by Error'.

Definition: *Create*(Q) brings into existence an empty queue $Q' = ()$, sets $n' = 0$, and initializes the global Error' = false, provided that Q does not previously exist. Otherwise, the operator Create is undefined.
Preconditions: Q does not exist.
Postconditions: $Q' = ()$, $n' = 0$, and Error' = false.

Definition: *Enter*(Q,x) inserts the element x immediately after the nth element e_n in Q if $n > 0$, and as the sole element e_1 in Q if $n = 0$.
Preconditions: Q and x exist, and $0 \leq n <$ Maxqueue.
Postconditions: If $0 \leq n <$ Maxqueue, then $Q' = (e_1\ e_2 \ldots e_n\ x)$, Error' = false, and $n' = n + 1$. If $n \geq$ Maxqueue, then Error' = true and $Q' = Q$.
Example:
  Let $Q = (49\ 42\ 23\ 80\ 25\ 46\ 39\ 96\ 73)$ and $x = 74$.
  Then Enter(Q,x) leaves $Q' = (49\ 42\ 23\ 80\ 25\ 46\ 39\ 96\ 73\ 74)$, and $n' = 10$.

Definition: *Leave*(Q) deletes the element e_1 from Q and returns it.
Preconditions: Q exists, and $0 < n$.
Postconditions: If $0 < n$, then $Q' = (e_2\ e_3\ \ldots\ e_n)$, Error' = false, $n' - 1$, and e_1 is returned. On the other hand, if $n = 0$, then Error' = true and $Q' = Q$.
Example:
  Let $Q = (49\ 42\ 23\ 80\ 25\ 46\ 39\ 96\ 73\ 74)$.
  Then Leave(Q) leaves $Q' = (42\ 23\ 80\ 25\ 46\ 39\ 96\ 73\ 74)$, $n' = 9$, and returns 49.

The following three queue operator definitions are given only for completeness; their implementations are identical with their counterparts for linear lists and stacks and will not be further belabored here.

Definition: *Size*(Q) returns the current number of elements, n, in Q.

Definition: *Display*(Q) displays the individual elements e_i of Q, for each $i = 1, \ldots, n$.

Definition: *Dump*(Q) displays the elements of Q, the value of n, and the current values of global variables Maxqueue and Error. Moreover, the memory addresses of the elements e_i and their hex representations are also shown.

6-2-1 Implementation of Queues in Modula-2

As for stacks, we can implement queues with the linked, rather than the contiguous, strategy without sacrificing efficiency of retrieval. That is, if we maintain for each queue not only a pointer to the current "head" element but also a pointer to the current "tail" element (to avoid a search in the event that an Enter operator is encountered), then each Enter and Leave operation will be executable in O(c) complexity. This is ideal, since in the process of regaining the efficiency of the contiguous implementation we have retained the storage flexibility afforded by the linked implementation. This combination is especially powerful for applications of queues in which large amounts of insertions and deletions will occur.

For the linked implementation of queues, the following declarations are appropriate. Note that these declarations are similar to the ones for our implementation of stacks; they are the same except for the addition of the new "tail" pointer in the queue's first record.

```
CONST Maxqueue = 10000;  (*This limit is arbitrary and can
                           be reset to reflect the actual
                           amount of storage available.*)

TYPE Queue=POINTER TO QueueHead;
     QueueLink=POINTER TO QueueNode;
     QueueHead=RECORD
                  n: CARDINAL;
                  head: QueueLink;
                  tail: QueueLink
               END;
     QueueNode=RECORD
                  e: QueueElement;
                  link: QueueLink
               END;
```

The following Modula-2 DEFINITION MODULE is appropriate as a basis for developing an implementation of the Queue abstract data type.

```
DEFINITION MODULE Queues;

EXPORT QUALIFIED Queue, QueueElement, QueueIndex,
                 QueueError, CreateQueue, Enter,
                 Leave, QueueSize, DisplayQueue,
                 DumpQueue;

TYPE Queue;
     QueueElement=INTEGER;
     QueueIndex=CARDINAL;
VAR QueueError: BOOLEAN;
```

```
PROCEDURE CreateQueue (VAR Q: Queue);

PROCEDURE Enter (VAR Q: Queue; x: QueueElement);

PROCEDURE Leave (VAR Q: Queue): QueueElement;

PROCEDURE QueueSize (VAR Q: Queue): QueueIndex;

PROCEDURE DisplayQueue (VAR Q: Queue);

PROCEDURE DumpQueue (VAR Q: Queue);

END Queues.
```

A queue's QueueHead record has *two* major POINTERs: "head" permanently addresses the queue's next element to leave (e_1), while "tail" permanently addresses the queue's most recent element to enter (e_n). Proper maintenance of head and tail are the responsibilities of the Create, Enter, and Leave operators. With these considerations, the implementation of Enter is given below.

```
PROCEDURE Enter (VAR Q: Queue; x: QueueElement);
VAR ilink: QueueLink;
BEGIN
   WITH Q^ DO
      IF n< Maxqueue THEN
         n:=n+1;
         NEW(ilink);
         ilink^.e:=x;
         ilink^.link:=NIL;
         IF head=NIL THEN
            head:=ilink
         ELSE
            tail^.link:=ilink
         END;
         tail:=ilink;
         QueueError:=FALSE
      ELSE
         QueueError:=TRUE
      END
   END
END Enter;
```

Here, we see that the local POINTER ilink is used to reference the new node to enter the queue and that node's link is NIL (since it will become the new tail element). If the queue is empty (head=NIL), then head must also be adjusted to point to the new node (since it simultaneously becomes both the head and the tail of the queue). Otherwise, the new node's predecessor is linked to it (by tail^.link:=ilink). In either case, the

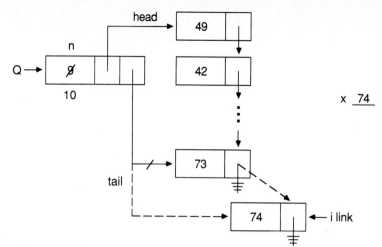

Figure 6-10
The Enter(Q,x) operator implementation for x = 74.

tail POINTER is finally adjusted to address this new node, and the global Error is established appropriately. These actions are summarized in Figure 6-10, for our example queue of INTEGER values and the new entry x = 74.

The implementation of Leave appears in the following way, remaining careful to maintain the integrity of both head and tail pointers in all cases.

```
PROCEDURE Leave (VAR Q: Queue): QueueElement;
VAR ilink: QueueLink;
    x: QueueElement;
BEGIN
  WITH Q^ DO
    IF n>0 THEN
      n:=n-1;
      x:=head^.e;
      ilink:=head;
      head:=head^.link;
      IF head=NIL THEN
        tail:=NIL
      END;
      DISPOSE(ilink);
      QueueError:=FALSE;
      RETURN x
    ELSE
      QueueError:=TRUE;
      RETURN 0
    END
  END
END Leave;
```

Here, the important special case is the one in which the *last* element leaves the queue, causing the queue to become empty. In that case, we must

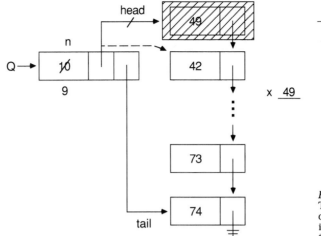

Figure 6-11
The Leave(Q) operator implementation.

set both tail and head to NIL, in order to maintain the queue's integrity for future actions. A second special case is the one in which the queue is already empty (and hence no elements are available to leave), whereby we simply set the global Error to TRUE and exit the procedure. All other cases are exemplified by the illustration in Figure 6-11, where the head element 49 leaves the queue.

Implementation of the queue operators Create, Size, Display, and Dump is left as an exercise.

6-2-2 Verification and Complexity of Queue Operators

We see now that the complexity of our queue operator implementations Enter and Leave is, indeed, $O(c)$. A total of nine steps is needed for the Enter procedure, while a total of eight steps is needed for Leave, under normal circumstances for a typical invocation.

Verification of each queue operator implementation can be done by inserting its pre- and postconditions at its beginning and end and then systematically observing that the postconditions are satisfied under all cases. We leave this also as an exercise.

6-2-3 Operating Systems: An Overview

The study and design of operating systems is a central topic in computer science, and a semester course in this subject is usually required for advanced undergraduate majors. An *operating system* is a collection of computer programs that serves as the interface between the application program and the hardware of the computer system. This is shown schematically in Figure 6-12.

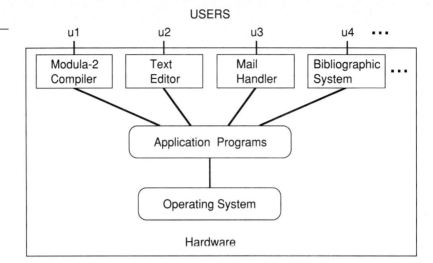

Figure 6-12
Conceptual view of an operating system.

Here, we see several users simultaneously sharing the resources of a computer system, and each one is using a different application program: a Modula-2 compiler, a text editor, a mail handler, and a bibliographic system, for example.

The programs of an operating system are many and diverse; they cooperate to manage the effective utilization of resources in a computer system—memory, registers, input-output devices (terminals, printers), storage and networking media—so that a maximum amount of computing activity can be accomplished over a continuous period of time with minimal interruption. Functionally, these programs allocate memory, perform input-output operations, manage queues waiting for the printer, schedule input-output devices according to incoming requests, and monitor the progress of each application program as it serves an individual user. Whenever an individual user logs off, the operating system disconnects all files that had been serving his or her session and returns the memory and other resources that were allocated to that user to the system for some other application. Whenever a user logs on, the operating system assigns appropriate system resources—memory, application program, file space, and so forth—to that user in accordance with his or her application. Thus, in general, the operating system manages the dynamic flow of activity through the computer system.

Different computers and application domains require different species of operating systems. For instance, the single-user domain of the personal computer requires an operating system like MS-DOS. System resources usually consist of memory, a single application program (a word processor, a spreadsheet program, or a Modula-2 compiler), one or two disk drives, and a printer. Control of this environment is relatively simple, and the operating system's responsiveness to the user is always maximal.

At another level, the time-sharing operating systems—such as UNIX, VMS, and CMS—typically support anywhere from 4 to 100 or more simultaneous users and run on appropriate minicomputers and mainframes like Digital's VAX. Here, system resources are shared among the several users who are active at any time, and the operating system must manage resources in such a way that users' requests are optimally served. This requires, in particular, the establishment of waiting lines, or queues, of requests for resources that are in high demand and short supply. For example, a system having only one or two printers and a larger number of user requests for printed listings of files (programs and data files of various kinds) than can be serviced by the combined capacities (speeds) of its printers must establish within its operating system a method of queueing print files (saving them in a waiting line on disk storage) until they can be serviced by the printers themselves.

At yet another level, the mainframe computers (IBM and others) are often set up to serve their users by maintaining a queue of "batch" jobs along with a large pool of time-shared terminals. Here, the jobs are typically those which can be prescheduled on a regular basis—the weekly payroll calculation, the monthly billing, the annual tax accounting, and so forth—by an organization. Operating systems that support these functions well are IBM's OS and MVS, for example.

Figure 6-13 identifies the major functional elements of an operating system for a minicomputer or mainframe that is designed to serve several time-sharing users at terminals, a batch job queue, and a queue of files waiting to be printed. Here, we see how the major resources of the computer—the memory, the terminals, the printer, and the disk storage—are used by the active processes p_1 through p_{12} at a typical moment in time. In the memory are the operating system's *control program*, one active process for each interactive terminal user or active batch job, a queue of batch jobs awaiting initiation, a queue of print jobs awaiting service by the printer, and drivers for each of the three input-output media (terminals, disk, and printer). Also, we note that the disk storage, whose capacity is very large in comparison with that of

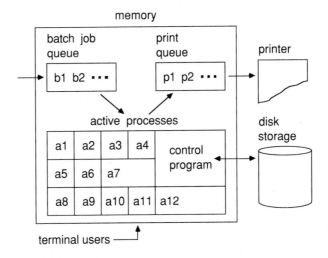

Figure 6-13
Main functional elements of an operating system.

memory, is used to store user files that are inactive, various application program that are available through the operating system, and additional inactive parts of the operating system in addition to its control program. The control program is the major system manager; all process activations, terminations, queueing actions, and so forth are performed by the control program.

This is only the most elementary level of description for an operating system. Most actual configurations are much more complex, containing several disk storage devices and printers, some additional kinds of input-output devices (magnetic tape, optical readers, plotters, and so forth), networking interfaces with other computers, and so forth. This basic discussion serves our purposes, however, because it reveals immediately the need to manage queues in order to properly serve the active processes in the system.

Let's fix our attention on the print queue, for example, in Figure 6-13. There, two basic events can take place. On the one hand, a print job can be initiated (by virtue of a request from one of the active processes in the memory), in which case an Enter command is issued by the control program and the queue increases in size. On the other hand, the printer may complete an active print job (it can do only one at a time), in which case it notifies the control program. The control program responds by issuing a Leave command, thus assigning the printer the next job in the queue.

Similar kinds of events can occur when considering the batch job queue and the active processes. The memory of the system is fixed in size, thus allowing only a finite number of active processes to exist at any one time. When such a process terminates (e.g., an interactive user logs off), the control program recovers the memory block that had been allocated to that process and may reallocate it to the first job in the batch queue so that that job may be initiated. This results, therefore, in a Leave command being issued for the batch job queue. Conversely, an Enter command is issued whenever a new batch job arrives in the system and insufficient memory is available to immediately initiate a process for that job.

6-2-4 Priority Queues

The two queues shown in Figure 6-13, in addition to their FIFO character, may exhibit an additional characteristic. That is, the operating system may be equipped to recognize different classes of users and give higher priority to users in one class over those in another whenever their jobs enter the batch queue or the print queue. For instance, it is not unusual in computer installations to discriminate between "production" jobs and "test" jobs in this way. A production job is one that must run as soon as possible whenever it is submitted to the queue (perhaps it calculates the weekly payroll or the monthly sales figures for a corporation), while a test job is one that can wait (perhaps it is a program under development, and its immediate execution is less urgent than a production job).

To make these distinctions effective, the queueing process must be able to select that job in the queue that has highest priority and, if there is more than one such job, the one closest to the head of the queue. Implementation of a priority queue requires, therefore, an additional field in each node that reflects the priority of that node (typically, a CARDINAL value) in the queue. The following modifications to the previous declaration for Queue, which we call PQueue, will accommodate this change.

```
TYPE PQueue=POINTER TO PQueueHead;
     PQueueLink=POINTER TO PQueueNode;
     PQueueHead=RECORD
                n: CARDINAL;
                head: PQueueLink;
                tail: PQueueLink
            END;
     PQueueNode=RECORD
                e: PQueueElement;
                priority: CARDINAL;
                link: PQueueLink
            END;
```

Implementation of the Enter and Leave operators for priority queues is governed by the need to remove nodes of highest priority first. This can be done using either of two strategies. The first strategy would leave the Enter operator essentially unchanged (from its implementation for ordinary queues) and alter the Leave procedure to take into account variations in priorities among nodes. The second strategy would alter the Enter operator so that a newly added node would immediately be moved ahead of all nodes having lower priority in the queue (but remain behind all nodes of equal or higher priority). In this case, the Leave procedure would not need to be altered from its original version, because the head of the queue will always contain the next node to be removed.

We implement the first of these strategies below and leave the implementation of the second alternative as an exercise. To do this, the LeavePQ procedure is implemented to search the queue from the head to find the highest priority for all nodes that are present and then delete the first occurrence of a node that has that particular priority.

```
PROCEDURE LeavePQ (VAR Q: PQueue): PQueueElement;
VAR ilink,jlink,klink: PQueueLink;
    x: PQueueElement;
BEGIN
  WITH Q^ DO
    IF n>0 THEN
      ilink:=NIL;
      jlink:=head;
      klink:=jlink;
```

```
        WHILE klink^.link<>NIL DO    (*Search for highest
                                        priority.*)
          IF klink^.link^.priority > jlink^.priority THEN
            ilink:=klink;
            jlink:=klink^.link
          END;
          klink:=klink^.link
        END;
        n:=n-1;
        x:=jlink^.e;       (*Assign the jth node's element.*)
        IF ilink=NIL THEN  (*It was first in the queue.*)
          IF head=NIL THEN
            tail:=NIL      (*It was also last.*)
          END;
          head:=head^.link
        ELSE
          ilink^.link:=jlink^.link   (*It was not first in
                                        the queue.*)
        END;
        DISPOSE(jlink);    (*Dispose the removed node.*)
        PQueueError:=FALSE;
        RETURN x
      ELSE
        PQueueError:=TRUE;
        RETURN 0
      END
    END
END LeavePQ;
```

Here, the POINTERs ilink, jlink, and klink are used to locate that node with the highest priority closest to the head of the queue. POINTER klink^.link indicates the current node in the search, while klink follows along immediately behind it. POINTERs ilink and jlink are paired so that jlink points to the node with the highest priority found so far in the search (initially, it points to the head node), and ilink points to the node immediately before it. This pairing is needed so that when the node to be removed is found, the link field in the immediately preceding node can be properly altered to implement the deletion. This situation is shown in Figure 6-14, where we see the following example priority queue being altered by a Leave operation. In this notation, the elements in the queue are assigned bracketed subscripts to denote their respective priorities.

PQ=(49[1] 42[6] 23[1] 80[3] 25[6] 46[7] 39[1] 96[7]
    73[7] 74[3])

It should be clear to the reader that the complexity of the Leave operator for a priority queue is no longer $O(c)$, as it had been for ordinary

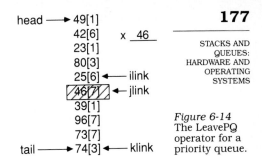

Figure 6-14
The LeavePQ operator for a priority queue.

queues. In particular, the complexity of Leave for priority queues is necessarily O(n), since the priority levels of new entries in the queue cannot be assumed to be in anything but random order. An arbitrary Leave operation can expect to search the entire list before finding the entry with the highest priority. If we had adopted the alternative implementation strategy mentioned above (in which the Enter procedure would basically maintain the queue in diminishing order of priority), we would simply have transferred this O(n) complexity from the Leave operator to the Enter operator.

However, significant improvements in the complexity of priority queue management can be gained if we can assume that there are a small number of distinct priority levels (say, five), rather than an arbitrarily large number (as we tacitly assumed above). This is, in fact, a realistic assumption since actual operating systems are often managed using a small, fixed number of priority levels. In that case, we abandon the single-queue strategy for a multiple-queue strategy, in which a different queue is managed for every different priority level. This is illustrated in Figure 6-15, for a system with five distinct priority levels.

Now the complexity of Enter and Leave operators returns to O(c), since each Enter or Leave takes place only at the tail or head of a single queue. The queue selection for an Enter operation is governed by the priority of the incoming job. The queue selection for a Leave operation is determined by polling each queue in turn (beginning with the one holding the jobs with the highest priority) until a nonempty one is found, and then the head job is deleted from that queue. Further details of the Create, Enter, and Leave implementations for this revised situation are left as an exercise.

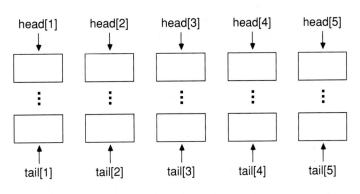

Figure 6-15
Muliple queues for five priority levels.

6-2-5 Problem 3: Job Scheduling

One of the functions of an operating system, therefore, is to manage the scheduling of jobs as they need to enter and leave each of the active queues in the system. To illustrate some of these dynamics, let us assume that we have an operating system that must manage a single batch job queue and a single print queue, as pictured in Figure 6-13. A job may enter either of these queues at any time, as keyed by one of the following requests, respectively:

```
J    jobno    priority    memorysize
P    jobno
```

Here, "jobno" is a preassigned identifying number for the job, "priority" is an integer from 1 to 5 identifying the job's priority, and "memorysize" is an integer from 1000 to 100000 indicating the memory requirements for initiating the job as an active process in the system.

Moreover, the active processes in the system are allocated fixed blocks of memory for their duration (called "address spaces"), and a linked list of these processes and their respective address spaces is also maintained by the operating system. In conjunction with this, a linked list called the "available space list" is maintained to keep track of all available contiguous blocks of memory in the system. Whenever an active process terminates, the following message is sent to the operating system: T jobno. This is a signal to the operating system for deleting a job from the active processes list, returning its address space to the available space list, and searching the batch job queue to find one or more new jobs that can now be initiated. This search is made with respect to priorities. If one or more such jobs is found, it is removed from the queue, allocated an appropriate address space (in accordance with its memory requirements), and the available space list is updated accordingly.

The other event that can occur is the termination of a print job, in which case the printer sends the following signal to indicate that it is ready to accept the next job in the print queue: R. Thereby, the operating system removes the next job from the head of the print queue and passes it to the printer.

These events can, of course, occur in any sequence and in any number. Furthermore, the occurrence of such an event does not guarantee that it will receive immediate satisfaction. For example, the signal R may occur before any jobs have entered the print queue, or the signal T may result in termination of a job and the freeing of insufficient memory space to satisfy *any* jobs waiting in the batch job queue. A typical sequence of events in this context is given in Figures 6-16a and 6-16b, where the resulting effects on the two queues, the active process list, and the available space list are shown on the right.

Development of the program to simulate the handling of these events is left as a team project at the end of the chapter. Most of the important tools for completing this simulation are, nevertheless, already available in the abstract data type Queue.

events	initial queue contents		events	final queue contents	
⋮	batch jobs	printer	J 15 8 2000 0	batch jobs	printer
J 12 8 10000	11 5 10000	7	J 16 5 3000 0	15 8 20000	8
J 13 5 40000		8	P 11	17 7 20000	9
		9	T 12		10
J 14 7 20000					11
	active processes				12
T 13	10 (5000-19999)			active processes	
P 10			P 12	10 (5000-19999)	
	available space list			11 (20000-29999)	
R	(0-4999)			16 (30000-59999)	
	(20000-100000)			14 (70000-89999)	
			J 17 7 2000 0	available space list	
			⋮	(0-4999)	
				(60000-69999)	
	(a)			(90000-100000)	
				(b)	

Figure 6-16 Queue management events.

EXERCISES

6-1. Implement the operators Create, Size, Display, and Dump for the Stack and Queue data types, using the same style as that suggested for the linked implementation of linear lists in Chapter 3. To what degree can any or all of these operators be direct *copies* of their counterparts in Chapter 3?

6-2. Verify the queue operator implementations for Enter and Leave.

6-3. Referring to Figure 6-3, suppose the MainProgram example were changed to contain, in addition, an invocation of Q embedded within itself (i.e., suppose Q is recursive). Using the style of Figure 6-3, show how the run-time stack now behaves by tracing its contents, under the same assumptions that are given in the discussion there.

6-4. Reconsidering the same MainProgram example, what would be the impact on the stack's contents if we assumed that any of the procedure invocations there could be embedded within a loop?

6-5. Convert each of the following arithmetic expressions to Polish form and then show all steps in evaluating that form.
  (a) $3 - 7 - 4$
  (b) $3 - (7 - 4)$
  (c) $0 - b + (b^2 - 4 * a * c)^{0.5} / (2 * a)$

6-6. In part (c), assume that a, b, and c are variable names in Modula-2 and they have the values 5, 10, and 3, respectively. Assume further that the operator ^ denotes exponentiation and has higher precedence than * and /. Evaluate that expression.

6-7. Extend the definition of Polish expressions to include unary operators, such as "sqrt" and "--" (denoting the square root and negation, respectively). How could the rules for evaluating a Polish expression be changed to accommodate unary operators? Show how the expression in part (c) of the previous exercise would be rewritten and evaluated, using this extended notion of Polish expressions.

6-8. In the program EvaluatePolish, we have assumed the presence of a function Power in the library module MiscLib. Implement that module and that function so that for any arguments x and i, the invocation Power(x,i) computes the result x^i. Be sure to include consideration for the special cases $i=0$ and $i<0$, as well as the usual $i>0$. Suggest additional functions that can be added to the library MiscLib, which appear neither as a Modula-2 operator nor among the standard Modula-2 libraries (see Appendix D).

6-9. Refine the program EvaluatePolish so that it recognizes each of the two additional error situations described in the text and displays an appropriate message in each of these events.

6-10. Implement the second of the two strategies described for maintaining priority queues by rewriting the Enter procedure for queues so that it places each new node ahead of all nodes in the queue that have lower priority than itself.

6-11. Implement the revised versions of Create, Enter, and Leave for priority queues that are suggested by the assumption of a fixed number (say, five) of priority levels exist for the system. Your implementations of Enter and Leave should both have complexity O(c).

TEAM PROJECT: JOB SCHEDULING

Implement the operating system queue management process simulation that is defined at the end of the chapter. Assume, in addition to the four events that are described there, that the signal D indicates that the contents of all active queues and lists be displayed, with appropriate documentary labels. Exercise this simulation using the stream of events that appears in Figure 6-16 and demonstrate that your program gives the same queue contents that are indicated after these events are serviced by the system. Then add more events to the stream, testing especially how the system responds when the event cannot be immediately serviced (e.g., occurrence of a P event and an empty print queue).

7

STRINGS: TEXT PROCESSING AND INFORMATION RETRIEVAL

In the last chapter, we began to see the general usefulness of algorithms and data structures in nonnumeric application domains. In particular, the Polish expression is a mixture of numeric operands and nonnumeric operators (+, −, *, /, and ^). The order in which these appear in a left-to-right scan is generally unpredictable by the program, and therefore each must be read initially as a character string and then classified (as either "number" or "operator") before further action is taken in the evaluation of the expression itself.

The character string is a most appropriate unit of information for a large class of problems, as we shall see in this chapter and elsewhere. For example, word processing software, library information retrieval systems, natural language interfaces to database systems, and other types of user interfaces all rely on the notion of a "text" as their basic medium of representation. Yet, the basic features of most programming languages, including Modula-2, are inadequate for supporting these applications well. The mere presence of the CHAR type, the string assignment, and the ReadString and WriteString procedures in the standard module InOut provide only the bare bones of a beginning to meet the requirements of text processing applications in Modula-2.

For these applications, it therefore makes sense to define an abstract data type *String* and an associated collection of basic operators, which can serve as a set of powerful programming tools. In this chapter we define such an abstraction, and then we illustrate its use in an information retrieval application. In doing this, we simultaneously provide an overview of information systems as a distinct area of study within the broad field of computer science.

7-1 STRING DEFINITION AND OPERATORS

Intuitively, a string is a finite sequence of characters taken from a relatively small set of distinct symbols, called an *alphabet*. For example, the set of characters in our own alphabet {a,b,...,z,A,B,...,Z} allows us to form strings that are "words" in the English language, such as the words of this sentence. The decimal digits {0,1,2,3,4,5,6,7,8,9} are an alphabet that allows us to form strings that are unsigned integers, such as 10 and 235.

In computer applications involving strings, the ASCII character set provides a useful alphabet. The ASCII set was introduced in Chapter 2 and is summarized in Appendix B. We shall use the ASCII set as our basis for defining character strings and their operators throughout this chapter. Thus, a complete sentence, paragraph, or larger unit of text can also be visualized as a string, since its individual characters (including the blanks and punctuation marks that separate words, clauses, and sentences) are all members of the ASCII character set. With these ideas in mind, we define the abstract data type string as follows:

Definition: A *string* s is a finite sequence of characters, $s = s_1 s_2 \ldots s_n$, with $n \geq 0$, taken from the ASCII character set. When $n = 0$, s is said to be the *empty string*, which is often denoted by ϵ. The value of n itself is known as the *length* of s. The associated operators for strings, which will be defined in later paragraphs, are identified as: Create, Assign, SubString, LT, EQ, LE, StrInt, StrReal, IntStr, RealStr, Insert, Delete, Search, Length, Read, ReadLex, ClassifyLex, Display, and Dump. Strings also have an associated global Error, whose Boolean value serves as a flag to indicate whether or not the last executed operator was successful.

Throughout the operator definitions that follow, the notations s and t denote arbitrary strings of characters, $s_1 s_2 \ldots s_m$ and $t_1 t_2 \ldots t_n$, from a basic set (typically the ASCII set), with lengths m and n, respectively. Moreover, s' and m' denote the result of applying an operator to the string s, with initial length m. The notations i and j denote arbitrary integers, x denotes an arbitrary decimal number, and thus i', j', and x' represent their a posteriori values, respectively. *Maxstring* is an implementation-dependent constant that is the upper limit for the length of any string.

When we write a string in a text such as this, we enclose it within apostrophes ('), so that it will be distinguished from the text itself. If a string properly contains an apostrophe as one of its constituent characters, the enclosing characters are changed to quotes (") so that no ambiguity arises about the beginning and end of the string. Also, blanks and other punctuation characters are significant within a string, and all such occurrences contribute to the string's length (but the enclosing apostrophes do not). With these ideas in mind, the following strings and accompanying lengths are given as examples.

String	Length
'mccarthy'	8
'Hello World!'	12
"Here's an implementation."	25
'turing'	6
''	0
ϵ	0
'32 33 + 65 –'	12

For many string operators, it is useful to identify a "substring" of a given string. A *substring* is understood to be any contiguous sequence of (zero or more) characters within a given string. For example, if the given string s is 'Hello World!', the following are some of its substrings:

'Hello World!'

'Hello World'

'Hello'

'World'

'lo W'

'e'

''

Note, specifically, that the empty string ϵ is a substring of every string. Also, every string is a substring of itself.

The first three string operators, *Create*, *Assign*, and *SubString*, respectively, create a string variable, assign a value to such a variable, and extract a substring from that variable's value.

Definition: *Create*(s) brings the string s into existence.
  Preconditions: The string s does not exist.
  Postconditions: s' = '' and Error' = false.

Definition: *Assign*(s,t) assigns the value of the string t to the string variable s.
  Preconditions: String variable s exists, and t is a string variable or value $t_1 t_2 \ldots t_n$.
  Postconditions: s' = $t_1 t_2 \ldots t_n$ and Error' = false.

Definition: *SubString*(s,t,i,j) assigns to t the substring of s that spans positions i through j.
  Preconditions: String variables s = $s_1 s_2 \ldots s_m$ and t exist, and $0 \le i \le j \le m$.
  Postconditions: If $0 \le i \le j \le m$, then t' = $s_i \ldots s_j$ and Error' = false. Otherwise, t' = t and Error' = true.

The next three string operators, *LT*, *EQ*, and *LE*, are used to define the relations "less than," "equal," and "less than or equal" between a pair of strings. For these to be well defined, we must adopt a definition of *ordering* among strings themselves. Assuming that our strings are taken from the ASCII character set, we may proceed with this definition as follows.

String ordering can be defined as a natural extension of the ordering that exists among the individual characters in the ASCII set. Recall from Appendix B that each such character has a unique ordinal value (derived by ORD in Modula-2) from 0C to 177C. Thus, if c_1 and c_2 are any ASCII characters, then $c_1 < c_2$ if $ORD(c_1) < ORD(c_2)$. This definition yields some "intuitive" relationships, such as 'a'<'b', 'b'<'c', and so forth. The following definition gives an ordering among all strings of ASCII characters:

Definition: If s and t are strings $s_1 s_2 \ldots s_m$ and $t_1 t_2 \ldots t_n$, then s is *lexically less than* t [written LT(s,t)] if there exists an integer i>0 for which:
    (i) $s_k = t_k$, for all k = 1, 2, ..., i−1, and either
    (ii) $s_i < t_i$ with i≤m and i≤n, or
    (iii) i = m + 1 ≤ n.

This definition yields the following results of LT(s,t) for the sample strings s and t given on the left.

String s	String t	LT(s,t)	Condition Satisfied
'Hello'	'Help'	TRUE	(i) and (ii), for i = 4 and 'l'< 'p'
'Hello'	'Hello'	FALSE	neither (ii) nor (iii)
'Hell'	'Hello'	TRUE	(i) and (iii), for i = m + 1 = 5
'Hello'	'hello'	TRUE	(i) and (ii), for i = 1 and 'H'<'h'
'Hello'	'aardvark'	TRUE	(i) and (ii), for i = 1 and 'H'<'a'

These five examples show some of the subtleties of this definition of lexical ordering. The first example shows a typical case, which happens to agree with the dictionary ordering of 'Hello' and 'Help'. The third example shows that any string that is identical with an initial part (i.e., is a prefix) of a longer string is lexically less than that longer string. The fourth example shows that the capitalized version of a word is lexically less than the lower case version of the same word. Yet normal dictionary ordering is not fully maintained by this definition, as shown rather dramatically in the last example of this list.[1]

---

[1]Different programming languages define lexical ordering among strings in different ways. Interested readers should review the equivalents of LT and EQ in C, PL/I, and SNOBOL. Furthermore, the EBCDIC character set yields a different ordering among the strings, since the individual characters in that set have different ordinal values than their ASCII counterparts. For instance, the EBCDIC string 'hello' is lexically less than the EBCDIC string 'Hello', since 'h'<'H' in the EBCDIC ordering of its characters. Thus, neither the ASCII nor the EBCDIC character set provides a natural basis for defining an ordering among strings fully consistent with normal dictionary ordering.

Lexical equality between two strings is defined as identity. That is, the following definition holds:

Definition: If s and t are strings $s_1s_2...s_m$ and $t_1t_2...t_n$, then s and t are *lexically equal* [written EQ(s,t)] if both m = n and $s_k = t_k$ for all k = 1, 2, ..., m.

Thus, none of the following pairs s and t are lexically equal, even though they are similar:

String s	String t	Reason that EQ(s,t) = FALSE
'Hello'	'Hello '	m = 5 and n = 6
' Hello'	'Hello '	$s_1 = $ ' ' and $t_1 = $ 'H'
'Hi there'	'Hithere'	$s_3 = $ ' ' and $t_3 = $ 't'
''	' '	m = 0 and n = 1

To complete the definitions of the ordering operators for strings, the less than or equal operator is defined as follows:

Definition: If s and t are strings $s_1s_2...s_m$ and $t_1t_2...t_n$, then s is *lexically less than or equal* to t [written LE(s,t)] if either LT(s,t) or EQ(s,t).

Once an ordering is defined for strings, we may use the relations LT, EQ, and LE as a basis for defining other operators, such as Search, for strings. String comparison, therefore, is enabled by these operators in the same way that number comparison is enabled by the operators <, =, and <= ordinarily found in programming languages. With such operators, for instance, a binary search of an ordered list of strings (names in a directory or words in a dictionary, for instance), can be implemented using exactly the same strategies as a binary search of an ordered list of integers. The only difference between the two implementations is that the relational operators <, =, and <= (for comparing numbers) must be replaced by the operators LT, EQ, and LE (for comparing strings) wherever they appear in the implementations.

The next set of string operators, *StrInt*, *StrReal*, *IntStr*, and *RealStr*, serve to "coerce," or convert, a value between its representation as a numeric type (INTEGER or REAL) and its representation as a string type. These operators serve as an interface between the normal terminal screen representation of a numeric value (essentially a character string) and its equivalent internal representation, as described in Chapter 2. As the previous chapter's EvaluatePolish example illustrates, we often encounter applications in which both representations must be available to the program, in order for the program to achieve an appropriate level of generality.

Definition: *StrInt(s,i)* coerces the string of characters s to an equivalent integer value i.

Preconditions: $s = s_1 s_2 \ldots s_m$ exists, $0 < m \leq$ Maxstring, $'0' \leq s_j \leq '9'$ for all $j = 2, \ldots, m$, and either $'0' \leq s_1 \leq '9'$ or $s_1 = '-'$ or $'+'$ (when $m > 1$).

Postconditions: If $'0' \leq s_1 \leq '9'$, then compute:

$$i' = \sum_{j=1}^{m} 10^{m-j} \times s_j$$

Otherwise, compute:

$$i' = -\sum_{j=2}^{m} 10^{m-j} \times s_j$$

Example:
Let $s = '-245'$. Then StrInt(s,i) leaves:
$i' = -(2 \times 10^2 + 4 \times 10^1 + 5 \times 10^0)$
$= -245$

Definition: *StrReal(s,x)* coerces the string of characters s to an equivalent decimal number x.

Preconditions: $s = s_1 s_2 \ldots s_k \ldots s_m$ exists, $1 < k < m \leq$ Maxstring, $s_k = '.'$, $'0' \leq s_j \leq '9'$ for all $j = 2, \ldots, k-1, k+1, \ldots m$, and either $'0' \leq s_1 \leq '9'$, or $s_1 = '-'$ or $'+'$.

Postconditions: If $'0' \leq s_1 \leq '9'$, then compute:

$$x' = \sum_{j=1}^{k-1} 10^{k-j-1} \times s_j + \sum_{j=k+1}^{m} 10^{k-j} \times s_j$$

Otherwise, compute:

$$x' = -\left(\sum_{j=2}^{k-1} 10^{k-j-1} \times s_j + \sum_{j=k+1}^{m} 10^{k-j} \times s_j \right)$$

Example:
Let $s = '245.31'$. Then StrReal(s,x) leaves:
$x' = (2 \times 10^2 + 4 \times 10^1 + 5 \times 10^0) + (3 \times 10^{-1} + 1 \times 10^{-2})$
$= 245.31$

Definition: *IntStr*(i,s) coerces the integer value i to an equivalent string value s.
Preconditions: i exists.
Postconditions: s' = $s_1 s_2 \ldots s_m$ such that if j' = StrInt(s',j), then j' = i, and m ≤ Maxstring. Otherwise, Error' = true.
Example:
Let i = −245. Then IntStr(i,s) leaves s' = '−245', because StrInt('−245',j) = −245.

Definition: *RealStr*(x,s) coerces the decimal number x to an equivalent string value s.
Preconditions: x exists.
Postconditions: s' = $s_1 s_2 \ldots s_m$ such that if y' = StrReal(s',y), then y' = x, and m ≤ Maxstring. Otherwise, Error' = true.
Example:
Let x = 245.31. Then RealStr(x,s) leaves s' = '245.31', because StrReal('245.31',y) = 245.31.

We have in these definitions provided protection against exceeding the maximum string length (Maxstring) for the implementation, but we have not provided the reverse protection: exceeding the maximum integer or real value for the implementation. Strictly speaking, that should also be done in these definitions, acknowledging the fact that such limits do exist.

The string operators *Insert, Delete, Search,* and *Length* are provided to allow insertion and deletion of a substring from a larger string, a string to be searched for the first occurrence of a particular substring, and a string's length to be determined.

Definition: *Insert*(s,t,i) inserts string t as a new substring of string s, immediately after the ith character of s.
Preconditions: s and t exist, with s = $s_1 s_2 \ldots s_m$, t = $t_1 t_2 \ldots t_n$, 0 ≤ i ≤ m, and m + n ≤ Maxstring.
Postconditions: If m + n ≤ Maxstring, then s' = $s_1 s_2 \ldots s_i t_1 t_2 \ldots t_n s_{i+1} \ldots s_m$, and m' = m + n. Otherwise, s' = s and Error' = true.
Example:
Let s = 'Hello World!' and t = 'there, '. Then Insert(s,t,6) leaves s' = 'Hello there, World!' and m' = 19.

Definition: *Delete*(s,i,j) deletes that substring in s that spans positions i through j.
Preconditions: s exists, with s = $s_1 s_2 \ldots s_m$ and 0 < i ≤ j ≤ m.
Postconditions: If 0 < i ≤ j ≤ m, then s' = $s_1 s_2 \ldots s_{i-1} s_{j+1} \ldots s_m$ and m' = m − (j−i+1).
Example:
Let s = 'Hello there, World!'. Then Delete(s,7,13) leaves s' = 'Hello World!' and m' = 12.

Definition: *Search*(s,t,i) searches string s, from left to right beginning in position i, for the leftmost occurrence of string t, and returns the position in s of the first character of that occurrence.

Preconditions: s and t exist, with $s = s_1 s_2 \ldots s_m$, $t = t_1 t_2 \ldots t_n$, and $0 < i \leq m$.

Postconditions: If there is a substring $s_k \ldots s_{k+n-1}$, of s for which $EQ(s_k \ldots s_{k+n-1}, t_1 t_2 \ldots t_n)$, $k \geq i$, and k is the smallest such index, then the value k is returned. Otherwise, Error' = true and the value Length(s) + 1 is returned.

Example:
Let s = 'Here we are!'. Then Search(s,'re',5) returns the value 10.

Definition: *Length*(s) returns the current length of string s.

Preconditions: $s = s_1 s_2 \ldots s_m$ exists, and $0 \leq m \leq$ Maxstring.

Postconditions: No change to s or m takes place, and m is returned.

Example:
Length('Hello World!') returns the value 12.

The final group of operators allows convenient input, output, and classification of string values. This set includes the operators *Read*, *ReadLex*, *ClassifyLex*, *Display*, and *Dump*.

Definition: *Read*(s) reads an input string, enclosed within apostrophes (') or quotes ("), and assigns it to s.

Preconditions: The input string's length is no greater than Maxstring.

Postconditions: s is assigned the string value of that input.

Example:
ReadLex(s), where the terminal input sequence is: 'Hello World!' leaves s with the value 'Hello World!'. Note that the enclosing apostrophes must be keyed at the terminal.

Definition: *ReadLex*(s) reads the next nonblank sequence of characters c for which LT(' ',c), from the terminal, and assigns that sequence to s.

Preconditions: The next nonblank sequence of characters is not greater than Maxstring in length.

Postconditions: s is assigned the string value of that sequence of characters.

Example:
ReadLex(s), where the terminal input sequence is: Hello World! leaves s with the value 'Hello'. Note that enclosing apostrophes must not be keyed.

Definition: *ClassifyLex*(s) determines and returns the lexical class of string s, as either "number," "identifier," "operator," or "other."

Preconditions: s exists.

Postconditions: No change to s takes place. The result returned is "number" if s consists of a series of digits, possibly including an embedded decimal point and a leading plus or minus sign (i.e., s satisfies the preconditions for either StrInt or StrReal). The result returned is "identifier" if s consists of a series of letters (A-Z, a-z) and digits (0-9), the leftmost of which is a letter. The result returned is "operator" if s is any of the single-character strings '+', '−', '*', '/', or '↑'. Otherwise, the result returned is "other."

Example:
ClassifyLex('Hello') = identifier, while ClassifyLex('Hello World!') = other.

Definition: *Display*(s) displays the individual characters s_i of string s, with its enclosing apostrophes.

Definition: *Dump*(s) displays the characters s_i of s, its length, its lexical class, and the current value of the global Error. Also, the memory addresses and hex representations of the characters s_i are displayed.

7-2 IMPLEMENTATION OF STRINGS IN MODULA-2

Our strategy for implementing the abstract data type String will be to build upon existing declaration, assignment, and string representation conventions that already exist in Modula-2. This strategy has the advantage of internal consistency, providing a smooth extension of basic notions already well understood in the language. On the other hand, this strategy bears with it the shortcomings and restrictions that accompany these conventions. Most serious is the Modula-2 requirement that a string variable be declared as an ARRAY[0..n] OF CHAR fixes its maximum length at n+1 characters. For some applications, this is a serious constraint; for others, it is not. We shall not, however, develop alternative implementations for strings in this chapter.

Thus, we intend to build upon existing implementations of the Create and Assign string operators, as they are both predefined in Modula-2. Specifically, Create is realized through the declaration of string variable s as an ARRAY[0..n] OF CHAR, and Assign(s,t) is realized through the regular Modula-2 assignment statement:

```
s:=t
```

For instance, if s is declared in the following way:

```
VAR s: ARRAY[0..80] OF CHAR;
```

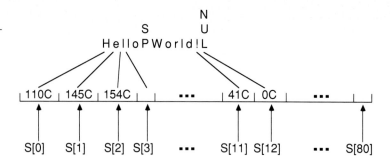

Figure 7-1
Modula-2
assignment of
the string
'Hello World!'.

Then the assignment statement:

```
s:='Hello World!'
```

assigns the ASCII values of the characters 'H', 'e', 'l', ... to the entries S[0], S[1], S[2], ..., as shown in Figure 7-1.

This brings us to an additional inconvenience for implementing strings after the built-in Modula-2 conventions. That is, an assignment of string $s_1 s_2 \ldots s_m$ (having length m) to a variable s = ARRAY[0..n] OF CHAR, leaves the character s_1 in array entry s[0], s_2 in entry s[1], ..., and s_n in entry s[n−1]. That is, the subscripts are offshifted by 1 in the implementation of the abstract definition of strings given in the foregoing section. Furthermore, a Modula-2 string assignment appends an additional ASCII character NUL (designated as 0C in Modula-2) in entry s[n] of the array s to mark the righthand end of the character sequence that is the string. The Length of the string s is thus not *explicitly* stored as an integer, but instead may be obtained by a left-to-right search of the array s for the first occurrence of the character NUL, and then returning the subscript value of the position where that NUL occurs. In the infrequent case where the length of the assigned string completely fills the array (that is, where m = n + 1), there is no room remaining for the NUL character, and so Modula-2 does not insert that character in this event. Instead, the length of s is n + 1 (fortunately, given by HIGH(s) + 1 in the event that s is an ARRAY OF CHAR parameter to a procedure).

With these points in mind, the example of Figure 7-1 shows the character NUL inserted in position s[12], from the assignment statement given above, yielding a length of 12 for this string stored in positions s[0] through s[11]. If, on the other hand, s had been declared as:

```
VAR s: ARRAY[0..11] OF CHAR;
```

the same assignment would have been successful, but the NUL character would not have been appended. In this case, too, the length of the value of s is 12. For the empty string assignment, s:='', the NUL character will be stored in position s[0], giving a length of 0 as desired.

In accordance with the foregoing operator definitions and accompanying discussion, a Modula-2 DEFINITION MODULE appropriate for implementing the remaining operators in the String abstract data type is shown below.

```
DEFINITION MODULE Strings;

EXPORT QUALIFIED StringIndex, StringError, LexClass, Eof,
                 Length, LT, EQ, LE, ReadString, ReadLex,
                 ClassifyLex, StrInt, StrReal, IntStr,
                 RealStr, SubString, InsertString,
                 DeleteString, SearchString, DisplayString,
                 DumpString;

(*All occurrences of ARRAY OF CHAR parameters below are to
  be interpreted as designating the type String. That is,
  the following type declaration is implicit throughout:

   TYPE String = ARRAY[0..MaxString] OF CHAR; *)

TYPE StringIndex = CARDINAL;
     LexClass = (number,identifier,operator,other);

VAR Eof, StringError: BOOLEAN;

PROCEDURE SubString (VAR s,t: ARRAY OF CHAR;
                     i,j: StringIndex);
(*Assign to string t that substring of s that spans
  positions i through j.*)

PROCEDURE LT (s,t: ARRAY OF CHAR): BOOLEAN;

PROCEDURE EQ (s,t: ARRAY OF CHAR): BOOLEAN;

PROCEDURE LE (s,t: ARRAY OF CHAR): BOOLEAN;

PROCEDURE StrInt (s: ARRAY OF CHAR; VAR i: INTEGER);

PROCEDURE StrReal (s: ARRAY OF CHAR; VAR x: REAL);

PROCEDURE IntStr(i: INTEGER; VAR s: ARRAY OF CHAR);

PROCEDURE RealStr (x: REAL; VAR s: ARRAY OF CHAR);

PROCEDURE InsertString (VAR s,t: ARRAY OF CHAR;
                        i: StringIndex);
(*Insert string t within string s immediately after
  the ith chararacter in s.*)
```

```
PROCEDURE DeleteString (VAR s: ARRAY OF CHAR;
                                 i,j: StringIndex);
(*Delete from string s that substring that spans positions
   i through j.*)

PROCEDURE SearchString (s,t: ARRAY OF CHAR;
                                 i: CARDINAL): CARDINAL;
(*Search for the leftmost occurrence of string t in
   string s, beginning in position i, and return the
   index of the leftmost character in that occurrence.*)

PROCEDURE ReadString (VAR s: ARRAY OF CHAR);

PROCEDURE ReadLex (VAR s: ARRAY OF CHAR);

PROCEDURE ClassifyLex (s: ARRAY OF CHAR): LexClass;

PROCEDURE Length (s: ARRAY OF CHAR): StringIndex;

PROCEDURE DisplayString (s: ARRAY OF CHAR);

PROCEDURE DumpString (s: ARRAY OF CHAR);

END Strings.
```

As we see, all procedures use the open array parameter convention for strings s and t. Furthermore, we export the types LexClass and StringIndex (for subscripting), as well as the globals Eof (for indicating end-of-input in the implementations of Read and ReadLex operators) and StringError, in addition to the operators themselves. Note also that these naming conventions preserve the Modula-2 preference for strong typing; thus, we have the names StringError, InsertString, DisplayString, and so forth corresponding to the abstract notions Error, Insert, Display, and so forth, which were defined in the previous sections.

Our implementations of the various string operators also use the following external procedures and declarations.

```
FROM InOut IMPORT Read, Write, WriteString, WriteInt,
                    WriteCard, WriteLn;
FROM SYSTEM IMPORT ADR, SIZE;
FROM MiscLib IMPORT ShowStorage, WriteBool;

CONST NUL=0C;
      EOL=36C;

VAR ch,lastch: CHAR;
```

The variables "ch" and "lastch" are used in the implementations of Read and ReadLex operators, and their use will be explained below.

The first procedure below implements the SubString operator. In a sense, this is a generalization of the Assign operator, in which any substring of a given string s is assigned to t.

```
PROCEDURE SubString (VAR s,t: ARRAY OF CHAR;
                    i,j: StringIndex);
(*Assign to string t that substring of s that spans
  positions i through j. *)
VAR k: StringIndex;
BEGIN
   IF (0<i) AND (i<=j) AND (j<=Length(s)) AND (j-i<=HIGH(t))
   THEN
(*Copy elements s[i-1..j-1] into t[0..j-i]. *)
      FOR k:=i TO j DO
         t[k-i]:=s[k-1]
      END;
      IF j-i<HIGH(t) THEN
         t[j-i+1]:=NUL
      END;
      StringError:=FALSE
   ELSE
      StringError:=TRUE
   END
END SubString;
```

This implementation points out the care that must be taken when referencing the individual characters of a string $s_1...s_n$, because they are stored in positions s[0] through s[n-1] of the corresponding array. Therefore, we see that the desired substring is taken from positions s[i-1] through s[j-1] rather than from positions s[i] through s[j].

The next two procedures implement the lexical ordering operators Length and and LT. Implementation of EQ and LE is left as an exercise.

```
PROCEDURE Length (s: ARRAY OF CHAR): StringIndex;
VAR i: StringIndex;
BEGIN
    FOR i:=0 TO HIGH(s) DO
       IF s[i]=NUL THEN
          RETURN(i)
       END
    END;
    RETURN HIGH(s)+1
END Length;

PROCEDURE LT (s,t: ARRAY OF CHAR): BOOLEAN;
VAR i: StringIndex;
BEGIN
   i:=0;
```

```
    WHILE (i<Length(s)) AND (i<Length(t)) AND (s[i]=t[i]) DO
      i:=i+1
    END;
    IF (i<Length(s)) AND (i<Length(t)) THEN
    (*initial substrings of s and t are equal, but s[i]<>t[i]*)
      RETURN s[i]<t[i]
    ELSIF Length(s)>=Length(t) THEN
    (*s is an initial substring of t and not shorter than t.*)
      RETURN FALSE
    ELSE
    (*s is an initial substring of t and is shorter than t.*)
      RETURN TRUE
    END
  END LT;
```

The procedure Length searches through the string s until either a NUL character is found (in which case the length is identical with the subscript value where that NUL appears) or not (in which case the entire array is filled and the length of the string is HIGH(s)+1).

The procedure LT compares corresponding characters in s and t, until one of three major events takes place:

(i) s and t have identical initial substrings, and s[i]<>t[i] for the next character that follows those initial substrings.
(ii) s is identical with an initial substring of t but is not shorter than t.
(iii) s is identical with an initial substring of t and is shorter than t.

In event (i), LT(s,t) is TRUE only if s[i]<t[i] for that next character. In event (ii), LT(s,t) is always FALSE. In event (iii), LT(s,t) is always TRUE. This is a delicate programming exercise, as are the implementations of EQ and LE.

The purpose of the procedure ReadLex is to read a sequence of input characters, skipping over initial blank, end-of-line, and carriage-return characters, and store them in s[0], s[1],... until the next blank or or smaller character (ASCII 40C or less) is reached. At that time, ReadLex fills the next position in s with the NUL character value (if s is not completely full). If two successive end-of-line (ASCII 36C) characters are encountered, ReadLex sets the global Eof to TRUE. In accordance with the postconditions of its abstract definition, ReadLex also sets the global variable StringError to TRUE in the event that the length of this input sequence exceeds the maximum length of the string variable where the characters are stored. The variable "ch" is used in this procedure to monitor the most recently read character from the terminal throughout the execution of the ReadLex procedure.

```
PROCEDURE ReadLex (VAR s: ARRAY OF CHAR);
VAR i: StringIndex;
```

```
    continue: BOOLEAN;
BEGIN
  i:=0;
  lastch:=ch;
  Read(ch); Write(ch);
  WHILE NOT Eof AND (ch<=' ') DO
    IF (ch=EOL) AND (lastch=ch) THEN
      Eof:=TRUE
    END;
    lastch:=ch;
    Read(ch); Write(ch)
  END;
  WHILE (NOT Eof) AND (ch>' ') AND (i<=HIGH(s)) DO
    s[i]:=ch;
    i:=i+1;
    lastch:=ch;
    Read(ch); Write(ch)
  END;
  IF (i>HIGH(s)) AND (ch>' ') THEN     (* string too long *)
    StringError:=TRUE
  ELSE
    IF i<=HIGH(s) THEN
      s[i]:=NUL
    END;
    StringError:=FALSE
  END
END ReadLex;
```

The procedure ClassifyLex classifies the string s as either an identifier, number, operator, or other, based on its lexical characteristics. Recall that the definitions of these classes were given in Chapter 6.

```
PROCEDURE ClassifyLex (s: ARRAY OF CHAR): LexClass;
(*Determine LexicalClass of s and return identifier, number,
  operator, or other accordingly. *)
VAR i: StringIndex;
BEGIN
  CASE s[0] OF
  'A'..'Z','a'..'z':
    FOR i:=1 TO Length(s)-1 DO
      IF NOT (Alphabetic(s[i]) OR Numeric(s[i])) THEN
        RETURN other
      END
    END;
    RETURN identifier
```

```
'+','-','*','/','^','0'..'9':
   IF (Length(s)=1) AND NOT Numeric(s[0]) THEN
      RETURN operator
   ELSE
      i:=0;
      IF (s[0]='+') OR (s[0]='-') THEN
         i:=i+1
      END;
      WHILE (i<=Length(s)-1) AND (s[i]<>'.') DO
         IF NOT Numeric(s[i]) THEN
            RETURN other
         END;
         i:=i+1
      END;
      i:=i+1;            (*Bypass '.' if present*)
      WHILE i<=Length(s)-1 DO
         IF NOT Numeric(s[i]) THEN
            RETURN other
         END;
         i:=i+1
      END;
      RETURN number
   END
ELSE
   RETURN other
END
END ClassifyLex;
```

Beyond the Length operator, ClassifyLex also uses the auxiliary procedures Alphabetic and Numeric. These determine, respectively, whether a single character c is an alphabetic character (in the range a, b, ...z or A, B, ...Z) or a numeric character (in the range 0, 1, ...9). Implementation of these procedures is left as an exercise.

Implementation of the operator ReadString is similar to that of ReadLex and is therefore also left as an exercise. Readers should note that the main logical difference between the two is in the condition for recognizing the beginning and end of a string. In the case of ReadLex, the end of a string is indicated by the next blank or lower character. In the case of ReadString, the end of a string is indicated instead by the next apostrophe (') or quotation mark ("), whichever was used to mark the beginning of that string.

The following procedure implements the coercion operator StrInt, which converts a string to an INTEGER. It follows specifications given in that operator definition. Local variable "minus" is used to flag whether or not the string begins with the character '−', and the procedure ClassifyLex is used to assure that the string is properly classified as a number.

```
PROCEDURE StrInt (s: ARRAY OF CHAR; VAR i: INTEGER);
VAR minus: BOOLEAN;
    j: StringIndex;
BEGIN
  IF ClassifyLex(s)=number THEN
    minus:=FALSE;
    i:=0;
    j:=0;
    IF s[j]='-' THEN
      minus:=TRUE;
      j:=j+1
    ELSIF s[j]='+' THEN
      j:=j+1
    END;
    WHILE (j<=Length(s)-1) AND (s[j]<>'.') DO
      i:=10*i+INTEGER(ORD(s[j])-ORD('0'));
      j:=j+1
    END;
    IF minus THEN
      i:=-i
    END;
    StringError:=FALSE
  ELSE
    StringError:=TRUE
  END
END StrInt;
```

The WHILE loop in the middle of the procedure scans the characters s[j] of the string, accumulating the integer representation i by adding s[j]'s integer equivalent [calculated by the expression INTEGER(ORD(s[j])−ORD('0'))] into the appropriate decimal digit position of i (achieved by computing 10∗i and adding s[j]'s integer equivalent into the units position).

Note that the loop is terminated by either the end of the string s or the appearance of a decimal point in the string s. In the latter case, s is the string representation of a REAL value, and its integer equivalent is thus achieved by truncation.

Implementation of the remaining coercion operators, IntStr, StrReal, and RealStr, is left as an exercise.

The Insert and Delete operators are implemented below. Note here also that the index value i, wherever it is used in the expression s[i], denotes the i+1st character of the string s. That is, s[0] denotes s_1, s[1] denotes s_2, and so forth.

```
PROCEDURE InsertString (VAR s,t: ARRAY OF CHAR;
                            i: StringIndex);
(*Insert string t within string s, right after the
```

```
                    ith chararacter in s, which is in position s[i−1]*)
        VAR m,n,j: StringIndex;
        BEGIN
          m:=Length(s);
          n:=Length(t);
          IF (0<=i) AND (i<=m) AND (m+n<=HIGH(s)+1) THEN
            (*Shift the tail of s right to make room for t*)
            FOR j:=m TO i+1 BY −1 DO
              s[j+n−1]:=s[j−1]
            END;
            (*Insert t into the vacated spaces of s*)
            FOR j:=i+1 TO i+n DO
              s[j−1]:=t[j−i−1]
            END;
            IF m+n<=HIGH(s) THEN
              s[m+n]:=NUL
            END;
            StringError:=FALSE
          ELSE
            StringError:=TRUE
          END
        END InsertString;
```

To illustrate the Insert procedure in detail, consider the invocation InsertString('Hello World!','there, ',6). The values of m and n are, respectively, 12 and 7. The first FOR loop shifts characters s_{i+1} through s_m (referenced as s[i] through s[m−1] in the procedure) to the right by n locations, as shown in Figure 7-2(a). The second FOR loop then inserts the characters t_1 through t_n (referenced by t[0] through t[n−1] in the procedure) into the vacated locations s_{i+1} through s_m, as shown in Figure 7-2(b).

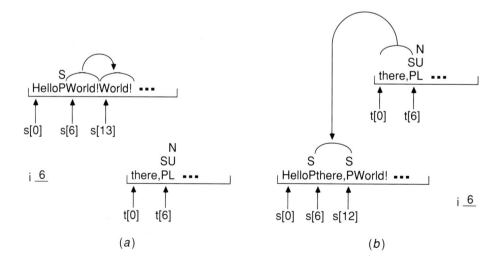

Figure 7-2
Details of the Insert string operator.

In the case of Delete, a similar shifting activity takes place, but now from right to left rather than from left to right. The effect of this implementation, shown below, is therefore to "cover up" the substring being deleted by the tail end of the string s, which is immediately to the right of the substring.

```
PROCEDURE DeleteString (VAR s: ARRAY OF CHAR;
                        i,j: StringIndex);
(*Delete from string s that string that spans
  positions i through j, denoted by s[i-1..j-1]. *)
VAR m,k: StringIndex;
BEGIN
  m:=Length(s);
  IF (0<i) AND (i<=j) AND (j<=m) THEN
    (*Shift position j+1 to i, j+2 to i+1, ..., and m to
      i+m-j+1. *)
    FOR k:=i TO i+m-j+1 DO
      s[k-1]:=s[k+j-i]
    END;
    s[i+m-j+1]:=NUL;
    StringError:=FALSE
  ELSE
    StringError:=TRUE
  END
END DeleteString;
```

The DeleteString procedure's operation is illustrated by the example Delete('Hello there, World!',7,13) in Figure 7-3. In this case, a single FOR loop moves characters s_{14} through s_{19} leftward, so that they replace characters s_7 through s_{12} in the string s. Note that the final statement after this loop reestablishes the NUL character at the end of the string s, after its rightmost characters are shifted to the left.

The Search string operator is implemented below in a most straightforward manner. More efficient implementations exist, but their efficiency

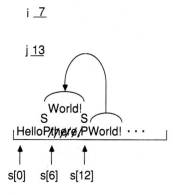

Figure 7-3
Details of the Delete string operator.

is only an advantage if the string length is significantly large. Here, the local variable "found" is used to indicate whether or not an occurrence of the desired string t has been located within s, and the index k is used to mark the leftmost character of such an occurrence.

Thus, the FOR loop in the procedure SearchString repeatedly marks the beginning of each such candidate substring for a match with t, and the embedded WHILE loop controls the comparison of each individual character within that substring with a corresponding character of t. If any such comparison locates a mismatch, s[j–1]<>t[j–k], then the entire substring beginning at position k is disqualified and the FOR loop begins again with a new value of k.

```
PROCEDURE SearchString (s,t: ARRAY OF CHAR;
                        i: StringIndex): StringIndex;
(*Search for the leftmost occurrence of string t in
  string s, beginning in position i, and return the
  position of the leftmost character in that occurrence.
  If t does not occur in s, then StringError is set to
  TRUE and the value Length(s)+1 is returned. *)
VAR m,n,j,k: StringIndex;
    found: BOOLEAN;
BEGIN
  m:=Length(s);
  n:=Length(t);
  StringError:=FALSE;
  IF (0<i) AND (i<=m) THEN
    FOR k:=i TO m–n+1 DO
      found:=TRUE;
      j:=k;
      WHILE (j<=k+n–1) AND found DO
        IF s[j–1]<>t[j–k] THEN
          found:=FALSE
        END;
        j:=j+1
      END;
      IF found THEN
        RETURN k
      END
    END;
    RETURN m+1
  ELSE
    StringError:=TRUE;
    RETURN m+1
  END
END SearchString;
```

As an illustration, Figure 7-4 shows the result of applying the Search operator implementation to find the leftmost occurrence of the string

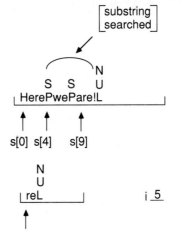

Figure 7-4 Details of the Search string operator.

$t = $ 're', beginning in position 5 of the string $s = $ 'Here we are!'. In this case, the result returned by SearchString('Here we are!','re',5) is 10.

7-3 VERIFICATION AND COMPLEXITY OF THE SEARCH OPERATOR

In this section, we analyze the Search operator implementation given above, both for correctness and for efficiency. This analysis will assure us that our implementation accurately reflects the specifications given in its abstract definition at the beginning of the chapter. Further, it will give us a measure of expected performance for this implementation without the need to run extensive benchmark tests and record execution times. For the purposes of both aspects of this analysis, we reproduce the body of the SearchString procedure below, with its individual lines numbered and preconditions, postconditions, loop invariants, and other helpful assertions inserted in appropriate places.

```
BEGIN
(**PRE:  0<i<=m**)
1    m:=Length(s);
2    n:=Length(t);
3    StringError:=FALSE;
4    IF (0<i) AND (i<=m) THEN
5        FOR k:=i TO m-n+1 DO
(**INV:   i<=k<=m-n+2 and NOT   EQ(s[i-2..i+n-2],t[0..n-1] **)
6            found:=TRUE;
7            j:=k;
8            WHILE (j<=k+n-1) AND found DO
```

```
(**INV: k<=j<=k+n and EQ(s[k-1..j-2],t[0..j-k-1])         **)
9         IF s[j-1]<>t[j-k] THEN
10             found:=FALSE
11         END;
12         j:=j+1
13       END;
(** found=TRUE and EQ(s[k-1..k+n-2],t[0..n-1]), or
    found=FALSE and NOT EQ(s[k-1..k+n-2],t[0,n-1])       **)
14       IF found THEN
15         RETURN k
16       END
17     END;
(** found=FALSE and NOT EQ(s[k-1..k+n-2],t[0,n-1])
    for any k from i to m-n+1.                            **)
18     RETURN m+1
19  ELSE
20     StringError:=TRUE;
21     RETURN m+1
22 END
(**POST: There is a k for which EQ(s[k-1..k+n-2],t[0..n-1]),
         i<=k<=m, and k is the smallest such value, or else
         there is no k for which EQ(s[k-1..k+n-2],t[0..n-1]).
         In the former case, the value of k is returned and
         Error'=FALSE, while in the latter case the value
         m+1 is returned and Error'=TRUE. **)
END SearchString;
```

First, consider the verification of this procedure. Note that five local variables are declared, m and n (permanently assigned the lengths of strings s and t, by statements 1 and 2, respectively), j, k, and "found" (whose purposes were briefly described above).

The goal of the inner loop in lines 6-13 is to determine whether or not the substring $s_k...s_{k+n-1}$ is identical with the string $t_1...t_n$, for a particular value of k. After initializing "found" to TRUE (line 6) and j to k (line 7), we repeatedly compare pairs of characters s_j and t_{j-k+1} (denoted by s[j−1] and t[j−k], respectively), until either of two events occurs. One event, the detection of an unequal pair, sets "found" to FALSE and thus sends us out of the loop. The other event, the detection of no unequal pairs, is signaled by the loop running its course (for all n values of j from k to k+n−1), whereby "found" remains TRUE. This is described succinctly by the assertion that precedes line 14.

Thus, we arrive at line 14 with either found=TRUE, in which case the current value of k marks the beginning of the leftmost matching substring in s for t, or found=FALSE, in which case we must repeat this matching process for the next appropriate value of k. In the former case, we simply return the value of k.

In the latter case, we continue the outer loop, which is controlled by the FOR statement in line 5. There, we see that the first candidate substring of s begins with the value of k=i and that the last possible substring of s that could match with t, if all others fail to match, begins with the value of k=m−n+1. Exit from that FOR loop therefore results in the assertion that follows line 17, which essentially admits failure to find a match after all candidate substrings of s have been compared with t.

If all such substrings of s fail to match with t, the statement "RETURN k" on line 15 will never be executed (since "found" will never be left at TRUE for an entire pass of the inner loop). Instead, the statement "RETURN m+1" on line 18 will be executed, satisfying the postcondition for the case that t occurs nowhere as a substring of $s_{1..n}$.

The remaining point to verify in this procedure is that the failure of i, m, and n to satisfy the precondition $0 < i \leq m$ results in the value m+1 being returned, along with the setting of StringError to TRUE. This event is confirmed by lines 4, 19, and 20, where we see that the body of the procedure is guarded by a test that this precondition is satisfied, combined with the assignment of StringError=TRUE (line 20) if it is not.

Turning to the complexity of the procedure StringSearch, we begin as usual by assuming that all lines (except END's) in the program text represent a single step each time they are executed. Here, we note that lines 1-4 are each executed once (thus counting a constant 4 steps for any execution of StringSearch). The remaining lines contribute a variable number of steps, depending on the lengths of s and t (m and n), the value if i, and the position of the leftmost occurrence of t in s (including the case where t occurs nowhere in s). Our analysis assumes the "average" case, in which t is assumed to be equally likely to occur in every possible position of s or not at all. That is, we assume that there are m−n−i+2 different possible leftmost occurrences of t in s and one more case in which none of these occurrences takes place. This is shown graphically in Figure 7-5, for s='Here we are!', t='re', and i=5. Therefore, the likelihood of the leftmost occurrence of t being either at a particular position k of s, or nowhere in s, is 1/(m−n−i+3). The average number of repetitions for the outer FOR loop in the procedure SearchString is therefore (m−n−i+3)/2.

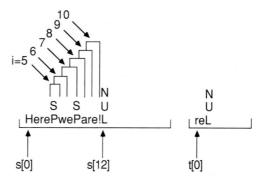

Figure 7-5 Average number of cases for StringSearch.

Similarly, for an arbitrary value of k, we must also estimate the likelihood that character t_j (for each $j = 1,\ldots,n$) will be the first to mismatch in a comparison with s_{j-k+1}. Assuming again that all characters of t are equally likely to be the first to mismatch, we have an average number of repetitions for the inner WHILE loop (lines 8-13) of $(n+1)/2$.

Combining these observations with the facts that there are two steps in each repetition of the inner WHILE loop except for the last (which has three steps) and there are three additional steps in each repetition of the outer FOR loop (besides those in the inner loop), we have the following expression for the average number of steps in the SearchString procedure:

$$4 + (m - n - i + 3)/2 \times (4 + 2(n - 1)/2 + 3/2)$$
$$= 4 + (m - n - i + 3)/2 \times (n + 4.5)$$
$$= (8 + mn - n^2 - in + 3n + 4.5m - 4.5n - 4.5i + 13.5)/2$$
$$= [mn + 4.5m - n(n + i + 1.5) - 4.5i + 5.5]/2$$

The dominant term here, as m and n increase, is the first one, so that the complexity of SearchString is O(mn). This we had expected all along, and thus our arithmetic serves to corroborate our intuition about the StringSearch procedure's complexity.

7-4 REGULAR EXPRESSIONS AND PATTERN MATCHING

The Search operator, as defined and implemented in this chapter, only allows us to find an occurrence of a *single* string within a larger text. For instance, suppose we want to find the leftmost occurrence of the string 'the' within a sentence, such as:

```
s='Here is an answer to the question.
```

Then we would write SearchString(s,'the',1), resulting in a return of the position of the leftmost character in the first occurrence of 'the' within s, or 22.

Although this is often useful, such a facility is not nearly as versatile as one that allows us to designate an *entire class* of strings to be sought in a larger text. For instance, suppose in the sentence above, we want to find the first occurrence of *any one* of the strings 'the', 'a', or 'an'. Such an expression is used to designate symbolically a whole group of strings having certain properties and is called a "regular expression." For example, the following is a regular expression denoting "any one of the three strings 'the', 'a', or 'an'":

```
the|a|an
```

Here, the special symbol vertical bar (|) designates the logical "or" when used in a regular expression.

In general, regular expressions contain provisions to conveniently express many different classifications of strings. The symbols in the following table have the special uses summarized on the right when they appear within a regular expression.

Symbol	Designation
c	Denotes exactly the character c in the ASCII set. E.g., the regular expression 'the' denotes exactly the characters t, h, and e in that order.
.	Denotes *any* single character in the ASCII set. E.g., the regular expression 't.e' denotes any 3-character sequence, beginning with t and ending with e.
[ ]	Encloses a set of alternative single characters. E.g., the regular expression '[Tt]he' denotes either of the strings 'The' or 'the'.
c_1–c_2	Denotes any character in the range c_1 through c_2, according to the ordering of ASCII characters. E.g., '[A-Za-z]' denotes any single letter of the alphabet, capitalized or not.
e_1|e_2	Denotes an alternative choice between the strings given by expression e_1 and those given by e_2. E.g., 'the|a|an' denotes any one of the strings 'the', 'a', or 'an'.
( )	Is used to override the normal precedence of concatenation over alternation (|). E.g., the expression 'John Doe|Brown' denotes either of the strings 'John Doe' or 'Brown', whereas the expression 'John (Doe|Brown)' denotes either of the strings 'John Doe' or 'John Brown'.
*	When used as a suffix, denotes "0 or more occurrences of the expression that precedes it." E.g., 'abba(dabba)*' denotes any string that begins with 'abba' and may have any number of occurrences of 'dabba' appended on the right.
+	When used as a suffix, denotes "1 or more occurrences of the expression that precedes it."
?	When used as a suffix, denotes "0 or 1 occurrence of the expression that precedes it."

One additional possibility for regular expressions allows any one of these symbols to be used to denote itself (literally) within an expression, provided it is preceded by the "escape" character \. For instance, the regular expression '...' represents any 3-character sequence, whereas the regular expression '..\.' represents any 2-character sequence followed by a period.

These conventions provide a rich basis for describing sets of strings, in the same way that ordinary arithmetic expressions provide a rich expressive basis for describing sequences of numerical calculations. In fact, regular expressions are used in many areas of computer science that deal formally with transformations on strings of characters. For instance, in programming language design, there is the need to describe precisely that class of strings that constitute valid elements of a program: identifiers, constants, declarations, and so forth. For this purpose, regular expressions are most useful.

Consider, for example, the notion of "identifier" in Modula-2, which is defined rather precisely as "any sequence of letters and digits, the first of which must be a letter." We are very familiar with this notion, since we use it every time we need to invent a new variable or procedure name in a program. The following are valid Modula-2 identifiers: StringError, SubString, i, j, and LT. Equivalently, the following regular expression defines precisely that class of strings we know as the "identifiers":

[A-Za-z][A-Za-z0-9]*

As another example, consider the description of "real number" that appeared in the StrReal operator definition in an early part of this chapter.

$s = s_1 s_2 \ldots s_k \ldots s_m$, with $1 < k < m \leq \text{Maxstring}$,
$s_k = \text{'.'}$, $\text{'0'} \leq s_j \leq \text{'9'}$ for $j = 2, \ldots, k-1, k+1, \ldots, m$,
and either $\text{'0'} \leq s_1 \leq \text{'9'}$, or $s_1 = \text{'-'}$ or '+'.

This is a rather awkward way of saying, "a real number is any sequence of two or more decimal digits, containing an embedded decimal point, and optionally preceded by a plus or minus sign." The same definition could have been rendered even more easily by the following equivalent regular expression:

[+|−]?[0–9]+\.[0–9]+

These two examples show the expressive power and simplicity of regular expressions, compared with English and other means, for describing classes of strings that occur in the syntax of programming languages.

For this reason, regular expressions are widely used in text editors and other text processing applications. The UNIX operating system, for instance, contains a powerful function called "grep" (for *global regular expression printer*). Grep is a useful programming tool for locating strings that match various complex patterns within a text.

Implementation of a regular expression pattern matching operator is, however, somewhat more complicated than the scope of this chapter permits. For the remainder of this chapter, we shall instead rely on the simpler Search operator that was implemented above. Readers who study advanced topics in computer science will encounter regular expressions in several different contexts. They are a useful formal description device for many different text processing applications.

7-5 INFORMATION SYSTEMS: AN OVERVIEW

A large segment of the computer science community works to support the needs of various activities known as "information systems." Information systems are concerned generally with the storage, retrieval, and maintenance of large volumes of information that serve the interests of a particular group of professionals. For instance, that volume of information that resides in a typical university library—consisting of card catalogues, books, periodicals, and other materials—is supported by a so-called "library information retrieval system." The collection of information that serves the interests of management of a large corporation—including sales information, operating cost information, market survey information, and so forth—is supported by a so-called "management information system," or MIS for short. That volume of federal and state laws that lawyers probe in search of legal precedents related to a current case is supported by a "legal information retrieval system."

Within an information system, there are several basic capabilities that require support. These fall into two general classes: maintenance and retrieval. The maintenance of an information system is that activity that keeps its information up-to-date and accurate. For instance, in a library information system, its maintenance activities include adding an entry for each new book that the library purchases, recording the names of persons who check books out, and so forth. In a management information system, maintenance includes the updating of sales figures on a regular basis, the timely recording of year-to-date payroll information, and so forth. A legal information system's maintenance activities include recording of new federal and state court decisions on a regular basis.

The retrieval function in an information system serves the interests of a person who has the need to know and wishes to obtain timely information from the system. To obtain this information, the person issues a specific, formalized request, which is known as a "query." For instance, in a library information retrieval system, queries are formulated by students and faculty in ways suggested by the following examples:

"Find all citations on the French Revolution."
"Find all works on Lincoln published in the 1870s."
"Find all research articles on actinomycosis published
 by the National Institutes of Health."

Queries for a management information system, on the other hand, are formulated by managers who are responsible for making planning decisions for their company. For instance, a manager may need to find out the names of all employees who may retire at the end of the year 1995. That manager would then formulate the following query for the corporation's information system:

"Find the names of all employees whose birth date is 1930 or earlier."

Queries for a legal information retrieval system are formulated in a similar manner by lawyers, and those for a medical information system are formulated by doctors and other medical researchers.

There are two basic differences in nature between the needs of a management information system (MIS) and a library information retrieval system. First, the data in a MIS is typically stored in a more rigid format (using a so-called "database management system," or DBMS) than the data in a library information retrieval system. The former contains "records" with fixed-length fields (i.e., strings with a fixed number of characters). In a library information retrieval system, the information is divided only into a series of documents, each containing a continuous text, represented by a variable-length character string.

This exposes the second basic difference between the MIS and the library information system. That is, in a MIS the nature of a query is relatively exact: the manager wants to know, for example, exactly the names of those employees who will retire in 1995, no more and no less. In contrast, the scholar who asks for all citations on the French Revolution may want only to make an "approximate cut," which will serve as an initial collection of citations for further refinement. A subsequent query will narrow this list to a more manageable group of citations, perhaps by requesting: "Select only those that were published in Europe."

7-6 PROBLEM 4: TEXT SEARCH AND INFORMATION RETRIEVAL

As part of the larger problem of library information retrieval, we pose the simpler one of searching a *single* entry in a bibliography and determining whether or not that entry contains all of a series of user-specified "keywords." For example, to determine whether a particular entry is on French art, one may supply the keywords "French" and "art." Our program should make no pretense about the relative positions of the keywords provided, so that the above example would succeed whether the words "French" and "art" appear side by side in that order or not. For instance, if the entry contained the phrase, "...the history of art in Persia; from the French of Georges Perrot...," it would result in just as successful a search as if it contained the phrase "French art" itself. This illustration tends to underscore that contemporary bibliographic search systems are inexact information retrieval systems. The user of such a system must be prepared to make several refinements on a search before obtaining the information that is really desired.

In any event, our problem is to read from a text file a *single* bibliographic entry, read from the terminal a series of keywords, determine whether or not the bibliographic entry contains all of the given keywords, and display the entry, the keywords, and one of the following messages appropriately.

"All of the keywords appear in the entry."
"Not all of the keywords appear in the entry."

The entry itself is assumed to contain a series of lines in the following format (this happens to be a variant of the standard UNIX format, used as a basis for implementing the UNIX bibliographic tools "addbib," "refer," and so forth):

%A	Author's name
%B	Book containing article referenced
%C	City (place of publication)
%D	Date of publication
%E	Editor of book containing article referenced
%G	Government order number
%H	Header commentary, printed before reference
%I	Issuer (publisher)
%J	Journal containing article
%K	Keywords to use in locating reference
%N	Number within volume
%O	Other commentary, printed at end of reference
%P	Page number(s)
%Q	Corporate or Foreign Author (unreversed)
%R	Report, paper, or thesis (unpublished)
%S	Series title
%T	Title of article or book
%V	Volume number
%X	Abstract
%#	Local library catalog number

For example, the following two entries may appear in a bibliography.

%T	Characteristics of French art,
%A	Fry, Roger Eliot,
%C	London,
%I	Chatto & Windus;
%D	1932.
%P	xo. 148 p., 1 l.
%K	Painting, French.
%#	709.44/F945

```
%T    History of art in Persia;
%S    from the French of Georges Perrot . . .
%A    Perrot, Georges,
%C    London,
%C    New York,
%I    Chapman and Hall, limited;
%I    A. C. Armstrong and son,
%D    1892.
%P    xii, 508 p.
%K    Art, Persia, History
%#    709.355/P427h
```

The solution to this problem is quite straightforward, if we assume the availability of powerful abstract data type implementations for lists and strings. To solve this problem from scratch, without such implementations, would be a more formidable task. Furthermore, the systematic verification of the resulting program becomes much easier when we are sure of the correctness of the underlying operator implementations. A sketch of the solution to this problem can be made as follows:

1. Obtain an entry from the bibliography file, consisting of, say, *b* lines of text.
2. Obtain, with appropriate prompting, a series of *k* keywords from the terminal.
3. Repeat step 4 for each keyword in the series until either all of the keywords are exhausted or a keyword is encountered that appears nowhere in the bibliographic entry.
4. Search the bibliographic entry for the given keyword.
5. Display the entry, the keywords, and an appropriate message based on the outcome of step 3.

We have a need for two different data types to solve this problem: the List and the String. Two variables of type list are needed: one for the individual lines of the bibliographic entry and one for the individual keywords themselves. Furthermore, the two data types are compounded upon each other, since the general ListElement for each of the two lists is ARRAY[0..n] OF CHAR (rather than INTEGER as given in Chapter 3). The following program assumes that the task of converting Chapter 3's list implementation in this way has been done.

```
MODULE TextSearch;

FROM Strings IMPORT StringIndex, Length, ReadString, Eof,
                    SearchString, DisplayString;
FROM Lists   IMPORT List, ListIndex, ListElement, ListError,
                    CreateList, Insert, Retrieve, ListSize,
                    DisplayList;
FROM InOut   IMPORT WriteString, WriteLn;
```

```
PROCEDURE ObtainBibentry; BEGIN END ObtainBibentry;
PROCEDURE ObtainKeywords; BEGIN END ObtainKeywords;
PROCEDURE DisplayOutcome; BEGIN END DisplayOutcome;

VAR  Bibentry, Keywords: List;
     b,k: ListIndex;      (*List indexes to Bibentry *)
                          (*and Keyword lists, respectively. *)
     i: StringIndex;      (*String index*)
     KeyFound,            (*switch for a single keyword*)
     AllFound: BOOLEAN;   (*switch for all keywords. *)
BEGIN
  ObtainBibentry;              (*Step 1 of the sketch. *)
  ObtainKeywords;              (*Step 2 of the sketch. *)
  AllFound:=TRUE;
  k:=1;
  WHILE (k<=ListSize(Keywords)) AND AllFound DO
                               (*Step 4 repeated. *)
    KeyFound:=FALSE;
    b:=1;
    WHILE (b<=ListSize(Bibentry)) AND NOT KeyFound DO
      i:=SearchString(Retrieve(Bibentry,b),
                      Retrieve(Keywords,k),1);
      IF i<=Length(Retrieve(Bibentry,b)) THEN
        KeyFound:=TRUE
      END;
      b:=b+1
    END;
    IF NOT KeyFound THEN
      AllFound:=FALSE
    END;
    k:=k+1
  END;
  DisplayOutcome               (*Step 5 of the sketch. *)
END TextSearch.
```

As shown, the details of steps 1, 2, and 5 of the above sketch are also not given in this implementation; completion of the procedures ObtainBibentry, ObtainKeywords, and DisplayOutcome is left as an exercise. The main logic for this program can nevertheless be revealed in Figures 7-6 and 7-7, using as an example the first bibliographic entry that appeared above and the keywords "art" and "French." In Figure 7-6, we see the situation immediately after the Bibentry and Keywords are stored, wherein the switch AllFound is initialized to TRUE. That switch remains TRUE as long as all keywords indexed so far appear at least once in Bibentry. The outer loop is thus repeated once for each Keyword in the list (using k as an index to this list). The inner loop is repeated once for each line in Bibentry, using b as an index. There, the switch KeyFound becomes TRUE as soon as the

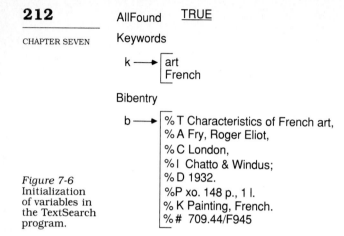

Figure 7-6
Initialization of variables in the TextSearch program.

first occurrence of the desired keyword (given by "Retrieve(Keywords,k)") is found by the SearchString procedure. If that event occurs nowhere in the Bibentry list, the switch KeyFound remains FALSE and AllFound is accordingly set to FALSE as well. The output for this particular example run of the program TextSearch is shown in Figure 7-7.

7-7 GENERICS, STRING IMPLEMENTATION, AND MODULA-2

The foregoing example provides a powerful illustration of a case where the *generic* implementation of an abstract data type would be very useful. Specifically, we desire a single implementation of Lists in which the List-Element can be any reasonable type—INTEGER, REAL, ARRAY[0..n] OF

Bibliographic entry:

%T Characteristics of French art,
%A Fry, Roger Eliot,
%C London,
%I Chatto & Windus:
%D 1932.
%P xo. 148 p., 1 l.
%K Painting, French.
%# 709.44/F945

Keywords:
art
French

All of the keywords appear in the entry.

Figure 7-7
Sample output of the TextSearch program.

CHAR, and so forth—without having to rewrite the implementation of Lists separately for each of these types. As suggested earlier, Modula-2's strong typing philosophy doesn't support generic implementations of abstract data types in a graceful way.

We should also emphasize that alternative strategies for implementing the string abstract data type, different from the one we adopted in this chapter, can be adopted to provide greater flexibility than ours. That is, the type String could have been implemented with a fully dynamic character, so that its length can grow arbitrarily large after the Create operator brings it into existence. Our implementation prevented this, since we aligned the Create operator with the string declaration ARRAY[0. .n] OF CHAR in the application program itself. Alternatively, we could have implemented the String as a linked list of fixed-length substrings. Every time the length of a string variable increased beyond the maximum length of such a substring, an additional node could be created to provide additional capacity. Implementation of each string operator would, of course, need to be rewritten to accommodate this new representation strategy.

The advantage of providing a fully dynamic implementation for strings is offset by the disadvantage of diverging from Modula-2's built-in basic support for strings. String assignment is directly realized within the language using the ordinary assignment statement, which assumes a conventional representation scheme using ARRAY[0. .n] OF CHAR and the NUL character to mark a string's end. Modula-2's basic input-output procedures for strings, ReadString and WriteString, are also built around this representation scheme. To replace that representation scheme would, therefore, nullify the conventional use of these assignment and input-output statements for strings; separate implementations of these operators would have to be used in their place.

EXERCISES

7-1. For the string 'Hello World!', how many substrings does it have? How many substrings does an arbitrary string of length n have?

7-2. Implement the procedures EQ, LE, Display, and Dump for the String abstract data type. Can you make use of any Modula-2 library procedures in place of either of these?

7-3. Give abstract definitions for the auxiliary operators Alphabetic and Numeric, which are used by the procedure ClassifyLex. Then implement these operators as Modula-2 procedures.

7-4. Implement the operators ReadString, IntStr, StrReal, and RealStr in accordance with the specifications given in their respective abstract definitions.

7-5. Strings are implemented in the C programming language in a similar way as described in this chapter; each string value is terminated by the NUL character. String functions are built into C that coerce numbers to strings (called "itoa," short for "integer-to-alphanumeric") and strings to numbers (called "atoi" and "atof," for "alpha-to-integer" and "alpha-to-float"). The C function strcat(s,t) forms a single string out of juxtaposing, or concatenating, strings s and t. For example, strcat('Hello ','World!') yields the single string 'Hello World!'. The function strcpy(s,t) assigns the string value of s to the variable t. The function strcmp(s,t) compares the strings s and t and delivers the result −1, 0, or +1, respectively, as LT(s,t), EQ(s,t), or LT(t,s). Determine how each of these C functions can be defined as a revision of our String abstract data type and then implement appropriate procedures for them.

7-6. The following two procedures could have been implemented as part of our String data type. Give appropriate specifications for each of these, by writing appropriate preconditions and postconditions.

```
PROCEDURE AppendString (VAR s,t: String);
(*Add the string t at the end of string s. *)


PROCEDURE ReplaceString (VAR s,t: String; i: CARDINAL);
(*Replace by the string t that substring of s that
   begins at position i and has the same length as t. *)
```

7-7. The operators in exercise 7-6 can be implemented either using the predefined procedures DeleteString and InsertString or from scratch. Implement them using each of these two alternatives and then compare the relative complexity of each implementation.

7-8. Logitech's Modula-2 implementation of the String abstract data type is also called "Strings." Like ours, it is based on the type declaration for String as an ARRAY[0..n] OF CHAR. Its DEFINITION MODULE contains the following procedures.

```
Assign (VAR s,t: ARRAY OF CHAR);
   (*Assigns the value of the string s to the string
     t. *)
Length (VAR s: ARRAY OF CHAR): CARDINAL;
   (*Returns the length of the string s. *)
Pos (s,t: ARRAY OF CHAR): CARDINAL;
   (*Returns index of the first occurrence of s in t,
     or else a value greater than HIGH(str) if s does
     not occur in t. *)
Insert (s: ARRAY OF CHAR; VAR t: ARRAY OF CHAR;
                           i: CARDINAL);
   (*Inserts s into t, starting at position t[i].
     If i>HIGH(t), then s is appended at the end of t. *)
```

```
Delete (VAR s: ARRAY OF CHAR; i,m: CARDINAL);
   (*Deletes the substring from s that begins in s[i]
     and has length m. *)
Copy (VAR s: ARRAY OF CHAR; i,m: CARDINAL;
      VAR t: ARRAY OF CHAR);
   (*Assigns to t that substring of s beginning with
     s[i] and having length m. *)
Concat (s,t: ARRAY OF CHAR; VAR u: ARRAY OF CHAR);
   (*Assigns to u the string that results from
     concatenating strings s and t together. *)
CompareStr (s,t: ARRAY OF CHAR): INTEGER;
   (*Compares strings s and t and returns −1, 0, or 1,
     accordingly, as s<t, s=t, or s>t. *)
```

Compare this set of operators with the one defined in this chapter. Identify how each operator in one set can be recast as a collection of appropriate operations in the other. Moreover, identify operators in each set that have no immediate counterpart in the other.

7-9. Borland's Modula-2 implementation contains a separate Number-Conversion module, which contains procedures for converting a value between its string representation and a CARDINAL or INTEGER value. It contains procedures named StringToInt, StringToCard, IntToString, and CardToString. If you have access to this implementation and its documentation, compare and contrast these with the coercion procedures that are defined in this chapter.

7-10. Analyze the implementations of the Insert and Delete operators given in this chapter, verifying their correctness and determining their complexity.

7-11. Reimplement the linked implementation of the list abstract data type from Chapter 3, using ARRAY[0..n] OF CHAR as the ListElement type, rather than INTEGER. In this implementation, import from our Strings implementation the operators that are needed by its procedures.

7-12. Choose any one of the sort procedures from Chapter 5 and reimplement it so that it sorts lists of strings rather than lists of integers, using the results of your work in exercise 7-11. Which operators from the Strings module need to be imported by this implementation? Exercise this sort by writing a sort driver that reads a list of names, invokes the sort procedure, and displays the resulting list in ascending order (as given by our definition of ordering for strings). To what degree does this sorted list of strings conform in its ordering with the ordering found in a dictionary or a telephone book?

7-13. Implement the procedures ObtainBibentry, ObtainKeywords, and DisplayOutcome that are used by the TextSearch program. Your implementation of DisplayOutcome should produce output in the style shown in Figure 7-7.

TEAM PROJECT: A SIMPLE TEXT EDITOR

Suppose you are given a text guaranteed to fit on the top twelve lines of an ordinary ASCII screen (each line contains eighty characters), a global "cursor" that contains a pair of integers marking the line (1 through 12) and position (1 through 80) of the currently scanned character in the text, together with the following primitive text editing commands:

```
top       move cursor to the leftmost character in the
          first line on the screen.
bot       move to the last character in the last line of
          the text.
ins s     insert string s at the current cursor position.
del i     delete the next i characters at the current
          position.
nxt s     search for the next occurrence of string s,
          beginning at the current cursor position.
mov i j   move the cursor to line i, position j.
end       end of execution.
```

Develop a program that reads such a text from a file and displays it, prompts the terminal operator for one of the above commands, carries out that command, and redisplays (refreshes) the text on the screen after the command is carried out. The program should repeat this cycle of prompting, carrying out commands, and refreshing the display until the command "end" is typed by the operator. For simplicity, assume that the commands "ins," "del," and "nxt" do not cross line boundaries; that is, a string inserted or deleted affects only the contents of the current line, and a string searched will be found only if it occurs in its entirety on a single line.

TREES: COMPILERS AND ARTIFICIAL INTELLIGENCE

All of the data abstractions discussed in the first seven chapters have been linear, or one-dimensional, in nature. Even the string data type could have been implemented as a linked list of CHAR elements. As noted at the end of Chapter 7, strings are often implemented in this way to provide more flexibility in the range of a string's length.

However, any broad exploration of topics in the field of computer science soon encounters situations in which a linear representation is inadequate, both in a conceptual sense and in a practical sense. An important basic step away from the linear list can be taken by studying the *binary tree*. The next step is realized by the more general notion of *tree*. These two abstract data types form the basis for our study in this chapter.

8-1 TREES AND THEIR PROPERTIES

Intuitively, we can visualize a tree as a way of organizing information in a hierarchical fashion, with a single entry point and a series of paths fanning out vertically from each point to its successors. An example tree is illustrated in Figure 8-1. The entry point, marked as point A in the figure, is known as the *root* of the tree, and each point (including the root) is known as a *node* (points A through G in the figure). Those nodes that have no nodes immediately below them are known as *leaves* (nodes D through G in the figure).

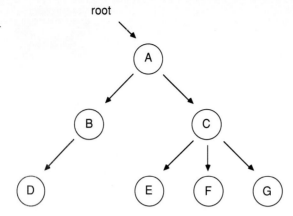

Figure 8-1
General notion of a tree.

Thus, the analogy between these data structures and the class of living organisms which we know as "trees" is strong. The idea of a "tree" as an abstract data type can be defined more precisely as follows:

Definition: A *tree* T is either empty or a finite set of nodes, each containing a value of the same type, in which:
 (i) One node is designated as the *root* of the tree, and
 (ii) The remaining nodes are divided into $m \geq 0$ disjoint sets $T_1, \ldots, T_m$, each of which is itself a tree. These sets are called the *subtrees* of the root.

For example, we see that the tree in Figure 8-1 follows this definition. The nodes are the individual capital letters, the root is node A, and there are two subtrees (one with nodes B and D and the other with nodes C, E, F, and G). Further, the subtree (B D) has its own subtree (with node D alone), and the subtree (C E F G) has three of its own subtrees (one with node E alone, one with node F, and one with node G). These, in turn, have empty subtrees.

From this definition, we may give precise characterizations of several features of trees. First, a *leaf* of a tree is any node that has no subtrees (nodes D, E, F, and G in Figure 8-1 are leaves also by this definition). Second, a *branch* or *edge* of a tree is designated by a line connecting a node to (the root of) any of one of its own subtrees. Branches appear in the figure between nodes A and B, A and C, B and D, C and E, C and F, and C and G.

The order in which the subtrees of a given tree are presented is also significant. For instance, the tree in Figure 8-1 is different from the tree in Figure 8-2, even though the two have the same collection of nodes and edges. Thus, subtrees of a tree are assumed to be *ordered* in this sense. Reflecting the importance of subtree ordering and the need to have a convenient linear representation for describing trees, we often use the following notational conventions for trees.

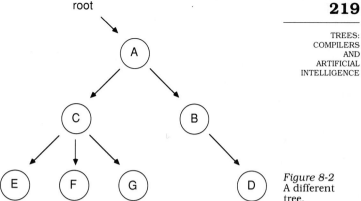

Figure 8-2
A different tree.

(i) The empty tree is written as ( ).
(ii) The tree with root node r and subtrees $T_1,\ldots,T_m$, for $m \geq 0$, is written as $(r\ T_1\ T_2\ \ldots\ T_m)$.
(iii) Any subtree consisting of a single (root) node alone is written without its enclosing parentheses.

These conventions unambiguously reveal the structure of all the nodes and subtrees within a tree. For instance, the trees of Figures 8-1 and 8-2 may be written in the following linear style, respectively:

(A (B D) (C E F G))
(A (C E F G) (B D))

Readers will notice the similarity between this notation for trees and the record structure of Modula-2. That is, a record is a hierarchical collection of data elements, which may be grouped at any level to form "subrecords." The tree of Figure 8-1, for instance, has the same structure as the following Modula-2 record.

```
RECORD
    A;
    RECORD
        B;
        D
    END;
    RECORD
        C;
        E;
        F;
        G
    END
END
```

Yet, there is an important difference between Modula-2 records and the tree data type that we will study in this chapter. Records are static in size and shape, while the tree data type is dynamic: its size and shape changes constantly during program execution, in order to effectively model the process that it represents.

We identify as a *path* in a tree any series of nodes from the root to a leaf. Thus, for instance, the tree in Figure 8-3 has root A, and paths A-B-C-D, A-B-E, A-F, and A-G-H. The *path length* of any path in a tree is one less than the number of nodes that the path contains. For instance, the four paths identified for the tree in Figure 8-3 have lengths 3, 2, 1, and 2, respectively.

In this context, we may also define the *depth* of any node in a tree as the number of nodes from the root to the node, proceeding along the path from the root to that node. Looking at the tree in Figure 8-3, we see that node A (the root) has depth 0; nodes B, F, and G have depth 1; nodes C, E, and H have depth 2; and node D has depth 3. The *height* of a tree is the maximum among all the depths of its nodes. The height of our example tree in Figure 8-3, for instance, is 3.

The tree structure has been used throughout history to represent the geneologies of families. An example is shown in Figure 8-4, where a portion of the Tucker family tree appears. (This particular portion documents the historical connection between the English ancestors and the first American settlers from the Tucker family. The settlers are identified by the towns in colonial America to which they first immigrated.) Out of the family tree notations, several terminological conventions for trees have emerged. For instance, all nodes that emanate directly from the same node are called *children* of that node, and furthermore they are called *siblings* of each other (brothers and sisters). For example, we see in the tree of Figure 8-4 that

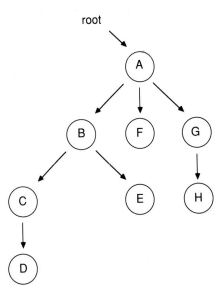

Figure 8-3
The tree
(A(B(C D)E)
F(GH)).

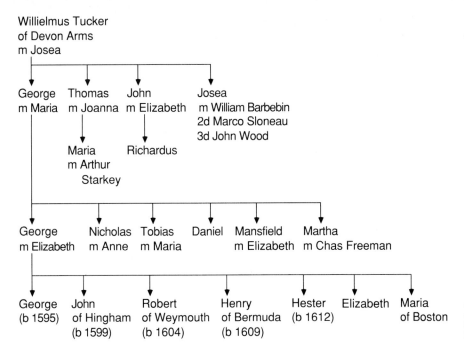

Figure 8-4 A portion of the Tucker family tree.

George, Thomas, John, and Josea are children of Willielmus (and Josea) Tucker and are siblings of each other. The node from which such a group of children directly emanates is called (predictably) their *parent*. Thus, in our figure, we see that the parent of George, Thomas, John, and Josea is Willielmus (and Josea). Furthermore, a node's *ancestors* are all nodes that lie on a path between it and the root, while a node's *descendents* are all nodes that lie on a path between it and a leaf. Thus, for instance, the ancestors of Daniel are George and Willielmus, while Daniel has no descendents.

When we visit every node in a tree exactly once, we are said to "traverse" the tree. Unlike a linear list, which is intuitively traversed in the order that its elements occur, a tree has more than one different order in which it may be traversed. One order, called "breadth-first" traversal, proceeds by visiting the root r first, then the roots of its subtrees $T_1,...,T_m$ (i.e., each of its children) in left-to-right order, then each of T_1's children, and so forth. For example, a breadth-first search of the family tree in Figure 8-4 will proceed chronologically from generation to generation, as follows:

Willielmus George Thomas John Josea George Nicholas Tobias Daniel Mansfield Martha Maria Richardus George John Robert Henry Hester Elizabeth Maria

A second natural order in which to traverse a tree is called "depth-first" traversal. This order starts at the root r, proceeds to the root of the leftmost subtree T_1, and then to the root of *its* leftmost subtree until a leaf is reached. This leaf is identified as the first node to be visited. Then, the path is retraced backwards (this is called "backtracking") until a node is found that has a second subtree, and the leftmost nodes of its subtrees are visited vertically until a leaf is found. This leaf becomes the second node to be visited, and so forth. This backtracking process continues until there are no more nodes to visit. For example, a depth-first traversal of the tree in Figure 8-4 yields the following order of visited nodes:

> George John Robert Henry Hester Elizabeth Maria George Nicholas Tobias Daniel Mansfield Martha George Maria Thomas Richardus John Josea Willielmus

Later in the chapter we shall identify applications in artificial intelligence where breadth-first and depth-first search are useful.

8-2 BINARY TREES

A rich subclass of the general data type called Trees is the *Binary Tree*. We shall see that it has many applications in computer science, and we define it below as an abstract data type as a basis for further development throughout this chapter.

> **Definition:** A *binary tree* is any tree in which no node has more than two children, and has the following basic collection of associated operators: Create, Destroy, Step, Store, Retrieve, Insert, Delete, Search, BinarySearch, Graft, Prune, Balance, Size, Depth, Height, Display, and Dump. In addition, the global variable Error is used to mark the occurrence of an error during the execution of any of these operators. The exact meanings, implementations, and uses of these and other operators will be defined throughout the remainder of this chapter.

For each node in a binary tree that has either one or two children, the lefthand child is identified as the root of that node's *left subtree,* and the righthand child is identified as the root of that node's *right subtree*. These characteristics are shown diagrammatically in Figure 8-5.

Thus, none of the trees among the foregoing examples is a binary tree. However, a particularly useful illustration of binary trees can be made using the familiar arithmetic expression. In this illustration, each leaf node is used to represent an operand (constant or identifier) in the expression, and each interior (nonleaf) node represents an operator. For example, the two binary trees in Figure 8-6 below represent the Modula-2 expressions $a+b+c$ and $a+2*(b-c)$, respectively.

8-2-1 Binary Search Trees

Another important application of binary trees is found when information is stored so that optimal searching can be done. Recalling the binary search

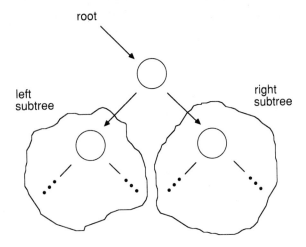

Figure 8-5
A binary tree with left and right subtrees.

strategy from Chapter 2, we noted there that such a search could only be done when the linear lists were ordered and implemented in contiguous storage. Here, we reincarnate that search strategy using a *binary search tree*, which can be defined as follows, instead of a linear list.

Definition: A *binary search tree* is a binary tree in which each node has all nodes in its left subtree less than or equal to it and all nodes in its right subtree greater than or equal to it.

For example, the linear list (23 25 39 42 46 49 73 74 80 96) from Figure 3-6 in Chapter 3 is recast in Figure 8-7 as a binary search tree.

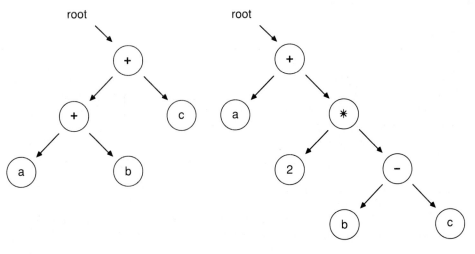

Figure 8-6
Two binary trees for arithmetic expressions.

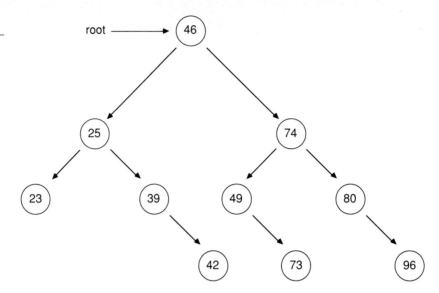

Figure 8-7
Binary search tree representation for a linear list.

Why is this important? It is important because the advantages of dynamic storage allocation over contiguous allocation, in flexibility and generality, can be preserved when we need to search the data structure in $O(\log_2 n)$ complexity. That is, a binary search with a contiguous list implementation (like the one in Chapter 3) can be directly simulated using a binary search tree representation instead.

8-2-2 Binary Tree Balance and Search

Before examining this algorithm, however, we need to introduce the notion of "balance." That is, there are many different binary search tree representations for a given list of numbers, but only a few yield to the kind of search efficiency which we desire. For instance, two alternative binary search tree representations for our example list of numbers are shown in Figures 8-8a and 8-8b. There, we see the numbers first organized in such a way that the left subtree is much larger than the right and next organized in such a way that every node has an empty left subtree; that is, the tree is essentially a linear list because its height is (nearly) equal to its number of nodes, or its *size*. Thus, a particular ordered collection of integers has many different binary search trees, and these trees can have significantly different heights. For instance, considering our sample of ten integers, the binary search tree of Figure 8-7 has a height of 3, while in the worst case (Figure 8-8b) the same collection of integers can form a binary search tree with height 9.

In general, every binary tree with n nodes has a maximum height of n−1 and a minimum height of $\lfloor \log_2 n \rfloor$. This is not difficult to prove, using induction on n. When n = 1, the height is necessarily 0. Assume, for the induction step, that the maximum and minimum heights are k−1 and

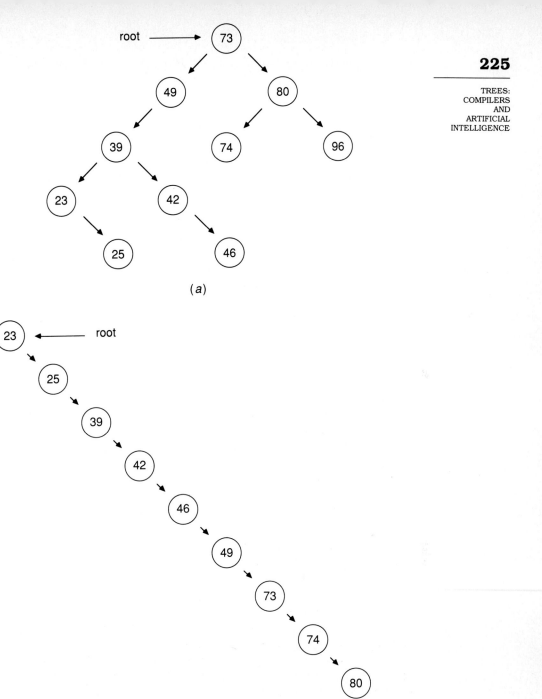

Figure 8-8 Two more binary search trees for the same list.

$\lfloor \log_2 k \rfloor$ respectively, for some $n = k \geq 1$. Then for $n = k+1$, we may add 1 to the height of a maximum-height tree by simply appending the new node to the leaf at depth k−1, giving a new tree of height k.

For the minimum-height tree, we have two cases: one where $k+1 = 2^p$ for some $p > 0$, and the other where $k+1 \neq 2^p$ for any $p > 0$. In the first case, the minimum-height tree of k nodes is said to be a *complete binary tree*, since all of its nonleaf nodes have exactly two children. For instance, this occurs in Figure 8-9, where we have a complete binary tree of seven nodes. Appending the next node to this kind of tree necessarily adds 1 to its height, since we have nowhere to append that node except to a leaf, which is at depth p−1. In Figure 8-9, for instance, we see that $p = 3$ and the only place where a new node may be appended is to a leaf at depth 2. For this case, $\lfloor \log_2(k+1) \rfloor = \lfloor \log_2 k \rfloor + 1$.

In the second case, we observe that there is always at least one "spare" location within the tree for appending the $k+1$st node without increasing the tree's height. For instance, looking back at Figure 8-7, we see five places where an 11th node may be appended without increasing the height of the 10-node tree. For these cases, $\lfloor \log_2(k+1) \rfloor = \lfloor \log_2 k \rfloor$ since $k+1$ is not a power of 2. The table on the next page identifies the points where the minimum height h of a binary tree changes as we increment the number of nodes n, for values of n up to 34.

Thus, we anticipate that the mere existence of a binary search tree is not sufficient for assuring optimal search time; the tree must also have minimum height in order to guarantee that the longest path from the root is as short as possible. We therefore define the idea of "balance" for binary search trees as follows:

Definition: A *balanced binary search tree* is a binary search tree having minimum height. That is, if the tree has n nodes and its height is $\lfloor \log_2 n \rfloor$, the tree is balanced.

The strategy for searching a balanced binary search tree can be modeled after that which was developed for an ordered contiguous list. That

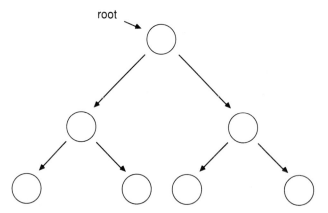

Figure 8-9
A complete binary tree with seven nodes.

Number of Nodes (n)	Minimum Height (h)	Number of Nodes (n)	Minimum Height (h)
1	0	18	4
2	1	19	4
3	1	20	4
4	2	21	4
5	2	22	4
6	2	23	4
7	2	24	4
8	3	25	4
9	3	26	4
10	3	27	4
11	3	28	4
12	3	29	4
13	3	30	4
14	3	31	4
15	3	32	5
16	4	33	5
17	4	34	5

is, consider the balanced tree in Figure 8-7, which is a reincarnation of the linear list that was binary searched in Chapter 3. Note in this rendition that, at the outset, the "middle" value is exactly the one at the root, or 46. Supposing (as we did in Chapter 3) that we are searching for the argument $x=80$, we may employ exactly the same search strategy. That is, if the argument is less than the root, we may proceed to the root's left subtree (and concurrently eliminate the entire right subtree from further consideration). If the argument is greater than the root, we proceed to the right subtree instead (and eliminate the entire left subtree). This strategy is made possible by the ordering characteristics that are required by the definition of the binary search tree. Finishing our example, we see that the same sequence of nodes is visited with $x=80$ (until x is found in the tree) as was visited when we used the original "divide in half" strategy with the contiguous list implementation.

The complexity of a balanced binary search tree search will necessarily be $O(\log_2 n)$, because of the characteristics of balance that were discussed above. A slightly more difficult problem is the one of building a balanced binary search tree itself: that is, a binary tree that has both the characteristic of ordering needed for the binary search strategy and the characteristic of minimum height needed to control the complexity of search. Since this algorithm is somewhat involved, we will return to it in a later section.

8-2-3 Binary Tree Traversal

Because binary trees are somewhat more specialized than trees in general, it is useful to define a more specialized collection of traversal strategies than the breadth-first and depth-first methods that were introduced above. These strategies are three in number and correspond to three basic ways that we normally peruse the individual nodes of a particular tree's root, its left subtree, and its right subtree. If we look first at the root itself, then at its left subtree, and finally at its right subtree, we are said to be traversing that tree in *preorder* sequence. If, on the other hand, we choose to look at the left subtree first, then at the root, and finally at the right subtree, we are traversing in *inorder* sequence. Finally, looking at the left subtree, the right subtree, and then the root is called *postorder* traversal.[1] These three traversal strategies are pictured in Figures 8-10a, b, and c, where the sequence of numbers attached to the nodes indicates the order in which they are visited.

Each of these three traversal methods for binary trees has unique intuitive justifications, in the context of computer science applications. For instance, we have seen already that binary trees are particularly useful for representing arithmetic expressions (Figure 8-6). If we have such a tree, then a postorder traversal of its constituent operators and operands yields the Polish representation (cf., Chapter 3) for that expression. Postorder traversal is particularly useful for compilers when they generate machine code from the tree representations of Modula-2 programs. We introduce the rudiments of compiler design in a later section of this chapter. On the other hand, a preorder traversal yields the linear, or LISP-like, representation for that expression, in which each operator precedes its constituent operands. We return to LISP in our discussion of artificial intelligence, which also appears later in this chapter.

8-2-4 Binary Tree Operators

With these elementary concepts defined, we proceed to give specifications, in the form of preconditions and postconditions, for the various binary tree operators that were identified in the definition of the Binary Tree abstract data type at the beginning of this section. This definition will provide a basis for our subsequent implementation of binary trees in Modula-2 and our exploration of binary tree applications in computer science later in the chapter.

In the following operator definitions, the notation $T = (r\ T_1\ T_2)$ denotes an arbitrary binary tree, having root r, left subtree T_1, and right subtree T_2. An index k is used throughout to identify the so-called "current" node t_k of the tree T (in a similar fashion that was introduced in Chapter 3). The integer n denotes the size (number of nodes) of T, and x will denote a separate element that has the same type as the individual nodes of T. The notations T′, r′, k′, n′, and x′ will denote the resulting values of T, r, k, n, and x after an operator has been applied to the binary tree T. As noted

---

[1] Sometimes these three traversal styles are called VLR, LVR, and LRV traversals respectively, where L denotes the left subtree, R denotes the right subtree, and V denotes the root. We prefer to use the more common "preorder," "inorder," and "postorder" denotations instead.

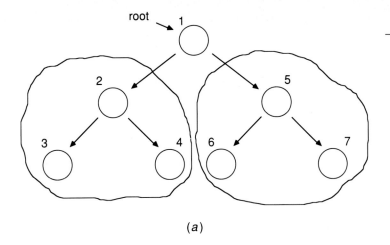

(a)

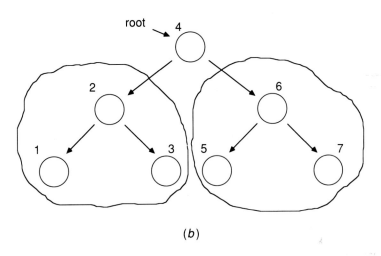

(b)

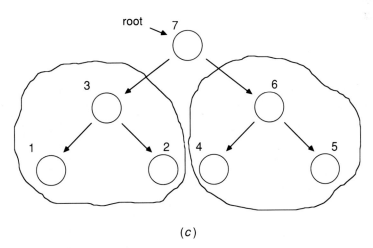

(c)

Figure 8-10
Preorder, inorder, and postorder traversals.

above, the global variable Error will be used to signal the success or failure of an operator, given the current values of T, x, r, k, or n. That is, Error' will become true if either an operator's precondition is not satisfied or its postcondition cannot be fulfilled.

When dealing with a binary tree, it is very useful to keep track, in a global way, of the most recently visited node (called here the "current node" or t_k) in the tree T. The current node concept is a carryover from our implementation of the linear list in Chapter 3, except here the current node is explicitly alterable via the Step operator in the binary tree abstract data type definition. Certain other binary tree operators will also implicitly alter the location of t_k, in an intuitive way, so that the transition from one operator to the next in an application program can usually be done smoothly—without having to relocate redundantly a particular node all the way from the root when moving from one operator to another. An example of the utility of the current node concept occurs when we use the Search operator to locate a particular value in the tree and then use a different operator (an Insert or a Delete, perhaps) to alter the shape of the tree at that location.

Relative to the current node t_k, we will also use a special parameter called "where," whose sole purpose is to directly locate the current node's parent, left child, right child, or root. These values are called, respectively, "toparent," "toleft," "toright," and "toroot" as depicted in Figure 8-11. The Step operator can thus be defined in the following way:

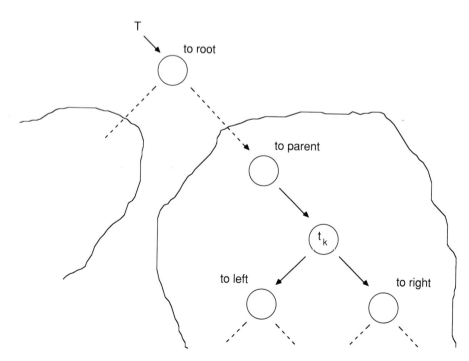

Figure 8-11
Locating nodes relative to the current node.

Definition: *Step*(T, where) alters the index k of the current node t_k, so that the current node becomes t_k's parent, left child, right child, or else the root of the tree T.
  Preconditions: T exists and where = toroot, or else T and t_k both exist and where = toleft, toright, or toparent.
  Postconditions: If where = toroot and T's root exists, then $t_{k'}$ = T's root; otherwise, $t_{k'}$ is unchanged. If where = toleft, toright, or toparent and t_k's left child, right child, or parent exists accordingly, then $t_{k'}$ = t_k's left child, right child, or parent, respectively; otherwise, $t_{k'}$ is unchanged.
  Example:
    Suppose T = (A B (C D (E F G))) and t_k = D. Then Step(T,toroot) leaves $t_{k'}$ = A, Step(T,toleft) and Step(T,toright) leaves $t_{k'}$ unchanged (since D has no left or right child), and Step(T,toparent) leaves $t_{k'}$ = C.

With this useful operator defined, we proceed to give specifications for the remaining operators that were identified in the definition of the binary tree abstract data type.

Definition: *Create*(T) brings into existence an empty binary tree T′, sets n′ = 0, and initializes the global Error′ = false.
  Preconditions: T does not already exist.
  Postconditions: T′ = ( ), n′ = 0, $t_{k'}$ is undefined, and Error′ = false.

Definition: *Destroy*(T) takes out of existence the binary tree T.
  Preconditions: T exists.
  Postconditions: T, together with all of its associated variables, does not exist.

Definition: *Store*(T,x) stores the value of x as the new value of the current node t_k.
  Preconditions: T, x, and t_k exist.
  Postconditions: If t_k exists, then t_k' = x. Otherwise, Error′ = true and T is unchanged.
  Example:
    If T = (A B (C D (E F G))), t_k = D, and x = X, then T′ = (A B (C X (E F G))) and no other change takes place.

Definition: *Retrieve*(T,x) retrieves the value of the current node, t_k, of T and assigns it to x.
  Preconditions: T, x, and t_k exist.
  Postconditions: If t_k exists, then x′ = t_k. Otherwise, Error′ = true and x is unchanged.
  Example:
    If T = (A B (C D (E F G))) and t_k = D, then x′ = D and no other change takes place. Note, this particular example tree has the same shape as the tree in Figure 8-6b for the expression (+a (∗2 (− b c))).

Definition: *Insert*(T,x,where) inserts a new node into the tree T and assigns it the value of x, according to the location given by the parameter "where." If where = toroot, toleft, or toright, an insertion of x as T's new root node, or else t_k's new left child or right child takes place.

Preconditions: T and x exist, and one of the following is true: where = toroot and T = ( ), where = toleft and t_k's left child does not exist, or where = toright and t_k's right child does not exist.

Postconditions: If where = toroot, then T' = (x), n' = 1, and $t_{k'}$ = x. If where = toleft, then T must be either of the form (... t_k ...), where t_k has neither left nor right child, or of the form (... (t_k ( ) U) ...) where U is t_k's nonempty right subtree. In the former case, T' = (... (t_k x) ...), and, in the latter case, T' = (... (t_k x U) ...). In either case, n' = n + 1 and $t_{k'}$ = x. If where = toright, then T must be either of the form (... t_k ...) or of the form (... (t_k U) ...) where U is t_k's nonempty left subtree. In the first case, T' = (... (t_k ( ) x) ...), and, in the latter case, T' = (... (t_k U x) ...). In either case, n' = n + 1 and $t_{k'}$ = x.

Example:
If T = (A B (C D (E F G))), n = 7, t_k = D, and x = X, then *Insert*(T,x,toleft) leaves T' = (A B (C (D X) (E F G))), $t_{k'}$ = X, and n' = 8.

This example is illustrated in Figure 8-12.

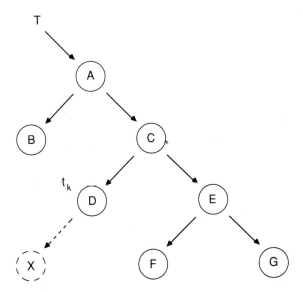

Figure 8-12
Insertion into a binary tree.

Definition: *Delete*(T) deletes the current element t_k from T, leaving T in inorder sequence if it had been already.

Preconditions: T and t_k exist.

Postconditions: If t_k has neither left nor right subtrees, then T is either of the form (... (t t_k U) ...) or (... (t U t_k) ...) where t is the parent of t_k, or of the form (t_k). In the first case, either T' = (... (t () U) ...) or T' = (... (t U ()) ...), respectively. In the second case, T' = ().
If, on the other hand, t_k has a left or right subtree only, then either t_k is not the root and T is one of the forms:
(... (t U (t_k V)) ...)
(... (t U (t_k () V)) ...)
(... (t (t_k V) U) ...)
(... (t (t_k () V) U) ...),
or t_k is the root and T is one of the forms:
(t_k V)
(t_k () V).
In the event that t_k is not the root, then T' = (... (t U V) ...) if T is either of the first two forms, and T' = (... (t V U) ...) if T is either of the second two forms. In the event that t_k is the root, then T' = (V).
Finally, consider the case in which t_k has both left and right subtrees. In the event that t_k is not the root, T must be one of the forms:
(... (t (t_k U V) W) ...)
(... (t W (t_k U V)) ...)
Here, deletion of t_k results in the tree T' = (... (t (V U) W) ...) or (... (t W (V U)) ...), respectively. In the event that t_k is the root, then T must be of the form (t_k U V). Here, deletion of t_k results in the tree T' = (V U).
In all of the above cases, $n' = n-1$ and $t_{k'}$ becomes undefined. Otherwise, Error' = true and $t_{k'} = t_k$.

Example:
Suppose T is the binary search tree in Figure 8-7. The purpose of the particular prescription for deletion given in the final case above, where the current node has both left and right subtrees, is to enforce a method of deletion that preserves the binary search tree's property of ordering. That is, deletion of any node from a binary search tree should still leave the nodes in ascending order with respect to an inorder traversal. If T = (46 (25 23 (39 () 42)) (74 (49 () 73) (80 () 96))) and $t_k = 74$, the above definition forces the subtree (80 () 96) to replace 74 in the tree and the subtree (49 () 73) to be reattached to (80 () 96) as its new left subtree. Thus, in this case, the resulting tree will be: T' = (46 (25 23 (39 () 42)) ((80 (49 () 73) 96))).

This particular deletion is pictured graphically in Figure 8-13.

The operators Search and BinarySearch are defined to permit the systematic examination of individual nodes in a binary tree in either of two distinct patterns. The first pattern proceeds through the tree in an inorder traversal, while the second is a binary search, carrying with it the additional requirement that the elements are ordered in such a way that the tree is a binary search tree.

Definition: *Search*(T,x) traverses the binary tree T in an inorder sequence, looking for the first occurrence of x, and marks that node as the new current node.

Preconditions: T and x exist.

Postconditions: If x occurs in T, and t_j is the first occurrence of x in an inorder traversal of T, then $t_{k'} = t_j$ and Error' = false. Otherwise, t_k is unchanged and Error' = true.

Example:
Assume that T is the binary tree in Figure 8-7 and that x = 39. Then, Search(T,x) will leave $t_{k'} = 39$ and Error' = false. However, Search(T,34) will leave t_k unchanged and Error' = true.

Definition: *BinarySearch*(T,x) examines a series of nodes in the binary search tree T, in "binary search" sequence, looking for the first occurrence of x, and marks that node as the new current node.

Preconditions: T and x exist, and T is a binary search tree.

Postconditions: If x occurs in T, and t_j is the first occurrence of x in a binary search of T, then $t_{k'} = t_j$ and Error' = false. If x does not occur in T, or if T is not a binary search tree, then $t_{k'}$ is the last node visited during the binary search and Error' = true.

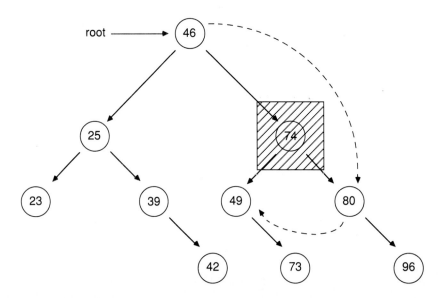

Figure 8-13
Deletion from a binary tree.

Example:
Assume again that T is the (binary search) tree in Figure 8-7, and that x=39. Then, BinarySearch(T,x) will leave $t_{k'}=39$ and Error'=false. However, BinarySearch(T,34) will leave $t_{k'}=39$ also, but Error'=true. In the binary search, nodes 46, 25, and 39 are visited on the way to determining that 34 is not in the tree, while in the ordinary inorder search all of T's nodes 46, 25, 23, 39, 42, 74, 49, 73, 80, and 96 will be visited before this determination can be made.

The rationale behind this particular definition of the BinarySearch operator is to provide application programs with a direct means to build a binary search tree "from scratch" by combining the BinarySearch operator with the Insert operator, whose definition relies upon an appropriate setting of the current node t_k. That is, consider the example of finding a proper place for inserting the value 34 into the binary search tree T of Figure 8-7, so that the resulting tree after the insertion retains the ordering that is required by a binary search tree. This insertion is correctly realized by the following sequence of (pseudo)instructions for an application program.

```
BinarySearch(T,34);
if 34<t_k then
   Insert(T,34,toleft)
elsif 34>t_k then
   Insert(T,34,toright)
end
```

Here, we see that the Insert operator's execution relies upon the proper setting of t_k by the BinarySearch operator that precedes it. This strategy for a single insertion can be easily extended in the following way, so that an entire binary search tree is built from scratch. A simple loop, whose body incorporates the instructions above, is all that we need:

```
Create(T);
read(x);
Insert(T,x,toroot);
read(x);
while not eof do
   BinarySearch(T,x);
   if x<t_k then
      Insert(T,x,toleft)
   elsif x>t_k then
      Insert(T,x,toright)
   end;
   read(x)
end
```

Readers should also note that duplicates are discarded in this process. Although the pseudocode is not exact Modula-2, it does suggest a basic strategy of combining BinarySearch, Insert, and the current node concepts to form cooperating sequences of instructions for solving problems involving binary tree traversal.

8-2-5 Whole Tree Operators—Graft and Prune

Unlike the above operators, which perform modifications to a tree on an element-by-element basis, the following two operators allow an entire tree to be appended as a new subtree of another tree (called "grafting," which is appropriate to suggest the analogy with living organisms), or separated from another tree (called "pruning," for similar reasons).

Definition: $Graft(T,U,where)$ attaches the tree U as a new subtree of the tree T, at a location specified by "where."

Preconditions: T, t_k, and U exist, and either where = toleft and t_k's left subtree is currently vacant, or where = toright and t_k's right subtree is currently vacant.

Postconditions: If $T = (\ldots (t_k \; () \; W) \ldots)$ and where = toleft, then $T' = (\ldots (t_k \; U \; W) \ldots)$. If, on the other hand, $T = (\ldots (t_k \; W \; ()) \ldots)$ and where = toright, then $T' = (\ldots (t_k \; W \; U) \ldots)$. In either of these two cases, $t_{k'} = t_k$ and U' is undefined (that is, U ceases to exist). If neither of these two grafts can be made, then Error' = true and T and U are unchanged.

Example:
Consider the binary trees $T = (+ \; a)$ and $U = (* \; b \; c)$, with $t_k = '+'$. Then Graft(T,U,toright) leaves $T' = (+ \; a \; (* \; b \; c))$, as shown in the illustration of Figure 8-14.

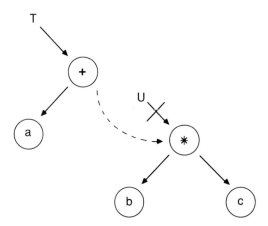

Figure 8-14
Example of the Graft operator.

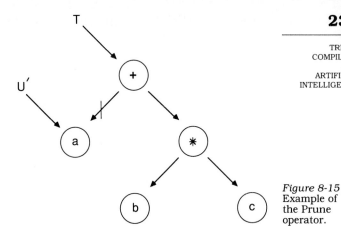

Figure 8-15 Example of the Prune operator.

Definition: *Prune*(T,U,where) separates the subtree designated by the specification "where" from the tree T and identifies it as the entirety of tree U.
Preconditions: T, t_k, and U exist, and either where = toleft or where = toright.
Postconditions: If T = (... (t_k V W) ...) and where = toleft, then T' = (... (t_k () W) ...) and U' = V. If, on the other hand, where = toright, then T' = (... (t_k V) ...) and U' = W. If neither of these two prunings is possible, then Error' = true and T and U are unchanged.
Example:
Consider the binary tree T = (+ a (* b c)) and $t_k = '+'$. Then Prune(T,U,toleft) leaves T' = (+ () (* b c)) and U' = (a), as shown in the illustrations of Figure 8-15.

8-2-6 Additional Binary Tree Operators

In this section, we give specifications for the remaining binary tree operators that were identified in the definition of the Binary Tree abstract data type.

Definition: *Balance*(T) converts the binary search tree T into a balanced binary search tree.
Preconditions: T exists, and T is a binary search tree.
Postconditions: T' contains the same nodes as T, except that Height(T') = $\lfloor \log_2 n \rfloor$ and $t_{k'}$ is undefined.
Example:
If T is either of the trees in Figure 8-8, then Balance(T) will leave T' as shown in Figure 8-7.

Definition: *Size*(T) returns the number of nodes n in the binary tree T.
Preconditions: T exists.
Postconditions: The value of n is returned, and no change to T or t_k occurs.

Definition: *Depth*(T) returns the depth of the current node t_k in the binary tree T.
Preconditions: T and t_k exist.
Postconditions: If t_k exists, its depth is returned; otherwise, Error' = true. No other change to T or t_k occurs.

Definition: *Height*(T) returns the maximum depth of all nodes in the binary tree T.
Preconditions: T exists.
Postconditions: No change to T, t_k, or n occurs.

Definition: *Display*(T) displays the elements of the binary tree T in an inorder sequence and with appropriate parenthesization to indicate the structure of T.
Preconditions: T exists.
Postconditions: T is displayed in its ordinary parenthesized representation, and no other changes to T occur.

Definition: *Dump*(T) displays the binary tree T "vertically" on the screen, with each element indented to indicate its depth, and also the current element t_k, together with the tree's size, height, ordering, balance, maximum size, and status of the Error global.
Preconditions: T exists.
Postconditions: T is displayed as indicated, and no other changes to T occur.

8-3 IMPLEMENTATION OF BINARY TREES IN MODULA-2

Because it is basically a two-dimensional data structure, the binary tree has more detail in its procedures that implement its operators than any of the simpler linear abstract data types that were studied in previous chapters. We use a linked implementation strategy for binary trees, in which each node has the structure shown in Figure 8-16. As shown, the node for any element t_k contains four entries; the element value t_k itself (which is

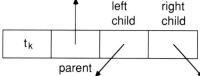

Figure 8-16 Node structure for implementing binary trees.

assumed throughout the remainder of this chapter to be of type String), together with a pointer to each of the element's parent, left child, and right child. At the outset, a binary tree will also have a "defining" node, in which will appear a pointer to the tree's root node, an integer n keeping track of the tree's size, and a pointer k to the tree's current node t_k, and (when the tree is in the process of being traversed) a record of the "backtrack stack" contents. More will be said about the backtrack stack when we discuss the implementation of binary tree traversal. All of this information appears in the following way in the DEFINITION and IMPLEMENTATION MODULEs for binary trees.

```
DEFINITION MODULE Trees;

EXPORT QUALIFIED BinaryTree, TreeIndex, String, TreeError,
                 ToWhere, CreateTree, DestroyTree, TreeStep,
                 StoreTree, RetrieveTree, InsertTree,
                 DeleteTree, TreeSearch, TreeBinarySearch,
                 Graft, Prune, Balance, TreeSize, Depth,
                 Height, DisplayTree, DumpTree;

TYPE BinaryTree;
     TreeIndex;
     String = ARRAY[0..20] OF CHAR;   (*Tree element type. *)
     ToWhere = (toroot, toleft, toright, toparent);

VAR TreeError: BOOLEAN;

PROCEDURE CreateTree (VAR T: BinaryTree);

PROCEDURE DestroyTree (VAR T: BinaryTree);

PROCEDURE TreeStep (VAR T: BinaryTree; where: ToWhere);

PROCEDURE StoreTree (VAR T: BinaryTree; x: String);

PROCEDURE RetrieveTree (T: BinaryTree; VAR x: String);

PROCEDURE InsertTree (VAR T: BinaryTree; x: String;
                                         where: ToWhere);

PROCEDURE DeleteTree (VAR T: BinaryTree);

PROCEDURE TreeSearch (VAR T: BinaryTree; x: String);

PROCEDURE TreeBinarySearch (VAR T: BinaryTree; x: String);

PROCEDURE Graft (VAR T,U: BinaryTree; where: ToWhere);

PROCEDURE Prune (VAR T,U: BinaryTree; where: ToWhere);

PROCEDURE Balance (VAR T: BinaryTree);

PROCEDURE TreeSize (T: BinaryTree): CARDINAL;

PROCEDURE Depth (T: BinaryTree): CARDINAL;
```

```
    PROCEDURE Height (T: BinaryTree): CARDINAL;

    PROCEDURE DisplayTree (T: BinaryTree);

    PROCEDURE DumpTree (T: BinaryTree);

    END Trees.


    IMPLEMENTATION MODULE Trees;

    CONST Maxtree = 10000;

    TYPE BinaryTree = POINTER TO TreeRoot;
         TreeIndex = POINTER TO TreeNode;
         TreeRoot = RECORD
                root: TreeIndex;
                n: CARDINAL;         (*current tree size*)
                k: TreeIndex;        (*current node index*)
                backtrack: AdStack (*stack for traversal*)
              END;
         TreeNode = RECORD
                t: String;
                parent: TreeIndex;
                left: TreeIndex;
                right: TreeIndex
              END;
```

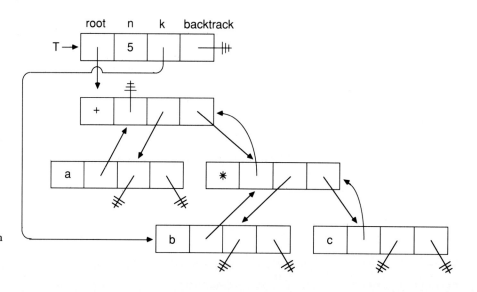

Figure 8-17 Representation of the tree T=(+a(*b c)).

For instance, suppose we have the binary tree T = (+ a (* b c)), with current node t_k = 'b'. Its internal representation, using this implementation scheme, is shown in Figure 8-17.

8-3-1 Basic Operator Implementations

Implementations of the operators Create, Destroy, Step, Store and Retrieve are given below. They are self-explanatory, except for the initiation of the "backtrack stack," whose purpose will be explained later. Also, our procedure naming conventions follow Modula-2's standard conventions, which reflect its commitment to strong typing. Thus, for instance, we implement the binary tree operator Create as the procedure named CreateTree, to distinguish it from CreateList, CreateStack, and so forth.

```
PROCEDURE CreateTree (VAR T: BinaryTree);
BEGIN
   NEW(T);
   TreeError:=FALSE;
   WITH T^ DO
      root:=NIL;
      n:=0;
      k:=NIL;
      CreateAdStack(backtrack)
   END
END CreateTree;

PROCEDURE DestroyTree (VAR T: BinaryTree);
BEGIN
   WITH T^ DO
      k:=root;
      WHILE k<>NIL DO
         DeleteTree(T);
         k:=root
      END;
      DestroyAdStack(backtrack)
   END;
   DISPOSE(T)
END DestroyTree;

PROCEDURE TreeStep (VAR T: BinaryTree; where: ToWhere);
BEGIN
   WITH T^ DO
      TreeError:=FALSE;
      IF where=toroot THEN
         k:=root;
         RETURN
```

```
      ELSIF k=NIL THEN
        TreeError:=TRUE;
        RETURN
      ELSE
        CASE where OF
          toleft:   k:=k^.left    |
          toright:  k:=k^.right   |
          toparent: k:=k^.parent
        END;
        RETURN
      END
    END
END TreeStep;

PROCEDURE StoreTree (VAR T: BinaryTree; x: String);
BEGIN
  WITH T^ DO
    IF k<>NIL THEN
      TreeError:=FALSE;
      k^.t:=x
    ELSE
      TreeError:=TRUE
    END
  END
END StoreTree;

PROCEDURE RetrieveTree (T: BinaryTree; VAR x: String);
BEGIN
  WITH T^ DO
    IF k<>NIL THEN
      TreeError:=FALSE;
      x:=k^.t
    ELSE
      TreeError:=TRUE
    END
  END
END RetrieveTree;
```

Implementation of the operators Insert and Delete is more involved, since it depends on the setting of the current node t_k. The procedure InsertTree uses the auxiliary procedure called NewNode (not exported), which handles the details of creating a new node, assigning the value of x to it, and initializing its left and right pointers to NIL. The procedures NewNode and InsertTree are shown below.

```
PROCEDURE NewNode (VAR T: BinaryTree; VAR i: TreeIndex;
                                      x: String);
(*This procedure creates a new node for a binary tree, and
  sets its left and right children to NIL and its value t
  to x.  It is used by the InsertTree and BalanceTree
```

```
                procedures, and is not exported. *)
BEGIN
  WITH T^ DO
    NEW(i);
    i^.t:=x;
    i^.left:=NIL;
    i^.right:=NIL
  END
END NewNode;

PROCEDURE InsertTree (VAR T: BinaryTree; x: String;
                                         where: ToWhere);

VAR i: TreeIndex;
BEGIN
  TreeError:=FALSE;
  WITH T^ DO
    CASE where OF
    toroot: IF n=0 THEN
              NewNode(T,i,x);
              root:=i;
              i^.parent:=NIL;
              k:=i;
              n:=1
            ELSE
              TreeError:=TRUE
            END                    |
    toleft,toright:
        IF (k<>NIL) AND (n<Maxtree) THEN
          CASE where OF
          toleft: IF k^.left=NIL THEN
                    NewNode(T,i,x);
                    k^.left:=i;
                    i^.parent:=k;
                    k:=i;
                    n:=n+1
                  ELSE
                    TreeError:=TRUE
                  END              |
          toright:IF k^.right=NIL THEN
                    NewNode(T,i,x);
                    k^.right:=i;
                    i^.parent:=k;
                    k:=i;
                    n:=n+1
                  ELSE
                    TreeError:=TRUE
                  END
          END
```

```
            ELSE
                TreeError:=TRUE
          END
        ELSE
            TreeError:=TRUE
        END
      END
   END InsertTree;
```

The InsertTree procedure, following the specifications for Insert in the previous section, requires an available space in the tree at the location where the insertion is to be made. For instance, if an insertion is to be made at the left child of the current node, then that left child should be vacant. This vacancy is indicated by the presence of a NIL left pointer in the current node (i.e., "IF k^.left = NIL").

Reconsidering the Insert example shown in Figure 8-12, its implementation details are revealed in Figure 8-18. In this, we assume that the current node t_k is 'D' and we want to make an insertion of the new node 'X' as t_k's left child. Readers should note that we will arrive at the second CASE statement in the InsertTree procedure, and the following essential sequence of statements will be executed.

```
NewNode(T,i,x);
k^.left:=i;
i^.parent:=k;
k:=i;
n:=n+1
```

The first statement in this sequence establishes the new node for 'X' (see Figure 8-18), and the next two provide the essential linkages of the new node into the tree, as shown by the dotted lines in Figure 8-18. The last two statements in this sequence reassign this new node as the current node for T and increment the size of T.

A similar sequence of instructions is executed in the event that an insertion is made either at the right child or at the root of the tree; readers should recognize these as simple variations of the above example.

The Delete operator implementation is shown below. The first significant sequence of statements in this procedure is aimed at locating where the reattachment of the left or right child for the current node (i.e., the node to be deleted) should be made. That is, it determines whether t_k is the root, a left child, or a right child of another node.

```
PROCEDURE DeleteTree (VAR T: BinaryTree);
VAR i: TreeIndex;
    where: ToWhere;
```

245

TREES:
COMPILERS
AND
ARTIFICIAL
INTELLIGENCE

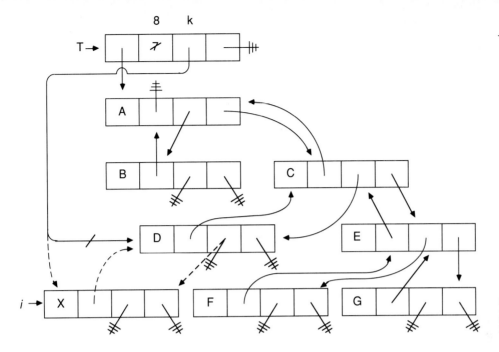

Figure 8-18
Implementation details for an insertion.

```
BEGIN
  TreeError:=FALSE;
  WITH T^ DO
    IF k<>NIL THEN
      IF k^.parent=NIL THEN      (*Locate where the attachment *)
        where:=toroot             (*should be made. Is k the*)
      ELSIF k^.parent^.left=k THEN (*root, the right
                                            child, or*)
        where:=toleft             (*the left child?*)
      ELSE
        where:=toright
      END;
      IF IsVacant(T,k,toleft) THEN (*Attach k^.parent to
                                        k^.right*)
        Attach(T,k^.parent,k^.right,where)
      ELSIF IsVacant(T,k,toright) THEN (*Attach to k^.left. *)
        Attach(T,k^.parent,k^.left,where)
      ELSE i:=k^.right;          (*Search and attach k^.parent*)
        WHILE i^.left<>NIL DO    (*to k^.right, and k^.left *)
          i:=i^.left             (*to first empty left subtree*)
        END;                     (*on k's right. *)
        Attach(T,k^.parent,k^.right,where);
        Attach(T,i,k^.left,toleft)
      END;
```

```
        n:=n-1;
        DISPOSE(k);
        k:=NIL
      ELSE
        TreeError:=TRUE
      END
    END
END DeleteTree;
```

Once that is determined, the remainder of the procedure carries out the deletion, according to the specifications given in the previous section. To aid in this task, the auxiliary procedures IsVacant and Attach perform the necessary reconnections of the relevant pointers. The procedure IsVacant is used to determine whether the left or right child of the kth node is currently "vacant;" that is, available for reattachment. For instance, the statement "IF IsVacant(T,k,toleft)..." is equivalent to saying "IF T^.k^.left = NIL...." Implementation of IsVacant is left as an exercise. Implementation of Attach is shown below.

```
PROCEDURE Attach (VAR T: BinaryTree; VAR i,j: TreeIndex;
                                     where: ToWhere);
(*This procedure reattaches node j as a left child or a
  right child of node i, or as a new root of the tree T,
  depending on the parameter "where." It is not an exported
  procedure; it is used by the procedures DeleteTree and
  BalanceTree. *)
BEGIN
  WITH T^ DO
    CASE where OF
    toroot: root:=j;
      IF j<>NIL THEN
        j^.parent:=NIL
      END
    toleft: i^.left:=j;
      IF j<>NIL THEN
        j^.parent:=i
      END
    toright: i^.right:=j;
      IF j<>NIL THEN
        j^.parent:=i
      END
    END
  END
END Attach;
```

To illustrate, reconsider the example of Figure 8-13 where the deletion of $t_k = 74$ from the binary search tree T = (46 (25 23 (39 ( ) 42))(74 (49 ( )

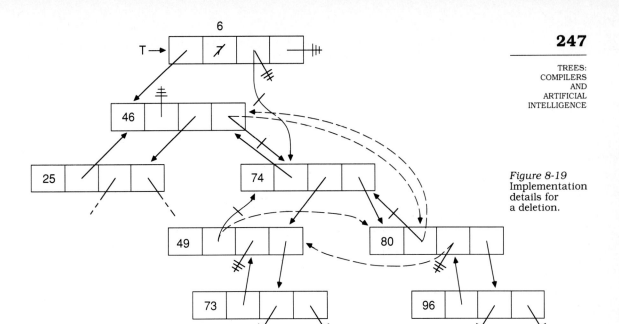

Figure 8-19
Implementation details for a deletion.

73)(80 ( ) 96))) is shown. The implementation details of that deletion appear in Figure 8-19. Here, we see that the parent of t_k is the node 46 and that 74 is the right child of 46. We also see that neither of 74's left or right subtrees is vacant and therefore two reattachments must be made. One attaches t_k's entire left subtree to the leftmost vacant left subtree of t_k's right subtree. The other attaches the root of t_k's right subtree to t_k's parent. The final actions for a deletion, of course, are to decrement the size n of the tree T and to DISPOSE the node t_k itself (leaving k undefined).

8-3-2 Tree Traversal, Inorder Search, and Binary Search

Implementation of the operator Search requires that the tree be traversed in an inorder sequence, continuing until either a match is found or the tree is fully traversed without a match. The auxiliary procedures TraverseStart and TraverseNext are defined to aid this process.

To implement a preorder, inorder, or postorder binary tree traversal algorithm requires the use of some kind of backtracking mechanism, as suggested earlier in the chapter. Backtracking is necessary because, at any point in the traversal of a binary tree, we need to keep track of "return points" as we proceed downward from the root, so that as we back up for resumption of the traversal we know where to resume. For instance, consider the inorder traversal of the tree in Figure 8-10b. Before visiting the root node (numbered 4 in the figure), we must inorder traverse the entire left subtree. Before inorder traversing the entire right subtree, we must visit the root. At the moment we initiate the inorder traversal of the left subtree, we must make a record somewhere that when that traversal is complete we should return to visit the root.

Similarly, when we proceed to perform an inorder traversal of the left subtree, we should make a record somewhere that when *its* left subtree is traversed we should return to *its* root. Thus, it makes sense to save a pointer to the root and then a pointer to the root of the left subtree as return points for backtracking. Continuing in this way, we see the need to recover the most recently saved pointer after node 2's left subtree has been completely traversed and then again to recover the most recently saved pointer after node 4's left subtree has been completely traversed. This suggests, therefore, that the record of return points for backtracking generally has the form of a stack, since the last recorded return point in the traversal process is the first to be recalled.

An algorithm for the inorder traversal of a binary tree can be sketched as follows, keeping these ideas in mind. Here, the pointer k indicates the current node in the tree, the stack of return points for backtracking is called "backtrack," and the PushAd and PopAd operators are adaptations of the Push and Pop operators (from Chapter 6), taking into account that the *type* of elements stored in the stack are now addresses (POINTERs), rather than INTEGERs.

```
k:=root;
WHILE k^.left<>NIL DO
   PushAd(backtrack,k);
   k:=k^.left
END;
WHILE k<>NIL DO
   IF k^.right<>NIL THEN
      k:=k^.right;
      WHILE k^.left<>NIL DO
         PushAd(backtrack,k);
         k:=k^.left
      END
   ELSIF AdStackSize(backtrack)=0 THEN
      k:=NIL
   ELSE
      k:=PopAd(backtrack)
   END
END
```

To illustrate, a trace of this algorithm for the binary tree in Figure 8-8a appears below, with the backtrack stack contents shown at the outset of each iteration of the second WHILE loop.

Second WHILE Loop Iteration	Backtrack Stack (left = top)	Node in Fig. 8-8a Referenced by k
1st	39 49 73	23
2nd	39 49 73	25
3rd	49 73	39
4th	49 73	42
5th	49 73	46
6th	73	49
7th	empty	73
8th	80	74
9th	empty	80
10th	empty	96
11th	empty	NIL

If we wanted to display the node values of this tree in an inorder sequence, one-by-one, the following loop and accompanying procedures named TraverseStart and TraverseNext, will be effective. TraverseStart embodies the logic of the first WHILE loop above, and TraverseNext embodies a *single* iteration of the second WHILE loop.

```
TraverseStart(T);
WHILE k<>NIL DO
   WriteString(k^.t);     (*Display the current node.*)
   WriteLn;
   TraverseNext(T)
END


PROCEDURE TraverseStart (VAR T: BinaryTree);
(*Initialize current node pointer k for an inorder
   traversal.*)
BEGIN
   TreeError:=FALSE;
   WITH T^ DO
      IF n=0 THEN
         k:=NIL;
         RETURN
      END;
      TreeStep(T,toroot);
      WHILE NOT IsVacant(T,k,toleft) DO
         PushAd(backtrack,k);
         TreeStep(T,toleft)
      END;
      RETURN
   END
END TraverseStart;
```

```
PROCEDURE TraverseNext (VAR T: BinaryTree);
VAR i: TreeIndex;
BEGIN
   TreeError:=FALSE;
   WITH T^ DO
     IF k=NIL THEN
       TreeError:=TRUE;
       RETURN
     END;
     IF NOT IsVacant(T,k,toright) THEN
       TreeStep(T,toright);
       WHILE NOT IsVacant(T,k,toleft) DO
         PushAd(backtrack,k);
         TreeStep(T,toleft)
       END
     ELSIF AdStackSize(backtrack)=0 THEN
       k:=NIL
     ELSE
       k:=PopAd(backtrack)
     END;
     RETURN
   END
END TraverseNext;
```

It may be evident that the inorder (or preorder or postorder, for that matter) traversal of a binary tree can also be accomplished in different ways than the iterative method suggested by the particular procedures TraverseStart and TraverseNext. For example, a recursive realization of the above display of node values can be written in the following way.

```
TreeStep(T,toroot);
InorderDisplay(T,k);

PROCEDURE InorderDisplay (VAR T: BinaryTree; k: TreeIndex);
BEGIN
   WHILE k<>NIL DO
     InorderDisplay(T,k^.left);
     WriteString(k^.t); WriteLn;
     InorderDisplay(T,k^.right)
   END
END InorderDisplay;
```

This variation displays the same sequence of nodes that the foregoing code displays, and evidently with a much simpler approach. That is, we have no need to establish and maintain an explicit backtrack stack, since the natural return address stack that accompanies the recursion process accomplishes the same end. A trace of InorderDisplay, using once again the tree in Figure 8-8a, will reflect the same pattern of control that was explicit in our backtrack stack from the foregoing trace.

Despite its simplicity, the recursive implementation of traversal is not always more useful than the pair of iterative operators, TraverseStart and TraverseNext. We shall use the latter approach, for instance, in implementing the tree balancing operator Balance in a later section.

Returning to the Search operator, its implementation is shown below. Its purpose is solely to reset the current node pointer k for accessing t_k in subsequent steps of an application program.

```
PROCEDURE TreeSearch (VAR T: BinaryTree; x: String);
BEGIN
  WITH T^ DO
    TreeError:=FALSE;
    TraverseStart(T);
    WHILE (k<>NIL) AND NOT EQ(x,k^.t) DO
      TraverseNext(T)
    END;
    IF k=NIL THEN
      TreeError:=TRUE
    END
  END
END TreeSearch;
```

This operator implementation is made simple by the presence of the TraverseStart and TraverseNext operators described above. Without them, this implementation of the Search operator would have been far more lengthy.

The search of a binary search tree is implemented below. It follows the specifications, especially in the case where the argument x is not anywhere in the tree. Note that this case leaves the current node t_k set at the last node visited before the absence of x in T is determined. This peculiarity is specified to facilitate the pairing of the BinarySearch operation in an application program with the Insert operation, which can immediately insert x in the tree at the exact point that would preserve T as a binary search tree.

```
PROCEDURE TreeBinarySearch (VAR T: BinaryTree; x: String);
VAR j: TreeIndex;
BEGIN
  WITH T^ DO
    TreeError:=FALSE;
    j:=NIL;                  (*j follows along behind k*)
    k:=root;
    WHILE (k<>NIL) AND NOT EQ(x,k^.t) DO
      j:=k;
      IF LT(x,k^.t) THEN
        k:=k^.left
```

```
      ELSE
        k:=k^.right
      END
    END;
    IF k=NIL THEN
      k:=j;                    (*k=last visited node*)
      TreeError:=TRUE          (*before search fails*)
    END
  END
END TreeBinarySearch;
```

As noted above, however, a series of such insertions will not necessarily maintain *balance* for T. We return to the problem of binary tree balance in a later section.

8-3-3 Graft and Prune Operator Implementations

The two operators Graft and Prune are useful in situations where an entire subtree should be attached to, or detached from, a particular tree. Their implementations are shown below.

```
PROCEDURE Graft (VAR T,U: BinaryTree; where: ToWhere);
VAR i,j: TreeIndex;
BEGIN
  TreeError:=FALSE;
  WITH T^ DO
    IF (k<>NIL) AND (n+U^.n<=Maxtree) THEN
      CASE where OF
      toleft:  IF IsVacant(T,k,toleft) THEN
                 k^.left:=U^.root;
                 n:=n+U^.n;
                 DISPOSE(U)
               ELSE
                 TreeError:=TRUE
               END                            |
      toright: IF IsVacant(T,k,toright) THEN
                 k^.right:=U^.root;
                 n:=n+U^.n;
                 DISPOSE(U)
               ELSE
                 TreeError:=TRUE
               END
    ELSE
      TreeError:=TRUE
    END
```

```
        ELSE
            TreeError:=TRUE
        END
    END
END Graft;


PROCEDURE Prune (VAR T,U: BinaryTree; where: ToWhere);
VAR i,j: TreeIndex;
BEGIN
    TreeError:=FALSE;
    WITH T^ DO
        IF k<>NIL THEN
            CreateTree(U);
            CASE where OF
            toleft:
                U^.root:=k^.left;
                k^.left:=NIL            |
            toright:
                U^.root:=k^.right;
                k^.right:=NIL
            END;
            n:=TreeSize(T);
            U^.k:=U^.root;
            U^.n:=TreeSize(U)
        ELSE
            TreeError:=TRUE
        END
    END
END Prune;
```

These implementations follow directly from the respective abstract definitions for operators Graft and Prune.

8-3-4 Building a Balanced Binary Search Tree

The operator that balances a binary search tree is more intricate to implement than the others, so we shall develop that implementation carefully in this section. To begin, consider the (unbalanced) binary search trees in Figures 8-8a and 8-8b. Either one of these, when traversed in an inorder sequence, yields an ascending sequence of integers. However, the heights of these two trees are 4 and 9, respectively, while the height of a *balanced* binary search tree with 10 nodes should be 3. The problem, then, is to take an unbalanced binary search tree, like one of these, and convert it to another binary search tree that has the same collection of node values and that is also balanced (as in Figure 8-7).

We can realize such a tree-balancing algorithm in the following way. For the original tree, suppose we visit its nodes one by one, using an inorder traversal. For each node visited, t_k, we then consider the subproblem of adding it to a new balanced tree of size k−1, in such a way that the result will be new balanced tree of size k. When this subproblem is solved (readers will recognize it as a loop invariant), then the final iteration of this process, where k = Size(T), will solve the original problem. Now let us reconsider the subproblem, for a few small values of k, wherein we make the following observations:

- For k = 1, the new tree has height 0 and node t_k is at level 0.
- For k = 2, the new tree has height 1 and node t_k is at level 0 (see Figure 8-20a).
- For k = 3, the new tree has height 1 and node t_k is at level 1 (see Figure 8-20b).
- For k = 4, the new tree has height 2 and node t_k is at level 0 (see Figure 8-20c).
- For k = 5, the new tree has height 2 and node t_k is at level 2 (see Figure 8-20d).

As we add each node t_k to the new tree with the aspiration of keeping it balanced and ordered (given that the sequence of nodes t_k is appearing in order), the height of the tree must be maintained at $\lfloor \log_2 k \rfloor$, and the level for adding node t_k can be calculated as the difference between the height

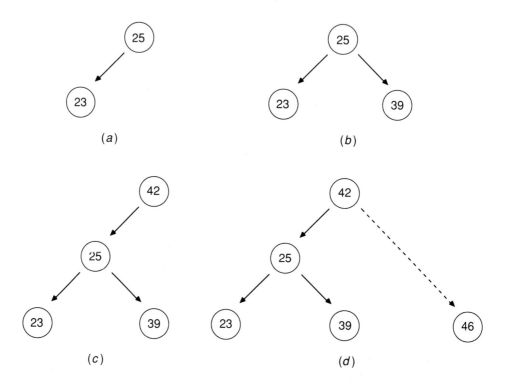

Figure 8-20
The first few balanced binary trees.

and the highest power of 2 that evenly divides k. This last assertion is a bit tricky, but a little arithmetic will convince us that it is the appropriate one. For example, consider the problem of having a 4-node balanced tree (necessarily of height 2) and adding a 5th node, as shown in Figure 8-20d. The 5th node is added at level 2, which is the difference between the new height (2) and the highest power of 2 that divides 2 (0).

This particular power of 2 is called the "age" of the node t_k in our new tree, because it characterizes the distance from the leaf to the level where the addition is to take place. For instance, the age of the 5th node is 0 (since it is a leaf), while the age of the 4th node is 2 (since it is two levels removed from the leaf level). Once the age of a node is determined, it never changes throughout the remainder of the tree-building process. The level of a node, however, may change, depending on the number of nodes that occur after that node is added to the tree.

Thus, the height of the resulting tree is guaranteed to be minimal. That the resulting tree is also ordered may be established by induction, considering the way in which each new node is attached to the partially reconstructed tree. In particular, consider the addition of t_k to a k–1 node tree and assume that the k–1 node tree is ordered. If the last node added to this tree at the next lowest age is immediately made the *left* child of the new node t_k, that node is guaranteed to be less in value than the value of t_k (by the initial ordering assumption). Moreover, if the last node added to this tree at the next higher age has no right child, then t_k also becomes the new right child of that node; again, this attachment is order-preserving. These two attachments enable the second and third attachments to be made, as shown in Figures 8-20c and 8-20b, respectively.

Sometimes, however, the last node added at the next higher age already has a right child, so that the new node cannot be immediately attached. That is, there is an "age gap" between the age of t_k and its ultimate parent. This situation is exemplified in Figure 8-20d, where the 5th node to be added (which will have age 0) cannot be attached as the right child of the most recently added node of age 1, since that node already has a right child. It is thus viewed temporarily as the right child for the node of age 2, since that node has no right child at the moment. However, if the 5th node is not the last node to be added to the tree, then the next node is guaranteed to have age 1, to be the 5th node's parent, and to be instated as the right child for the node of age 2. Thus, for the moment, it is useful to leave the 5th node temporarily unattached to any parent.

When we finish this process, we are guaranteed to have a balanced binary search tree in which all connections are made between parents and children whose ages differ by 1. However, connections will remain to be made for those parents whose ages differ from their right children by 2 or more. Finally, the root node of the new tree will typically be a different node than that of the old tree and must be relocated. That is simply done, however, since it is identical to the last node added to the new tree at the highest age. These two steps are accomplished in the auxiliary procedure RootAndReconnect, shown below.

The main procedure Balance is given first. In it, the array "last-added" keeps track of the last (rightmost) node added to the new tree at each age level, and the variable "age" denotes the age of each new node t_k as it is appended to the new tree U. Two auxiliary procedures are used by the main procedure: MaxPower (which calculates highest power of 2 that divides k, or the age of t_k) and NewNode (which creates a new node for adding t_k to the tree U). Note also that the main procedure uses the operators TraverseStart and TraverseNext to visit systematically the nodes of tree T in an inorder sequence and disconnects t_k from T after its value is added to U. Thus, the tree T is empty at the end of the loop in this procedure. The remaining steps reconnect the fragments of U, relocate its root, and reassign the entire tree U to T.

```
PROCEDURE Balance (VAR T: BinaryTree);
CONST agemax = 20;
VAR U: BinaryTree;
    m,age: INTEGER;  (*age is the "age" of a new node to be
                        added to U, measured in its distance
                        from a leaf; it is the opposite of
                        the node's height.  A leaf has age 0,
                        its parent has age 1, and so forth. *)
    i,j: TreeIndex;
    lastadded: ARRAY[-1..agemax] OF TreeIndex;
                     (*lastadded is an array used to keep
                        track of the last (rightmost) node
                        added to U at each age level. *)

BEGIN
  TreeError:=FALSE;
  WITH T^ DO
    IF IsOrdered(T) AND (Log2(n)<agemax) THEN
      FOR m:=-1 TO agemax DO
        lastadded[m]:=NIL
      END;
      m:=0;
      CreateTree(U);
      TraverseStart(T);
      WHILE k<>NIL DO
        m:=m+1;
        age:=MaxPower(2,m);
        NewNode(U,i,k^.t);
        i^.right:=NIL;
        i^.left:=lastadded[age-1];
        IF lastadded[age-1]<>NIL THEN
          lastadded[age-1]^.parent:=i
        END;
```

```
            lastadded[age]:=i;
            IF lastadded[age+1]<>NIL THEN
               IF lastadded[age+1]^.right=NIL THEN
                  lastadded[age+1]^.right:=i;
                  i^.parent:=lastadded[age+1]
               END
            END;
            TraverseNext(T)
         END;
         U^.n:=m;                    (*Establish the size of U.*)
                                     (*find U's new root, re-*)
         RootAndReconnect;           (*connect its partial*)
         DestroyTree(T);             (*trees, get rid of T,*)
         T:=U                        (*and rename U.*)
      ELSE
         TreeError:=TRUE
      END
   END
END Balance;
```

The RootAndReconnect procedure appears below. This procedure is assumed to be internal to the Balance procedure, so that it can access the common variables and arrays that are declared locally.

```
PROCEDURE RootAndReconnect;
(*At the end of the process of creating U, this procedure
  finds U's root and reconnects any fragments that are left
  by the process.*)
BEGIN
   WITH U^ DO
      age:=agemax;
      WHILE (lastadded[age]=NIL) AND (age>1) DO
         age:=age-1
      END;
      root:=lastadded[age];
      root^.parent:=NIL;
      IF age=1 THEN                  (*0- or 1-node tree*)
         RETURN
      ELSE
         WHILE age>1 DO
            IF lastadded[age]^.right<>NIL THEN
               age:=age-1
            ELSE
               i:=lastadded[age]^.left;
               m:=age-1;
```

```
            REPEAT
                i:=i^.right;
                m:=m-1
            UNTIL (i=NIL) OR (i<>lastadded[m]);
            lastadded[age]^.right:=lastadded[m];
            lastadded[m]^.parent:=lastadded[age];
            age:=m
          END
        END;
        RETURN
      END
    END
END RootAndReconnect;
```

8-3-5 Verification and Complexity of Operator Implementations

Looking back at the binary tree operators, we observe that some operator definitions are more elaborate than their corresponding implementations (Delete, for instance), while others are less elaborate (Balance, for instance). Verification of these operator implementations is more difficult in either case, since there is no obvious symmetry between the individual parts of an operator's postconditions and the individual parts of the corresponding procedure implementation. Such symmetry was much more apparent and useful in the verification of linear data types in the foregoing chapters.

Nevertheless, let's look at the problem of informal verification in the case of the Delete operator. Its postconditions separate into three cases, for an arbitrary tree T and current node t_k:

(i) t_k has an empty left subtree.
(ii) t_k has a nonempty left subtree and an empty right subtree.
(iii) t_k has nonempty left and right subtrees.

In all three cases, t_k must be deleted, and its left and right subtrees (if they exist) must be reattached to the tree in place of t_k in the manner described by the postconditions for Delete. A further detail is added to this problem by the need to distinguish between the case where t_k is the root of T and the case where it is not the root.

To aid the DeleteTree procedure, we have the auxiliary procedure Attach(T,i,j,where). This procedure reattaches a subtree with root j as either the left or right child of node i in T, or at the root of T, depending on the value of "where." We assume in this verification exercise that Attach correctly performs that task.

Turning to the DeleteTree procedure, we reproduce below its body with preconditions, postconditions, line numbers, and certain additional assertions added to distinguish each of the three cases described above.

```
     BEGIN
     (**PRE: T exists and t[k] exists.                     **)
1      TreeError:=FALSE;
2      WITH T^ DO
3        IF k<>NIL THEN
4          IF k^.parent=NIL THEN
5            where:=toroot
6          ELSIF k^.parent^.left=k THEN
7            where:=toleft
8          ELSE
9            where:=toright
10         END;
11         IF IsVacant(T,k,toleft) THEN
12           Attach(T,k^.parent,k^.right,where)
     (** (i) T=(...(t[k] () V)...) and T'=(...(V)...)      **)
13         ELSIF IsVacant(T,k,toright) THEN
14           Attach(T,k^.parent,k^.left,where)
     (** (ii) T=(...(t[k] U ())...) and T'=(...(U)...)     **)
15         ELSE i:=k^.right;
16           WHILE i^.left<>NIL DO
17             i:=i^.left
18           END;
19           Attach(T,k^.parent,k^.right,where);
20           Attach(T,i,k^.left,toleft)
     (** (iii) T=(...(t[k] U V)...) and T'=(...(V U)...)   **)
21         END;
22         n:=n-1;
23         DISPOSE(k);
24         k:=NIL
25       ELSE
26         TreeError:=TRUE
27       END
28     END
     (**POST: t[k] is deleted from T, n'=n-1, and t[k]'
              is undefined. **)
     END DeleteTree;
```

When execution reaches line 10 in this procedure, the determination of whether t_k is the root, a left child, or a right child has been made. The three cases are thereafter distinguished by line groups 11-12, 13-14, and 15-20, respectively. The three assertions placed at the end of each group describe the kind of reattachment that is made to form T' out of T. The first two cases are self-explanatory. The third requires a loop to locate the first vacant left child in t_k's right subtree, in order to reattach t_k's left subtree properly. Finally, lines 22 and 23 guarantee satisfaction of postconditions $n'=n-1$ and $t_{k'}$ is undefined, respectively.

The complexity of each BinaryTree operator is easily determined by reviewing the code of its implementation and asking whether, in each case, a traversal of the tree is needed for the operator to satisfy its postconditions. If not, the operator's complexity is O(c) — that is the case for our implementations of the operators Create, Step, Store, Retrieve, Insert, Delete, Graft, Prune, and Size. In many of these cases, O(c) complexity is enabled because their implementation relies on the presence of a current node t_k.

The complexity of most remaining operators is O(n), where n is the size of the tree, since their implementations require a traversal. This is the case for Search, Balance, Display, and Dump.

The complexities of Depth and Height are a bit tricky to determine. If we assume the tree is balanced, the depth of each leaf node can be computed in $O(\log_2 n)$ complexity (that is the maximum depth of recursion in our implementation of the Depth operator). For each node in the traversal found in our implementation of Height, its depth is computed and checked against the maximum depth determined so far. Thus, the complexity of our Height implementation is $O(n \log_2 n)$, in the case where the tree is balanced.

Finally, the complexity of our BinarySearch implementation is also $O(\log_2 n)$, also under the assumption that the tree is balanced.

8-4 AN OVERVIEW OF COMPILERS

A *compiler* is a very special sort of computer program, often written (either partially or fully) in a language like Modula-2, which has as its sole task the translation of programs from a "high-level language" (like Modula-2 again) into a "machine-level language" (like the machine languages introduced in Chapter 2). A functional diagram of a compiler is shown in Figure 8-21. As we can see, a compiler processes the text of a Modula-2 program in four

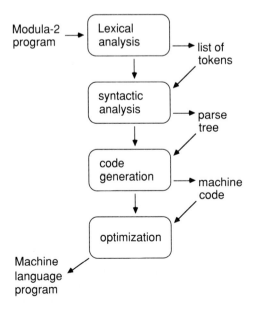

Figure 8-21
Overview of a compiler.

major stages, called lexical analysis, syntactic analysis, code generation, and optimization. Many compilers have more stages (in fact, the PL/I Optimizing Compiler developed by IBM has over fifty separate stages), but these four are the essential ones.

The task of the lexical analysis stage is to transform the text of a program into a list of lexical "tokens" (identifiers, constants, operators, reserved words, delimiters, and so forth) from its original form, which is essentially a character string. This transformation often results in the generation of a so-called "symbol table," which is a list of all identifiers defined in the program and their associated types. For example, Figure 8-22 shows a simple Modula-2 program, and Figure 8-23 shows the result of lexical analysis on that program.

Syntactic analysis, sometimes called "parsing," takes this list and transforms it into a structural description of the program, called a "parse tree." This tree is generated under the guidance of the formal syntactic description of Modula-2, such as the BNF syntax given in Appendix C. An abbreviated portion of the parse tree for the program in Figure 8-22 is shown in Figure 8-24, using a pidgin version of the Modula-2 syntax from Appendix C.

The code generation phase of a compiler traverses the parse tree and generates a list of machine language instructions from that traversal. The traversal method is essentially depth-first, in order that the correct sequence of machine instructions is generated. In the case of arithmetic expressions within a program's parse tree, they generally take the form of binary trees, and a postorder (LRV) traversal is appropriate for generating the machine instructions in the correct sequence. (In fact, as we have seen, the

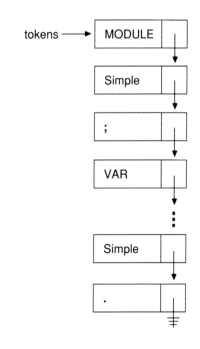

```
MODULE Simple;
VAR x,a,b : CARDINAL;
BEGIN
    a : = 2;
    b : = 3;
    x : = a + 2 ∗ b
END Simple.
```

Figure 8-22
Simple program input to a compiler.

Figure 8-23
Result of lexical analysis for that program.

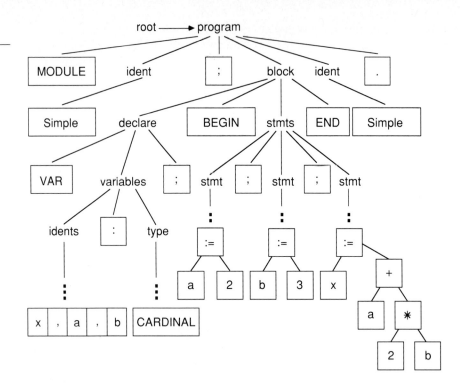

Figure 8-24
Abbreviated parse tree for that program.

postorder traversal strategy for binary trees is just a special case of the depth-first search strategy for general trees.) An illustration of code generation for a portion of this sample parse tree is shown in Figure 8-25.

The optimization phase of a compiler is an optional phase, and its purpose is to improve the run-time efficiency of the code generated by the previous phase (while maintaining the semantic integrity of the code with respect to the intentions of the original Modula-2 program). For instance, most code generators are equipped with heuristic procedures for finding redundant subexpressions within an arithmetic expression, such as (a + b) in the following:

```
x:=(a+b)*c+(a+b)*d
```

Once found, the generated code for this expression is replaced by code that mirrors a more efficient equivalent program, such as the following:

```
temp:=a+b;
x:=temp*(c+d)
```

This alternative is superior to the original, since it involves only one multiplication and two additions, rather than the original two multiplications

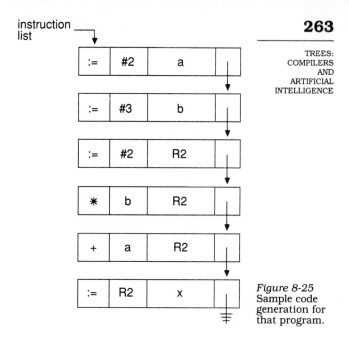

Figure 8-25
Sample code generation for that program.

and three additions. If such a statement had been placed within a loop that executed, say, thousands of times each day, the savings yielded by such an optimization step would be significant.

8-4-1 Problem 5:
Parsing Arithmetic Expressions

Although it is not practical here for us to pursue the implementation of even a small compiler in its entirety, that particular "slice" of a compiler's syntactic analysis phase that produces a parse tree from an arithmetic expression does serve as a healthy application of the binary tree abstract data type. Therefore, our goal in this problem will be to develop a program that takes an arithmetic expression like the one given in the sample program of Figure 8-22 and perform the equivalent of lexical and syntactic analysis, generating a parse tree like the one shown in Figure 8-24. The output of the program will be a binary tree for the expression, displayed in standard parenthesized notation.

This exercise is also valuable because it combines the implementations of several different abstract data types—BinaryTrees, Strings, Lists, and Stacks—in designing a robust solution to a rather difficult problem.

For the purposes of this problem, we assume that an arithmetic expression is a series of strings, each representing either an identifier, a number, an operator (as defined by the type LexClass from Chapter 7), or a left or right parenthesis, and separated from each other by one or more blanks. These strings must occur in such a way that they satisfy the following syntax:

```
arithmeticexpression ::= term { + term | - term }
term ::= factor { * factor | / factor }
factor ::= ident | number |
           ( arithmeticexpression ) |
           ident ^ factor | number ^ factor |
           ( arithmeticexpression ) ^ factor
```

This syntax, the reader will notice, forms a subset of the general syntax for Modula-2's "simple expression" (see Appendix C), except that Modula-2 has no operator for exponentiation (^).

Examples of arithmetic expressions appear throughout the text. Our strategy for parsing arithmetic expressions is derived from the more general technique called "precedence parsing," which was developed in the 1960s when compiler design was in its infancy. This particular method is still widely used in compilers, and also has particularly strong intuitive appeal.

The idea behind precedence parsing is that when one scans an arbitrary arithmetic expression from left to right, certain relationships should be preserved in the resulting parse tree for that expression. First, the operands (identifiers and numbers) that appear in the expression form the leaves of the resulting parse tree, and their left-to-right order is preserved. This is shown, for instance, in the parse trees of Figure 8-6. Second, the operators in the expression always appear as the nonleaf nodes, and their positions in the tree reflect the order in which they will be applied to their operands (using a postorder traversal for execution), rather than their textual order of appearance in the original expression. For instance, the expression a+2*(b-c) contains the operators +, *, and - in that order; yet, the corresponding parse tree contains these operators in a different (postorder traversal) order, in which - appears first, followed by *, and finally followed by +.

For this reason, a left-to-right scan of the original expression can be designed in such a way that the operands are converted into a list of single-leaf trees, immediately as they are encountered. But when we encounter an operator during such a scan, we cannot determine its structural position in the resulting parse tree until we have examined the next operator to its right and compared the precedences of the two. Consider, for example, the two expressions a+2+b and a+2*b. In the first expression, the operands a and 2 are joined directly in the tree by the operator + as their parent, because the precedence of the next operator in the expression (also +) is not greater than that of the first +. In the second expression, the operands a and 2 cannot be joined directly by + as their parent because the second operator (*) has higher precedence than +. Instead, 2 and b are joined by * as their parent, and this subtree ultimately becomes the right child of the parent + in the final tree for the expression a+2*b. These two situations are distinguished in Figure 8-26.

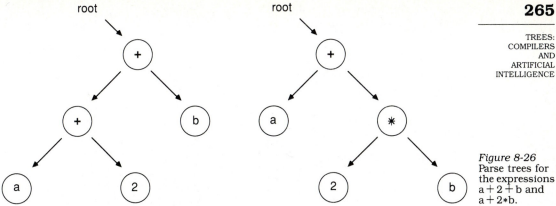

Figure 8-26
Parse trees for the expressions a+2+b and a+2*b.

An additional consideration must be made in a left-to-right scan when we encounter a parenthesized (sub)expression as an operand. The parse of the expression enclosed within the parentheses must also take precedence over the currently scanned operator, in the sense that all operations embedded between the left and right parentheses must be attached to the parse tree in such a way that they are executed *before* that operator.

These two considerations suggest that we have two supporting data structures in the formation of a parse tree for an arithmetic expression: a stack for holding operators and left parentheses, and a list for holding single-leaf trees for each of the operands as well as partially constructed subtrees as primary operations in the parse are discovered. In the following program, this stack is called "operators," and this list of trees is called "parsetrees."

The algorithm proceeds as follows: the expression is scanned from left to right, one token (operand, operator, left parenthesis, or right parenthesis) at a time. If the token is an operand, it is immediately converted into a single-leaf tree and added to the parsetrees list. This is shown for the first token, a, in the expression a+2*b in Figure 8-27a. If, on the other hand, the token is an operator, its priority is compared with that of the top operator on the stack (if there are any). If the topmost operator (called "top-token" below) has lower priority than the current token (or if the stack is empty or the current token is a left parenthesis), then the current token is pushed onto the stack. This is the case when the token + is encountered in the expression a+2*b (Figure 8-27b) and again when the * is encountered (Figure 8-27c).

If the topmost operator in the stack has equal or higher priority, then it is popped from the stack and combined with the two most recently added trees in the list to form a new tree in the list in their place. This would occur, for example, in the expression a*2+b when the token + is encountered, causing the * to be popped from the stack and combined with the two trees (a) and (2) forming the new tree (* a 2).

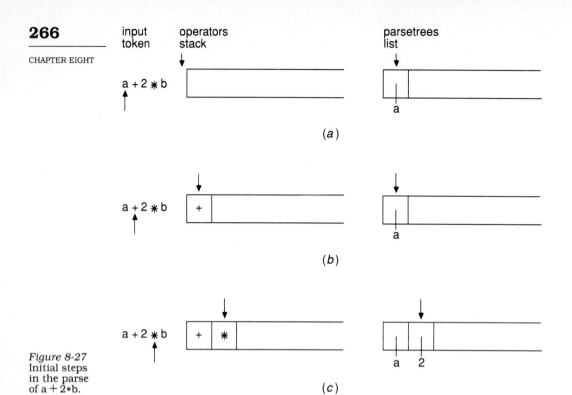

Figure 8-27 Initial steps in the parse of a + 2*b.

Finally, encountering a right parenthesis in an expression (or the end of the expression itself) causes the stack to be emptied, one operator at a time, with each operator combined with the rightmost two parse trees in the output list to form a new parse tree. This emptying process is stopped by the next occurrence of a left parenthesis (denoting completion of the parse for a parenthesized subexpression) or the bottom of the stack, respectively.

The entire program is shown below. It includes three auxiliary procedures called WriteError (to display an error message), Priority (to compute the priorities of the operators +, −, *, /, and ^ as 0, 0, 1, 1, and 2, respectively), and CombineTrees (to combine an operator with two trees as its left and right children, forming a new tree in their place).

```
MODULE ExpressionParser;

FROM Trees    IMPORT BinaryTree, String, TreeIndex, TreeError,
                     ToWhere, CreateTree, DestroyTree,
                     StoreTree, TreeStep, InsertTree, Graft,
                     Prune, DisplayTree;
FROM TrLists IMPORT TrList, TrListIndex, TrListError,
                     CreateTrList, InsertTr, DeleteTr;
FROM StStacks IMPORT StStack, StStackIndex, StStackError,
                     CreateStStack, PushSt, PopSt;
```

```
FROM Strings IMPORT StringError, LexClass, ReadLex, Eof,
                    ClassifyLex, EQ;
FROM InOut   IMPORT WriteString, WriteLn;

VAR token,toptoken: String;        (*String type*)
    operators: StStack;            (*Stack of Strings*)
    parsetrees: TrList;            (*List of BinaryTrees*)
    T: BinaryTree;                 (*Tree of Strings*)

PROCEDURE WriteError;
BEGIN
  WriteString('Syntax Error: processing stops.'); HALT
END WriteError;

PROCEDURE Priority (operator: ARRAY OF CHAR): CARDINAL;
BEGIN
  CASE operator[0] OF
    '+','-': RETURN 0          |
    '*','/': RETURN 1          |
    '^'    : RETURN 2
  ELSE
    WriteError
  END
END Priority;

PROCEDURE CombineTrees;
  (*Form a new tree T with toptoken as its root,
    parsetrees[2] and parsetrees[1] as its left and right
    subtrees, respectively. Replace parsetrees[2] by this
    new tree and delete parsetrees[1]. *)
VAR t: BinaryTree;
BEGIN
  CreateTree(T);
  InsertTree(T,toptoken,toroot);
  DeleteTr (parsetrees,1,t);
  Graft(T,t,toleft);
  TreeStep(T,toroot);
  DeleteTr(parsetrees,0,t);
  Graft(T,t,toright);
  InsertTr(parsetrees,0,T);
END CombineTrees;

BEGIN
  CreateStStack (operators);
  CreateTrList (parsetrees);
  PushSt (operators,'$$');    (* Stack bottom marker.   *)
  WriteString ('Enter an arithmetic expression, '); WriteLn;
  WriteString ('with tokens separated by spaces:'); WriteLn;
```

```
ReadLex (token);
WHILE NOT Eof DO
   CASE ClassifyLex(token) OF
   number,identifier:
      CreateTree(T);
      InsertTree(T,token,toroot);
      InsertTr(parsetrees,0,T)            |
   operator:
      PopSt(operators,toptoken);
      LOOP
         IF EQ(toptoken,'$$') THEN
            PushSt(operators,toptoken);
            EXIT
         ELSIF EQ(toptoken,'(') THEN
            PushSt(operators,toptoken);
            EXIT
         ELSIF Priority(toptoken)<Priority(token) THEN
            PushSt(operators,toptoken);
            EXIT
         ELSE
            CombineTrees;
            PopSt(operators,toptoken)
         END
      END;
      PushSt(operators,token)             |
   other:
      IF EQ(token,'(') THEN
         PushSt(operators,token)
      ELSIF EQ(token,')') THEN
         PopSt(operators,toptoken);
         WHILE NOT EQ(toptoken,'(') DO
            CombineTrees;
            PopSt(operators,toptoken)
         END
      ELSE
         WriteError
      END
   END;
   ReadLex (token)
END;


PopSt(operators,toptoken);
WHILE NOT EQ(toptoken,'$$') DO
   CombineTrees;
   PopSt(operators,toptoken)
END;
```

```
DeleteTr(parsetrees,0,T);
WriteString('Parsetree=');
DisplayTree(T)

END ExpressionParser.
```

To illustrate the activity of this program, a trace of the operators stack and the output list of parse trees is shown in Figure 8-28, for certain key steps in the expression $((a+b)^2-c^2)/(2*a)$.

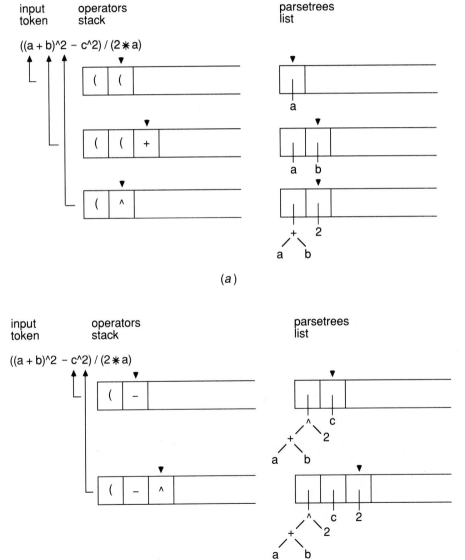

Figure 8-28 Steps in the parse of $((a+b)^2 - c^2)/(2*a)$.

A careful reading of the IMPORT lists for this program reveals that most of our abstract data type implementations from previous chapters—Lists, Strings, Stacks, and Trees—are needed in the solution of this program, but with two slight variations. First, the basic element type for the list in this problem is tree (that is, we are dealing here with a list of trees) rather than INTEGER, as was the case in Chapters 3 and 4 where Lists were originally implemented. Second, the basic element type for the stack in this problem is string rather than INTEGER, as was the case in Chapter 6 where Stacks were originally implemented.

Thus, we have implemented simple variations called TrLists (for Lists of Trees) and StStacks (for Stacks of Strings) and added affixes to the names of their respective operators (e.g., StoreTr and RetrieveTr instead of Store and Retrieve), in keeping with the Modula-2 spirit of strong typing. Realization of these implementations is straightforward and will not be belabored here.[2]

8-5 SOFTWARE ENGINEERING AND OBJECT-ORIENTED DESIGN

The program in the foregoing section provides a good example of how the effective use of tools can help us avoid reimplementing common data structures and utility functions when solving a complex problem. Knowing when a stack, tree, or linear list is appropriate for solving a problem is often a matter of style and judgment gained from experience with other related problems. Once their usefulness is determined, however, the ability to exploit appropriate modules containing their implementations should become second nature for the serious programmer. The practice of designing and implementing effective solutions to complex software problems is called "software engineering". An important element of software engineering is the mastery of tools (data abstractions such as stacks, lists, strings, and their operators) and their effective use in problem solving.

The entire process of realizing an engineered software solution to an application problem is called the "software life cycle," and contains the following general steps:[3]

1. *Needs analysis* determines the set of requirements that the software should fulfill (i.e., the application is defined).

---

[2]Alternatively, we could have implemented the Lists and Stacks abstract data types more generically at the outset and avoided this penultimate problem in the long run. Yet, such an effort would have been significantly distractive to the main themes of this course and excessive of the design goals of Modula-2 itself.

[3]This presentation of software engineering is necessarily cursory. A more thorough introduction to the subject can be found in various texts, including Weiner and Sincovec's *Software Engineering with Ada and Modula-2* (John Wiley & Sons, 1984), and Booch's *Software Engineering with Ada*, (Benjamin Cummings, 1983).

2. *Specifications* are formally drawn for all of the input, output, and functional processes that will be embodied by the software.
3. *Design* takes place, in which the major data types and operators (i.e., data abstractions) are identified, along with the major functional modules of the solution, their interfaces, and their individual functional requirements.
4. *Implementation*, or programming, of these modules in a programming language (such as Modula-2) then takes place.
5. *Installation and testing* of the resulting programs verifies their correctness and adequacy for meeting the original specifications that were derived in step 2.
6. *Maintenance* of the programs, after they have been placed into productive use, involves the regular evaluation of their performance and adequacy, the location and correction of occasional errors, and the modification of the programs as minor changes in the application take place.

An important element of software engineering, therefore, is the art of design itself. That is, considering the parser of the foregoing section, it is one thing to implement a correct program that parses arithmetic expressions, but it is quite another to design the solution that leads to the implementation of the program in the first place. This text is not as fundamentally concerned with the design of solutions as it is with the understanding and effective use of basic tools (abstract data types, effective programming techniques, and effective verification techniques) in the implementation of predesigned solutions. Such fundamental concern with design is elaborated in several later courses in the computer science curriculum, such as the compiler course, the software engineering course, the database course, or the systems analysis and design course.

Yet, a certain design technique inevitably emerges as we continue through this presentation. That is, as the book progresses, we tend to tackle increasingly complex problems, building upon our experience with relatively easier problems in the earlier chapters. To solve these complex problems, we initially rely on "assimilation," which is simply identifying the problem at hand as a variant of some other related problem that we have recently seen solved. Such is the case, for instance, in the Team Project at the end of this chapter; the reader should see that this is a variant of the arithmetic expression parsing problem solved in the foregoing section, and therefore should use many of the same techniques in the solution of the regular expression parsing problem.

This design technique is sometimes called "object-oriented design" and is a relatively newer concept than its more widely known predecessors: top-down design and bottom-up design. (Top-down design methodology is based on the premise that arriving at a solution to a problem is a hierarchical process, in which each stage in the hierarchy represents an elaboration of a set of relatively general specifications into sets of relatively more detailed specifications. Bottom-up design, on the other hand, begins with the most detailed parts of a solution and works upward in the hierarchy to increasingly more general levels of design, until the top of the hierarchy is reached. It is, virtually, the opposite of top-down design in its development of the problem solution.)

Object-oriented design represents a kind of middle ground between these two positions. It relies on the preexistence of powerful sets of tools (data objects and their operators, or data abstractions) in libraries, such as stacks and strings, and begins by asking the question: "Which of these objects are most appropriate to the solution of the problem at hand, and how are they to be used?" Thus, a substantial part of the older bottom-up design process can be bypassed. Once the appropriate objects and operators are identified, then the rest of the design proceeds in a relatively top-down fashion. When this design methodology is properly used, substantial gains in software reliability and productivity can be realized.

8-5-1 Import-Export Trees

A useful tool in the object-oriented design process is what we will call the "import-export tree." This is simply a tree-structured diagram representing the data types and operators that are imported and exported by each module that participates in the solution to a problem, with the main program module serving as the root of the tree. For example, the import-export tree representation of the NaiveInstructor program in Chapter 1 of this text is shown in Figure 8-29.

Here, the notation is nearly self-explanatory. The name at the top corner of each oval identifies a module from/to which individual data types and procedures are exported/imported. The names inside each oval identify the types and procedures themselves, together with their nature ("ty," "pr," or "gl" denoting type, procedure, or global variable, respectively). The direction of the arrows distinguishes between imported and exported entities. Thus, for instance, the diagram of Figure 8-29 tells us that the main program NaiveInstructor imports the procedures WriteString and WriteLn from module InOut, the global variable Done from module InOut, the global type score from the module NaiveLib, and the procedures GetScores and ShowAverage from the module NaiveLib.

A more elaborate example appears in Figure 8-30, which is a partial import-export tree for our solution to the arithmetic expression parser problem in the foregoing section.

8-6 AN OVERVIEW OF ARTIFICIAL INTELLIGENCE

The field of *artificial intelligence* (AI) is a research area of computer science that aims to use computers to simulate various aspects of intelligent behavior. These aspects include deductive reasoning, vision, natural language understanding, speech, and various associated mechanical, or robotic, activities that are associated with such behavior.

273

TREES:
COMPILERS
AND
ARTIFICIAL
INTELLIGENCE

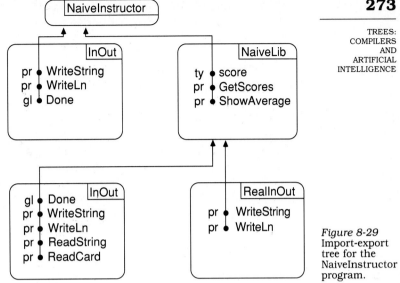

Figure 8-29 Import-export tree for the NaiveInstructor program.

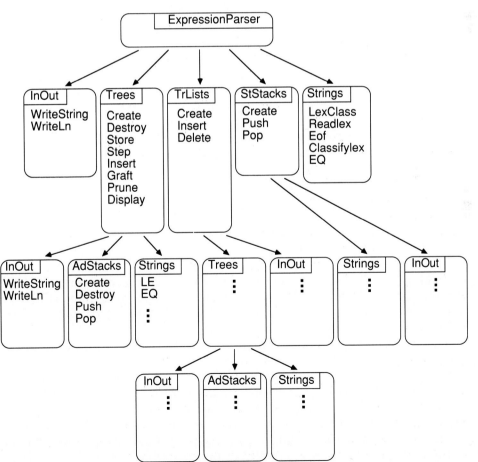

Figure 8-30 Import-export tree for the Expression-Parser program.

For instance, the discipline and knowledge required by a medical diagnostician who identifies possible diseases from a given set of symptoms can, in a limited way, be simulated by a computer. Early AI experiments of this sort were called MYCIN and R1. This class of simulation is called an "expert system" and is one of the more active AI research and development areas today. Other areas of expert systems applications appear as aids in the configuration of computer systems from component parts to meet different customers' specifications.

Another area of AI research is that of natural language understanding. Here, the goal is to develop sufficient linguistic and world knowledge (of a situational sort) to be able to simulate "machine understanding" of the content of the story being told by a narrative text. Examples can be found in early research projects done by Terry Winograd and by Yorick Wilks. These examples helped AI researchers to appreciate the complexity of the whole area of natural language understanding by machine.

An AI area that also shows promise of practical results is that known as computer vision: the analysis of photographic and x-ray images with the aim of understanding the nature of the object(s) in the image, in the same way that a person understands what he or she sees. Applications of this research have brought results in the field of medical diagnosis and satellite photo analysis. Ideally, of course, computer vision should simulate the activity of the human eye, operating in real time and transmitting to the "brain" an interpretation of the scene in the field of vision. That capability, however, is a long way from realization.

One of the early applications of AI was that of automatic theorem proving. That is, given an assertion and a set of axioms and theorems, write a program that either proves the assertion or proves that it is not a theorem. Certain subclasses of this problem have been solved. A classical example of a software system that supports the development of certain kinds of theorem-proving programs is called MACSYMA. It is particularly useful in the area of solving systems of linear and nonlinear equations algebraically.

In all of these AI areas, as well as the areas of knowledge acquisition, computer learning, and robotics, researchers must confront the problems of *combinatorial explosion* of alternatives and *search*. That is, the number of feasible alternatives that must be considered, or evaluated, in the process of making a single logical deduction (such as choosing the next move in a chess game) is typically immense. These alternatives are usually stored in a more general data structure called a "network." But sometimes they have the simpler hierarchical structure of a tree.

When the number of nodes in a tree is large—say, tens or hundreds of thousands—the efficiency of traversal has immediate impact on the process of finding feasible solutions to these problems. This problem is characterized in AI research as the problem of search. The choice of search strategies varies from one application to another and often involves the intelligent "skipping" of entire subtrees (as in the binary search) as a practical method for avoiding the overhead that accompanies an "exhaustive" search of the entire tree (as in breadth-first or depth-first search).

8-6-1 Trees and LISP Expressions

The predominant programming language in AI research is LISP. Its style of programming is called "functional programming," and its syntax and basic data types are fundamentally different from those of Modula-2. LISP is, however, eminently well suited for the manipulation of symbols and symbolic expressions.

The basic building block for LISP programming—both its programs and its data—is called the "expression." The LISP expression bears no resemblance to the arithmetic expressions of Modula-2, but it has an exact resemblance to the linear (parenthesized) representation of the tree. A LISP program is always written as this sort of expression, and so is its input and output data. This fundamental simplicity, combined with a powerful set of standard functions for manipulating data structures (that is, trees), makes LISP an especially elegant language for AI programming.

Although it is not our purpose to teach LISP in this text (for an excellent treatment of LISP with data structures, see Abelson and Sussman's *Structure and Interpretation of Computer Programs,* MIT Press, 1985), we illustrate briefly how LISP programs have a fundamental structural correspondence with trees. To do this, let's consider the Modula-2 averaging program which appears at the beginning of Appendix A, and compare it with the following equivalent LISP program:

```
(defun average ()
   (princ 'enter the list of numbers to be averaged')
   (setq x (read))
   (setq av (/ (apply '+ x) (length x)))
   (princ 'their average = ')
   (print av)
)
```

Here, the first line of the program serves to name the program as a defined function, via the command "defun." The second and fifth lines are commands to display a literal message on the terminal, while the sixth line displays the computed average itself. The third line performs the input of a list and assigns it to the variable x, and the fourth line computes the average "av" as the quotient of the sum of x's values (apply '+ x) and the number of values in the list x (length x). The operator "setq" in each of these two lines is the LISP assignment operator (equivalent to the operator ":=" in Modula-2).

Thus, a typical execution of this program will show the following dialogue:

```
enter the list of numbers to be averaged
(89 91 93 95)
their average = 92
```

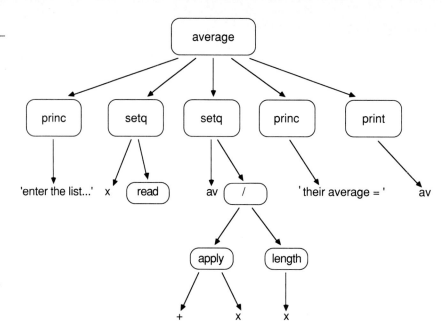

Figure 8-31
Tree representation of the LISP function "average."

To emphasize the point that LISP programs correspond structurally with trees, Figure 8-31 shows the tree representation of the LISP function "average."

This brief example illustrates the simple tree structure of LISP programs, even though it does not reveal the power and utility of the language in dealing with symbol manipulation problems, which is its natural domain. A thorough appreciation of that can be gained by browsing through an introductory text on artificial intelligence or LISP, such as the one mentioned above.

EXERCISES

8-1. For each of the three trees in Figure 8-32 below, identify its root, its subtrees, all of its paths and their lengths, and its height. Give the linear (parenthesized) representation for each of these trees. Which, if any, are binary trees?

8-2. For each of the trees in Figure 8-32, give a depth-first traversal. Now give a breadth-first traversal for each.

8-3. For the tree in Figure 8-7, give a preorder traversal, an inorder traversal, and a postorder traversal of its nodes.

8-4. Show the sequence of nodes visited for a binary search of the tree in Figure 8-7, for $x=25$. Do the same for $x=99$ and again for $x=46$.

8-5. Show the resulting tree after each of the following operators is applied to the binary tree $T=(A\ B\ (C\ D\ (E\ F\ G)))$:

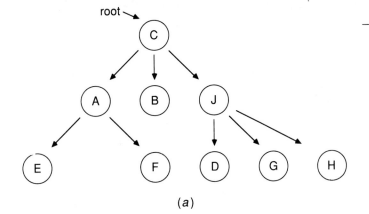

(a)

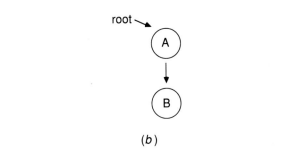

(b)

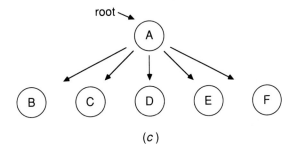

(c)

Figure 8-32
Three trees.

(a) Insert(T,'X',toleft), with t_k = 'F'.
(b) Delete(T), with t_k = 'F'.
(c) Insert(T,'X',toright), with t_k = 'B'.

8-6. What is the only case in which Insert(T,x,toroot) will not give an error, for arbitrary tree T and element x?

8-7. Implement the procedure IsVacant(T,i,where), which is invoked by the operator implementations DeleteTree, Graft, and others. That is, for a tree T, index i, and where = toleft or toright, IsVacant should return TRUE if the left or right child, accordingly, in node i is NIL. If that child is not NIL, then FALSE should be returned. If i is NIL, then TreeError should be set to TRUE. Once this procedure is implemented, give appropriate preconditions and postconditions for the corresponding abstract operator IsVacant.

8-8. Give nonrecursive procedures that will perform a preorder traversal of a binary tree in the same style as the procedures TraverseStart and TraverseNext. Trace their behavior by showing the sequence of values for k (the current node pointer) and the backtrack stack contents as the binary tree in Figure 8-7 is traversed in preorder sequence.

8-9. Complete the implementation of binary trees by defining, verifying, and compiling procedures for the operators TreeSize, Depth, Height, DisplayTree, and DumpTree in accordance with their respective specifications.

8-10. Implement the procedure MaxPower(i,j), whose purpose is to compute the highest power of i that evenly divides j. Assume that i, j, and the result are CARDINAL values.

8-11. The Balance procedure uses an auxiliary procedure IsOrdered, which determines whether or not a binary tree T is a binary search tree, that is, whether its nodes are in ascending sequence during an inorder traversal. Implement the procedure IsOrdered and give appropriate preconditions and postconditions for it.

8-12. Define and implement the operator IsBalanced, which determines whether an arbitrary binary tree is balanced. What is the complexity of your implementation? Explain.

8-13. The Balance procedure, which creates a balanced binary search tree U, is defined on the assumption that the original tree T is already ordered, but not necessarily balanced. What if we needed to create a balanced binary search tree from a tree T that was neither ordered nor balanced? What tree and list operators would be needed, and how could this be accomplished?

8-14. Using the procedure IsVacant, implement procedures to determine each of the following characteristics for the current node of a binary tree T:
 (a) IsLeaf(T) determines whether the current node is a leaf.
 (b) IsNonLeaf(T) determines whether the current node is a nonleaf.
 (c) IsRoot(T) determines whether the current node is the root.

8-15. Trace execution of the program ExpressionParser by showing the sequence of values in the stack and output list of trees when it is applied to each of the following input expressions:
 (a) a + b * c / d * e − f
 (b) a * (b + c * (d + e * f))
 (c) a * b − c * d − e * f

8-16. Give a complete import-export tree for the program TextSearch in Chapter 7 and another for the program EvaluatePolish in Chapter 6.

TEAM PROJECT: PARSING REGULAR EXPRESSIONS

In the style of the arithmetic expression parser, you are asked in this project to design and implement a regular expression parser. Assume that regular expressions are that class of expressions defined in Chapter 7, except for the constraints listed below:

- Concatenation is explicitly marked in the expression by the operator '^', which has higher precedence than '|'.
- The operators '?', '+', '.', '−', and '[ ]' are disallowed.
- The Individual tokens of regular expressions are any strings of non-blank ASCII characters (i.e., anything that is classified by ClassifyLex as identifier, number, operator, or other).
- The priorities of the remaining operators are such that the closure operator (*) has highest priority, followed by concatenation (^) at the next-highest level, and alternation (|) at the lowest priority.
- As in arithmetic expressions, parentheses are used to override these priorities.

For example, the input regular expression (a | b) * ^ c represents any sequence of a's and b's that is terminated by a single c. The parse tree for this expression is shown in Figure 8-33.

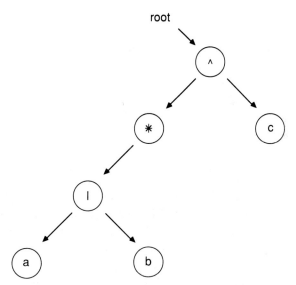

Figure 8-33 Parse tree for the regular expression (a|b)*^c.

FILES AND HASHING: DATABASE MANAGEMENT SYSTEMS

All of the data abstractions already introduced in this text were implemented under the assumption that the complete data structure, for a single run of the application program that uses it, resides entirely in memory. For example, when we used the binary tree abstract data type implementation in Chapter 8 to develop an expression parser, we assumed (reasonably) that no expression will ever be so large that its parse tree exceeds the size of available memory.

Of course, many realistic applications do not permit such an assumption to govern their design. Such applications typically require information to be stored in very large quantities—sometimes millions of individual records, each record containing thousands of bytes of data. For example, Chapter 7 showed the beginnings of a fairly typical information retrieval problem; there, a *single* bibliographic entry was searched to determine whether or not it contained certain user-specified "keywords." The completion of that problem, of course, would require the program to search an *entire file* of such entries—hundreds of thousands for an average university library—to find *all* entries that contain the designated keywords.

It is usually not practical to store such a large file in its entirety within the memory of a single computer. Auxiliary memory, called "secondary storage," must be used, because it has the capacity to accommodate such large amounts of information and make it available (one record at a time) to the application program. To service an information retrieval request such as the kind suggested in the previous paragraph, the programmer must design and implement a strategy for obtaining several individual records of data (each record representing a single bibliographic entry) from the file in secondary storage, so that it can be searched individually for the presence of keywords. Such a design must also be accomplished so that the resulting program is relatively efficient; the user should receive reasonably quick response from each individual search request.

In this chapter, we introduce the principles of file processing so that readers can understand and master applications such as the one introduced above. The first section contains a general discussion of files and their storage media, together with the basic operations on files that are usually available to programmers. In this sense, a "file" can be viewed as an abstract data type in the same general way as a "tree" or a "queue." The second section of this chapter describes Modula-2's standard procedures that support file processing. Here, we shall review the features of the familiar system module InOut and then introduce and discuss the more general file processing features of the standard system module FileSystem.

The third section of this chapter gives an overview of the important area of "database management systems" within computer science. The fourth section then resumes our discussion of files by introducing the notion of "random access files," whose records are not generally accessed in the same order in which they are stored. Techniques for retrieving records from such a file are many and varied, and we shall study the notion of "hashing," which provides a basis for some of these techniques. Finally, the fifth section concludes the chapter by progressing further toward a conclusion to the Advanced Instructor's Problem, which was first introduced in Chapter 1. The conclusion itself is realized in the form of a Team Project at the end of the chapter; this also incorporates a conclusion for the Advanced Registrar's Problem that was introduced in Chapter 1. When viewed together, these two problems comprise a basis for implementing an actual database management system.

9-1 SECONDARY STORAGE MEDIA AND FILE PROCESSING PRINCIPLES

Abstractly, a *file* can be viewed as a linear list (e_1 e_2 . . . e_n) that resides *permanently*—that is, before, during, and after the program that uses it is executed—on a *secondary storage medium*, and whose individual elements e_i are only accessible to the program on a one-at-a-time basis. The individual elements of a file are generally called "records," and, like linear lists, all the records in a particular file are of the same type. This type may be elementary (a single character or number) or composite (an entire array or record structure).

The term "secondary storage" characterizes any electronic or mechanical medium where information may be stored and retrieved by command from a Modula-2 program, *except* the memory itself (which is frequently called "primary storage"). Examples of secondary storage media are magnetic disks (such as floppy disks), magnetic tapes, mass storage devices, optical scanners, printers of all types (dot matrix, letter quality, laser graphic, and line printers), the terminal keyboard, and the terminal screen. A

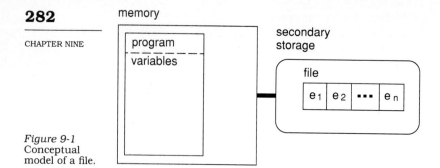

Figure 9-1
Conceptual model of a file.

conceptual model of the file, and its relationship to any program that uses it, is shown in Figure 9-1.

Because of their physical characteristics, some secondary storage media can be used only for input files (such as a terminal keyboard) or only for output files (such as a printer). Magnetic disks and tapes, on the other hand, are used both for input files and for output files.

When accessed by a program, a file is usually used only for input or only for output. An exception occurs in the case where some of the records in a file are to be changed, added, or deleted in a single run of the program, but where most of the records remain unchanged. In this case, a record may be read by the program, altered in some of its fields, and then the altered version rewritten back to the file in place of the original one. We shall return to this case later in the chapter. Further, the records in a file may be accessed either "sequentially" or "randomly." That is, the records of a file may be accessed by the program in the same order in which they are physically stored (first e_1, then e_2, and so forth), or else in another order determined by the nature of the application program.

When sequentially accessing a file, the program must perform three basic operations. First, the file must be "opened," which means that the program establishes a physical connection between itself and the file. Second, the file is "read" (or "written") one or more times; each read or write operation transfers a single record physically from (to) the file's location in secondary storage to (from) a memory area where the program can subsequently access the record. Third, the file must be "closed," which means that all processing of the file by the program is complete and the program is physically disconnected from the file.

When randomly accessing a file, a program also performs these three operations, along with an additional operation called "seek." The seek operation precedes each read or write and serves to reposition physically the access mechanism at the next record to be read or written. Thus, it allows the program to jump randomly among the records within a file, not necessarily starting with the first record, and not necessarily accessing the records in the same physical (sequential) order in which they are stored. An important requirement of random access files is that the program establish an effective convention for associating unique disk "addresses" with the

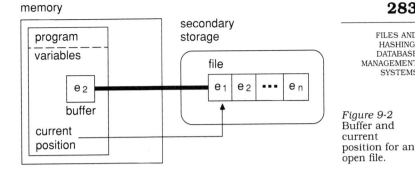

Figure 9-2
Buffer and current position for an open file.

individual records that are stored there. Such a convention is called "hashing"; we will illustrate hashing in a later section of this chapter.

Random access file storage can thus be viewed as an extension of main storage, since the latter is also a random access medium (as we learned in Chapter 2). Continuing this parallel, a random access disk file occupies an "address space," in which each individual record has a unique preassigned address. This address serves as a pointer to the record residing in that area of the disk.

After it is opened, the file has an associated area within main memory known as the file's "buffer." The size of a file's buffer is exactly the size of a physical "block" of data as it is stored on the disk (or other medium). The system physically transfers data to and from the program in complete blocks, rather than individual elements or records, because it is more efficient to do so. The "current position" in a file refers to the position (relative to the beginning of the file) of the next record to be read or written. These characteristics are portrayed schematically in Figure 9-2.

9-2 MODULA-2 FILE PROCESSING FACILITIES: THE MODULE FILESYSTEM

Returning to a concrete example, let us consider the Modula-2 standard module FileSystem. (This discussion resumes our treatment of Modula-2 file processing where the discussion in Appendix A concluded. A brief review of that portion of Appendix A may serve as a useful refresher at this point.) Recall that the standard module InOut provides a complete set of procedures for reading and writing various types of data at the terminal and that this activity can be temporarily redirected to any appropriate disk file by using one of the procedures OpenInput or OpenOutput. However, this redirection temporarily suspends the use of the terminal as long as that disk file is open; that is, not both the terminal and another disk file can be attached to the Modula-2 file "in" or "out" at the same time.

Many programming problems, of course, call for one or more files, beyond the terminal keyboard and screen, to be sending and receiving data at the same time. Modula-2 supports this activity through the standard system module FileSystem, which is summarized in Appendix D. For the purposes of this text, we can view FileSystem as an implementation of the abstract data type File, with an appropriate set of associated operators. This implementation and its usage comprise the remaining discussion in this chapter.

9-2-1 Modula-2 File Characteristics

The DEFINITION MODULE FileSystem exports the type File. This is implemented as a collection of characteristics, in the form of a RECORD, which describe any variable declared as a File in an application program. For the following discussion, suppose we have IMPORTed from FileSystem this type File, and that we have declared the file variable f for our program, as follows:

```
VAR f: File;
```

The important characteristics that are inherited by our file f, by virtue of this declaration, are the following:

- "f.res"—gives the Response from the system resulting from the most recently executed file operation. Among others, the responses are "done" and "notdone." For instance, the program may test for successful completion of a file operation by using the expression "IF f.res = done..."
- "f.flags"—is a SET OF type Flag, indicating the result that occurred from the most recently executed file operation. The Flag values "er," "ef," "rd," "wr," and "ag" indicate an error, an end-of-file, a read mode, a write mode, and an "Again" call after the last read.
- "f.bufa"—is the ADDRESS of the buffer for file f.
- "f.eof"—indicates whether or not the last file operation for file f went beyond the end of the file.

Thus, if the program wants to use either of f.res or f.flags, it must also IMPORT the type Response or Flag, respectively, from FileSystem.

9-2-2 Opening and Closing Files in Modula-2

The module FileSystem implements three operators for opening and closing files: Create, Lookup, and Close. Create and Lookup open a file, while Close closes a file. Create is used for opening a temporary file—one that will exist only while the program is executing—while Lookup is used for opening a file that exists (before and) after program execution is competed. These are invoked in the following way:

- *Create(f,'')* creates and opens the file f for temporary use by the program. After program execution completes, this file is normally not retained by the system. The current position of the file is set to byte 0 of its address space.
- *Lookup(f,s,new)* opens the file f with system name s (a character string). A value of TRUE for the BOOLEAN parameter "new" indicates the program's desire to create a new file with system name s. Conversely, a value of FALSE for "new" indicates the program's desire to open a file that already exists with system name s. Here, the system checks to see that s does indeed exist and then opens the file f. If s *does not* exist, f.res is set to "notdone" and the file f is not opened. In either case, the current position of the file is set to byte 0 of the file's address space.
- *Close(f)* closes the file f, either deleting it from the system (if it had been opened by Create) or releasing it for use by other programs in the system (if it had been opened by Lookup).

9-2-3 Reading, Writing, and Repositioning Within a Modula-2 File

The module FileSystem permits information to be transferred to and from a file either sequentially or randomly. Random file access will be discussed in a later section. Sequential access is the most typical file processing mode and should be mastered first.

When sequentially accessing a file, either for input or for output, the program may transfer data from/to the file either word by word or character by character. As soon as the file is opened, the system maintains a pointer indicating the current position (word or byte, relative to the beginning of the file) where the next read or write operation will take place within the file. As soon as that read or write is complete, the system increments the file's current position accordingly.

For an input file, the two operators ReadWord and ReadChar are provided, and their usage is described below.

- *ReadWord(f,v)* transfers the word at the current position of file f to the variable v and increments the current position of f to the next word. v may be a variable of *any* type that occupies a single word of memory for the implementation: typically, CARDINAL, INTEGER, and ADDRESS. In the event that the current position of f is at the end of the file at the time ReadWord is invoked, f.res will be set to "notdone." If the result

of executing ReadWord leaves the current position at the end of the file f, f.eof will be set to TRUE.
- *ReadChar(f,v)* transfers the character (byte) value at the current position of file f to the variable v and increments the current position of f to the next character. v should be a CHAR variable. Setting of f.res and f.eof occurs in the same way as described for ReadWord.

For an output file, two corresponding operators, WriteWord and WriteChar, are provided. Their usage is described below:

- *WriteWord(f,v)* transfers the word value of variable v to the file f at the current position and increments the current position accordingly.
- *WriteChar(f,v)* transfers the character value of variable v to the file f at the current position and increments the current position accordingly.

When a Modula-2 program accesses a file whose individual records are composite—either ARRAYs or RECORDs—a series of ReadWord or WriteWord (ReadChar or WriteChar) instructions is needed. The program can always determine the number of bytes in such a composite by invoking the TSIZE procedure from the module SYSTEM. Knowing this, the program should have a loop that repeats ReadChar (or WriteChar) that number of times, in order to transfer the entire composite from (or to) the file. Addressing individual bytes within such a composite is accomplished by using the ADR procedure (from the SYSTEM module) and exploiting the fact that arithmetic can be done with ADDRESS variables in Modula-2.

To illustrate, suppose we have the following RECORD type and variables declared in our program, and we wish to create a file full of such records—one for each student in the class.

```
TYPE StudentRecord = RECORD
                        name: ARRAY [0..15] OF CHAR;
                        ngrades: CARDINAL;
                        grades: ARRAY [1..10] OF CARDINAL
                     END;
VAR Student: StudentRecord;
    n,a: ADDRESS;
```

Suppose further that we are obtaining individual student data (names, grades, and so forth) from a dialogue at the terminal, which is completely managed by invoking some auxiliary procedure, say GetStudent. Here, we are concerned only with the process of writing a student's entire record to the disk file f, and we assume for that purpose that we have IMPORTed the procedures ADR and TSIZE from the module SYSTEM. The following loop will accomplish the task of writing a single student record to file f.

```
a:=ADR(Student);
n:=a+TSIZE(StudentRecord);
```

```
WHILE a<n DO
    WriteWord(f,a^);
    INC(a,2)      (*implementation-dependent; 2 bytes/word*)
END
```

Here, note that the procedure TSIZE returns the size, in words, of StudentRecord, so that the WHILE loop's WriteWord instruction is repeated once for each word. However, addressing for our implementation is byte by byte (see Chapter 2), while the size of a single word is two bytes. Thus, an INCrement of 2 for "a" is appropriate. If we were to port this program to a system with a different word size, we would need to modify the INC statement accordingly.

A similar strategy applies to the process of reading from an input file containing these records, as shown in the following code segment.

```
a:=ADR(Student);
n:=a+TSIZE(StudentRecord);
WHILE a<n DO
    ReadWord(f,a^);
    INC(a,2)      (*implementation-dependent; 2 bytes/word*)
END
```

Thus, the length in bytes of a record (such as StudentRecord) in a file can always be obtained directly by the program from the TSIZE procedure in the SYSTEM module. We can also obtain information about the current position (i.e., the next available byte location, relative to byte 0) in the file where the next record will be written or read, from the operator GetPos, which is also exported by FileSystem. The statement

```
GetPos(f,high,low)
```

leaves the CARDINAL variables "high" and "low" with values that allow the calculation of the current position for file f, using the following relationship:

```
current position = high*blocksize + low
```

Here, "blocksize" denotes the physical size of a single block of records as they are stored on the disk, and this value varies among different Modula-2 implementations. For instance, the Logitech MS-DOS implementation of Modula-2 has a blocksize of 2^{16}, or 65536 bytes.

9-2-4 An Example of File Processing in Modula-2

To illustrate a complete Modula-2 program that sequentially creates an output disk file and then reopens that file and reads it as input, we have finished the foregoing example in the form of a program called CreateFile, shown below. Here, the separate procedure GetStudent reads a student name and a series of grades from the terminal. The procedure WriteStudent then appends that record to the disk file f, which has system name 'students.dat'. That file is then closed and reopened for input, at which time the records are individually read (by the procedure ReadStudent) and displayed on the terminal screen.

```
MODULE CreateFile;
   FROM InOut IMPORT ReadString, ReadCard, Read, Write,
        OpenInput, WriteCard, WriteLn, WriteString, EOL,
        termCH;
   FROM SYSTEM IMPORT ADDRESS, ADR, TSIZE;
   FROM FileSystem IMPORT File, Response, Flag, Lookup,
        ReadWord, WriteWord, Close, GetPos, Length;

CONST EOF=32C;     (*ctrl-z is ASCII 32C, or end-of-input*)

TYPE StudentRecord = RECORD
                        name: ARRAY [0..15] OF CHAR;
                        ngrades: CARDINAL;
                        grades: ARRAY [1..10] OF CARDINAL
                     END;

VAR Student: StudentRecord;
    n,a: ADDRESS;
    i,high,low: CARDINAL;
    f: File;

PROCEDURE GetStudent;
(*This procedure obtains a student's name and test scores
   from the terminal.*)
BEGIN
   WITH Student DO
      ReadString(name); WriteString('   ');
      i:=1;
      WHILE (i<=10) AND (termCH#EOL) AND (termCH#EOF) DO
         ReadCard(grades[i]); WriteString('  ');
         i:=i+1
      END;
      WriteLn;
      ngrades:=i-1
   END
END GetStudent;

PROCEDURE WriteStudent;
(*This procedure writes a complete student record to the
   disk file 'students.dat'. Note that this procedure is
   system dependent, assuming byte addressing and 2-byte
```

```
      word size.*)
BEGIN
  a:=ADR(Student);
  n:=a+TSIZE(StudentRecord); (*record size in bytes*)
  WHILE a<n DO
    WriteWord(f,a^);
    INC(a,2)
  END
END WriteStudent;

PROCEDURE ReadStudent;
(*This procedure reads a complete student record from the
  disk file 'students.dat'*)
BEGIN
  a:=ADR(Student);
  n:=a+TSIZE(StudentRecord);
  WHILE a<n DO
    ReadWord(f,a^);
    INC(a,2)
  END
END ReadStudent;

BEGIN
  WriteString('Enter student name and up to 10 scores on');
  WriteString(' each line.  End last line with ctrl-z.');
  WriteLn;
  Lookup(f,'students.dat',TRUE);     (*opening for output*)
  WriteString('size of student record:');
    WriteCard(TSIZE(StudentRecord),5); WriteLn;
  IF f.res<>done THEN
    WriteString('error: unable to open output file.')
  ELSE
    REPEAT
      GetStudent;
      WriteString('high & low before next write:');
      GetPos(f,high,low);
      WriteCard(high,5); WriteCard(low,5); WriteLn;
      WriteStudent
    UNTIL termCH=EOF;
    Close(f)
  END;
  WriteLn;
  WriteString('Now the file is reread and displayed.');
  WriteLn;
  Lookup(f,'students.dat',FALSE);    (*opening for input*)
  IF f.res<>done THEN
    WriteString('error: unable to open input file.')
```

```
      ELSE
        WriteString('high & low for complete input file:');
        Length(f,high,low);
        WriteCard(high,5); WriteCard(low,5); WriteLn;
        WITH Student DO
          WriteString('Name          Grades'); WriteLn;
          ReadStudent;
          WHILE NOT f.eof DO
            WriteString(name);
            FOR i:=1 TO ngrades DO
              WriteCard(grades[i],4)
            END;
            WriteLn;
            ReadStudent
          END
        END
      END
END CreateFile.
```

Note that several tracing statements appear in this program, and they report the values of variables "high" and "low." The variable "low" is the current position of the file just before each new record is added to the file by WriteStudent. The variable "high" is incremented every time a complete block of data is passed during file processing. Recalling that the size of a block is 2^{16} bytes, the program would have to write nearly 2000 38-byte records before the value of "high" is incremented from 0 to 1.

An example of executing this program is shown in Figure 9-3. Note there that the creation of a sequential file leaves its individual records stored in the order in which they are written by the procedure WriteStudent. That is, opening the file f for output initiates its current position at byte 0, and every invocation of WriteStudent increments the current position by the length of a single student record, or 38 bytes.

```
Enter student name and up to 10 scores on
each line. End last line with ctrl-z.
size of student record:   37
backus  75   85   95
high & low before next write:           0        0
turing      90   80
high & low before next write:           0       38

Now the file is reread and displayed.
high & low for complete input file:  0       76
Name          Grades
backus    75   85   95
turing    90   80
```

Figure 9-3 Example output for running program CreateFile.

9-3 DATABASE MANAGEMENT SYSTEMS: FURTHER DISCUSSION

Chapter 7 introduced the concepts of a database management system (DBMS) and an information retrieval system, as contemporary models for organizing and retrieving information from files. In this chapter, we can see already that a system's underlying file structure and file management capabilities form essential foundations for any DBMS design.

The sequential file processing conventions introduced in the foregoing section are the most elementary, and simultaneously the most common, methods of organizing information in files. Often sequential files are known as "flat files" because they require only a linear list, or "flat" structure (as compared, for instance, with the "nonflat" structure of a tree), in the way they are stored and accessed.

By contrast, the next section will discuss in detail the notion of a random access file, which is the next step away from the sequential file in complexity and flexibility. There, we shall introduce techniques of accessing the individual elements of a flat file in a random order, not just sequentially in the order in which they are stored. A further step away from the sequential file is the so-called "database," which is comprised of a collection of two or more files that are logically interrelated. Organizing a database is a complex matter, and there are several general strategies for doing so. The most common among these strategies are known as the "network" strategy, the "hierarchical" strategy, and the "relational" strategy. Every database organization strategy is designed to provide a mechanism for efficient storage of large quantities of information while maintaining fast retrieval of such information in response to a user's request, or "query."

A database management system is usually organized in two major parts: one part for the programmer to design and implement the database maintenance activities (addition, deletion, and modification of records in its constituent files) and the other part for the user to retrieve information from the database. The former is often called the "data definition and data manipulation language," and it has many of the declarative and imperative aspects of an ordinary programming language like Modula-2. The latter is often called a "query language," and it is styled in such a way that nonprogrammers—managers and professionals in the application area that uses the database—can easily write statements, or queries, that allow direct and efficient retrieval of information from the database (ideally, without the need for intervention by a programmer or technician).

The differences among the hierarchical, network, and relational data base organization schemes can be briefly characterized as follows. A hierarchical database has its constituent files arranged in a hierarchical, or treelike, structure (cf., Chapter 8). Thus, information retrieval from such a database requires tree traversal to be implemented efficiently. Examples of hierarchical DBMSs are found in IBM's IMS (Information Management System) and MRI's System 2000.

A database management system with a networked organization allows more general relationships to be defined among its constituent files than

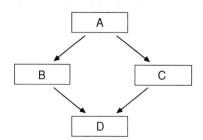

Figure 9-4
A network of four files.

the treelike structures that characterize hierarchical systems. Unlike trees, networks are a more general class of abstract data type that allows any pair of nodes (files) to be connected. Thus, Figure 9-4 shows a network among four files. There, files B and C are descendents of file A, and D is a descendent of both B and C. This last relationship disqualifies the structure in Figure 9-4 from being a tree, since a tree does not permit any of its nodes to have more than one parent. The most widespread system for realizing networked DBMS designs is the so-called "CODASYL model," which is generally implemented as an extension to the COBOL programming language for a number of different mainframe computers. Other networked database systems include TOTAL and ADABAS.

A relational database management system organization allows perhaps the most flexibility and generality in information retrieval. Its file organization scheme is generally tabular, and the same field can be repeated in more than one file in the database. This redundancy contributes to the generality of access, but at a significant cost in system overhead. Abstractly, relational database systems are perhaps the most interesting to study because of their strong connections with the theoretical principles of relational algebra. Examples of relational database systems are found in INGRES (implemented on many UNIX systems) and System R.

A basic characteristic of all database management and information retrieval systems, in practice, is that they are comprised of many files. These files are functionally related to each other and are typically accessed by different managers and other professionals within the organization that maintains the database.

For instance, consider the student records file we use as an example in this chapter. The instructor is the person who keeps track, during the semester, of all the students' grades in that file. But related to this file is the university's complete registration file, which contains, for each student, a record of all the courses in which he or she is currently enrolled, as well as records for all the courses that he or she has taken in the past.

Are these two files functionally related? Yes. At the beginning of the semester, the university registrar sends to each instructor a "class list" containing the names of all students who are enrolled in that class. During the semester, as individual students add into that course or withdraw from that course, the registrar sends the instructor a record of those changes. Thus, the responsibility for maintaining the information in this database is shared by the registrar, on the one hand, and the instructor, on the other. The database itself is comprised of (at least) these two different files: the instructor's file of grades for a course and the registrar's file of who is registered for what courses.

9-4 RANDOM ACCESS FILES AND HASHING

Returning to our previous discussion, let us consider the more basic problem of randomly accessing records in a single flat file. Generally speaking, a random access file is one whose individual records are not accessed in the same physical order in which they are stored. With such a file, one field in each record is designated as the "key" field; this field is so named bacause its value is used to uniquely distinguish that record from all the other records in the file. For example, in our file of student records illustrated above, the student's name can be designated as the key field if we can assume that no two students in a class will have the same name. (In practice, this particular choice of key field and its underlying assumption is not the best, but we shall use it in the following example nevertheless.)

Thus, when reading a record randomly from a file, the program must know beforehand the key (e.g., the student's name) for the record that it desires. Conversely, when writing a record randomly into a file, the program must be sure that the key field is different from the key fields of all other records in the file.

When implementing a random access file, we must also identify an address space for all the records in the file. That is, assuming that a file on disk is a contiguous sequence of bytes, with relative addresses 0, 1, 2, and so forth, the program must reserve a large enough area of contiguously addressed disk space to accommodate the maximum number of records that can occur for the file, considering the nature of the application. For instance, for our student records file, we may wish to assume that no class size will exceed 200 students (that might, for instance, represent the size of the largest lecture hall on campus). The absolute maximum number of bytes, therefore, for a file of student records like those shown above is 7600 for the entire file (38 bytes per record times 200 records). Thus, a byte address space of 0-7599, corresponding to a record address space of 0-199, would be adequate for this application.

Another consideration also affects this planning. When we store or retreive a record from this file, we must have a method for translating its key field (the student's name) into a unique record address within this space. Such a method is called a "hashing" algorithm, and there are many different hashing algorithms that have been effectively used in practical applications. For a complete discussion of hashing, the reader may wish to scan Knuth's definitive work, *Sorting and Searching*.

For our purposes, we wish only to introduce the flavor of hashing. Therefore, let's suppose we adopt a hashing algorithm in which the byte address of the record whose key field is the string k, say addr(k), is defined as:

$$\text{addr}(k) = 38 \sum_{i=1}^{\text{Length}(k)} \text{ORD}(k_i) \bmod 200$$

where $\text{ORD}(k_i)$ denotes the ASCII value of each individual character k_i in the string k which is the key field (in our case, the student's name) of the student's record. Our general goal in defining such an algorithm is that it will result in a fairly even spread of hashed names across the address space. Let's look at a few examples from our student records file, where the key k is the student's name.

Key (k)	Ordinal ASCII	Hashed Record address
backus	98 97 99 107 117 115	33
wirth	119 105 114 116 104	158
turing	116 117 114 105 110 103	65
gries	103 114 105 101 115	138
vonneumann	118 111 110 110 101 117 109 97 110 110	93

So far, so good; no one's name hashes to the same address as anyone else's. Figure 9-5 shows the hashed distribution of these five names over the 200-record address space. But suppose now that we want to add a record to this file for a new student named "siger" or "writh" or "buckas." Each of these names, and many others, hash to the same addresses as those occupied by our five original students. This event, when two or more records' keys hash to the same address, is known as a *collision*. Although we always want to find a hashing algorithm that minimizes the number of collisions for our particular file, we cannot practically eliminate collisions altogether.

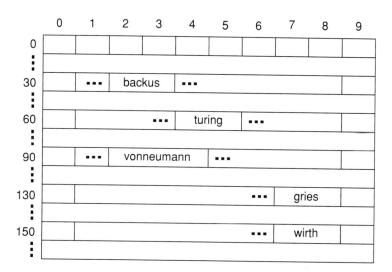

Figure 9-5
Hashed record addressing for five students.

That is, if we try to define an address space large enough to eliminate *all* possibilities for collisions for 16-letter keys, we need an address space of $\sum_{i=1}^{16} 26^i$ records! This is a very large number, much larger than the capacity of most conventional disk storage devices. Thus, we are generally confined to define a file's address space within the much smaller magnitude of the practical limits of disk storage devices, but which will nevertheless be large enough to minimize the likelihood of a collision.

Assuming that collisions will eventually occur, how can we handle them effectively when they *do* occur? That is, since two different records cannot simultaneously occupy the same disk address, we must find a strategy for assigning an alternate address for a record, in the event that its hashed address is already occupied by another record. Just like the choice of a hashing algorithm, the choice of a good collision-management algorithm has also been widely studied, since it is a difficult problem in general. For our file, a simple collision management scheme for adding a new record can be defined as follows:

> If the new record's hashed address (computed by the algorithm above) is already occupied by another record, *increment* this address repeatedly (in multiples of the record length) until an unoccupied address occurs. The first such unoccupied address is thus the hashed address for the new record.

For instance, if we were to add a record for "buckas" to the file shown in Figure 9-5, we first compute its hashed address 1254. We then detect that this address is already occupied by "backus," and thus we increment this address (more than once if necessary) until we find an unoccupied address (1292 for our example). This collision management strategy is illustrated in Figure 9-6 for our example.

To retrieve a record using this collision management scheme, we first recompute the hashed address for the key of the record we want, retrieve the record (if it is, in fact, there!), and then compare that record's key literally with our key, in order to be sure that no collision occurs at that

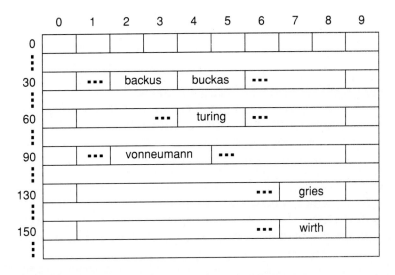

Figure 9-6
Collision Management for adding "buckas."

address. If a collision does occur, we successively read records from subsequent addresses, until we either find the record with our key or find an unoccupied address (which indicates that no record with our key is anywhere in the file).

Finally, to make this scheme effective, we must initially define a convention for creating the file's address space and then mark every record area in that space as "unoccupied." We also must provide for protecting the integrity of our hashing, collision management, and retrieval strategies in the event that the file becomes full (not likely, but nevertheless possible). These considerations are accommodated in our implementation of the student grade records file in the next section.

9-4-1 Creating and Randomly Accessing a File in Modula-2

Recall that the module FileSystem keeps track of the next available position in a sequential file for reading or writing a record and that its address (that is, the byte number, relative to 0) is obtained by the GetPos procedure. If we want to randomly access a record in that file, we must first *seek* the address of the record we want by resetting the file's current position to that address. Fortunately, FileSystem provides a companion operator called SetPos, which accomplishes exactly this task:

```
SetPos(f,high,low)
```

resets the current position in file f to the relative byte number given by the formula

```
current position = high * blocksize + low
```

where "blocksize" has the same meaning that it did for GetPos.

We anticipate that, in implementing a random access file, the program will intermittently read *and* write records from the file. For instance, suppose we want to add a fourth grade to the record for "vonneumann" in our file of students. To accomplish this, the program must first *seek* and *read* the original record (with the three grades shown in the foregoing illustration), then it must alter the record to reflect the addition of a fourth grade, and finally it must *rewrite* that altered record in place of the original record that had occupied that hashed address.

To support these kinds of actions, FileSystem provides three procedures—SetRead(f), SetWrite(f), and SetModify(f)—that allow the program to alter the "state" of the file f. SetRead sets the state of the file to read, which means that the program may only use the file for sequential input. SetWrite sets the state of file f to write, which means that records may be sequentially appended only at the end of f. SetModify sets the file's state to modify, which allows both reading and writing to take place, but the current position of the file is not automatically incremented by the system (as it is for the read and write states). That is, the program *must* use SetPos whenever a new record is to be read or written in the file, if the file is in the modify state, while randomly seeking each individual record that it wants to modify.

We now have all the tools we need for creating and randomly accessing our student grades file. Creating the file is done by a separate program, which simply initializes 200 38-byte empty records full of NUL characters. Any program that subsequently accesses the file randomly will therefore detect a collision by testing the first character of the student's name for NUL; a non-NUL value indicates that the address is occupied by another student's record. This program, CreateRandom, is given below; it creates the file named "rstudent.dat" on the disk.

```
MODULE CreateRandom;
  FROM InOut IMPORT ReadString, ReadCard, Read, Write,
    OpenInput, WriteCard, WriteLn, WriteString, EOL, termCH;
  FROM SYSTEM IMPORT ADDRESS, WORD, ADR, TSIZE;
  FROM FileSystem IMPORT File, Response, Flag, Lookup,
    SetModify, WriteWord, SetPos, Close;
(*This program initializes an empty random access file of
  200 student records for a course*)

CONST NUL=0C;
TYPE StudentRecord = RECORD
                      name: ARRAY [0..15] OF CHAR;
                      ngrades: CARDINAL;
                      grades: ARRAY [1..10] OF CARDINAL
                    END;

VAR Student: StudentRecord;
    n,a: ADDRESS;
    i,low,high: CARDINAL;
    f: File;

PROCEDURE InitStudentRecord;
(*This procedure fills a student's record with
  NUL characters. *)
BEGIN
  a:=ADR(Student);
  n:=a+TSIZE(StudentRecord);
  WHILE a<n DO
    a^:=WORD(NUL);
    INC(a,2)
  END
END InitStudentRecord;

PROCEDURE WriteStudent;
(*This procedure writes a student record in the
  file 'rstudent.dat.' *)
```

```
BEGIN
  a:=ADR(Student);
  n:=a+TSIZE(StudentRecord);
  WHILE a<n DO
    WriteWord(f,a^);
    INC(a,2);
    INC(low,2)              (*Move file address along.*)
  END
END WriteStudent;


BEGIN
  WriteString('Initializing file rstudent.dat to empty.');
  WriteLn;
  Lookup(f,'rstudent.dat',TRUE); (*opening for output *)
  IF f.res<>done THEN
    WriteString('error: unable to open output file.')
  ELSE
    high:=0; low:=0;
    SetModify(f);           (*Set up for program to*)
    InitStudentRecord;      (*fill record with NUL.*)
    FOR i:=1 TO 200 DO
      SetPos(f,high,low);   (*Maintain current position*)
      WriteStudent          (*Write 200 NUL records.*)
    END;
    Close(f);
    WriteString('Initialization completed.'); WriteLn
  END
END CreateRandom.
```

Once "rstudent.dat" is created, a second program can be written to add, modify, and delete individual student records within this file, conducting a dialogue with the terminal user to obtain the desired information. Unlike a sequential file process, this dialogue should accommodate the following different kinds of functions:

- When a new student "adds in" to the class, a new record should be added to the file rstudent.dat with this student's name. Assurance must be made by the program that this name is distinct from all other names in the entire class.
- When a student's grade is added to his or her record in the file rstudent.dat, that record should be appropriately modified. Existence of a record in the file with that student's name must first be confirmed by the program, as well as the availability of space in that record for adding the new grade.
- When a student "withdraws" from the class, his or her record should be deleted from the file rstudent.dat. Assurance must be made by the

program that a record with this name already exists in the file before it can be deleted.
- When a student's entire set of current grades is requested for review by the operator, the entire record should be displayed on the screen.

These functions are implemented in the procedures named NewStudent, GradeAdd, Withdraw, and ShowStudent respectively. An additional procedure, ShowAll, is provided which displays all the students in the file, along with their grades. These five procedures appear below. For documentation, the procedures ShowStudent and ShowAll are also equipped to display each student's hash address.

```
PROCEDURE NewStudent;
BEGIN
  found:=TRUE;
  REPEAT
    ReadStudent (collision);
    IF NOT collision THEN
      found:=FALSE
    ELSIF CompareStr(desiredname,Student.name)=0 THEN
      currentaddress:=hashaddress
    ELSE
      currentaddress:=(currentaddress+recordsize) MOD
                      filesize
    END
  UNTIL NOT found OR (currentaddress=hashaddress);
  IF NOT found THEN
    Assign(desiredname,Student.name); (*Set up the record*)
    Student.ngrades:=0;    (*and initialize no of grades.*)
    low:=currentaddress;
    WriteStudent
  ELSE
    WriteString('addition impossible; duplicate name or ');
    WriteString('fullfile.');
    WriteLn
  END
END NewStudent;


PROCEDURE GradeAdd;
BEGIN
  WITH Student DO
    found:=FALSE;
    REPEAT
      ReadStudent (collision);
      IF NOT collision THEN
        currentaddress:=hashaddress
```

```
      ELSIF CompareStr(desiredname,name)=0 THEN
        found:=TRUE
      ELSE
        currentaddress:=(currentaddress+recordsize) MOD
                        filesize
      END
    UNTIL found OR (currentaddress=hashaddress);
    IF NOT found THEN
      WriteString('grade not added; student not in file.');
      WriteLn
    ELSIF ngrades=10 THEN
      WriteString('grade not added: student has 10 grades.');
      WriteLn
    ELSE
      ngrades:=ngrades+1;
      WriteString('Enter new grade: ');
      ReadCard(grades[ngrades]); WriteLn;
      low:=currentaddress;
      WriteStudent
    END
  END
END GradeAdd;

PROCEDURE Withdraw;
BEGIN
  found:=FALSE;
  REPEAT
    ReadStudent (collision);
    IF NOT collision THEN
      currentaddress:=hashaddress
    ELSIF CompareStr(desiredname,Student.name)=0 THEN
      found:=TRUE
    ELSE
      currentaddress:=(currentaddress+recordsize) MOD
                      filesize
    END
  UNTIL found OR (currentaddress=hashaddress);
  IF NOT found THEN
    WriteString('withdrawal not performed; ');
    WriteString('student missing.');
    WriteLn
  ELSE
    Student.name[0]:=NUL;   (*Set byte 0 of name to NUL
                                for deletion.*)
    low:=currentaddress;
    WriteStudent
  END
END Withdraw;
```

```
PROCEDURE ShowStudent;
BEGIN
   found:=FALSE;
   REPEAT
      ReadStudent (collision);
      IF NOT collision THEN
         currentaddress:=hashaddress
      ELSIF CompareStr(desiredname,Student.name)=0 THEN
         found:=TRUE
      ELSE
         currentaddress:=(currentaddress+recordsize) MOD
                        filesize
      END
   UNTIL found OR (currentaddress=hashaddress);
   IF NOT found THEN
      WriteString('display impossible; student not in file.');
      WriteLn
   ELSE
      WriteString('Name       Hash Address     Grades');
      WriteLn;
      WriteString(Student.name); WriteString('    ');
      WriteCard(currentaddress,5);
      FOR i:=1 TO Student.ngrades DO
         WriteCard(Student.grades[i],4)
      END;
      WriteLn
   END
END ShowStudent;

PROCEDURE ShowAll;
BEGIN
   WriteString('Here is the entire file.');
   WriteLn;
   WITH Student DO
      currentaddress:=0;
      WriteString('Name       Hash Address     Grades');
      WriteLn;
      ReadStudent (collision);
      FOR i:=1 TO 200 DO
         IF name[0]#NUL THEN     (*Skip unoccupied addresses. *)
            WriteString(name);
            WriteCard(currentaddress,5);
            FOR i:=1 TO ngrades DO
               WriteCard(grades[i],4)
            END;
            WriteLn;
         END;
         currentaddress:=currentaddress+recordsize;
```

```
            ReadStudent (collision)
        END
    END
END ShowAll;
```

To understand how these procedures work, we must first examine the procedure ReadStudent, which is invoked by all of them. When ReadStudent is invoked, it uses the current hash address value (in the variable 'currentaddress') and reads a record from that address in the file f and stores it in the RECORD variable Student. It then checks to see if that record is NUL or not, and sets the BOOLEAN parameter 'collision' accordingly. 'Collision' is TRUE or FALSE depending on whether or not the student record area at the 'currentaddress' on disk is already occupied or not, respectively. ReadStudent is shown below.

```
PROCEDURE ReadStudent (VAR collision: BOOLEAN);
(*This procedure reads a complete student record from the
  disk file rstudent.dat beginning at byte
  ''currentaddress.'' The parameter ''collision'' is set
  to indicate whether or not a non-NUL record already
  occupies the current address. *)
BEGIN
    a:=ADR(Student);
    n:=a+recordsize;
    low:=currentaddress;
    SetPos(f,high,low);
    WHILE a<n DO
        ReadWord(f,a^);
        INC(a,2);
        INC(low,2);
        SetPos(f,high,low)
    END;
    IF Student.name[0]=NUL THEN
        collision:=FALSE
    ELSE
        collision:=TRUE
    END
END ReadStudent;
```

Each of the foregoing procedures uses the information returned by ReadStudent in a slightly different way. For example, look at the procedure NewStudent. It repeatedly invokes ReadStudent, incrementing the variable "hashaddress" after each invocation, until either a record is found whose name is identical with that of the new student (in the variable 'desiredname') or a NUL record is found. In the former case, no addition can be made and a message is displayed to that effect. In the latter case, the NUL record is replaced at the 'currentaddress' in the file f by a record with the new student's name. A final consideration for adding a new student arises when the file f is full (all 200 records are non-NUL), and that is handled by an appropriate message as well.

The GradeAdd, Withdraw, and ShowStudent procedures, on the other hand, use the procedure ReadStudent in the opposite way; they invoke it *expecting* to find a collision and a record in the file with a name that matches the 'desiredname' variable. If not, an error message is displayed. Finally, the ShowAll procedure sequentially accesses all 200 records in the file f and displays the names, hash addresses, and grades of all records that are non-NUL.

The other auxiliary procedure that is used by these four is called Write-Student, shown below. The reader will notice that this procedure is a simple variation of its counterpart in the earlier program that sequentially accessed the file student.dat, with the added provision of appropriate "seek" commands—implemented in Modula-2 by SetPos—which explicitly adjust the file's current position as individual words are written. Recall that when the file f is set to the "modify" mode, the current position is not automatically incremented, as it would be in the "read" or "write" mode.

```
PROCEDURE WriteStudent;
(*This procedure writes a complete student record to the
   disk file 'rstudent.dat'*)
BEGIN
   a:=ADR(Student);
   n:=a+recordsize;
   low:=currentaddress;
   SetPos(f,high,low);
   WHILE a<n DO
     WriteWord(f,a^);
     INC(a,2);
     INC(low,2);            (*Move file address along.*)
     SetPos(f,high,low)
   END
END WriteStudent;
```

9-5 THE ADVANCED INSTRUCTOR'S PROBLEM REVISITED

This example program draws us a lot closer to a complete solution to the Advanced Instructor's Problem that was first introduced in Chapter 1. The need for files in this problem is central and essential, since the useful life of a class record generally extends for an entire academic term rather than a single run of a program. Each single run should access only certain students' records in that file for the purpose of adding new grades; the majority of information in the file should remain unchanged from one run of the program to the next. Below is the remainder of a program, with the foregoing procedure bodies ellipsed, that interactively updates randomly selected student records, using information from prompts issued at the terminal.

```
MODULE UpdateRandom;
   FROM InOut IMPORT ReadString, ReadCard, Read, Write,
                OpenInput, WriteCard, WriteLn, WriteString,
                EOL, termCH;
   FROM SYSTEM IMPORT ADDRESS, ADR, TSIZE;
   FROM FileSystem IMPORT File, Response, Flag, Lookup,
                SetRead, SetModify, ReadWord, WriteWord,
                GetPos, SetPos, Close;
   FROM Strings IMPORT CompareStr, Assign;
(*This program updates individual student records in a
  random access file for a course.  The functions supported
  are: a=add a new student to the course, g=add a new grade
  for a student in the course, w=withdraw a student record
  from the course, and s=show the current record for a
  student in the course.*)

CONST EOF=32C;     (*ctrl-z is ASCII 32C or end-of-input.*)
      NUL=0C;      (*Missing record is marked by NUL char.*)

TYPE StudentRecord = RECORD
                       name: ARRAY [0..15] OF CHAR;
                       ngrades: CARDINAL;
                       grades: ARRAY [1..10] OF CARDINAL
                     END;

VAR Student: StudentRecord;
    n,a: ADDRESS;
    i,low,high,
      hashaddress, currentaddress,
      recordsize,filesize: CARDINAL;
    collision,found: BOOLEAN;
    f: File;
    command: CHAR;
    desiredname: ARRAY[0..15] OF CHAR;

PROCEDURE NewStudent ...
PROCEDURE GradeAdd ...
PROCEDURE Withdraw ...
PROCEDURE ShowStudent ...
PROCEDURE ShowAll ...
PROCEDURE ReadStudent ...
PROCEDURE WriteStudent ...
```

```
PROCEDURE GetNameAndHash;
(*This procedure obtains the name of a desired student
  from the terminal and computes its corresponding hash
  address.*)
BEGIN
  WriteString('Enter the name of a student:');
  ReadString(desiredname); WriteLn;
  hashaddress:=0; i:=0;
  WHILE (desiredname[i]#NUL) AND (i<=15) DO
    hashaddress:=hashaddress+ORD(desiredname[i]);
    i:=i+1
  END;
  hashaddress:=recordsize * (hashaddress MOD 200);
  currentaddress:=hashaddress;
  WriteString('hash address=');
  WriteCard(hashaddress,5); WriteLn
END GetNameAndHash;



BEGIN
  WriteString('Enter a series of new students (a), ');
  WriteLn;
  WriteString('new grades (g), and/or withdrawals (w).');
  WriteLn;
  WriteString('Enter s to display a student, and d to');
  Writestring(' display all.');
  WriteLn;
  WriteString('Terminate session by ctl-z.'); WriteLn;
  Lookup(f,'rstudent.dat',FALSE);    (*opening for update*)
  IF f.res<>done THEN
    WriteString('error: unable to open random file.');
    WriteLn;
  ELSE
    SetModify(f);
    high:=0;
    low:=0;
    recordsize:=TSIZE(StudentRecord);
    filesize:=200*recordsize;
    REPEAT
      WriteString('Enter a,g,w,d,l, or ctl-z: ');
      Read (command);
      WriteLn;
      CASE command OF
        'a': GetNameAndHash;
             NewStudent    |
        'g': GetNameAndHash;
             GradeAdd      |
```

```
              'w': GetNameAndHash;
                   Withdraw      |
              'd': GetNameAndHash;
                   ShowStudent   |
              'l': ShowAll       |
              EOF:
            ELSE WriteString('invalid command; try again.');
                 WriteLn
            END
          UNTIL command=EOF;
            Close(f)
        END;
END UpdateRandom.
```

In addition to the main body of the program, we also have a procedure GetNameAndHash. Its purpose is to read a student's name from the terminal and compute the corresponding hash address (using the variable 'hashaddress') from it. Once computed, this value is assigned to the variable 'currentaddress' as well, so that the first probe of file f for a record with the 'desiredname' will begin at that address. The body of the program UpdateRandom should otherwise be self-explanatory.

To demonstrate the functionality of this program, we created an empty file (using program CreateRandom) and then added five student records and grades to it. A portion of that dialogue is shown in Figure 9-7, where two new students are added, and the entire file is listed (using the 'a' and 'l' options, respectively) on the terminal screen.

In concluding this section, one should not assume that the Advanced Instructor's Problem is satisfactorily completed here in its entirety. Recall, for instance, that the original statement of the problem placed no limit on the number of grades recorded for any student in a course. Lifting this restriction from the above design is a nontrivial matter; we need to simulate a linked list within a disk address space, using techniques developed in Chapter 3 combined with techniques for list traversal via random-access disk addressing (GetPos and SetPos procedures) instead of memory adddressing (ADDRESS type and ADR procedure).

```
Enter a,g,w,d,l, or ctl-z: a
Enter the name of a student: vonneumann
hash address= 3534
enter a,g,w,d,l, or ctl-z: a
Enter the name of a student: backus
hash address= 1254
Enter a,g,w,d,l or ctl-z: l
Name          Hash Address         Grades
backus            1254
vonneumann        3534
Enter a,g,w,d,l, or ctl-z: <ctl-z>
```

Figure 9-7
A sample session with program Update-Random.

Furthermore, an improved solution would use our abstract data type Strings as defined in Chapter 7, rather than the implementation-dependent functions CompareStr and Assign that the foregoing program imports from the Logitech Modula-2 library named Strings. Finally, an improved solution would display a class list of student grades in alphabetical order, rather than in the order that their hash addresses occur. For a class of five students, such as the one in our examples, the latter ordering poses only a mild inconvenience. But consider the problem that an unsorted display would cause for a class size of 50 or 150 students! Thus, an appropriate sort procedure from Chapter 5 is also necessary for completing the Advanced Instructor's Problem.

The design challenges suggested by these additions render the Advanced Instructor's Problem an ideal final team project to conclude this text. Thus, we leave it as such at the end of this chapter. This problem is also an excellent example of the broadly synthetic nature of problem solving in computer science. The solution of such realistic problems draws upon a collection of different skills, principles, and abstractions, none of which is trivial and all of which are essential.

EXERCISES

9-1. Alter the program CreateFile so that it will interactively retrieve the file name from the terminal, and thus each run will potentially create a different file on the disk. If the file name reflects the course number (e.g., cosc101.dat or phil320.dat), what advantage does that give us?

9-2. Continuing this line of thought, write a program that will report the names of all students in the sequential file named "x.dat," where the string x is obtained interactively from the terminal.

9-3. One way to sort the records in a sequential file (if the file is not too large) is to read the individual key fields (student names, for example) and their corresponding disk addresses, building a linear list in memory, then sort this list internally (using an algorithm from Chapter 5), and finally rearrange the records in the file accordingly (using a simple swap procedure). This method is often referred to as a "tag sort." Implement this idea by appending a tag sort procedure to the program CreateFile, using the list abstract data type from Chapter 3 and an appropriate sorting algorithm from Chapter 5.

9-4. When a file has too many records for a tag sort, other sorting methods can be used. One such method involves reading a small group of records from a file, say f, into an internal linear list, sorting this list, and appending this sorted group to an initially empty separate file, say g. This procedure is repeated, alternating the output of the sorted groups between two different separate files, g and h. Once file f is exhausted, it is closed and reopened for output, and files g and h are closed and reopened for input. Now the sorted groups are read in pairs, one from g and one from h, and merged (as in the merge sort of Chapter 5) into a single sorted group, but twice as long, back into file f. When g and h are exhausted, we now have half as many sorted groups in file f as we did on files g and h. Now we split these groups between files g and h again and repeat this merge process. This splitting and merging continues $\log_2 n$ times (where n is the original number of sorted groups in files g and h), until we arrive at a single group in file f that is sorted. Implement this file sorting procedure and exercise it using a large file of random numbers (which can be created using the Random procedure from Chapter 2).

9-5. The hashing algorithm shown in this chapter is only one of several different algorithms that have been developed over the years. Find a different hashing algorithm, perhaps from Knuth's *Sorting and Searching*, and implement it within the program UpdateRandom by altering the procedure GetNameAndHash accordingly. What are the hash addresses of our five students, using this new algorithm? Does this algorithm seem to give a better spread of hash addresses than the one we gave? Try them both, using a significantly large file of names (perhaps a few pages out of the phone book) and have your program count the number of collisions that occur in each case.

9-6. The collision management scheme shown in this chapter is called "linear probing" (appropriately) because it looks to the series of records immediately following the record with the computed hash address in order to resolve a collision. For large files, this scheme tends to develop a *clustering* of records in bunches adjacent to these computed hash addresses, rather than to spread the records out evenly across the address space. One way of solving this clustering problem is to move away from the original hash address in a "quadratic" fashion. That is, when a collision occurs, move away from the hash address in successive increments of 1, 4, 9, 16, . . . records until an unoccupied space occurs. Implement this quadratic collision-management strategy by modifying the procedures NewStudent, GradeAdd, WithDraw, and ShowStudent appropriately. Suggest a way in which the collision management scheme can be isolated as a separate procedure (rather than replicated in all four of these procedures, as they currently are), so that it can be more efficiently maintained.

9-7. Design a record layout that will be appropriate for the Advanced Registrar's Problem introduced in Chapter 1. Each record should contain a student's name, number of courses, and course name for each of the courses in which the student is registered. The maximum number of courses per student is five.

9-8. Given a series of registrations in the form suggested in exercise 9-7, write a Modula-2 program that builds a random access file with each record area containing the registration information for a single student.

9-9. Write a second program that, using the file created in exercise 9-8, automatically builds a class list file for each different course mentioned in at least one student's registration record. This program is a kind of head start for the first team project described below. Once each such file is built, it should be sorted by student name (perhaps a separate program), and a summary of the number of students who have registered for each course should be displayed.

TEAM PROJECT: THE ADVANCED INSTRUCTOR'S AND REGISTRAR'S PROBLEMS CONCLUDED

Complete both the Advanced Instructor's Problem and the Advanced Registrar's Problem simultaneously by implementing the database suggested at the end of the chapter. Write separate programs that (1) create that database; (2) simulate a registration day, in which all students at the university register for courses and the initial class lists are created as separate subfiles (in alphabetical order) by the program; (3) simulate an instructor's session with his or her own course (subfile), updating the grades of students in that course; (4) simulate the registrar's "drop/add" record keeping by adding new students to a course or dropping students who withdraw from a course; (5) generate a grade-averaging report for one or more courses, on demand by any instructor, as an aid in determining final grades; and (6) record final grades for each student in each course (including withdrawals), issuing a separate grade report to each student in the university.

Your database design should allow a different maximum enrollment for each course, but no more than five courses per student. Any number of grades should be allowed for an individual student in a course, using the linked list strategy suggested at the end of the chapter.

TEAM PROJECT: BIBLIOGRAPHIC INFORMATION RETRIEVAL REVISITED

Returning to the Text Search and Information Retrieval problem introduced at the end of Chapter 7, recall that the procedure ObtainBibentry had a simple task: to read a single bibliographic entry that was the *entirety* of a text file on disk. In this team project, you should design a random access file that is a complete collection of such entries and then design an extension of the team project in Chapter 7 that searches this entire file and displays *every* entry that contains every one of a series of user-specified keywords.

Consider alternative schemes that you might use as a basis for hashing this file. Consider also the problem of handling variable-length records, which is an inherent feature of bibliographic entries. Discuss the problem of associating collections of user-specified keywords with hash addresses. As time permits, read about the designs of some contemporary library information retrieval systems and learn how they organize their databases for flexible search, fast retrieval, and efficient storage of large amounts of information.

10

COMPUTER SCIENCE: THE DISCIPLINE IN PERSPECTIVE

Since its emergence as a coherent academic discipline in the 1960's, computer science has evolved rapidly. The Association for Computing Machinery (ACM) has served throughout this period as the major professional society for computer scientists, while the Institute for Electrical and Electronic Engineers (IEEE) Computer Society serves the same purpose for the engineering side of the profession. These two organizations have as an ongoing activity the development and maintenance of computer science curriculum standards for colleges and universities throughout the nation. Any complete survey of the discipline, therefore, generally follows the contour established by current curriculum standards.[1]

Recently, ACM's curriculum standards have continued to undergo scrutiny at the introductory levels. In an effort to break away from the widespread and false notion that "computer science equals programming," many educators are recasting the introductory courses CS1 and CS2 so that they represent the broad field of computer science and not just its programming aspects. This text, for instance, reflects that contemporary view.

10-1 DEFINING COMPUTER SCIENCE

In defining "computer science," we therefore need to look to more contemporary sources than the present curriculum standard. One such source is a

---

[1] The ACM's curriculum standards have gone through two stages of evolution in the past three decades. These are known as "Curriculum 68" and "Curriculum 78," designating the years in which they were published. The two introductory courses in the 1978 standard, known as CS1 and CS2, were updated again in 1985. The IEEE Computer Society's curriculum standard, known as "The IEEE Model Curriculum," was published in 1983.

recent article by Peter Denning, former president of ACM and a widely recognized educator and scholar in the field. In an article for the January 1985 issue of *American Scientist*,[2] Denning gives a broad, historically-based, definition of computer science as an academic discipline. This article is highly recommended for students who contemplate further work in this field. The article begins with the following definition of computer science:

> Computer science is the body of knowledge dealing with the design, analysis, implementation, efficiency, and application of processes that transform information. The fundamental question underlying all of computer science is "what can be automated?".

The article continues to describe eleven broad subject matter areas that, together, comprise the discipline of computer science, and that have evolved over the last four or five decades. These areas and their approximate dates of emergence in a coherent body of knowledge are estimated by Denning as follows:

Area of Computer Science	Date of Emergence
Theory	1940
Numerical computation	1945
Architecture	1950
Programming languages and methodology	1960
Algorithms and data structures	1968
Operating systems	1971
Networks	1975
Human interface	1978
Database systems	1980
Concurrent computation	1982
Artificial intelligence	1986

Another work that provides a coherent definition of computer science as an intellectual and scientific discipline is known as the "Model Curriculum" for computer science.[3] This curriculum model was developed by computer scientists from several high quality liberal arts institutions for the purpose of identifying a more extensive theoretical core for the

---

[2] Denning, Peter, "The Science of Computing: What Is Computer Science?" *American Scientist* 73 (January 1985), 16-19.

[3] Gibbs, Norman E. and Allen B. Tucker, "A Model Curriculum for a Liberal Arts Degree in Computer Science," *Communications of the ACM* 29,3 (March 1986), 202-210.

discipline than that given by ACM's 1978 standard. There, computer science is defined as follows:

> Computer science is the systematic study of algorithms and data structures, specifically: i) their formal properties, ii) their mechanical and linguistic realizations, and iii) their applications.

In this definition, a basis was sought that would support the evolution of a curriculum standard for computer science as a *science*, including significant experimental (laboratory) aspects, on the one hand, and significant theoretical aspects, on the other. In this way, computer science can be viewed more properly in the same way as the other scientific disciplines: chemistry, biology, physics, and so forth. The resulting Model Curriculum described in this article is therefore quite different in content and emphasis from ACM's 1978 standard, because it is more strongly aligned with contemporary academic principles in these other sciences.

In 1986, ACM established a Task Force on the Core of Computer Science,[4] which has the task of developing an extensive definition of computer science, accompanied by recommendations for teaching an intensive three-semester introductory curriculum that would leave students with a comprehensive understanding of the entire field—especially those theoretical and topical aspects that exceed the programming elements that now dominate the introductory course. That work is in progress at this writing, and is expected to be completed by the end of 1987.

This brief survey of curriculum standards development serves as a testimony to the rapid evolution that has taken place in computer science education over the last three decades. The evolution has many positive results, not the least of which has been the education of undergraduates and the general public about the breadth, substance, and essential nature of the computer science field.

10-1-1 Tree Structure of the CR Categories

Another way of comprehensively viewing the broad subject matter of computer science is by looking at ACM's subject classification scheme. ACM maintains this scheme as a basis for cataloging, reviewing, and retrieving information from the steady flow of scholarly work that appears in books, journals, and conference proceedings. This scheme is called the "CR Categories" and is the basis for organizing information in the monthly publication of ACM's *Computing Reviews* of this literature.

This classification scheme is elaborate, but overall it has a hierarchical tree structure. Below appears a partial display of the CR Categories, which we might call the "Abbreviated CR Categories. " That is, the categories shown here are only the ones for which *actual* citations appeared

---

[4]Peter Denning (chair), Douglas Comer, David Gries, Michael Mulder, Allen Tucker, A. Joe Turner, and Paul Young.

during the period between December 1985 and May 1986. Students who are interested in the complete CR Categories should browse a recent issue of ACM's *Computing Reviews*. This abbreviated version is displayed below in a treelike fashion: the root is at the leftmost margin, and each new subtree level is introduced at an indented tab position from its parent.

Abbreviated CR Categories

A. General Literature
   1. Introductory and Survey
   2. Reference

B. Hardware
   1. Control Structures and Microprogramming
      1.1. Control Design Styles
   2. Arithmetic and Logic Structures
      2.1. Design Styles
      2.2. Performance Analysis and Design Aids
      2.3. Reliability, Testing and Fault-Tolerance
   3. Memory Structures
   4. Input/output and Data Communications
   5. Register-Transfer-Level Implementation
   6. Logic Design
   7. Integrated Circuits

C. Computer Systems Organization
   1. Processor Architectures
      1.1. Single Data Stream Architectures
      1.2. Multiple Data Stream Architectures (Multiprocessors)
      1.3. Other Architecture Styles
   2. Computer-communication Networks
      2.1. Network Architecture and Design
      2.2. Network Protocols
      2.3. Network Operations
      2.4. Distributed Systems
      2.5. Local Networks
   3. Special-purpose and Application-based Systems
   4. Performance of Systems
   5. Computer System Implementation
      5.3. Microcomputers
      5.4. VLSI Systems

D. Software
   1. Programming Techniques
      1.1. Applicative (Functional) Programming
      1.2. Automatic Programming

      1.3. Concurrent Programming
      1.4. Sequential Programming
   2. Software Engineering
      2.1. Requirements/Specifications
      2.2. Tools and Techniques
      2.3. Coding
      2.4. Program Verification
      2.5. Testing and Debugging
      2.6. Programming Environments
      2.7. Distribution of Maintenance
      2.8. Metrics
      2.9. Management
   3. Programming Languages
      3.1. Formal Definitions and Theory
      3.2. Language Classifications
      3.3. Language Constructs
      3.4. Processors
   4. Operating Systems
      4.1. Process Management
      4.2. Storage Management
      4.3. File Systems Management
      4.4. Communications Management
      4.5. Reliability
      4.6. Security and Protection
      4.7. Organization and Design
      4.8. Performance
      4.9. Systems Programs and Utilities

E. Data
   1. Data Structures
   2. Data Storage Representations
   3. Data Encryption
   4. Coding and Information Theory
   5. Files

F. Theory of Computation
   1. Computation by Abstract Devices
      1.1. Models of Computation
      1.2. Modes of Computation
      1.3. Complexity Classes
   2. Analysis of Algorithms and Problem Complexity
      2.1. Numerical Algorithms and Problems
      2.2. Nonnumerical Algorithms and Problems
      2.3. Tradeoffs among Complexity Measures
   3. Logics and Meanings of Programs
      3.1. Specifying and Verifying and Reasoning about Programs
      3.2. Semantics of Programming Languages
      3.3. Studies of Program Constructs

4. Mathematical Logic and Formal Languages
   4.1. Mathematical Logic
   4.2. Grammars and Other Rewriting Systems
   4.3. Formal Languages

G. Mathematics of Computing
   1. Numerical Analysis
      1.1. Interpolation
      1.2. Approximation
      1.3. Numerical Linear Algebra
      1.6. Optimization
      1.7. Ordinary Differential Equations
      1.8. Partial Differential Equations
   2. Discrete Mathematics
      2.1. Combinatorics
      2.2. Graph Theory
   3. Probability and Statistics
   4. Mathematical Software

H. Information Systems
   1. Models and Principles
      1.1. Systems and Information Theory
      1.2. User/Machine Systems
   2. Database Management
      2.1. Logical Design
      2.2. Physical Design
      2.3. Languages
      2.4. Systems
      2.5. Heterogeneous Databases
      2.6. Database Machines
      2.7. Database Administration
   3. Information Storage and Retrieval
      3.1. Content Analysis and Indexing
      3.2. Information Storage
      3.3. Information Search and Retrieval
      3.4. Systems and Software
      3.5. On-Line Information Services
      3.6. Library Automation
   4. Information Systems Applications
      4.1. Office Automation
      4.2. Types of Systems
      4.3. Communications Applications

I. Computing Methodologies
   1. Algebraic Manipulation
      1.1. Expressions and Their Representation
      1.3. Languages and Systems

2. Artificial Intelligence
    2.1. Applications and Expert Systems
    2.2. Automatic Programming
    2.3. Deduction and Theorem Proving
    2.4. Knowledge Representation Formalisms and Methods
    2.5. Programming Languages and Software
    2.6. Learning
    2.7. Natural Language Processing
    2.8. Problem Solving, Control Methods and Search
    2.9. Robotics
    2.10. Vision and Scene Understanding
3. Computer Graphics
    3.2. Graphics Systems
    3.3. Picture/Image Generation
    3.4. Graphics Utilities
    3.5. Computational Geometry and Object Modeling
    3.6. Methodology and Techniques
    3.7. Three-dimensional Graphics and Realism
4. Image Processing
    4.2. Compression (coding)
    4.3. Enhancement
    4.4. Restoration
    4.6. Segmentation
    4.7. Feature Measurement
    4.8. Scene Analysis
    4.9. Applications
5. Pattern Recognition
    5.1. Models
    5.3. Clustering
    5.4. Applications
    5.5. Implementation
6. Simulation and Modeling
    6.3. Applications
    6.4. Model Validation and Analysis
7. Text Processing
    7.1. Text Editing
    7.2. Document Preparation

J. Computer Applications
    1. Administrative Data Processing
    2. Physical Sciences and Engineering
    3. Life and Medical Sciences
    4. Social and Behavioral Sciences
    5. Arts and Humanities
    6. Computer-aided Engineering
    7. Computers in Other Systems

K. Computing Milieux
  1. The Computer Industry
  2. History of Computing
  3. Computers and Education
      3.1. Computer Uses in Education
      3.2. Computer and Information Science Education
  4. Computers and Society
      4.1. Public Policy Issues
      4.2. Social Issues
      4.3. Organizational Impact
  5. Legal Aspects of Computing
  6. Management of Computing and Information Systems
      6.1. Project and People Management
      6.2. Installation Management
      6.3. Software Management
      6.4. System Management
  7. The Computing Profession
      7.1. Occupations
      7.2. Organizations
  8. Personal Computing

Many of these topics should now be familiar to the reader, since they are introduced in earlier sections of this text. For instance, some of the topics in subtree B are introduced in Chapter 2 (hardware, memory structures), while topics in subtree D are introduced in Chapter 1 (program verification, testing and debugging) and emphasized throughout the text. Other topics in subtree D are found in Chapter 6 (operating systems), Chapter 8 (compilers, here called "programming language processors"). Topics in subtree E are found in Chapter 2 (data storage representations) and Chapters 3, 6, and 8 (data structures). The notion of computational complexity (subtree F) is a continuing theme throughout this text, and the regular expressions presented in Chapter 7 are also an elementary part of the topics in subtree F. Some of the information systems concepts of subtree H are introduced in Chapter 9. Some of the topics in subtree I are introduced in Chapter 7 (text processing), while others are introduced in Chapter 8 (artificial intelligence).

The next few sections of this chapter will review certain major subject areas of computer science as they were covered in the first nine chapters of the text, introducing at the same time some additional important subjects that did not appear there: notably, graphs (subtree G above), concurrency (subtree D), networks (subtree C), the human interface, programming languages (subtree D), and mathematical algorithms (subtree G). These new subjects are only briefly introduced here, thus serving to indicate the breadth of study that computer science majors will later encounter in advanced courses. The main body of the chapter then concludes with a review and refocusing of the definition of "computer science" and an overview of the computer science academic and professional community. An annotated bibliography of major texts and references in the various subject areas of computer science appears at the end of this chapter.

10-2 ALGORITHMS, DATA STRUCTURES, AND INFORMATION SYSTEMS

A major theme in this text has been the study of algorithms: their use in abstraction, design, implementation, evaluation, and verification. Principles of programming methodology introduced in Chapter 1—precise specification and verification, complexity measurement, and data abstraction—are reinforced throughout the entire text.

The fundamental data structures that accompany that study are also emphasized here. Chapters 3, 6, 7, and 8, successively, cover lists, stacks, queues, strings, and trees with substantial thoroughness. Finally, Chapter 9 gives careful attention to the subjects of files, hashing, and database management systems and their roles in the field of computer science.

10-2-1 Graphs

In later courses, readers will encounter additional species of data structures, and will examine them in depth. A most general class of data structures is called the "graph," which we briefly introduce and describe in this section.

One way of viewing graphs is that they are generalizations of trees. That is, a graph may be any collection of nodes and edges, but there is no "root node" and there is no hierarchy of levels, as we had with trees. Moreover, a graph may contain a "cycle," or a path that connects a particular node to itself. Two examples of graphs are shown in Figure 10-1.

Here, in the left-hand example, we have a cycle from node A to itself, consisting of the path A-B-D-A. Another difference between trees and

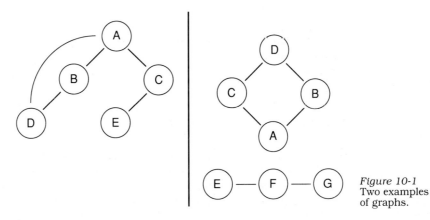

Figure 10-1
Two examples of graphs.

graphs is that a graph need not be connected. That is, there is no requirement that a path exists between every pair of nodes. That is the case in the right-hand example of Figure 10-1, which is not a connected graph since there is no path between nodes A and E.

The theory of graphs is well developed and originates from mathematics. A graph abstract data type can be developed as a generalization of the tree data type, with basic operators for insertion, deletion, and search for a node. The definition and Modula-2 implementation of this abstraction are left as exercises at the end of the chapter. By now, readers have developed sufficient understanding of this technique to begin the process of defining abstract data types themselves.

Graphs are useful in a wide variety of computer science applications. They are used especially to model various kinds of networks, from the geographic distribution of goods by a trucking company to the physical layout of circuits on a computer's integrated circuit board. Once the graph model is developed, one can ask questions about the shortest path length between two nodes. Such questions are important to the trucking company because their answers suggest the most economically feasible delivery routes. Such questions are also important to the integrated circuit designer because the shorter the path length between two nodes in a circuit the faster the circuit will perform its function.

Readers will encounter a rich variety of graph applications during their study of computer science and related fields. This brief glimpse, unfortunately, is an understatement of the importance of graphs (their theory and their applications) in this study.

10-2-2 Complexity Classes and the Limits of Computability

Throughout this text, we have been concerned with estimating the complexity of algorithms. This concern is essential in the process of measuring efficiency, as well as understanding that different algorithms have intrinsically different orders of magnitude in their execution efficiencies.

Most of the algorithms which we have studied in this text have complexities that can be measured in $O(n)$, $O(n \log_2 n)$, or $O(n^2)$ execution steps. That is, their execution times are bounded by a polynomial with degree n^2 or less. We don't have to venture very far, however, to discover an algorithm whose complexity exceeds these bounds. For instance, ordinary matrix multiplication has complexity $O(n^3)$, where n is the number of rows and columns in the two matrices being multiplied. In general, the class of *all* deterministic algorithms—such as the ones in this text—which have polynomial complexity is known as the class "P." The class of all nondeterministic algorithms which have polynomial complexity is known as the class "NP." The difference between determinism and nondeterminism in algorithmic behavior is difficult to explain briefly, and will not be covered here. Interested readers should consult other texts, such as Horowitz and Sahni's *Fundamentals of Computer Algorithms* for more discussion of this important topic.

On the other hand, there are algorithms whose complexity exceeds the bounds of *any* degree of polynomial, having instead execution times that grow exponentially—$O(2^n)$, $O(n^2 2^n)$, and so forth—with the size of their input. These are a very important class of algorithms because of the extraordinary amount of computing time that they require when they are executed. The study of these algorithms is therefore central subject matter for an algorithms course, which closely follows this one in the undergraduate curriculum.

Proceeding one step further, there are problems in computer science which, although describable, are provably unsolvable. That is, we can define a problem which is so difficult that *no* algorithm (i.e., no program whose execution terminates under all input conditions) can be written which solves it. Here, we are at the limits of computability, and much research remains to be done to characterize this class of problems precisely, and to determine which problems are solvable in this sense and which are not.

An excellent example of this latter class of problems is popularly known as the "halting problem." It can be stated as follows:

> Find an algorithm H which will determine, for an arbitrary program P and input I, whether P will halt after a finite number of steps or else enter an infinite loop.

It is well-known that such an algorithm H does not exist; that is, the halting problem is unsolvable. Further reading in this important area of computability and complexity can be found in any text on algorithms, including the one by Horowitz and Sahni cited above.

10-3 ARCHITECTURE AND CONCURRENCY

In Chapter 2, we gained enough knowledge of computer organization to understand how data and programs are represented in the memory of contemporary computers. A more comprehensive study of computer organization and architecture follows this course in the computer science curriculum. There, the different levels of computer organization are exposed and related, including the microprogramming level, the input-output programming level, the machine language level, and the assembly language level. That study continues with more advanced courses entitled "computer architecture," which introduce such additional topics as multiprocessing, interrupt handling, logic design, integrated circuits, and VLSI design. Many of these topics appear in subtrees B and C of the Abbreviated CR Categories.

Two driving forces in the study of computer architecture are *control* and *efficiency*. By control, we mean the design and implementation of algorithms that effectively manage and respond to the myriad of different events that can occur during the operation of a computer in executing a program. The simplest and oldest control model is the so-called "von Neumann machine," in which the instructions of a single program are executed in a one-at-a-time fashion. Variations on the von Neumann architecture—such as overlap, pipelining, and cache memories—have been introduced over the last two decades in the interest of efficiency.

10-3-1 Concurrency and Synchronization in Modula-2

Beyond the von Neumann architecture, substantial efficiency gains may be realized by developing computers and programming languages that allow the execution of several instructions at a time, several programs at a time, and/or several data streams at a time. This area is a relatively young one, in the sense that a significant amount of research remains to be done before the effective exploitation of the natural parallelism in algorithms for day-to-day applications is realized. Thus, we now have several competing theories and processor models that attempt to exploit parallelism and make quantum gains in efficiency over the conventional von Neumann machines and sequential programming styles.

In this section, rather than broadly surveying the subject of concurrency, we introduce the features of Modula-2 that support concurrent programming. We also illustrate here a situation where these features are useful, in order to provide a taste of their potential utility across a broad range of programming applications.

The concurrent programming features of Modula-2 assume the presence of several processors, any number of which may be simultaneously executing a different procedure, called a "process." Cooperation and information sharing among processes is enabled through the use of common (shared) variables called "signals." This general model is depicted in Figure 10-2.

Modula-2's primitives for concurrent programming are provided in the standard system module Processes shown on the next page:

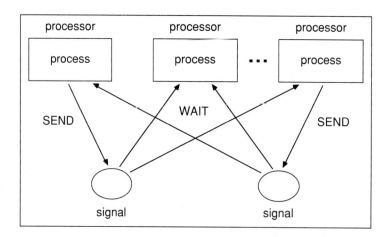

Figure 10-2
The setting for concurrent programming in Modula-2.

```
DEFINITION MODULE Processes;

TYPE SIGNAL;

PROCEDURE StartProcess (P: PROCEDURE; n: CARDINAL);

PROCEDURE SEND (VAR s: SIGNAL);

PROCEDURE WAIT (VAR s: SIGNAL);

PROCEDURE Awaited (s: SIGNAL): BOOLEAN;

PROCEDURE Init (VAR s: SIGNAL);

END Processes.
```

In this setting, the type SIGNAL is associated with any variable which is used to synchronize processes. Such a variable is used in a program to signal the occurrence of a specific event. As such, a signal can be "sent" from one process to other processes, via the SEND procedure. Moreover, other processes may "wait" for the occurrence of such a signal, via the WAIT procedure. These are the major operations that apply to signals, except for their initialization (via the Init procedure). Finally, the procedure Awaited is used to determine whether a particular signal is currently awaited by one or more processes.

The process itself is represented in Modula-2 as a procedure. Within the body of that procedure, one may include one or more SEND and WAIT statements, accordingly, as its own execution detects/needs a particular signal before continuing. Typically, representing a collection of concurrent events is accomplished by writing a so-called "monitor." A monitor is a module in which one or more signals are declared globally and shared among its constituent procedures (representations of processes) for the purpose of coordinating control as certain classes of events take place. We shall illustrate these principles by examples in the sections below.

10-3-2 An Application: The Producer-Consumer Model

In this model, we have a "buffer pool" of fixed size, which is shared by several programs simultaneously. The pool is managed by the operating system and may serve, for instance, as a queueing area for files destined for an input-output device (such as a printer). The situation here is different from that depicted in Chapter 6 (cf Figure 6-13), because this buffer does not gracefully grow as the number of print jobs in the queue increases. Instead, the printer is viewed as a "consumer" of print jobs from the buffer, and the programs that send print jobs to the buffer are viewed as "producers." This situation is pictured in Figure 10-3.

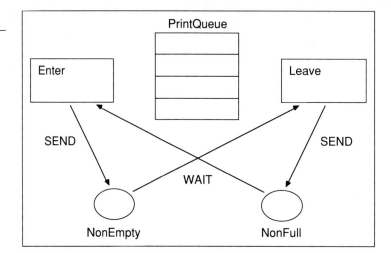

Figure 10-3
The producer-consumer model for monitoring a print queue.

The monitor for this model has two processes, which we shall call "Enter" and "Leave" (for conceptual association with their counterparts in Chapter 6). It also has four common variables: the buffer (called PrintQueue), an integer n (which keeps track of the number of print jobs in the queue), and two signals (called NonFull and NonEmpty), which are used to relay certain controlling events that may occur during the ongoing activities of maintaining the buffer.

The central idea to remember here is that any number of Enter and Leave operations may occur, and in any order. The monitor has no direct control over these occurrences; it must only respond intelligently to them when they do occur. To illustrate, suppose we have a buffer that can accommodate no more than four (4) print jobs at any one time. If that is the case, the fifth successive occurrence of an Enter operation, without an intervening Leave, should cause the Enter to interrupt itself and WAIT for the signal NonFull to be issued. Conversely, the first occurrence of a Leave operation with an empty buffer (for instance, before the first Enter) should cause a WAIT for the signal NonEmpty to be issued. Who issues these signals? The procedures (Leave and Enter, respectively) that are in a position to recognize these two events must therefore SEND the signals NonFull and NonEmpty, respectively. The complete print queue monitor is shown below:

```
MODULE Monitor[1];

FROM Processes IMPORT SIGNAL, SEND, WAIT, Init;
EXPORT Enter, Leave;

CONST BufferSize=4;
VAR n: [0..BufferSize];
    NonEmpty, NonFull: SIGNAL;
    i,j: [0..BufferSize-1];   (* indices for the queue *)
    PrintQueue: ARRAY [0..BufferSize-1] OF INTEGER;
```

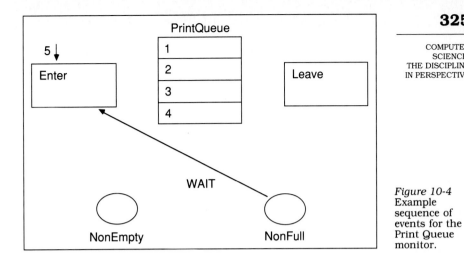

Figure 10-4
Example sequence of events for the Print Queue monitor.

```
PROCEDURE Enter (x: CARDINAL);
BEGIN
  IF n=BufferSize THEN
    WAIT(NonFull)
  END;
  n:=n+1;
  PrintQueue[i]:=x;
  i:=(i+1) MOD BufferSize;
  SEND(NonEmpty)
END Enter;

PROCEDURE Leave (VAR x: CARDINAL);
BEGIN
  IF n=0 THEN
    WAIT(NonEmpty)
  END;
  n:=n-1;
  x:=PrintQueue[j];
  j:=(j+1) MOD BufferSize;
  SEND(NonFull)
END Leave;

BEGIN
  n:=0;
  i:=0;
  j:=0;
  Init(NonEmpty);
  Init(NonFull)
END Monitor;
```

A sample trace of the activity of Enter and Leave, for a typical collection of invocations, is shown in Figure 10-4. Note here that the arrival the fifth successive Enter causes this process to WAIT until receiving the SIGNAL NonFull from the Leave process, which is executing simultaneously. Note also that the indices i and j keep track of the head and tail of the queue itself and that the four-element buffer is utilized in a circular fashion.

10-4 OPERATING SYSTEMS AND THE HUMAN INTERFACE

The introduction of operating systems in Chapter 6 was necessarily simple and omitted most of the more complex aspects of contemporary operating system design. Yet, it did unveil the importance of the Stack and the Queue as essential data types in any operating system model.

Contemporary research and development of operating systems also addresses issues of concurrency, distribution of operating systems over networks of cooperating computers, and sophisticated user interfaces involving graphics, mice, and windows as well as a natural command language. Traditional text terminals are giving way to the rapid evolution of "bit-mapped graphics" workstations, which provide powerful tools, through rapid and reliable user interfaces, for software development.

We cannot begin to scratch the surface of these areas in this text; the interested reader is referred to later courses in the curriculum for a more thorough study of operating systems principles and their application to contemporary hardware environments.

10-5 PROGRAMMING LANGUAGES, NATURAL LANGUAGES, AND THEIR PROCESSORS

Our discussions in this text are necessarily limited to a single programming language, Modula-2. In the broad area of computer science and computer applications there are many different programming languages in use.

We have seen, for instance, that LISP is an important programming tool in *artificial intelligence* applications. This field has also seen the rapid growth of PROLOG, a programming language which is especially useful in applications where the simulation of logical reasoning, or rule-based systems, is required. Some of these applications are the "expert systems" introduced in chapter 8.

Outside the artificial intelligence area, several other areas of computer science have different programming language preferences. In the area of *scientific and engineering* programming, for instance, premiums are placed on the availability of powerful tools for numerical and statistical analysis of data. Scientists and engineers rely heavily upon FORTRAN (Formula Translating System), one of the oldest programming languages, and its extensive library of mathematical routines for their computing needs. The main reason for this particular choice is FORTRAN's extensive support for mathematical analysis and its efficient implementation on very fast scientific computers and supercomputers. More recently, the languages C and Pascal have made substantial gains in usage by scientific programmers. Social scientists, on the other hand, often prefer to use commercially available packaged programs for their data analysis purposes, such as SPSS (Statistical Package for the Social Sciences) and SAS (Statistical Analysis System).

In *commercial data processing and information systems* applications, COBOL has been the dominant programming language. This domination is attributed to COBOL's extensive support for large data file definition and processing, its ease of learning by the large programming staffs of our nation's businesses and government organizations, and its widespread implementation and standardization dating back to the middle 1960s. More recently, however, the COBOL programming community has gradually migrated toward the use of "fourth generation languages" (4GLs for short) for many of their data processing applications. These languages are useful in the design of database applications and contain a higher level of expressive power than conventional programming languages. For instance, one typically finds in these languages powerful "query" commands for selectively searching and retrieving information from a database. In a conventional language like COBOL, such queries would not be directly supported in the language.

Another important general area of programming applications is known traditionally as *systems programming*. These applications produce our operating systems, our programming language compilers and interpreters, our text editors, our real-time embedded software systems, and all other software elements whose reliability and efficiency are most crucial in the effective utilization of computers by the applications programming communities themselves. Modula-2 has rapidly emerged as a systems programming language, and so have the languages Ada and C. Traditionally, however, most systems programming has been done in the assembly (machine) language of the host machine where the software systems are used. This choice, although arguably efficient, places serious constraints on software reliability and portability. The emergence of C, Ada, and Modula-2 in the systems programming area will likely provide effective means for addressing these reliability and portability problems, while maintaining acceptable levels of efficiency for systems software.

A great deal more can be said about the evolution and substance of various species of programming languages. The interested reader is referred to other references on the subject, including one by this writer, which are listed at the end of this chapter.

10-5-1 Mice, Windows, and What About English?

A great deal of effort has been spent, during the short history of computer science, to find ways of effectively bridging the gap between our natural, human modes of communication and the computer's unnatural, inhuman modes of communication. Although substantial progress has been made, this "human interface problem" (as it is often called) remains largely elusive. That is, professionals in various fields who need to use computers often cannot communicate their needs to these machines without some kind of intermediate restatement of such needs in a form and style that the computer can understand and service.

Sometimes that restatement can be made after the professional has directly learned the artificial language of an application package, such as Lotus 1-2-3 for solving "spreadsheet" problems that appear in all kinds of accounting applications. Furthermore, many authors (including this one) learn about the rudiments of word processing and laser graphic typesetting software, so that the tedium of manuscript preparation, revision, and publication can be reduced.

Other applications, however, require the utilization of an intermediary programmer between the professional and the computerization of his or her problem. Small accounting firms, medical organizations, and other businesses have data organization and processing requirements that exceed the limited capabilities of a spreadsheet program. They require some additional design and interface development by an experienced "systems analyst" before they can take full advantage of computing in their daily operations.

In any application, however, the final software product tends to be close to the "language" of the professional field it serves. Ideally, such software products are both easy to learn and efficient to operate by persons in that profession. Ease of use and efficient operation, therefore, are well served when the language at the interface is highly Anglicized and effectively integrates the technology of "mice," "windows," and the conventional keyboard at the user's terminal. (Voice and touchscreens are also designed for this purpose, although their effective utilization has been modest to date.) Readers have perhaps used mice and windows already in their computing experience. For example, the Apple MacIntosh employs these in its word processing and graphics software. Furthermore, many Modula-2 systems contain predefined modules that facilitate the development of applications using mouse and window techniques at the user interface.

So, what can be said about the use of English as an interface with computers? On the surface, this would appear to be an ultimate medium of communication. In fact, that goal has emerged at various times during the short history of computing. For instance, the designers of COBOL fashioned its syntax after the syntax of pidgin English, identifying paragraphs, sentences, clauses, and so forth in the structural hierarchy that comprises a COBOL program. However, the ultimate goal that COBOL would allow the broadest range of professionals to intelligibly read and understand computer programs was both naive in its conception and not even closely approximated at any time during the twenty-five year life of the language. Of course, that rather negative conclusion does not diminish COBOL's substantial contribution to the application of computers in the field of data processing.

Recent efforts to develop models and systems that simulate computer understanding of English have appeared in the field of artificial intelligence. Here, the goal is to concentrate on a relatively narrow subject matter area, such as weather forecasting, and to develop tools that exploit the computer's ability to simulate the understanding of utterances in that subject area. These tools can, for instance, serve as an aid to a person developing a weather forecast, or even as a basis for the computer to translate the text of a weather forecast from English into French. A system that does the latter, in fact, is called TAUM-METEO and is used regularly by the Canadian government to provide bilingual weather forecasts. As a general field of application, however, the development of computerized natural language understanding systems is in its infancy. However, this field shows rich promise as a research area for the next decade or two.

10-5-2 Language Processors: Compilers, Interpreters, and LISP Machines

Returning to the topic of programming languages, we recall from Chapter 2 the basic discontinuity that occurs between an utterance as it appears in a Modula-2 program and the same utterance as it is interpreted and executed, as a series of machine instructions, by a computer. The resolution of this discontinuity is accomplished in one of three different ways: *compilation, interpretation,* or *direct execution*.

The general structure of a compiler was introduced in Chapter 8. There, recall, the Modula-2 program passed through two stages of analysis, called "lexical analysis" and "syntactic analysis." Thereafter, the "code generation" stage developed an equivalent machine language program, while the "optimization" stage looked for ways of improving the efficiency of that program. Thus, after a Modula-2 program is compiled, an entirely separate and later step is required in order for the (equivalent machine language) program to be executed.

By contrast, the process of interpretation takes the original program's body, in a step-by-step fashion, carrying out each step directly. No prior translation of the entire program takes place; instead each step is dynamically interpreted (and in cases where the step is inside a loop, repeatedly *re*interpreted) at the time it is encountered. This process is shown in Figure 10-5. As our intuition would suggest, compilation has an execution-time efficiency advantage over interpretation. However, interpretation is preferred in many rapid-prototyping and program development environments, since information about the original Modula-2 program is more directly available to the programmer when working with an interpreter, versus working with a compiler. Important languages that are widely implemented by interpreters include LISP, PROLOG, and BASIC.

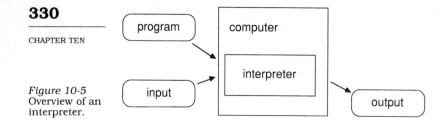

Figure 10-5
Overview of an interpreter.

The idea of designing machines that directly (and hence, interpretively) execute the statements of a program in a language such as LISP has more recently been brought to fruition. The so-called "LISP machines" are widely used in artificial intelligence research because they combine the conceptual advantages of interpreters with the run-time efficiency advantages of compilers. Under direct execution, the machine is no longer bound to the basic von Neumann architecture that was discussed in Chapter 2. Instead, the machine enjoys an architecture that directly mirrors the semantic structure of the language (say, LISP) it is interpreting. That is, its instructions and data types are matched with those of the LISP language itself. At this writing, LISP machines have been successfully marketed by several computer manufacturers, including Symbolics and Texas Instruments.

10-5-3 Fourth Generation Languages: The UNIX Environment

The idea of "fourth generation languages" attempts to address problems in software reliability, development, and maintenance by providing powerful problem-solving tools that are directly associated with the area of application itself. For instance, the programmer who is developing software for a bank should ideally have a repertoire of instructions that are semantically representative of the basic functions that occur in the bank: OPEN an account, DEPOSIT some money, WITHDRAW some money, CLOSE an account, and so forth.

The commands of a fourth generation language tend to be more imperative in substance, rather than algorithmic, when compared with those of an ordinary programming language. That is, programmers are enabled by these languages to describe what to do (via a simple verb like DEPOSIT) rather than how to do it (like write a loop that locates an account in a file, adds money to the balance, and rewrites that balance in the file). Examples of fourth generation languages are the database query languages (such as QUEL in the INGRES database system), the statistical packages (such as SPSS and SAS), and the so-called shell programming language of the UNIX operating system.

This latter language allows programmers to combine different commands, from the library of UNIX utilities, in creative ways to solve problems that would normally require many times the effort in a conventional programming language. Although these solutions are not always efficient, in a production sense, they do provide powerful tools to develop prototype solutions to problems rapidly (especially in the domain of text processing) and to demonstrate their feasibility.

10-6 MATHEMATICAL ALGORITHMS AND SIMULATION

The area of mathematical progamming is an especially important element of the computer scientist's field of view, since such an extensive array of engineering and scientific research and development areas depend critically upon mathematical methods. Briefly, mathematical programming applications are those that rely principally upon the computer's ability to perform rapid and accurate mathematical calculations, often involving very large numbers of individual data values and calculations.

The challenge here is that the digital computer is a discrete device (it represents a REAL value with a *finite* number of significant digits), while many of the physical and biological phenomena being studied actually have continuous mathematical representations (mathematically, some real numbers require infinite precision for accurate representation). Thus, the calculus of continuous variables provides theoretical foundations for a large class of mathematical algorithms.

10-6-1 Errors in Computer Arithmetic and Number Representation

The computer scientist must understand the ramifications of having inexact computer representations of scientific and statistical phenomena that have exact mathematical characterizations. The field of "error analysis" therefore seeks to analyze such errors: errors in the computer representation of real numbers (called "representation errors") and errors in the computer execution of arithmetic functions (called "propagated errors"). In order to gain a proper basis for studying errors and their control in mathematical algorithms, computer science students should therefore develop proficiency in the calculus.

To illustrate, suppose we have the decimal number 1.1. To represent this number in the computer as a REAL, we must convert it to an equivalent binary value (recall the discussion in Chapter 2). However, the *exact* equivalent binary number has an *infinite* number of binary digits, forming the repeated pattern: 1.00011001100110011001100110011....

Of course, the computer representation of real numbers disallows such values, which require an infinite number of bits for their representation. Instead, such values are *truncated* to that number of significant bits which the computer representation permits. That number varies among different computer species, but it is often 24 (using a 32-bit word for the entire value, including sign and scale factor), or 56 (for "extended precision," which is required by certain mathematical algorithms—see below), or higher. In any event, that number is always *finite*, and therefore the binary *approximation* of the decimal number 1.1 is as follows (assuming 24-bit representation): 1.00011001100110011001100.

Errors are also propagated during the computer execution of simple arithmetic functions, such as multiplication and division of REAL values. For instance, the real values 11.0 and 10.0 may have *exact* REAL representations, but their exact quotient (1.1 again) cannot be represented.

Because of the proliferation of representational and propagated errors, the computer solution of complex mathematical and statistical problems is necessarily an *approximate* process. A great deal of effort, therefore, goes into estimating and controlling the *degree* of such errors, and that varies widely among different classes of problems.

10-6-2 Mathematical Programming

Part G of the Abbreviated CR Categories, given at the beginning of this chapter, lists the major areas where mathematical programming and error analysis are used.

In the area of numerical analysis, the notion of "interpolation" suggests a general process of iterative refinement of an approximate solution to a problem. This iteration continues until either a tolerably small error (difference between the approximate solution and the exact solution) has been achieved, or else it is discovered that such a small error cannot be achieved. A classical example of interpolation is Newton's method for iteratively arriving at an approximation to a mathematical function (such as the square root of a real number) that cannot be computed directly.

The area of "numerical linear algebra" includes the broad spectrum of mathematical problems that requires the solution of a series of simultaneous linear equations. For instance, with two variables x_1 and x_2, the equations are:

$$a_{11}x_1 + a_{12}x_2 = b_1$$
$$a_{21}x_1 + a_{22}x_2 = b_2$$

Here, the problem is to find values for x_1 and x_2, given any particular set of values for the a's and b's. For some such sets the solution is exact, while for others the solution may only be approximated. Further, there are some sets of values for the a's and b's that lead to either *no* solution or *infinitely many* solutions to these equations.

Thus, any effective computer algorithm for solving such sets of linear equations must gracefully accommodate each of these different possible outcomes; it must find (reasonably accurate approximations for the exact) solutions when they do exist, and it must detect and report the nonexistence of solutions in all other cases. A widely used algorithm for this problem is known as "Gaussian elimination," and its mastery requires significant mathematical maturity as well as programming skill.

The area of "optimization" encompasses algorithms that serve the development of mathematical modeling of economic systems, in which different sets of strategic decisions lead to different levels of profit or loss. Finding optimal strategies, therefore, leads to maximization of profit (minimization of loss). Simulation of other kinds of strategic and physical systems also requires the use of optimization methods. For instance, in "fine tuning" the performance of an operating system in a particular application environment (such as a bank), one would like to determine the optimal amount of memory and on line disk space and the optimal number of interactive terminals for managing the daily average and peak numbers of transactions that the operating system will have to accommodate. Such a determination is governed by the constraint of minimizing computing costs (that is, not purchasing too much memory or disk) while maximizing terminal response time during peak periods of activity.

10-7 ARTIFICIAL INTELLIGENCE AND COGNITIVE SCIENCE

We have seen, at various times throughout this text, some perspectives on the area of computer science known as "artificial intelligence." Chapter 8 contains a fairly extensive introduction to this area, and its subfields are broken out again in part I of the Abbreviated CR Categories. The artificial intelligence field has reached dramatic levels of activity in the last few years, not only as an important field of research but also in industry and government where many of its theories and models have been brought into productive use.

The role of LISP and recursion is central to AI research and development. So are the problems of "combinatoric explosion of alternatives" and "knowledge representation and acquisition." That is, in simulating even the simplest aspects of human intelligent behavior, an AI system must be designed to manage effeciently the large number of elementary decisions that occur. Moreover, how can such a system acquire, store, and maintain the knowledge elements and structures that are needed for governing such decisions? These are difficult problems; some skeptics believe, in fact, that they are not solvable. Excellent readings on the philosophical as well as the practical issues surrounding AI are abundant. For instance, readers are referred to Pamela McCorduck's *Machines Who Think* (Freedman, 1979) for the former and Elaine Rich's *Artificial Intelligence* (McGraw-Hill, 1983) for the latter.

The 1980s is now seeing a new field of study emerging in certain distinctive academic settings, and this is known as "cognitive science." Based on the belief that the focus of AI research and development may have become too narrow for effectively studying and modeling human intelligent behavior, cognitive science combines certain areas of psychology, philosophy, linguistics, and AI itself into a coherent intellectual discipline. A prominent scholar in this new field is John Searle, and his writings on the subject are strongly recommended for the interested reader. Undergraduate and graduate programs in cognitive science are now evolving at many of the nation's leading colleges and universities.

10-8 COMPUTER SCIENCE: THE DISCIPLINE AND THE PROFESSION

With the Abbreviated CR Categories and the first nine chapters of this text providing topical overviews, we may now draw some conclusions about the essential nature of computer science as an academic and professional discipline, including both what it *is* and what it *is not*. First, our experience allows us to dispel some common myths about the nature of computer science:

- Computer science *is not* just programming. An accurate characterization of the role of programming in the field of computer science can be drawn by equating it with the role of narrative writing in the study of English or history.
- Computer science *is not* just the application of computers to those professions that need the services of a computer. Professionals in other fields sometimes tend to see computer scientists from a self-serving point of view; that is, they view computer science as "whatever computers can do for us." Since the largest single application of computers is business, some businesspersons tend to characterize computer science in its entirety as "the design and implementation of management information systems." This error often leads to fundamental misunderstandings among businesses and academic computer science programs, especially over the choice of subject matter that ought to be taught in the computer science undergraduate curriculum.
- Computer science *is not* just an engineering discipline, on the one hand, or a subdiscipline of mathematics, on the other. This does not mean, however, that computer science does not draw heavily in its methodology from engineering, or in its theory and style from mathematics. The body of this text, for instance, testifies to the fundamental contributions of both these fields to computer science.

On the positive side, our experience in this text suggests that the following are generally more accurate statements about the true nature of computer science as an academic field of study and a profession.

- Computer science *is* the study of algorithms and data structures, including their theories, their abstractions, their mechanical realizations, their verification and reliability, their efficiency and measurement, and their linguistic description.
- Computer science *is* a mathematical discipline, in the sense that its style of investigation and communication is necessarily rigorous in the same way that the other sciences and mathematics are rigorous.

- Computer science *is* an applied science, in the sense that its theories are continually evaluated in an empirical setting. Programs are not only designed and implemented, but they are also analyzed for efficiency and verified for correctness. Computer science applications are drawn from a wide variety of fields, including business, engineering, government, academia, medicine, and law.

A computer scientist, therefore, is a person who understands the discipline in its entire depth and breadth and who conducts research, design, or applications work in a particular subject matter area of computer science.

Having now seriously begun the study of computer science, interested readers may want to expand their involvement in the field. An ideal way to do this would be to become a (student) member of ACM or the IEEE Computer Society, the two principal computer science professional societies that were noted at the beginning of this chapter. Many colleges and universities have their own student chapters of ACM whose memberships are open to all who want to pursue such interests.

With membership in ACM, one receives a subscription to the *Communications of the ACM*, the principal monthly journal of the association. This journal contains not only technical articles and reports on contemporary issues in computer science, it also keeps an up-to-date calendar of conferences, it reports current events in the computer industry, and it publishes classified advertisements for employment in the computer industry and academia. Similar benefits accompany a student membership in the IEEE Computer Society, through a regular subscription to its monthly publication, *Computer*.

As a field of study, computer science offers academic degree programs at the bachelors, masters, and doctoral levels at most leading colleges and universities throughout the nation (indeed, throughout the world). This rapid evolution of computer science in the academic community has taken place mainly during the last two decades. With it have come many problems associated with the emergence of any new discipline: unevenness of understanding and support on the part of other disciplines in the sciences, overextension of industrial demand for computer science professionals, and the consequent severe shortage of teaching computer scientists in academia, and so on. However, these problems have recently shown signs of decline, and the field is entering a period of relative normalcy in its evolution.

Undergraduates who major in computer science gain access to a variety of options for further study and professional growth upon graduation. A good reference for these different postgraduate study and professional opportunities can be found in two *Peterson's Guides*: one lists the employment opportunities in the computer industry, while the other lists the graduate school opportunities in computer science. ACM also publishes an annual *Graduate Assistantship Directory*, which gives comprehensive and detailed information on all the computer science graduate programs that exist—their number of faculty, their research areas, their number of graduate assistantships, their research computer support, and so forth.

Graduate programs leading to the M.S. or the Ph.D. in computer science vary widely in their areas of emphasis. Major areas of emphasis include theory (formal languages, automata, computability, and so forth), hardware systems (architecture, networking, parallel processing, VLSI design, and so forth), software systems (operating systems, compilers, interpreters, human interfacing, graphics, and so forth), artificial intelligence (natural language understanding, vision, robotics, speech, expert systems, and so forth), database and information systems, and other applications areas.

Unlike many other fields of study, computer science has an unusual abundance of interdisciplinary ties. The field owes much to mathematics. Indeed, it is true that Alonzo Church, Alan Turing, John von Neumann, and many others who are recognized as the founders of this new discipline were mathematicians. On the other hand, much of the theory that underlies the design of modern programming languages originated in the field of linguistics, especially from the work of the linguist Noam Chomsky. The disciplines of logic and abstraction, which originated among the philosophers, also contribute to the foundations for the "switching theory" that guides the logical design of computer systems. The areas of artificial intelligence and cognitive science borrow much of their intellectual energy from psychology, linguistics, and philosophy. Mechanical engineering contributes to robotics, electrical engineering contributes to electronic circuit design, and so on. Thus, computer science is richly endowed with principles that originate in closely-allied fields; computer science has synthesized these principles in new and exciting ways.

As an undergraduate computer science major, you should now have gained an initial mastery of data abstraction, verification, and the related mathematical methods that support the rich variety of applications that computer scientists regularly encounter. In the future, you should expect to gain a really comprehensive overview of the field in its entirety, so that a strong motivation and perspective emerges for further study. Readings cited at the end of this chapter, together with this text itself, will provide the basis for your future work.

EXERCISES

10-1 Define, using the same style and precision in the earlier chapters, the abstract data type Graph, with operators Create, Store, Retrieve, Insert, Delete, Search, and Display.

10-2 Implement the abstract data type Graph in Modula-2, using the definitions you developed in exercise 10-1. Assuming the graph's element type is String, IMPORT the necessary operators from the Strings abstract data type that is implemented in Chapter 7. Use similar techniques for remembering the current node for a graph that were used in the implementation of Trees in Chapter 8.

10-3 Verify this implementation of Graphs in exercise 10-2 by writing a driver program that exercises all of your graph operator implementations.

10-4 For your implementation of the Search graph operator, verify its correctness by showing that its execution satisfies the postconditions given in exercise 10-1 whenever its preconditions are met.

10-5 Exercise this chapter's Monitor program, using different arrival sequences for the jobs shown in Figure 10-4. For each of these variations, discuss its impact on the amount of WAITing that the monitor experiences as it serves the individual requests in that sequence.

10-6 Another example of the use of concurrency in programming languages comes from a classical problem in logic, called the Dining Philosophers' Problem. Here, we assume there are five philosophers who spend all of their time in a villa that has a common dining room. All of their activity is limited to thinking (which is done alone) and eating (which is done in the common dining room). In the dining room is a table with five plates, five chairs, five forks, and a single platter of spaghetti in the center, as shown in Figure 10-6.

While thinking, a philosopher may decide to enter the dining room and eat. In order for eating to begin, the philosopher must find a place at the table where there is an available fork on the left. Further, the philosopher must obtain a portion of spaghetti from the common platter by picking up an available fork on the right, and using both forks to retrieve a serving from the platter. Thereafter, the philosopher can begin eating, after which he or she returns both forks to the table, gets up from the table, and leaves the room.

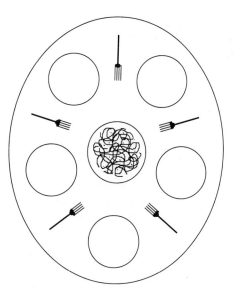

Figure 10-6
The dining philosophers' dining room.

As we can see, certain situations will interrupt the smooth flow of this process. First, a philosopher may enter the room and find that no empty seat has an available fork on its left. Second, the existence of such a seat does not guarantee that there is an available fork on its right! Thus, two distinct situations can occur that will cause a philosopher to wait. Identifying these situations by the SIGNALs SeatAvailable and ForkAvailable, respectively, discuss the requirements for designing a monitor that will correctly manage any sequence of events that can occur at this table. Implement such a Dining-Philosophers-Monitor by writing procedures that will handle these events. Your procedures should share a common data structure that reflects the current status of the seats and forks around the table.

10-7 Summarize your ideas about the nature of the field of computer science by writing a one- or two-page essay on computer science. In it, describe those aspects of the field that are most interesting to you for further study, as well as those aspects that are least interesting.

10-8 Find a current issue of *Communications of the ACM* in your library and read it from cover to cover. Do the same for the IEEE *Computer* magazine.

A SHORT ANNOTATED BIBLIOGRAPHY OF SELECTED TEXTS AND REFERENCES IN COMPUTER SCIENCE

The following texts and references are given to provide a representative sample of basic readings in the major topic areas in computer science. This sample may be useful as readers begin to probe further into these areas in their future studies. The entries listed below are annotated to identify computer science topic areas (in **boldface**) from the Abbreviated CR Categories tree for which they are written, as well as the level of audience (i. e. , introductory, intermediate, or advanced undergraduate text, or graduate-level reference) for which they are written.

Abelson, Harold and Gerald Sussman, *Structure and Interpretation of Computer Programs*, MIT Press (1985), 542 pages. **Algorithms and data structures, abstraction, symbol manipulation**. Sophomore-level undergraduate text; uses Scheme, a variant of LISP.

Aho, Alfred, John Hopcroft, and Jeffrey Ullman, *Data Structures and Algorithms*, Addison-Wesley (1983), 427 pages. **Algorithms and data structures, dynamic programming, memory management**. Intermediate undergraduate text.

Aho, Alfred, Ravi Sethi, and Jeffrey Ullman, *Compilers: Principles, Techniques, and Tools*, Addison-Wesley (1986), 796 pages. **Programming languages; theory, processors (compilers)**. Advanced undergraduate text and graduate-level reference.

Booch, Grady, *Software Engineering with Ada*, Benjamin Cummings (1983), 502 pages. **Software engineering**. Advanced undergraduate text.

Ghezzi, Carlo and Mehdi Jazayeri, *Programming Language Concepts*, John Wiley & Sons (1987), 428 pages. **Programming Languages**. Advanced undergraduate text.

Gries, David, *The Science of Programming*, Springer-Verlag (1981), 366 pages. **Software development, program verification, theory**. Advanced undergraduate text.

Hofstadter, Douglas, *Godel, Escher, Bach*, Vintage (1979), 777 pages. **Theory**. Pulitzer prize-winning novel on the confluence of certain themes in computer science, mathematics, music, and art.

Horowitz, Ellis, *Fundamentals of Programming Languages*, Computer Science Press (1983), 450 pages. **Programming languages, concurrency**. Advanced undergraduate text.

Horowitz, Ellis and Sartaj Sahni, *Fundamentals of Computer Algorithms*, Computer Science Press (1978), 626 pages. **Algorithms and data structures, complexity classes, mathematics of computing**. Intermediate undergraduate text; language-independent.

Knuth, Donald E. , *Fundamental Algorithms, 2e*, Addison-Wesley (1975), 634 pages. **Algorithms and data structures, theory, computer organization**. Advanced undergraduate text, graduate-level reference.

—, *Seminumerical Algorithms 2e*, Addison-Wesley (1981), 688 pages. **Mathematics of computing; combinatorics, interpolation, probability, random number generation; hardware, arithmetic and logic structures**. Advanced undergraduate text, graduate-level reference.

—, *Sorting and Searching*, Addison-Wesley (1975), 723 pages. **Algorithms, theory, computational complexity, information storage and retrieval, hashing**. Advanced undergraduate text, graduate-level reference.

Korth, Henry F. and Abraham Silberschatz, *Database System Concepts*, McGraw-Hill Computer Science Series (1986), 546 pages. **Database management systems, information retrieval**. Advanced undergraduate text.

Kruse, Robert L. , *Data Structures and Program Design, 2e*, Prentice-Hall (1987), 586 pages. **Data structures, algorithms, complexity**. Intermediate undergraduate text.

Lewis, Harry R. and Christos Papadimitriou, *Elements of the Theory of Computation*, Prentice-Hall (1981), 466 pages. **Theory of computation; formal languages, models of computation (automata, Turing machines), complexity, computability**. Advanced undergraduate text.

McCorduck, Pamela, *Machines Who Think*, Freedman (1979), 375 pages. **Artificial intelligence**. Historical survey of the origins and promise of the field of artificial intelligence.

McGilton, Henry and Rachel Morgan, *Introducing the UNIX System*, McGraw-Hill (1983), 556 pages. **Operating systems, the user interface, software development environments**. Text and reference.

Peterson, James L. and Abraham Silberschatz, *Operating Systems Concepts*, Addison-Wesley (1983), 548 pages. **Operating systems**. Advanced undergraduate text.

Rich, Elaine, *Artificial Intelligence*, McGraw-Hill Series in Artificial Intelligence (1983), 436 pages. **Artificial intelligence; knowledge representation, learning, logic, search**. Advanced undergraduate text.

Salton, Gerald and Michael McGill, *Introduction to Modern Information Retrieval*, Mcgraw-Hill Computer Science Series (1983), 448 pages. **Text analysis,

automatic indexing, information retrieval applications. Advanced undergraduate text and graduate-level reference.

Sedgewick, Robert, *Algorithms*, Addison-Wesley (1983), 552 pages. **Algorithms, computational complexity.** Intermediate undergraduate text.

Tanenbaum, Andrew S., *Structured Computer Organization, 2e*, Prentice-Hall (1984), 465 pages. **Hardware, logic design, computer systems organization, architecture.** Intermediate undergraduate text.

Tucker, Allen B., *Programming Languages, 2e*, McGraw-Hill Computer Science Series (1986), 590 pages. **Programming languages.** Advanced undergraduate text.

Ullman, Jeffrey D., *Principles of Database Systems 2e*, Computer Science Press (1982), 484 pages. **Database management systems, information retrieval.** Advanced undergraduate text.

Weiner, Richard and Richard Sincovec, *Software Engineering with Ada and Modula-2*, John Wiley & Sons (1984), 451 pages. **Software engineering, programming techniques.** Advanced undergraduate text.

Wirth, Niklaus, *Algorithms + Data Structures = Programs*, Prentice-Hall (1987), 366 pages. **Algorithms and data structures, programming techniques.** Intermediate undergraduate text.

APPENDIX

FROM PASCAL TO MODULA-2: AN INTRODUCTION

Linguists, who study the evolution of humanity's (natural) languages, use the idea of "language drift" to help explain how a language changes as the culture evolves through history. Obsolete words and phrases slowly disappear from the language as they become unused, and new words and phrases find their way into the dictionaries in place of the obsolete ones.

So it is with programming languages. A most apropos example of "programming language drift" is the evolution from Pascal to Modula-2. The decade from 1970 to 1980, which approximately marks the birth of Pascal at one end and the birth of Modula-2 at the other, witnessed a significant evolution in the "culture" of programming. Reflecting this evolution, some obsolete Pascal features, such as the **goto** statement, do not appear in Modula-2. More important, Modula-2 contains many new features that reflect the emergence of new methodologies and needs in the programming culture. Prominent among these are the need to define and implement abstract data types, the need to access system-level phenomena (binary representations of values, memory management, and so forth), and the need to implement concurrency in algorithms. These nonelementary subjects are addressed in various parts of this text.

In this appendix, we give a concise introduction to Modula-2 for readers who are already familiar with programming and Pascal. This material should not, however, be viewed as an introduction to programming.

A-1 BASIC PROGRAM STRUCTURE

The basic structure of a Modula-2 program is similar to that of its Pascal counterpart. Recall that the general form of a Pascal program is as follows:

```
program p (input,output);
  declarations
begin
  s; s; ...; s
end.
```

Here, the program name is p and the designation "(input,output)" indicates that the program will be reading and writing information at the terminal screen. (Often this designation is optional and may be omitted.)

The "declarations" include constants, types, variables, and any procedures and functions that the program itself invokes and are not provided as standard Pascal procedures. Some Pascal implementations allow separate compilation of these procedures, but that is a true language extension when it occurs. The statements of the program are designated above as "s; s; ...; s" to indicate that they are separated individually by semicolons. The reserved words **program**, **begin**, and **end** are required, and the entire program is terminated by a period. As an example, consider the following simple Pascal program, which averages a series of integers that are entered at the terminal.

```
program averager (input, output);
{This program computes the average AV of N input
 numbers X.}
var x, sum, av: real;
    n: integer;
begin
  n:=0; sum:=0;
  writeln ('Enter a series of numbers:');
  readln (x);
  while not eof do
    begin
      n:=n+1;
      sum:=sum+x;
      readln (x)
    end;
  av:=sum/n;
  writeln (n:5, ' numbers were given');
  writeln (av:5:1, ' is their average')
end.
```

A Modula-2 main program is called a "module" to indicate that it is a separately compiled unit of code. There are other kinds of modules that can be separately compiled besides main programs, and we introduce these in Chapter 1. In this elementary case, a Modula-2 main program has the following form.

```
MODULE p;
   import statements
   declarations
BEGIN
   s; s; ...; s
END p.
```

Here, the program name p must occur *both* in the heading *and* after the END in the program. The "declarations" and statements "s; s; ...; s" have generally the same usage and syntax as they do in Pascal; minor differences will be more fully explained below. The reserved words MODULE, BEGIN, and END are *necessarily* written in uppercase. Modula-2 is generally case-sensitive, so that the words BEGIN, Begin, and begin are three *different* identifiers. Only the first of these is the counterpart of the Pascal reserved word **begin**. (Some Modula-2 compilers relax this restriction, but we remain faithful to it throughout this text.)

The use of an "import statement" represents the first significant departure as we migrate from Pascal to Modula-2. Such a statement is *required* whenever the program uses *any* procedure (either standard or programmer-defined) that does not appear among its declarations. Unlike Pascal, the standard procedures in Modula-2 are grouped in several different packages, called "standard modules;" these provide basic input/output, arithmetic, storage management, type transfer, and other collections of procedures. When using such a procedure, the program must identify the name of the standard module from which it is being "imported" and the name of the procedure itself. This is done using an "import statement," which has the following form:

```
FROM module-name IMPORT procedure-names;
```

Two examples of the import statement appear in the Modula-2 program below. This program performs identically the same task as the foregoing Pascal program: it averages numbers that are entered at the terminal.

```
MODULE Averager;
   FROM RealInOut IMPORT ReadReal, Done, WriteReal;
   FROM InOut IMPORT WriteInt, WriteString, WriteLn;
```

```
(*This program computes the average AV of N input
  numbers X. *)
VAR x, sum, av: REAL;
    n: INTEGER;
BEGIN
  n:=0;
  sum:=0.0;
  WriteString('Enter a series of numbers:');
  WriteLn;
  ReadReal(x); WriteLn;
  WHILE Done DO
    n:=n+1;
    sum:=sum+x;
    ReadReal(x); WriteLn
  END;
  av := sum / FLOAT(n);
  WriteInt(n,10);   WriteString(' numbers were given');
  WriteLn;
  WriteReal(av,10); WriteString(' is their average');
  WriteLn
END Averager.
```

Here, the standard procedures ReadReal and WriteReal are imported from the module RealInOut, and the standard procedures WriteInt, WriteString, and WriteLn are imported from the module InOut. A complete summary of Modula-2's standard procedures is provided in Appendix D. We shall gain experience with most of these in different parts of this text.

A-2 GENERAL SYNTAX

Much can be learned about the similarities and differences between Pascal and Modula-2 by examining their respective sets of reserved words. The Pascal reserved words are listed alphabetically in Figure A-1, and their Modula-2 counterparts are listed beside them wherever there are direct correspondences in usage. For instance, we see that the Pascal reserved word **array** has a direct counterpart ARRAY in Modula-2, while the Pascal reserved words **downto** and **goto** (!) have none. There are some reserved words in Modula-2 that have no counterparts in Pascal, such as DEFINITION, LOOP, and EXIT. These reflect features of Modula-2 that are not in Pascal, and they will be more fully discussed in various parts of this text.

As shown in the foregoing example programs, a Pascal *comment* can be written as a string of text enclosed between the braces { and }, while a Modula-2 comment's text is enclosed between (* and *). While this latter notation can also be used in Pascal, the braces { and } *cannot* be used to enclose comments in Modula-2; instead, they are used to enclose the members of a SET (see below).

Pascal	Modula-2	Pascal	Modula-2
and	AND	nil	
array	ARRAY	not	NOT
begin	BEGIN	of	OF
	BY	or	OR
case	CASE	packed	
const	CONST		POINTER
	DEFINITION	procedure	PROCEDURE
div	DIV	program	MODULE
do	DO		QUALIFIED
downto		record	RECORD
else	ELSE	repeat	REPEAT
	ELSIF		RETURN
end	END	set	SET
	EXIT		
	EXPORT		
file		then	THEN
for	FOR	to	TO
	FROM	type	TYPE
function	PROCEDURE	until	UNTIL
goto		var	VAR
if	IF	while	WHILE
	IMPLEMENTATION	with	WITH
	IMPORT		
in	IN		
label			
	LOOP		
mod	MOD		

Figure A-1 Reserved word correspondences in Pascal and Modula-2.

A-3 DATA TYPES, VALUES, AND DECLARATIONS

Modula-2's elementary data types are comparable with those of Pascal and are slightly more extensive, as shown in Figure A-2. Specifically, Modula-2 adds the CARDINAL type as that set of integers from 0 to the maximum value supported by the implementation. This is an especially useful type for any application involving counting and arrays; that is, any variable that takes only nonnegative values, such as an array's subscript.

Note also here that Modula-2 has the additional type LONGINT, which allows integer values over a wider range than that supported by the INTEGER type. Moreover, Modula-2 string values are enclosed either by apostrophes (') or by double quotes ("); if the string properly contains one of these, then the other *must* be used as the enclosing character. Subranges in Modula-2 are written *with* their enclosing brackets, whereas Pascal subranges appear within brackets only if they occur in an array declaration.

Elementary Type	Pascal Declaration	Modula-2 Declaration	Pascal Example	Modula-2 Example
Numbers				
real	real	REAL	3.5	3.5
integer	integer	INTEGER	−17	−17, −11H, or −16C
		LONGINT		
nonnegative integer	n/a	CARDINAL	n/a	17
Logical values	Boolean	BOOLEAN	true false	TRUE FALSE
Characters	char	CHAR	'a'	'a' or "a"
Strings			'It''s here!'	"It's here!" 'It"s here!'
Subranges			0..7	[0..7]
Scalars			(red,green,blue)	(red,green,blue)

Figure A-2 Elementary types and values in Pascal and Modula-2.

The correspondence between Pascal and Modula-2 is also strong with respect to the syntax and semantics of declarations. These are illustrated in Figure A-3, with some familiar examples.

A few additional notes should also be made here. First, a multidimensional array in Modula-2 is declared with its individual subscript ranges individually enclosed in brackets and separated by commas. For instance, the familiar Pascal declaration of a 10x10 array of integers b:

Declaration Kind	Pascal Example	Modula-2 Example
constant	**const pi**=3.14159;	CONST pi=3.14159;
type	**type** color=(red,green,blue); octal=0..7;	TYPE color=(red,green,blue); octal=[0..7];
variable	**var** x,sum: real;	VAR x,sum: REAL;
array	**var** a: **array** [1..10] **of** integer;	VAR a: ARRAY [1..10] OF INTEGER;
character string	**type** String=**packed array** [0..20] **of** char;	TYPE STRING=ARRAY [0..20] OF CHAR;

record	**var** r: **record**
	  field1: type;
	  field2: type;
	  ...
	  fieldn: type
	end;
		VAR r: RECORD
		  field1: type;
		  field2: type;
		  ...
		  fieldn: type
		END;

Figure A-3 Declarations in Pascal and Modula-2.

```
var b: array [1..10,1..10] of integer;
```

must be written in Modula-2 strictly in the following way:

```
VAR b: ARRAY [1..10],[1..10] OF INTEGER;
```

However, a reference to the entry in the ith row and jth column of b, where i and j are appropriate variables, is still written as b[i,j]—just as it is in Pascal.

A second note concerns character strings; Modula-2 has more extensive (yet still incomplete, as Chapter 7 illustrates) support for character string manipulation than Pascal. For instance, procedures for string input/output are provided and string assignment is also directly supported (rather than looping through a **for** loop, character by character, as in Pascal). However, the Pascal notion of **packed** (which suggests an efficient storage scheme) is not carried forth into Modula-2. On the other hand, as we illustrate in Chapter 7, it tends to be more convenient to begin a Modula-2 string's subscript range with 0 rather than 1, and we use that convention throughout this text.

A third note on declarations is the way in which variant records are declared. As shown in Figure A-3, the fixed portion of a record is written in essentially the same way in the two languages. However, the variant part of a record declaration is written slightly differently, as shown in the following example: first in Pascal and then again in Modula-2. Here, we assume the existence of the predeclared type "String" as it is given in Figure A-3.

```
var person: record
   name: String;
   address: String;
   case status: char of
   'e': (employer: String;
         years: integer);
   'u': (reason: String);
   'r': (age: integer;
         pension: real)
end;

VAR person: RECORD
   name: String;
   address: String;
   CASE status: CHAR OF
   'e': employer: String;
        years: INTEGER     |
   'u': reason: String     |
   'r': age: INTEGER;
        pension: REAL
   END
END;
```

The main differences here are the use in Modula-2 of the vertical bar (|) to delimit the different CASE alternatives (where Pascal uses parentheses) and the requirement of an explicit END at the end of the last CASE alternative.

A-3-1 File, Pointer, and Set Types

Three additional classes of entities that carry over from Pascal to Modula-2 deserve an introduction here. These are files, pointers, and sets. While we may declare variables in each of these classes in Modula-2, such a declaration carries different constraints and possibilities than its Pascal counterpart. Thus, the Pascal to Modula-2 analogy is more complex than a mere syntactic change would suggest. Below are some examples:

Declaration Class	Pascal Example	Modula-2 Example
file	**var** f: **file of** person;	VAR f: File;
pointer	**type** ptr = ^person;	TYPE ptr = POINTER TO person;
set	**var** colorset: **set of** color;	VAR colorset: SET OF color;

Here, "color" and "person" are assumed to have been declared as shown in a previous illustration. Now for the differences.

The word **file** in Pascal is a reserved word, while in Modula-2 its analogy (File) is a type, which is IMPORTed by the program from a standard system module. This difference suggests a far different treatment of input/output in Modula-2, and that is indeed the case. We resume the discussion of Modula-2 input/output in a later section of this appendix and then again in Chapter 9.

Pointer variables are the foundation for dynamic memory allocation and data structure management in Modula-2, just as they are in Pascal. Since the great majority of subject matter in this text deals with data structures, and since readers may not have substantial experience with pointers already, we introduce them carefully in Chapter 3 of this text.

The type SET in Modula-2 is somewhat more constrained in its generality than its counterpart in Pascal. Recall in Pascal that one could declare a set of *any* scalar type: **integer, real, Boolean, char**, scalar, or subrange. In Modula-2, a SET can only be composed out of members that are INTEGERs in the range $0..w-1$ (where w is the word size of the host computer that runs the program) or out of members taken from an enumeration type (like our example "color" above) with, at most, w values. Thus, if the computer's word size is 16 (a typical case), any SET variable may have at most 16 different members at one time. Finally, the standard type BITSET is predefined in Modula-2 to be equivalent to the following explicit declaration:

```
TYPE BITSET = SET OF [0..w—1];
```

This type and its use are discussed more fully in Chapter 2.

A-3-2 Procedure Types

A new feature of Modula-2 is its support of so-called "procedure types." That is, we can declare a variable of type PROCEDURE in styles suggested by the following examples:

```
VAR p: PROCEDURE (REAL): REAL;
    q: PROCEDURE (REAL, VAR REAL);
```

Here, p is a variable whose value may be any function procedure that has one REAL parameter and returns one REAL result, while q is a variable that may be assigned the name of any procedure that has two REAL parameters (the second one a "varying" parameter, in the Pascal sense). Having p and q thus declared, we may assign to them the names of different procedures during program execution, using ordinary assignment statements (with the constraint that none of the Modula-2 standard procedures—see below—may be assigned to p or q).

A-4 EXPRESSIONS AND ASSIGNMENT

Expressions in Modula-2 are formed using almost the same set of operators that are found in Pascal. A summary of the Pascal and Modula-2 arithmetic, Boolean, and relational operators is given in Figure A-4.

In this summary, the columns labeled "Priority" and "Operand Types" apply to the corresponding Modula-2 operators only. The column labeled "Priority" indicates the levels of precedence in Modula-2 that will govern the order of evaluation whenever two or more operators appear in the same expression. For instance, the higher priority of multiplication over addition explains why, in the expression a+b*c, the multiplication occurs before the addition.

As in Pascal expressions, Modula-2 expressions require the use of parentheses to override the order imposed by these predefined priorities. Thus, for example, the Modula-2 expression

```
(a<b) AND (b<c)
```

requires parentheses in order to force the "less than" operation < to occur before the conjunction operation AND, which has higher priority.

All Modula-2 operators are binary infix operators—except NOT, which is a prefix operator. Moreover, the operator <> may be equivalently substituted for # (a carryover from Pascal), ~ may be substitued for NOT, and & may be substituted for AND, anywhere within a Modula-2 program.

A more important note is Modula-2's stricter adherence to "strong typing" of operands for each operator. Specifically, *both* operands for an operator must be of the same type; we cannot even mix INTEGER and REAL operands, as we could in the following common Pascal expression:

```
x+1
```

Operation	Pascal Operator	Modula-2 Operator	Priority	Operand Types
equal, unequal	=, <>	=, #(or <>)	0	INTEGER, REAL, LONGINT, CARDINAL, subrange, enumeration, CHAR, SET, POINTER
less, greater	<,>	<,>	0	INTEGER, REAL, LONGINT, CARDINAL, subrange, enumeration, CHAR
less or equal	<=	<=	0	"
greater or equal	>=	>=	0	"
addition	+	+	1	INTEGER, REAL, LONGINT, CARDINAL, subrange
subtraction	−	−	1	"
disjunction	**or**	OR	1	BOOLEAN
multiplication	*	*	2	INTEGER, REAL, LONGINT, CARDINAL, subrange
division	/	/	2	REAL
	div	DIV	2	INTEGER, LONGINT, CARDINAL, subrange
remainder	**mod**	MOD	2	"
conjunction	**and**	AND	2	BOOLEAN
negation	**not**	NOT	3	"

Figure A-4 Pascal and Modula-2 operators and operands.

where x is a REAL variable. In this instance, we must force either REAL addition to take place (by saying "x+1.0") or INTEGER addition to take place (by saying "TRUNC(x)+1"). This second alternative is made possible by the availability in Modula-2 of the "standard procedure" TRUNC. This means literally to "truncate x to an INTEGER and add 1, with the result being an INTEGER."

Another example of the use of standard procedures to make both operands conform to the required type appears in the example program (at the beginning of the appendix) as follows:

```
av := sum / FLOAT(n)
```

If this explicit conversion had not been specified, a syntax error would have resulted, since the types of sum (REAL) and n (INTEGER) are not both the same (REAL in this case, which is a requirement for the division operator "/" to be properly applied).

As in Pascal, some of Modula-2's arithmetic operators can be applied to SETs. The following interpretations apply to variables s and t of type SET, and where x has the element type of the set s.

Expression	Meaning	Result Type
s+t	set union	SET
s−t	set difference	SET
s*t	set intersection	SET
s/t	set symmetric difference	SET
s=t	set equality	BOOLEAN
s<>t or s#t	set inequality	BOOLEAN
s<=t	improper subset	BOOLEAN
x IN s	set membership	BOOLEAN

The assignment statement in Modula-2 is similar in form, but not always in usage, to that of Pascal. It has one of the following two general forms in either language:

```
v := e
p := e
```

In the first form, "v" denotes a variable and "e" denotes an expression, and the type of the variable must agree with that of the result delivered by the expression. In the second form, the meaning in Pascal is that "p" names a function procedure in which this assignment statement appears and the assignment fixes a result to be returned by the function. Returning a result from a Modula-2 function procedure is accomplished, on the other hand, by the RETURN statement (see below). The Modula-2 usage of "p:=e" serves, however, to assign to a procedure-typed variable the name of a procedure.

It is important to note also that Modula-2 assignment statements may be used directly with character strings, such as the following:

```
s := 'Hello World!'
```

Here, the variable s must be of type ARRAY [0..n−1] OF CHAR, where n is no less than the length of the string 'Hello World!', or 12. Further discussion of the use of strings in Modula-2 appears in Chapter 7 of the text.

A-5 BASIC STATEMENTS

Aside from the assignment statement, Modula-2 has nearly the same collection of basic statements that appear in Pascal, as summarized in Figure A-5. In this summary, the notations v, e, and s denote variables, expressions, and statements, respectively. Moreover, p denotes a function procedure name, and l denotes a list of case labels in the Pascal sense.

The procedure statement in Modula-2 carries over directly from Pascal. Example procedure statements for input/output appear in the Modula-2 program at the beginning of this appendix. More discussion of programmer-defined procedures appears in a later section. On the other hand,

Statement Type	Pascal	Modula-2
assignment	v: = e p: = e	v: = e p: = e
procedure	p(a,a,. . .,a)	p(a,a,. . .,a)
go to	**goto** label	not available
compound	**begin** s;s;. . .;s **end**	not available

conditional	**if** e **then**
	  begin
	    s;s;. . .;s
	  end
		IF e THEN
		  s;s;. . .;s
		END

	if e **then**
	  begin
	    s;s;. . .;s
	  end
	else
	  begin
	    s;s;. . .s
	  end
		IF e THEN
		  s;s;. . .;s
		ELSE
		  s;s;. . .;s
		END

	not available	IF e THEN
		  s;s;. . .;s
		ELSIF e THEN
		  s;s;. . .;s
		ELSIF e THEN
		  s;s;. . .;s
		. . .
		ELSE
		  s;s;. . .;s
		END

case	**case** e **of**
	  l: s;
	  l: s;
	  . . .
	  l: s
	end
		CASE e OF
		  l: s;s;. . .;s
		  l: s;s;. . .;s
		  . . .
		  l: s;s;. . .;s
		ELSE
		  s;s;. . .;s
		END

while	**while** e **do**
	  begin
	    s;s;. . .;s
	  end
		WHILE e DO
		  s;s;. . .;s
		END

repeat	**repeat**
	  s;s;. . .;s
	until e
		REPEAT
		  s;s;. . .;s
		UNTIL e

Figure A-5 Summary of basic statements in Pascal and Modula-2.

Statement Type	Pascal	Modula-2

for	**for** v: = e **to** e **do**
	  begin
	    s;s;...;s
	  end
		FOR v: = e TO e DO
		  s;s;...;s
		END

	for v: = e **downto** e **do**
	  begin
	    s;s;...;s
	  end
		not available

	not available	FOR v: = e TO e BY e DO s;s;...;s END
loop	not available	LOOP s;s;...EXIT...;s END

with	**with** v **do**
	  begin
	    s;s;...;s
	  end
		WITH v DO
		  s;s;...;s
		END

Figure A-5 Summary of basic statements in Pascal and Modula-2.

the use of Pascal's compound statement has been eliminated in Modula-2, due to the simplification of syntax that occurs in other Modula-2 statement types listed in Figure A-5. In Modula-2 programming, the only BEGIN...END sequence that appears is that which encloses the main body of executable statements in the program itself. This is illustrated in the example program at the beginning of this appendix.

The "go to" statement of Pascal is not available in Modula-2. This reflects the strong position that such a statement is not needed, and moreover may be undesirable, as a programming construct at this level of language. Readers will use variants of the "go to" statement when they encounter assembly language programming in other courses.

Modula-2's conditional statement provides some additional variations beyond Pascal's, in order to accommodate certain control structures more directly. Note first that *every* variation of the conditional terminates with END, but that *no* variation requires a BEGIN. Thus, the need for the compound statement in this context is eliminated, just as it is for Modula-2's WHILE and FOR statements as well. Note that the WHILE and FOR statements in Figure A-5 also have an obligatory END as a terminator.

Returning to the Modula-2 conditional statement, note that the last variation is a significant extension beyond Pascal. The reserved word ELSIF means exactly what it suggests—**else if** in Pascal—except that much of the cumbersome syntax that would accompany this variation in Pascal (lots of additional **begin**'s and **end**'s) is eliminated. Also note that the ELSE part of this last variation is optional (but the final END is not!).

The "case" statement in Modula-2 carries over rather directly from Pascal, except that it too has an optional ELSE part. That part is executed whenever the value of expression e matches *none* of the case labels l that precede the ELSE. This change corrects a widely cited deficiency of Pascal.

The "while," "repeat," and "for" statements carry over directly from Pascal to Modula-2. Note that the effect of the **downto** option in Pascal is subsumed by the more general BY option in Modula-2. That is, the following Pascal and Modula-2 for statements are equivalent:

```
for i:=10 downto 1 do
   sum:=sum+A[i]

FOR i:=10 TO 1 BY -1 DO
   sum:=sum+A[i]
END
```

As an historical note, the BY option is a revitalization of the same from Algol, which preceded Pascal during the 1960s and early 1970s as the dominant language in computer science education.

An additional looping control structure is provided in Modula-2 by the LOOP and EXIT statements, whose general syntax is shown in Figure A-5. A LOOP statement is written to specify continuous repetition of a sequence of statements s;s;...;s, which can only be terminated by execution of an EXIT statement (of which there must be at least one) embedded within that sequence. The EXIT statement is written simply as EXIT and typically appears within a conditional, such as the following:

```
IF e THEN
    EXIT
END
```

Loops written in this way occur infrequently in programming situations; normally the WHILE, REPEAT, or FOR is preferable.

Finally, the "with" statement carries over directly from Pascal to Modula-2. It serves to eliminate the need for explicitly qualifying individual field references for a record variable within a block of code by enclosing that block completely by the WITH statement. For instance, suppose we have the record variable "person" as declared in section A-3. Individual fields of this record are normally referenced by

```
person.name
person.address
```

If we enclose the block of code that contains all such references by the WITH statement:

```
WITH person DO
END
```

then we may abbreviate all such references by omitting the qualification "person." and just write:

name
address

instead. The same strategy can be used for a record referenced by a POINTER variable, as illustrated in Chapter 3 and other chapters of this text.

A-6 PROCEDURE DECLARATIONS

Pascal has two different forms for defining an algorithm separately from the main program: procedures and functions. In Modula-2, these two forms are syntactically more unified, and they are called "proper procedures" and "function procedures," respectively. Their syntax is summarized in Figure A-6.

Most of Pascal's features for declaring procedures and functions carry over to Modula-2, except for simple syntactic variations. For instance, the reserved word **function** is not carried over; this distinction is instead made evident in Modula-2 by the presence or absence of a "type" specification in the PROCEDURE's heading line. Parameters are specified in exactly the same way in Modula-2 as they are in Pascal, with the reserved word VAR placed before all parameters whose values will be reassigned during procedure invocation. Also, note that a return of control out of a Modula-2 procedure is signaled by the RETURN statement. This statement has the additional role of returning a result for the function procedure, in which case its form is:

RETURN e

Pascal	Modula-2
procedure p (parameters);	PROCEDURE p (parameters);
declarations	declarations
begin	BEGIN
s;s;. . .;s	s;s;. . .;s;
end;	RETURN
	END p;
function p(parameters): type;	PROCEDURE p (parameters): type;
declarations	declarations
begin	BEGIN
s;s;. . .;s;	s;s;. . .;s;
p: = e	RETURN e
end;	END p;

Figure A-6
Procedure declarations in Pascal and Modula-2.

One fundamental difference between Pascal and Modula-2 procedures is in the way they handle array parameters. Recall that Pascal procedures and functions require strict matching between the array parameter and its corresponding argument, with respect to upper and lower bounds as well as element type. For instance, suppose a procedure Sort were defined to sort the 50-element array a. Then, its heading would be written in Pascal as follows:

```
procedure Sort (var a: array50);
```

where the type "array50" is assumed to have been declared as:

```
type array50 = array [1..50] of real;
```

All invocations of this procedure must provide as an argument an array of exactly 50 reals; to sort a different sized array requires additional programming of one kind or another.

In Modula-2, the so-called "open array parameter" permits more flexibility for procedures that have array parameters. There, the procedure does not have to commit to a constant pair of bounds for the array parameter, like 1..50 in the above example. Instead, the parameter is declared *without* bounds, as in the following:

```
PROCEDURE Sort (VAR a: ARRAY OF REAL);
```

When this is done, the array parameter a is assigned the bounds 0 and HIGH(a) by default. Here, HIGH is a Modula-2 standard function that delivers a value that is one less than the number of entries in the corresponding argument array in the invocation. Thus, the procedure can be invoked at different times with different-sized actual arrays as arguments. Further discussion and an example of Modula-2's open array parameter appear in Chapter 1.

A-7 STANDARD PROCEDURES AND FUNCTIONS

Recall that Pascal's standard procedures and functions fall into several categories; input-output procedures, dynamic storage procedures, type transfer procedures and functions, arithmetic functions, and predicates. We shall discuss the correspondence between Pascal and Modula-2 input-output procedures in the next section of this appendix. In this section, we summarize the corresponding Modula-2 procedures and functions in the remaining categories.

The Pascal procedures "new" and "dispose" are used for dynamic storage allocation, in conjunction with the implementation of linked data structures of various sorts: lists, stacks, queues, trees, and so forth. Modula-2 also provides these procedures through the standard module SYSTEM. We introduce these more systematically in Chapter 3 of this text.

The Pascal procedures "pack" and "unpack" are not supported in Modula-2, since they apply only to the **packed** option in the declaration of character strings. This option does not carry over to Modula-2.

The Pascal standard functions, together with their Modula-2 counterparts, are listed in Figure A-7. There, the last column indicates the system module from which certain of these Modula-2 functions can be IMPORTed (the rest are built into the language proper and need not be explicitly imported).

In Figure A-7, "x" denotes any number of appropriate type, "c" denotes any character, "t" denotes any type, and "a" denotes any array. The last eleven functions in this list are Modula-2 extensions, in the sense that they do not appear in Pascal at all. Among these, we have an example of

Function	Pascal Realization	Modula-2 Realization	Module for IMPORT
absolute value	abs(x)	ABS(x)	
square	sqr(x)	n/a	
sine	sin(x)	sin(x)	MathLib0
cosine	cos(x)	cos(x)	"
exponential	exp(x)	exp(x)	"
natural logarithm	ln(x)	ln(x)	"
square root	sqrt(x)	sqrt(x)	"
arctangent	arctan(x)	arctan(x)	"
successor	succ(x)	INC(x)	
predecessor	pred(x)	DEC(x)	
is odd?	odd(x)	ODD(x)	
truncation	trunc(x)	TRUNC(x)	
entier	n/a	entier(x)	MathLib0
round off	round(x)	n/a	
ordinal value	ord(c)	ORD(c)	
character value	chr(x)	CHR(x)	
capital letter	n/a	CAP(c)	
CARDINAL-to-REAL	n/a	FLOAT(x)	
INTEGER-to-REAL	n/a	real(x)	MathLib0
high index value	n/a	HIGH(a)	
maximum value	n/a	MAX(t)	
minimum value	n/a	MIN(t)	
type size	n/a	SIZE(t)	
ordinal value	n/a	VAL(t,x)	
add to set	n/a	INCL(s,x)	
delete from set	n/a	EXCL(s,x)	
stop execution	n/a	HALT	

Figure A-7 Pascal and Modula-2 standard functions.

the FLOAT function in the program at the beginning of this appendix. The function HIGH is used in procedures that have "open array" parameters, as explained above.

The next three functions—MAX, MIN, and SIZE—are used to describe characteristics of a particular type (like CARDINAL) for the implementation. MAX(CARDINAL), for instance, returns the maximum CARDINAL value for the implementation. The utility of these functions is illustrated more fully in Chapter 2 of the text.

The functions INCL and EXCL are primitive operators on sets. INCL(s,x) is the set resulting from addition of the element x to the set s. Thus, INCL(s,x) is equivalent to the assignment s:=s+{x}. Conversely, EXCL(s,x) is equivalent to the assignment s:=s−{x}.

A-8 TERMINAL INPUT/OUTPUT AND SEQUENTIAL FILES

The foregoing sample program gave a glimpse of the input-output statements that are usually needed in Modula-2 programming. In this section, we summarize the input-output features for handling text files in standard Pascal and introduce their counterparts in Modula-2. This introduction is continued in Chapter 9, since the complete collection of Modula-2 input-output features is far more extensive than that found in standard Pascal. Moreover, such features are generally not as well covered in a first course in computer science as they are in a second course.

Recall in Pascal that the type "text" is used to identify any "**file of char**" and that the two special text files named "input" and "output" are predefined by the system, so that they need not be explicitly declared. (That is the reason for their appearance in the header of a typical Pascal program, such as the one at the beginning of this appendix.) The file named "input" is permanently assigned to the terminal keyboard as the default input file, and the file named "output" is similarly assigned to the terminal screen for displaying output. The Pascal procedures "read," "write," "readln," and "writeln" are normally used to designate the transmission of information between the terminal and certain variables (expressions) in the program. These four procedures are also generic, because they take as arguments any mixture of types: real, integer, char, or (in the case of output) string.

In Modula-2, procedures for terminal input and output are provided through two of its so-called "standard system modules," known as InOut and RealInOut. Each of these is a small library of procedures, which must be explicitly accessed by any application program that needs them. To access such a library in Modula-2, one uses a so-called "IMPORT statement" at the beginning of the program, such as the two shown in the example program. There, the statements

```
FROM RealInOut IMPORT ReadReal, Done, WriteReal;
FROM InOut IMPORT WriteInt, WriteString, WriteLn;
```

access the system modules RealInOut and InOut, respectively. From RealInOut, the program declares that it will be using the procedures ReadReal and WriteReal, as well as the global Done. From InOut, the program will be using the procedures WriteInt, WriteString, and WriteLn.

As suggested by their names, Modula-2's procedures for input and output are not generic, as they are in Pascal. If we want to transmit a REAL value in Modula-2, we use the procedure ReadReal; if we want to transmit an INTEGER value, we use the procedure ReadInt instead. This convention is consistent with Modula-2's insistence upon strong typing throughout, especially in the area of procedure and parameter linkage.

A complete list of Pascal and Modula-2 terminal input-output procedures is given in Figure A-8. The Modula-2 procedures ReadReal and WriteReal come from the system module RealInOut, while all of the others come from the system module InOut. In this figure, the symbol "v" denotes any variable, "x" denotes any numeric expression, "c" denotes any CHAR value, "s" denotes any string value, and "n" denotes the number of significant digits in the output representation of a value. In the Modula-2 column, the variables "v" and expressions "x" must also have appropriate types. Another major difference between Pascal and Modula-2 input-output procedures lies in the number of arguments that they take. Pascal procedures generally allow any number of arguments, while Modula-2 procedures allow only one argument (and WriteLn permits none; i.e., it serves strictly as a line feed command). Thus, in Figure A-8, the notation "$v_1,...,v_k$" denotes any number k of variables for the Pascal read, readln, write, and writeln statements.

Note finally that the Pascal global "eof," which is used to signal the end of the input file, has as a counterpart in Modula-2 the (nearly equivalent) global "Done," which denotes literally that the last read or write was *done*

Function	Pascal (standard procedure)	Modula-2 (system module InOut or RealInOut)
input	read ($v_1,...,v_k$)	ReadInt (x)
		ReadCard (x)
		Read (c)
		ReadReal (x)
	n/a	ReadString (s)
	readln ($v_1,...,v_k$)	n/a
	eof	NOT Done
	eoln	CONST EOLN = 36C
output	write ($x_1,...,x_k$)	WriteInt (x,n)
		WriteCard (x,n)
		Write (c)
		WriteReal (x,n)
		WriteString (s)
	writeln ($x_1,...,x_k$)	WriteLn

Figure A-8
Terminal input and output in Pascal and Modula-2.

successfully.[1] However, this convention only applies to numbers, which are automatically converted from their input (character) representation to an appropriate internal representation. Thus, the Pascal conditional "while not eof do ..." can in many cases be systematically replaced by the Modula-2 conditional "WHILE Done DO . . .," as illustrated in the foregoing sample program.

A-8-1 An Overview of Files in Pascal and Modula-2

Data that comes from other locations than the terminal (usually disk files) may be accessed from a Pascal or Modula-2 program through their standard facilities. However, the nature of external file connection is different between these two languages, and these important differences must be fully understood for them to be effectively exploited.

Recall the essential steps whereby a Pascal program accesses information in a file. First, the program declares the file:

```
var f: file of type;
```

Here, "type" designates the type that is in common to each individual record in the file f. For instance,

```
var f: file of char;
```

declares f to be a file in which each entry is a single ASCII character. (This particular type, "file of char," is so common that it has the natural abbreviation "text." That is, we could have equivalently declared f by saying "var f: text;" instead.)

Second, the program initiates the physical connection between this file name f and the name of an actual file, say s, as it is stored on the disk. The name s is a character string, and its composition reflects the system's conventions for naming files. For instance, suppose we have a series of integers in a disk file named 'grades.dat' and we want to connect our program's file named f to this disk file for the purpose of reading its contents. Then we would use the Pascal procedure "reset" in the following way:

```
reset(f,'grades.dat')
```

---

[1] The use of Done does not cover all the cases of end-of-input for Modula-2 programming, particularly those cases where input is a character string (rather than a number). Fortunately, the module InOut provides the global CHAR variable named termCH, which always contains the ASCII value of the last character typed at the terminal keyboard. Thus, the simple convention of reserving the ASCII character 32C (ctrl-z at the keyboard) to indicate a "handshake" agreement between the program and the terminal operator will always provide a reliable basis for identifying end-of-input. The first program in Chapter 1, called NaiveInstructor, illustrates the use of this valuable convention.

If, instead, our program were intended to *create* that text file, rather than use it as input, then the following Pascal procedure statement would appear instead:

```
rewrite(f,'grades.dat')
```

Thereafter, the program performs individual input (or output) operations on the file by using the ordinary read and readln (write and writeln) procedure statements, just as if the input (or output) data were coming from (going to) the terminal. The form of these statements, however, is slightly altered because they must include the file name f as their first parameter. For instance, to read an integer x as input from the file f (connected to the disk file named 'grades.dat' by the above reset statement), one writes

```
read(f,x)
```

which is equivalent to the statement "read(x)" when the input is coming from the terminal.

Finally, when input or output processing of a file is completed, the program may use the "close" procedure to disconnect the program from the physical disk file. If this procedure is omitted from the program, the file will be automatically disconnected upon normal termination of the program.

The file processing facilities in Modula-2 are slightly different, and significantly more extensive, than those found in standard Pascal. Our discussion here, therefore, is only an introduction; further discussion of this important subject appears in Chapter 9.

A fundamental difference between Pascal and Modula-2 lies in the way they handle the standard terminal files. (These are called "input" and "output" in Pascal, and "in" and "out" in Modula-2.) When a Pascal program uses an auxiliary disk file, such as the file f in the previous example, the terminal files remain intact throughout that process. That is, we may read and write information at the terminal intermittently as we are reading and writing information in a disk file.

In Modula-2, we have a choice: either we may proceed as in Pascal (keeping the terminal open for input-output dialogue while we are intermittently reading and writing information in a disk file), or we may *temporarily suspend* terminal input (or terminal output) while we input (or output) the contents of a disk file and then resume normal terminal activities after this file has been completely processed. If we choose the former, our input (or output) procedures are imported from the system module named Files. If we choose the latter, our input (or output) procedures are taken from the system module InOut, along with the following four additional procedures:

- OpenInput(s) redirects input away from the terminal and connects all subsequent read statements to the file with system name s.

- OpenOutput(s) redirects output away from the terminal and connects all subsequent write statements to the file with system name s.
- CloseInput disconnects the program from the file and redirects all subsequent input to the terminal.
- CloseOutput disconnects the program from the file and redirects all subsequent output to the terminal.

The impact of each of these statements is shown graphically in Figure A-9.

To illustrate these points, the Modula-2 program below is a modification of the averaging program shown at the beginning of this appendix, in which the program now takes the numbers to be averaged from a user-specified disk file named "numbers.dat" rather than from the terminal directly. The name of this file (or any other file of numbers to be averaged, for that matter) is supplied in response to an appropriate prompt to the user.

```
MODULE Averager;
   FROM RealInOut IMPORT ReadReal, Done, WriteReal;
   FROM InOut IMPORT WriteInt, WriteString, WriteLn,
                     ReadString, OpenInput, CloseInput;
(*This program computes the average AV of N input
  numbers X. *)
VAR x, sum, av: REAL;
    n: INTEGER;
    s: ARRAY[1..14] OF CHAR; (*s is the input file's name. *)
BEGIN
   n:=0;
   sum:=0.0;
   WriteString('This program averages numbers in a
                disk file.');
   WriteLn;
   WriteString('Enter the name of the file:');
   ReadString(s); WriteLn;
```

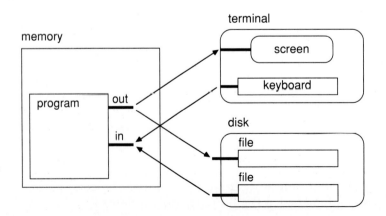

Figure A-9
Redirection of Files "in" and "out" in Modula-2.

```
    OpenInput(s);              (*Redirect input to file s.*)
    WriteString('Here are the numbers:'); WriteLn;
    ReadReal(x);
    WHILE Done DO
       WriteReal(x,10); WriteLn;
       n:=n+1;
       sum:=sum+x;
       ReadReal(x)
    END;
    CloseInput;                (*Redirect input to terminal.*)
    av := sum / FLOAT(n);
    WriteLn; WriteInt(n,10);
    WriteString(' numbers were given'); WriteLn;
    WriteReal(av,10); WriteString(' is their average');
    WriteLn
END Averager.
```

Note in this example that none of the input statements (ReadReal) are changed from the original program; they function the same way as they did before, except that they receive input from a different source than the keyboard. This kind of redirection is especially useful when testing or running a program that requires a large amount of input (or output) to be typed. Rather than retype it every time the program is run, we may instead type it once into a disk file and then redirect the program to that file every time we run the program.

A-9 ADDITIONAL MODULA-2 FEATURES

In this brief summary, we have introduced those elements of Modula-2 that correspond directly with the features of Pascal which the reader already understands. Moreover, we have begun to introduce facilities of Modula-2 that represent significant departures from Pascal. Notably, the IMPORT feature and the existence of several libraries of standard functions in Modula-2 suggest a much wider diversity of functional support than in standard Pascal.

Furthermore, we shall quickly see in Chapter 1 that Modula-2's MODULE concept permits programs to be dissected into smaller units, or groups of procedures, which may be independently compiled and archived into additional libraries. We use this essential feature throughout the text as our means of realizing "data abstraction" in Modula-2; this, too, is introduced quickly in Chapter 1.

Modula-2 contains many functional extensions beyond Pascal, and these will be introduced and illustrated at appropriate points throughout the text. For instance, the ability to access system-level information is explored and illustrated in Chapter 2. The ability to specify concurrently executing and communicating procedures is illustrated in Chapter 10. Modula-2's support for string manipulation and file manipulation is illustrated and developed in Chapters 7 and 9.

In all, we shall see that Modula-2 is a rich programming language: maintaining the expressive style and elegance of Pascal, on the one hand, and adding the power and versatility of a robust systems programming tool on the other. This text intends to help the reader to experience the adventure of Modula-2 programming, while at the same time mastering some additional principles in the study of computer science.

EXERCISES

A-1. Write Modula-2 statements that are equivalent to the following familiar Pascal code. Given coefficients a, b, and c, the following program segment finds solutions to the quadratic equation:

$$ax^2 + bx + c = 0$$

with a≠0. Assume here that the variables a, b, c, and d are REAL.

```
d := sqr(b) - 4*a*c;
if d<0 then
   writeln ('no solutions')
else if abs(d)<1.0E-8 then
   begin
      writeln('two identical solutions:');
      writeln(-b/(2*a))
   end
else
   begin
      writeln('two distinct solutions:');
      writeln((-b+sqrt(d))/(2*a));
      writeln((-b-sqrt(d))/(2*a))
   end
```

A-2. Write a Modula-2 function procedure AMAX that, using an open array parameter, returns the index i of the maximum CARDINAL value A[i] in that array. Assume that the number of integers in that array, say n, is given as an additional parameter, which may or may not be equivalent to HIGH(A).

A-3. Using the function AMAX defined above, write a Modula-2 program that inputs a series of CARDINAL values in random order and then displays them, one by one, in descending order on the screen. For example, if the input is:

43 21 36 57 54

then the output will be:

```
57 54 43 36 21
```

A-4. Reconsidering exercise A-3, create a data file of CARDINAL values and revise the program so that it will take its input from that file instead of the keyboard. Design appropriate prompts that will direct the program to the proper file.

A-5. Write a Modula-2 program that, IMPORTing the appropriate procedures from MathLib0, displays a table of trigonometric values for sin(x), cos(x), and tan(x) using a series of values of x between 0 and 2† at intervals of 0.4.

APPENDIX B

THE ASCII CHARACTER SET

The ASCII character set is summarized in the table below. The Modula-2 function ORD(c) returns the (decimal) byte value of ASCII character c, while the function CHR(x) returns the ASCII character whose decimal value is x.

Octal Byte Value

lefthand digit(s)	righthand digit(s)							
	0C	1C	2C	3C	4C	5C	6C	7C
0	nul	soh	stx	etx	eot	enq	ack	bel
1	bs	ht	lf	vt	ff	cr	so	si
2	dle	dc1	dc2	dc3	dc4	nak	syn	etb
3	can	em	sub	esc	fs	gs	rs	us
4	blank	!	"	#	$	%	&	'
5	(	)	*	+	,	−	.	/
6	0	1	2	3	4	5	6	7
7	8	9	:	;	<	=	>	?
10	@	A	B	C	D	E	F	G
11	H	I	J	K	L	M	N	O
12	P	Q	R	S	T	U	V	W
13	X	Y	Z	[	\	]	^	←
14	`	a	b	c	d	e	f	g
15	h	i	j	k	l	m	n	o
16	p	q	r	s	t	u	v	w
17	x	y	z	{			}	~	del

APPENDIX

MODULA-2 SYNTAX AND SEMANTICS

This is a complete summary of Modula-2 syntax, accompanied by some commentary on the related semantics. An introduction to this style of syntactic description is given in Chapter 4. In these BNF rules, the notation [] means "optional," {} means "0 or more occurrences," | means "or," juxtaposition of two words means "textual concatenation," and ::= means "is defined as." When any of the symbols [,], {, }, or | is part of the Modula-2 language itself, it is enclosed within quotation marks (") to denote this alternative usage.

In this presentation, we have taken the liberty to regroup, rearrange, and indent these BNF rules, in the interest of clarifying the hierarchy of syntactic and semantic ideas they represent. We hope that the result is both pleasant and useful as readers develop a mastery of Modula-2 syntax in the course of this study.

Minor changes in the syntax of Modula-2 occurred between the publication of the second and third editions of Wirth's *Programming in Modula-2* (Springer-Verlag, 1983 & 1985), which is the definitive reference for the language. The one key change is that the "export" part of a DefinitionModule is not allowed in the third edition, while it is required in the second edition. Throughout this text and the following syntax, we use the latter convention, since that is what our present compiler supports.

Readers who are using Modula-2 compilers that follow the third edition's conventions should systematically delete each instance of an "export" statement from every DefinitionModule that they write and ignore all such instances throughout this text. The third edition's change is based on the assumption that *every* constant, type, variable, and procedure that appears in the DefinitionModule is to be *automatically* exported—otherwise it wouldn't appear there at all. Thus, the use of an explicit "export" statement in a DefinitionModule becomes redundant.

C-1 MODULA-2 PROGRAMS AND COMPILATION UNITS

A Modula-2 main program, known as a ProgramModule, is a unit of code that can be separately compiled. A DefinitionModule, which can contain any collection of ProcedureHeadings, constant declarations, type declarations, and variable declarations, is also a separate compilation unit, as explained in Chapter 1. Every DefinitionModule has an associated implementation module, which gives complete ProcedureDeclarations for all of the ProcedureHeadings that appear in the DefinitionModule.

```
ProgramModule ::= MODULE ident [priority];
                  {import}
                  block ident.

CompilationUnit ::= ProgramModule                    |
                    DefinitionModule                 |
                    IMPLEMENTATION ProgramModule

priority ::= ''['' ConstExpression '']''

import ::= [FROM ident] IMPORT IdentList;
export ::= EXPORT [QUALIFIED] IdentList;

DefinitionModule ::= DEFINITION MODULE ident;
                     {import}
                     [export]
                     {definition}
                     END ident.

definition ::= CONST {ConstantDeclaration;}  |
               TYPE  {ident [= type];}       |
               VAR   {VariableDeclaration;}  |
               ProcedureHeading ;
```

Examples: For examples, see the discussions in Chapter 1, Appendices D and E, and Chapters 3, 5, 6, 7, and 8.

Note: In many Modula-2 compilers, the "export" part of a DefinitionModule is required. In others, it is prohibited. We assume the former throughout this text.

Note: A definition of the form "TYPE ident;" identifies a so-called "opaque type." As such, its declaration must be completed in the accompanying implementation module. Such specifications are thereby hidden from the view of the application program that imports that type.

C-2 BASIC ENTITIES IN MODULA-2 PROGRAMS

Modula-2 programs are constructed out of identifiers (ident), numbers, strings, and qualified identifiers (qualident). These are basic entities in a program and are described below.

```
ident      ::= letter {letter | digit}
number     ::= integer | real
integer    ::= digit {digit} |
               octalDigit {octalDigit} B |
               octalDigit {octalDigit} C |
               digit {hexDigit} H
real       ::= digit {digit} . {digit} [ScaleFactor]

ScaleFactor ::= E [+ | -] digit {digit}
digit       ::= octalDigit | 8 | 9
octalDigit  ::= 0 | 1 | 2 | 3 | 4 | 5 | 6 | 7
hexDigit    ::= digit | A | B | C | D | E | F
string      ::= ' {character} ' | " {character} "
qualident   ::= ident {. ident}
```

Examples: score, i, L, List, x, NaiveInstructor,
0, 65535,
177B, 36C,
012AH, 1010H,
−1.59, 0.112E−007
'Hello World!', "I'm here."
student.name

C-3 LISTS AND SEQUENCES OF ENTITIES IN MODULA-2 PROGRAMS

Lists of entities in a Modula-2 program are generally separated by commas (,), while sequences of entities are generally separated by semicolons (;).

```
IdentList      ::= ident {, ident}
ExpList        ::= expression {, expression}
CaseLabelList  ::= CaseLabels {, CaseLabels}
   CaseLabels  ::= ConstExpression [.. ConstExpression]

FormalTypeList ::= ([ [VAR] FormalType
                   {, [VAR] FormalType} ])
                   [: qualident]
```

```
FieldList           ::= [IdentList : type |
                        CASE [ident] : qualident OF
                            variant {"|" variant}
                        [ELSE FieldListSequence]
                        END]
   variant          ::= [CaseLabelList : FieldListSequence]

FieldListSequence   ::= FieldList {; FieldList}
StatementSequence   ::= statement {; statement}
```

C-4 EXPRESSIONS IN MODULA-2

We write arithmetic and other kinds of expressions in Modula-2 programs by following the syntax below.

```
expression          ::= SimpleExpression
                        [relation SimpleExpression]
   relation         ::= = | # | <> | < | <= | > | >= | IN
SimpleExpression    ::= [+ | —] term {AddOperator term}
   AddOperator      ::= + | — | OR
term                ::= factor {MulOperator factor}
   MulOperator      ::= * | / | DIV | MOD | AND
factor              ::= number | string | set          |
                        designator [ActualParameters]  |
                        ( expression )                 |
                        NOT factor

set                 ::= [qualident] "{"
                        [element {, element}] "}"
   element          ::= expression [.. expression]
designator          ::= qualident
                        { . ident | "[" ExpList "]" | ^ }
ActualParameters    ::= ( ExpList )
```

Examples: i+1
sum/FLOAT(HIGH(scores)+1)
(ilink<>NIL) AND (x>0.0)
NOT StringError

Note: The operators <> and # both mean "not equal."

C-5 DECLARATIONS IN MODULA-2

We can declare constants, types, variables, procedures, and modules within Modula-2 programs.

```
declaration ::= CONST ConstantDeclaration ;   |
                TYPE  TypeDeclaration ;       |
                VAR   VariableDeclaration ;   |
                ProcedureDeclaration ;        |
                ModuleDeclaration ;

ConstantDeclaration ::= ident = ConstExpression
   ConstExpression    ::= expression

TypeDeclaration ::= ident = type
   type ::= SimpleType  | ArrayType     |
            RecordType  | SetType       |
            PointerType | ProcedureType

SimpleType      ::= qualident | enumeration | SubrangeType
   enumeration  ::= ( IdentList )
   SubrangeType ::= [qualident]
                    ''[''ConstExpression .. ConstExpression'']''

ArrayType       ::= ARRAY SimpleType {, SimpleType} OF type
RecordType      ::= RECORD
                       FieldListSequence
                    END
SetType         ::= SET OF SimpleType
PointerType     ::= POINTER TO type
ProcedureType   ::= PROCEDURE [FormalTypeList]


VariableDeclaration  ::= IdentList : type


ProcedureDeclaration ::= ProcedureHeading ;
                         block ident
   ProcedureHeading  ::= PROCEDURE ident [FormalParameters]
   block             ::= {declaration}
                         [BEGIN
                            StatementSequence]
                         END
   FormalParameters ::= ( [ FPSection {; FPSection} ] )
                        [: qualident]
   FPSection        ::= [VAR] IdentList : FormalType
   FormalType       ::= [ARRAY OF] qualident

ModuleDeclaration ::= MODULE ident [priority];
                      {import}
                      [export]
                      block ident
```

C-6 STATEMENT TYPES IN MODULA-2 PROGRAMS

Statements in a Modula-2 program are of the following eleven varieties. The EXIT statement can be used only within a LoopStatement, for the purposes of terminating the loop. The RETURN statement is used only within the block of a ProcedureDeclaration (see above), and its optional expression may be used only when the procedure is a function procedure; that is, it returns a result to the invocation.

```
statement     ::= [ assignment      | ProcedureCall     |
                    IfStatement     | CaseStatement     |
                    WhileStatement  | RepeatStatement   |
                    LoopStatement   | ForStatement      |
                    WithStatement   | EXIT              |
                    RETURN [expression] ]

assignment       ::= designator := expression

ProcedureCall    ::= designator [ActualParameters]

IfStatement      ::= IF expression THEN
                         StatementSequence
                     {ELSIF expression THEN
                         StatementSequence}
                     [ELSE
                         StatementSequence]
                     END

CaseStatement    ::= CASE expression OF
                         case { | case}
                     [ELSE
                         StatementSequence]
                     END
    case ::= [ CaseLabelList : StatementSequence ]

WhileStatement   ::= WHILE expression DO
                         StatementSequence
                     END

RepeatStatement  ::= REPEAT
                         StatementSequence
                     UNTIL expression

ForStatement     ::= FOR ident := expression TO expression
                                 [BY ConstExpression] DO
                         StatementSequence
                     END
```

```
LoopStatement      ::= LOOP
                           StatementSequence
                       END

WithStatement      ::= WITH designator DO
                           StatementSequence
                       END
```

Note: The IF, WHILE, and FOR statements always require END's (unlike Pascal). Also, the FOR statement has an optional "BY clause," which allows the loop variable to increment or decrement by any constant value (not just $+1$ or -1, as in Pascal). The CASE statement provides an optional "ELSE clause," which is also not available in all versions of Pascal. The LOOP statement must contain an EXIT; that is the only way in which termination of the loop can be specified.

APPENDIX

MODULA-2
STANDARD
LIBRARY
DEFINITION
MODULES

This appendix summarizes the facilities provided in the essential Modula-2 standard library modules by listing their respective DEFINITION MODULES, along with brief descriptions of their constituent procedures' purposes in the form of preconditions and postconditions. This form of specification reinforces the notion that the standard library modules themselves ought to be viewed as implementations of abstract data types. As such, any of them can be reimplemented by the programmer to suit the need for refinements and/or extensions of the abstract definitions themselves. The development of such refinements and extensions is, however, beyond the scope of this text.

We note also that additional library modules are defined in Wirth's *Programming in Modula-2* (Springer-Verlag, 1985) and in the various implementations of Modula-2. However, such modules are not "standardized" at the present time, so we have decided not to try and document them in this text.

```
DEFINITION MODULE InOut;

EXPORT QUALIFIED EOL, Done, termCH, OpenInput, OpenOutput,
                 CloseInput, CloseOutput, Read, ReadString,
                 ReadInt, ReadCard, Write, WriteLn,
                 WriteString, WriteInt, WriteCard, WriteOct,
                 WriteHex;
```

```
CONST EOL=36C;          (*character that marks end-of-line, or
                          carriage return*)
VAR Done: BOOLEAN;      (*If executing any of the following
                          'Read' operators is successful, then
                          Done=TRUE; otherwise, Done=FALSE. *)
    termCH: CHAR;       (*the value of the next character
                          after the last character read by any
                          of the following 'Read' operators*)

PROCEDURE OpenInput (filename: ARRAY OF CHAR);
  (**PRE: input is at the terminal. **)
  (**POST: input is redirected to the file named
    'filename'. **)

PROCEDURE OpenOutput (filename: ARRAY OF CHAR);
  (**PRE: output is at the terminal. **)
  (**POST: output is redirected to the file named
    'filename'. **)

PROCEDURE CloseInput;
  (**PRE: input is not at the terminal. **)
  (**POST: input is redirected to the terminal. **)

PROCEDURE CloseOutput;
  (**PRE: output is not at the terminal. **)
  (**POST: output is redirected to the terminal. **)

PROCEDURE Read (VAR c: CHAR);
  (**PRE: c exists. **)
  (**POST: c'=the value of the next input character. **)

PROCEDURE ReadString (VAR s: ARRAY OF CHAR);
  (**PRE: s exists. **)
  (**POST: s'=the value of the next nonblank input
          string. **)

PROCEDURE ReadInt (VAR x: INTEGER);
  (**PRE: x exists. **)
  (**POST: x'=the result of reading the next nonblank
          input string and converting it to an INTEGER. **)

PROCEDURE ReadCard (VAR x: CARDINAL);
  (**PRE: x exists. **)
  (**POST: x'=the result of reading the next nonblank input
          string and converting it to a CARDINAL. **)
```

```
PROCEDURE Write (c: CHAR);
  (**PRE: c exists. **)
  (**POST: the value of c is displayed in the output. **)

PROCEDURE WriteLn;
  (**PRE: none. **)
  (**POST: the next line of output is initiated. **)

PROCEDURE WriteString (s: ARRAY OF CHAR);
  (**PRE: s exists. **)
  (**POST: s is displayed as output. **)

PROCEDURE WriteInt (x: INTEGER; n: CARDINAL);
  (**PRE: x and n exist. **)
  (**POST: x is displayed in the next n output positions. **)

PROCEDURE WriteCard (x,n: CARDINAL);
  (**PRE: x and n exist. **)
  (**POST: x is displayed in the next n output positions. **)

PROCEDURE WriteOct (x,n: CARDINAL);
  (**PRE: x and n exist. **)
  (**POST: the octal value of x is displayed in n
           positions. **)

PROCEDURE WriteHex (x,n: CARDINAL);
  (**PRE: x and n exist. **)
  (**POST: the hex value of x is displayed in n
           positions. **)

END InOut.



DEFINITION MODULE RealInOut;

EXPORT QUALIFIED Done, ReadReal, WriteReal, WriteRealOct;

VAR Done: BOOLEAN;    (*If executing the following 'Read'
                         operator is successful, then
                         Done=TRUE; otherwise, Done=FALSE.*)

PROCEDURE ReadReal (VAR x: REAL);
  (**PRE: x exists. **)
  (**POST: x'=the result of reading the next nonblank input
            string and converting it to a REAL. **)
```

```
PROCEDURE WriteReal (x: REAL; n: CARDINAL);
  (**PRE: x and n exist.**)
  (**POST: the value of x is converted to an n-character
          string and displayed as output.**)

PROCEDURE WriteRealOct (x: REAL; n: CARDINAL);
  (**PRE: x and n exist.**)
  (**POST: the octal value of x is converted to an
          n-character string and displayed as output.**)

END RealInOut.




DEFINITION MODULE FileSystem;

FROM SYSTEM IMPORT ADDRESS, WORD;
EXPORT QUALIFIED File, Response, Command, Flag, FlagSet,
          Create, Close, Lookup, Rename, SetRead,
          SetWrite, SetModify, SetOpen, Doio, SetPos,
          GetPos, Length, Reset, Again, ReadWord,
          WriteWord, ReadChar, WriteChar;

TYPE Response=(done, notdone, notsupported, callerror,
          unknownmedium, unknownfile, paramerror,
          toomanyfiles, eom, deviceoff, softparityerror,
          softprotected, softerror, hardparityerror,
          hardprotected, timeout, harderror);
     Command= (create, open, close, lookup, rename, setread,
          setwrite, setmodify, setopen, doio, setpos,
          getpos, length, setprotect, getprotect,
          setpermanent, getinternal);
     Flag=    (er, ef, rd, wr, ag, bytemode);
     FlagSet= SET OF Flag;
     File=    RECORD
               res: Response;
               bufa, ela, ina, topa: ADDRESS;
               elodd, inodd, eof: BOOLEAN;
               flags: FlagSet;
               CASE com: Command OF
                 create, open, getinternal:
                   fileno, versionno: CARDINAL
                 lookup:
                   new: BOOLEAN
                 setpos, getpos, length:
                   highpos, lowpos: CARDINAL
```

```
              setprotect, getprotect:
                wrprotect: BOOLEAN
              setpermanent, getpermanent:
                on: BOOLEAN
           END
        END;
```

```
PROCEDURE Create (VAR f: File; mediumname: ARRAY OF CHAR);
  (**PRE: f does not exist; mediumname is a valid medium
          name.**)
  (**POST: temporary file f exists for the duration
           of program execution, on the named medium.**)

PROCEDURE Close (VAR f: File);
  (**PRE: file f exists for the program.**)
  (**POST: file f does not exist; if f is a temporary file,
           it is also destroyed on the system.**)

PROCEDURE Lookup (VAR f: File; filename: ARRAY OF CHAR;
                              new: BOOLEAN);
  (**PRE: f does not exist, filename and new exist.**)
  (**POST: If new=TRUE and filename does not exist on the
           system, then a file with this name is created
           and f exists with this filename for the duration
           of the program.  If filename already exists
           on the system, then f exists with this filename
           for the duration of the program.**)

PROCEDURE Rename (VAR f: File; filename: ARRAY OF CHAR);
  (**PRE: f and filename exist**)
  (**POST: f is renamed to filename for the duration of the
           program; if filename='', then f becomes a
           temporary file**)

PROCEDURE SetRead (VAR f: File);
  (**PRE: f exists.**)
  (**POST: f is set for reading (ReadWord or ReadChar).**)

PROCEDURE SetWrite (VAR f: File);
  (**PRE: f exists.**)
  (**POST: f is set for writing (WriteWord or WriteChar).**)

PROCEDURE SetModify (VAR f: File);
  (**PRE: f exists.**)
  (**POST: f is set for reading and writing.**)
```

```
PROCEDURE SetOpen (VAR f: File);
  (**PRE: f exists. **)
  (**POST: any input or output operations on f are
          terminated. **)

PROCEDURE Doio (VAR f: File);
  (**PRE: f exists. **)
  (**POST: in conjunction with SetRead, SetWrite, and
          SetModify, Doio is used to read, write, or modify
          a file sequentially. **)

PROCEDURE SetPos (VAR f: File; highpos, lowpos: CARDINAL);
  (**PRE: f, highpos, and lowpos exist. **)
  (**POST: the currentposition of f is set to byte
          65536*highpos+lowpos. **)

PROCEDURE GetPos (VAR f: File;
                  VAR highpos, lowpos: CARDINAL);
  (**PRE: f exists. **)
  (**POST: highpos' and lowpos' are set to reflect the
          current byte position in file f, according to the
          formula given in the POSTcondition for SetPos. **)

PROCEDURE Length (VAR f: File;
                  VAR highpos, lowpos: CARDINAL);
  (**PRE: f exists. **)
  (**POST: highpos' and lowpos' are set to reflect the last
          byte position in file f, according to the formula
          given in the POSTcondition for SetPos. **)

PROCEDURE Reset (VAR f: File);
  (**PRE: f exists. **)
  (**POST: f is opened, and the current position is reset
          to its first byte. **)

PROCEDURE Again (VAR f: File);
  (**PRE: f exists. **)
  (**POST: backspaces the current position in f, so that
          the next ReadWord or ReadChar will return the
          same value again that it did the previous time. **)

PROCEDURE ReadWord (VAR f: File; VAR w: WORD);
  (**PRE: f and w exist. **)
  (**POST: w'=the value of the next word in file f. **)
```

MODULA-2
STANDARD
LIBRARY
DEFINITION
MODULES

```
PROCEDURE WriteWord (VAR f: File; w: WORD);
  (**PRE: f and w exist.**)
  (**POST: the value of w is appended to file f.**)

PROCEDURE ReadChar (VAR f: File; VAR c: CHAR);
  (**PRE: f and c exist.**)
  (**POST: c'=the value of the next character in file f.**)

PROCEDURE WriteChar (VAR f: File; c: CHAR);
  (**PRE: f and c exist.**)
  (**POST: the value of c is appended to file f.**)

END FileSystem.



DEFINITION MODULE MathLib0;

EXPORT QUALIFIED sqrt, exp, ln, sin, cos, arctan, real,
                 entier;

PROCEDURE sqrt (x: REAL): REAL;
  (**PRE: x>=0.0.**)
  (**POST: the square root of x is returned.**)

PROCEDURE exp (x: REAL): REAL;
  (**PRE: x exists.**)
  (**POST: the exponential of x is returned.**)

PROCEDURE ln (x: REAL): REAL;
  (**PRE: x>0.0.**)
  (**POST: the natural logarithm of x is returned.**)

PROCEDURE sin (x: REAL): REAL;
  (**PRE: x exists and represents an angle in radians.**)
  (**POST: the trigonometric sine of x is returned.**)

PROCEDURE cos (x: REAL): REAL;
  (**PRE: x exists and represents an angle in radians.**)
  (**POST: the trigonometric cosine of x is returned.**)

PROCEDURE arctan (x: REAL): REAL;
  (**PRE: x exists.**)
  (**POST: the arctangent, in radians, of x is returned.**)
```

```
PROCEDURE real (x: INTEGER): REAL;
   (**PRE: x exists.**)
   (**POST: the REAL value equivalent to x is returned.**)

PROCEDURE entier (x: REAL): INTEGER;
   (**PRE: x exists.**)
   (**POST: the INTEGER result of truncating x
            is returned.**)

END MathLib0.



DEFINITION MODULE Processes;

EXPORT QUALIFIED SIGNAL, StartProcess, SEND, WAIT, Awaited,
                        Init;

TYPE SIGNAL;

PROCEDURE StartProcess (P: PROC; n: CARDINAL);
   (**PRE: P and n exist.**)
   (**POST: start a process with procedure P and workspace
            size n.**)

PROCEDURE SEND (VAR s: SIGNAL);
   (**PRE: s exists.**)
   (**POST: send signal s.**)

PROCEDURE WAIT (VAR s: SIGNAL);
   (**PRE: s exists.**)
   (**POST: loop until signal s is sent by another
            process.**)

PROCEDURE Awaited (s: SIGNAL): BOOLEAN;
   (**PRE: s exists.**)
   (**POST: if at least one process is WAITing for s, then
            TRUE is returned; otherwise, FALSE is
            returned.**)

PROCEDURE Init (VAR s: SIGNAL);
   (**PRE: s does not exist.**)
   (**POST: s exists.**)

END Processes.
```

```
DEFINITION MODULE Storage;

FROM SYSTEM IMPORT ADDRESS;
EXPORT QUALIFIED ALLOCATE, DEALLOCATE, Available;

PROCEDURE ALLOCATE (VAR a: ADDRESS; size: CARDINAL);
  (**PRE: size exists. **)
  (**POST: a'=the address of a size-byte area, obtained
           from the system by the program. **)

PROCEDURE DEALLOCATE (VAR a: ADDRESS; size: CARDINAL);
  (**PRE: a and size exist. **)
  (**POST: the size-byte area a is returned to the system
           by the program. **)

PROCEDURE Available (size: CARDINAL): BOOLEAN;
  (**PRE: size exists. **)
  (**POST: if an area of at least size bytes is available
           to the program from the system, then TRUE is
           returned; otherwise, FALSE is returned. **)

END Storage.




DEFINITION MODULE SYSTEM;

EXPORT QUALIFIED WORD, ADDRESS, ADR, TSIZE, NEWPROCESS,
  TRANSFER;

TYPE WORD;
  ADDRESS=POINTER TO WORD;

PROCEDURE ADR (x: anytype): ADDRESS;
  (**PRE: x exists and may have any type. **)
  (**POST: the address of x is returned. **)

PROCEDURE TSIZE (anytype): CARDINAL;
  (**PRE: any type may be given as an argument. **)
  (**POST: the size, in words, of the given type is
           returned. **)
```

```
PROCEDURE NEWPROCESS (P: PROC; A: ADDRESS; n: CARDINAL;
                     VAR q: ADDRESS);
  (**PRE:  P, A, n, and q exist. **)
  (**POST: create a new process P, with workspace address
           and size A and n; q'=the address of process P. **)

PROCEDURE TRANSFER (a, b: ADDRESS);
  (**PRE:  a and b exist. **)
  (**POST: transfer control from the process at address a
           to the process at the address b. **)

END SYSTEM.
```

APPENDIX

ABSTRACT DATA TYPE DEFINITION MODULES

This appendix summarizes the abstract data type implementations for Lists, Stacks, Queues, Strings, and Binary Trees that are used throughout the text, by displaying their respective Modula-2 DEFINITION MODULES together with their respective defining preconditions and postconditions. The complete IMPLEMENTATION MODULES for these are separately available on a diskette, which is distributed by the publisher along with the Instructor's Manual for this text.

```
DEFINITION MODULE Lists;

EXPORT QUALIFIED List, ListElement, ListIndex, ListError,
            CreateList, Store, Retrieve,
            Insert, Delete, SearchList, ListSize,
            DisplayList, DumpList;

TYPE List;
     ListElement = INTEGER;
     ListIndex = CARDINAL;

VAR ListError: BOOLEAN;

(*In the following specifications, n denotes the size of
   list L, and Maxlist denotes an implementation-dependent
   constant that limits the maximum value of n for any list L.
```

When any of these operators is invoked and its precondition
is not met, the global ListError is set to TRUE;
otherwise, it remains FALSE. *)

PROCEDURE CreateList (VAR L: List);
  (**PRE: L does not exist. **)
  (**POST: L'=( ), n'=0, and ListError'=FALSE. **)

PROCEDURE Store (VAR L: List; i: ListIndex; x: ListElement);
  (**PRE: L=(e[1] e[2] ... e[i] ... e[n]), 0<i≤n, and
        x exists. **)
  (**POST: L'=(e[1] e[2] ... e[i−1] x e[i+1]
          ... e[n]). **)

PROCEDURE Retrieve (VAR L: List; i: ListIndex): ListElement;
  (**PRE: L=(e[1] e[2] ... e[i] ... e[n]) and 0<i≤n. **)
  (**POST: e[i] is returned. **)

PROCEDURE Insert (VAR L: List; i: ListIndex; x: ListElement);
  (**PRE: L=(e[1] e[2] ... e[i] ... e[n]), x exists, and
         0≤i≤n<Maxlist. **)
  (**POST: L'=(e[1] e[2] ... e[i] x e[i+1] ... e[n]),
          n'=n+1. **)

PROCEDURE Delete (VAR L: List; i: ListIndex;
              VAR x: ListElement);
  (**PRE: L=(e[1] e[2] ... e[i] ... e[n]), x exists,
         and 0≤i<n. **)
  (**POST: L'=(e[1] e[2] ... e[i] e[i+2] ... e[n])
          and n'=n−1. **)

PROCEDURE SearchList (VAR L: List; VAR i: ListIndex;
                 x: ListElement);
  (**PRE: L=(e[1] e[2] ... e[j] ... e[n]); i and x exist. **)
  (**POST: If e[j]=x for some j=1,...,n, then i' = the
          smallest such value of j. Otherwise, i'=0. **)

PROCEDURE ListSize (VAR L: List): CARDINAL;
  (**PRE: L=(e[1] e[2] ... e[i] ... e[n]). **)
  (**POST: n is returned. **)

PROCEDURE DisplayList (VAR L: List);
  (**PRE: L=(e[1] e[2] ... e[i] ... e[n]). **)
  (**POST: Output is of the form (e[1] e[2] ... e[n]). **)

```
PROCEDURE DumpList (VAR L: List);
  (**PRE: L=(e[1] e[2] ... e[i] ... e[n]).**)
  (**POST: Output is of the form (e[1] e[2] ... e[n]),
          followed by the values of n, Maxlist,
          ListError, and the memory addresses and
          hexadecimal representations of the elements
          e[i] in L.**)

END Lists.



DEFINITION MODULE Stacks;

EXPORT QUALIFIED Stack, StackElement, StackIndex, StackError,
                 CreateStack, Push, Pop, StackSize,
                 DisplayStack, DumpStack;

TYPE Stack;
     StackElement=INTEGER;
     StackIndex=CARDINAL;

VAR StackError: BOOLEAN;

(*In the following specifications, n denotes the size of
  stack S, and Maxstack denotes an implementation-dependent
  constant that limits the maximum value of n for any
  stack S.  When any of these operators is invoked and its
  precondition is not met, the global StackError is set
  to TRUE; otherwise, it remains FALSE. *)

PROCEDURE CreateStack (VAR S: Stack);
  (**PRE: S does not exist.**)
  (**POST: S'=(), n'=0, and StackError'=FALSE.**)

PROCEDURE Push (VAR S: Stack; x: StackElement);
  (**PRE: S=(e[1] e[2] ... e[n]), x exists,
         and 0<=n<Maxstack.**)
  (**POST: S'=(x e[1] e[2] ... e[n]); n'=n+1.**)

PROCEDURE Pop (VAR S: Stack): StackElement;
  (**PRE: S=(e[1] e[2] ... e[n]), and 0<n<=Maxstack.**)
  (**POST: S'=(e[2] ... e[n]), n'=n-1, and e[1] is
          returned.**)

PROCEDURE StackSize (VAR S: Stack): StackIndex;
  (**PRE: S=(e[1] e[2] ... e[n]).**)
  (**POST: n is returned.**)
```

```
PROCEDURE DisplayStack (VAR S: Stack);
  (**PRE: S=(e[1] e[2] ... e[n]).**)
  (**POST: Output is of the form (e[1] e[2] ... e[n]).**)

PROCEDURE DumpStack (VAR S: Stack);
  (**PRE: S=(e[1] e[2] ... e[n]).**)
  (**POST: Output is of the form (e[1] e[2] ... e[n]),
          followed by the values of n, Maxstack,
          StackError, and the memory addresses and
          hexadecimal representations of the elements
          e[i] in S.**)

END Stacks.



DEFINITION MODULE Queues;

EXPORT QUALIFIED Queue, QueueElement, QueueIndex, QueueError,
                 CreateQueue, Enter, Leave, QueueSize,
                 DisplayQueue, DumpQueue;

TYPE Queue;
     QueueElement=INTEGER;
     QueueIndex=CARDINAL;

VAR QueueError: BOOLEAN;

(*In the following specifications, n denotes the size of
  queue Q, and Maxqueue denotes an implementation-dependent
  constant that limits the maximum value of n for any queue
  Q.  When any of these operators is invoked and its
  precondition is not met, the global QueueError is set to
  TRUE; otherwise, it remains FALSE. *)

PROCEDURE CreateQueue (VAR Q: Queue);
  (**PRE: Q does not exist.**)
  (**POST: Q'=(), n'=0, and QueueError'=FALSE.**)

PROCEDURE Enter (VAR Q: Queue; x: QueueElement);
  (**PRE: Q=(e[1] e[2] ... e[n]), x exists, and
         0<=n<Maxqueue.**)
  (**POST: Q'=(e[1] e[2] ... e[n] x); n'=n+1. **)

PROCEDURE Leave (VAR Q: Queue): QueueElement;
  (**PRE: Q=(e[1] e[2] ... e[n]), and 0<n<=Maxqueue.**)
  (**POST: Q'=(e[2] ... e[n]), n'=n-1, and e[1] is
          returned.**)
```

```
PROCEDURE QueueSize (VAR Q: Queue): QueueIndex;
  (**PRE: Q=(e[1] e[2] ... e[n]).**)
  (**POST: n is returned.**)

PROCEDURE DisplayQueue (VAR Q: Queue);
  (**PRE: Q=(e[1] e[2] ... e[n]).**)
  (**POST: Output is of the form (e[1] e[2] ... e[n]).**)

PROCEDURE DumpQueue (VAR Q: Queue);
  (**PRE: Q=(e[1] e[2] ... e[n]).**)
  (**POST: Output is of the form (e[1] e[2] ... e[n]),
           followed by the values of n, Maxqueue, QueueError,
           and the memory addresses and hexadecimal
           representations of the elements e[i] in Q.**)

END Queues.




DEFINITION MODULE Strings;

EXPORT QUALIFIED StringIndex, StringError, LexClass, Eof,
                 Length, LT, EQ, LE, ReadString, ReadLex,
                 ClassifyLex, StrInt, StrReal, IntStr,
                 RealStr, SubString, InsertString,
                 DeleteString, SearchString, DisplayString,
                 DumpString;

(*All occurrences of ARRAY OF CHAR parameters below are to
  be interpreted as designating the type ''String.''  That
  is, the following type declaration is implicit throughout:

    TYPE String = ARRAY[0..Maxstring-1] OF CHAR; *)

TYPE StringIndex = CARDINAL;
     LexClass = (number,identifier,operator,other);

VAR Eof, StringError: BOOLEAN;

(*The operators CreateString and AssignString, which are
  defined in the Strings abstract data type, are not
  explicitly implemented in this module.  CreateString is
  realized by the application program in the process of
  declaring the TYPE String and its maximum length.
```

AssignString is provided by the Modula-2 language's
assignment statement, which directly supports the
assignment of strings. *)

(*In the specifications below, m and n denote the lengths of
strings s and t. Maxstring denotes an implementation-
dependent constant that is specified by the application
program. When any of these operators is invoked and its
precondition is not met, the global StringError is set to
TRUE; otherwise, it remains FALSE. *)

PROCEDURE SubString (VAR s,t: ARRAY OF CHAR;
                    i,j: StringIndex);
  (**PRE: s=s[1..m], t=t[1..n], and $0<i \leq j \leq m$. **)
  (**POST: t'=s[i..j], and n'=j-i+1. **)

PROCEDURE LT (s,t: ARRAY OF CHAR): BOOLEAN;
  (**PRE: s=s[1..m], t=t[1..n], and $0 \leq m,n \leq Maxstring$. **)
  (**POST: if there is an integer i, for which
          s[1..i-1]=t[1..i-1] and either $i=m+1 \leq n$ or
              $0 \leq i \leq m,n$ and ORD(s[i])<ORD(t[i]),
          then return the value TRUE. Otherwise, return
          FALSE. **)

PROCEDURE EQ (s,t: ARRAY OF CHAR): BOOLEAN;
  (**PRE: s=s[1..m], t=t[1..n], and $0 \leq m,n \leq Maxstring$. **)
  (**POST: if s[1..m]=t[1..n] and m=n, then return the value
          TRUE. Otherwise, return FALSE. **)

PROCEDURE LE (s,t: ARRAY OF CHAR): BOOLEAN;
  (**PRE: s=s[1..m], t=t[1..n], and $0 \leq m,n \leq Maxstring$. **)
  (**POST: if either LT(s,t) or EQ(s,t), then return the
          value TRUE. Otherwise, return FALSE. **)

PROCEDURE StrInt (s: ARRAY OF CHAR; VAR i: INTEGER);
  (**PRE: s=s[1..m], $m \geq 1$ and s[1..m] is a series of decimal
          digits, or $m \geq 2$ with s[1]=+ or - and s[2..m] a
          series of decimal digits.**)
  (**POST: i is the INTEGER value equivalent to s[1..m]. **)

PROCEDURE StrReal (s: ARRAY OF CHAR; VAR x: REAL);
  (**PRE: s=s[1..m], $m \geq 2$, and s[1..m] is a series of
          decimal digits including a decimal point, or $m \geq 3$
          with s[1]=+ or - and s[2..m] is a series of
          decimal digits including a decimal point.**)
  (**POST: x is the REAL value equivalent to s[1..m]. **)

```
PROCEDURE IntStr(i: INTEGER; VAR s: ARRAY OF CHAR);
  (**PRE: the INTEGER i exists.**)
  (**POST: s is the string value equivalent to the value
           of i.**)

PROCEDURE RealStr (x: REAL; VAR s: ARRAY OF CHAR);
  (**PRE: the REAL x exists.**)
  (**POST: s is the string value equivalent to the value
           of x.**)

PROCEDURE InsertString (VAR s,t: ARRAY OF CHAR;
                       i: StringIndex);
  (**PRE: s=s[1..m], t=t[1..n], 0<i<=m,
          and m+n<=Maxstring.**)
  (**POST: s'=s[1..i]t[1..n]s[i+1..m] and m'=m+n.**)

PROCEDURE DeleteString (VAR s: ARRAY OF CHAR;
                       i,j: StringIndex);
  (**PRE: s=s[1..m], and 0<i<=j<=m.**)
  (**POST: s'=s[1..i-1]s[j+1..m], and m'=m-(j-i+1).**)

PROCEDURE SearchString (s,t: ARRAY OF CHAR;
                       i: CARDINAL): CARDINAL;
  (**PRE: s=s[1..m], t=t[1..n], and 0<i<=m.**)
  (**POST: if there is a k, for which EQ(s[k..k+n-1],t) and
           i<=k, then return the smallest such k.
           Otherwise, return the value m+1.**)

PROCEDURE ReadString (VAR s: ARRAY OF CHAR);
  (**PRE: s exists.**)
  (**POST: s'=s[1..m'], where s[1..m'] is the next input
           sequence of characters entered, enclosed within
           quotes, and m'=the length of that sequence.**)

PROCEDURE HeadLex (VAR s: ARRAY OF CHAR);
  (**PRE: s exists.**)
  (**POST: s'=s[1..m'], where s[1..m'] is the next input
           sequence of characters entered, skipping all
           leading characters c for which ORD(c)<=ORD(' ').
           The end of that sequence is marked by a trailing
           occurrence of such a character c, and m' is the
           length of that sequence (excluding the
           trailing character).**)

PROCEDURE ClassifyLex (s: ARRAY OF CHAR): LexClass;
  (**PRE: s=s[1..m], and 0<=m<=Maxstring.**)
  (**POST: if s is a number, then return 'number';
           if s is an identifier, then return 'identifier';
```

               if s is +, —, *, /, or ^, then return 'operator';
               otherwise, return 'other'.**)

PROCEDURE Length (s: ARRAY OF CHAR): StringIndex;
  (**PRE: s=s[1..m] and 0<=m<=Maxstring.**)
  (**POST: return the value of m.**)

PROCEDURE DisplayString (s: ARRAY OF CHAR);
  (**PRE: s=s[1..m], and 0<=m<=Maxstring.**)
  (**POST: display the value s[1..m], enclosed within
           quotes.**)

PROCEDURE DumpString (s: ARRAY OF CHAR);
  (**PRE: s=s[1..m] and 0<=m<=Maxstring.**)
  (**POST: display the value s[1..m], enclosed within
           quotes, its length m, its lexical class, and the
           value of StringError.**)

END Strings.

DEFINITION MODULE Trees;

EXPORT QUALIFIED BinaryTree, TreeIndex, String, TreeError,
          ToWhere, CreateTree, DestroyTree, TreeStep,
          StoreTree, RetrieveTree, InsertTree,
          DeleteTree, TreeSearch, TreeBinarySearch,
          Graft, Prune, Balance, TreeSize, Depth,
          Height, DisplayTree, DumpTree;

TYPE BinaryTree;
     TreeIndex;
     String = ARRAY[0..20] OF CHAR;   (*Tree element type *)
     ToWhere = (toroot, toleft, toright, toparent);

VAR TreeError: BOOLEAN;

(*In the following specifications, n denotes the size of
  binary tree T, k indexes the current node, and Maxtree
  denotes an implementation-dependent constant that limits
  the maximum value of n for any binary tree T. When any
  of these operators is invoked and its precondition is not
  met, the global TreeError is set to TRUE; otherwise, it
  remains FALSE. The tree element type is assumed to be
  String throughout these specifications.*)

```
PROCEDURE CreateTree (VAR T: BinaryTree);
  (**PRE: T does not exist.**)
  (**POST: T'=(), n'=0, and TreeError'=FALSE.**)

PROCEDURE DestroyTree (VAR T: BinaryTree);
  (**PRE: T exists.**)
  (**POST: T does not exist.**)

PROCEDURE TreeStep (VAR T: BinaryTree; where: ToWhere);
  (**PRE: T=(r ... t[k] ... ), and where exists.**)
  (**POST: k' is reset to t[k]'s parent, left child, or
           right child, accordingly, as where=toparent,
           toleft, or toright. If where=toroot, then k' is
           reset to T's root.**)

PROCEDURE StoreTree (VAR T: BinaryTree; x: String);
  (**PRE: T=(r ... t[k] ... ), and x exists.**)
  (**POST: T'=(r ... x ... ); that is, T is unchanged,
           except that the current node t[k] is replaced
           by x.**)

PROCEDURE RetrieveTree (T: BinaryTree; VAR x: String);
  (**PRE: T=(r ... t[k] ... ), and x exists.**)
  (**POST: x'=t[k], and T is unchanged. That is, the value
           of the current node is assigned to x.**)

PROCEDURE InsertTree (VAR T: BinaryTree; x: String;
                      where: ToWhere);
  (**PRE: x exists, and one of T=() and where=toroot,
          T=(r ... (t[k] () ... )) and where=toleft, or
          T=(r ... (t[k] U () ... )) and where=toright.**)
  (**POST: If where=toroot, then T'=(x), n'=1, and t[k]'=T's
           root. If where=toleft, then
           T'=(r ... (t[k] x ... )), n'=n+1, and t[k]'=the
           new left child of t[k]. If where=toright, then
           T'=(r ... (t[k] U x ... )), n'=n+1,
           and t[k]'=the new right child of t[k].**)

PROCEDURE DeleteTree (VAR T: BinaryTree);
  (**PRE: T and t[k] exist.**)
  (**POST: If t[k] is a leaf, then it is deleted from T. If
           t[k] has no left subtree, then it is deleted from
           T and t[k]'s right subtree is reattached in place
           of t[k]. If t[k] has a left subtree, but no right
           subtree, then t[k]'s left subtree is reattached
           in place of t[k]. If t[k] has both left and right
           subtrees, then t[k]'s right subtree is reattached
           in place of t[k] and t[k]'s left subtree is
```

reattached to the first empty left child node
located in an inorder search of t[k]'s right
subtree. In any of these cases, t[k] becomes
undefined and n'=n−1. **)

PROCEDURE TreeSearch (VAR T: BinaryTree; x: String);
  (**PRE: T and x exist. **)
  (**POST: if there is a node t[j] in T for which
          EQ(t[j],x), and t[j] is the first such node that
          occurs in an inorder traversal of T, then the new
          current node is t[j] (that is, k'=j) and
          TreeError'=FALSE. Otherwise, k'=k and
          TreeError=TRUE. **)

PROCEDURE TreeBinarySearch (VAR T: BinaryTree; x: String);
  (**PRE: T and x exist, and T is a binary search tree. **)
  (**POST: if there is a node t[j] in T for which
          EQ(t[j],x), and t[j] is the first such node that
          occurs in a binary search of T, then the new
          current node is t[j] (that is, k'=j) and
          TreeError'=FALSE. Otherwise, k'=k and
          TreeError=TRUE. **)

PROCEDURE Graft (VAR T,U: BinaryTree; where: ToWhere);
  (**PRE: T=(r ... t[k] ...), U and where exist; where=
          toleft and t[k]'s left subtree is empty, or where=
          toright and t[k]'s right subtree is empty. **)
  (**POST: If where=toleft, then U is attached as t[k]'s
          new left subtree. If where=toright, then U is
          attached as t[k]'s new right subtree. In either
          case, U' becomes undefined.**)

PROCEDURE Prune (VAR T,U: BinaryTree; where: ToWhere);
  (**PRE: T=(r ... t[k] ...), U and where exist; where=
          toleft or where=toright. **)
  (**POST: If where=toleft, t[k]'s left subtree is removed
          and becomes the new value of U'. If where=
          toright, then t[k]'s right subtree is removed and
          becomes the new value of U'. **)

PROCEDURE Balance (VAR T: BinaryTree);
  (**PRE: T exists, and T is a binary search tree. **)
  (**POST: T' is a balanced binary search tree and has the
          same size and node values as T. **)

PROCEDURE TreeSize (T: BinaryTree): CARDINAL;
  (**PRE: T exists.**)
  (**POST: Returns the number of nodes, n, in T. **)

```
PROCEDURE Depth (T: BinaryTree): CARDINAL;
  (**PRE: T exists. **)
  (**POST: Returns the depth of the current node t[k]
          in T. **)

PROCEDURE Height (T: BinaryTree): CARDINAL;
  (**PRE: T exists. **)
  (**POST: Returns the height of the binary tree T. **)

PROCEDURE DisplayTree (T: BinaryTree);
  (**PRE: T=(r ... t[k] ... ) exists. **)
  (**POST: Displays the value (r ... t[k] ... ) of T, with
          the nodes given in an inorder sequence and
          parentheses inserted to show the proper depth for
          each node. **)

PROCEDURE DumpTree (T: BinaryTree);
  (**PRE: T=(r ... t[k] ... ) exists. **)
  (**POST: Displays the value of tree T vertically on the
          screen, with each node indented to indicate its
          depth, together with the value of T's current
          node t[k], T's size, height, ordering, balance,
          maximum size (Maxtree), and status of
          TreeError. **)

END Trees.
```

INDEX

Abelson, Harold, 338
Abstract data type, 2, 50
Abstraction, 9, 15, 50
ACC (*see* Accumulator)
Accumulator, 27, 28, 31
ACM, 311, 335
   Computing Reviews, 313
   CR Categories, 313
   Graduate Assistantship Directory, 335
Ada (*see* programming languages)
ADABAS, 292
Address space, 282
ADDRESS type, 33, 37
Addressing, 24, 28, 30
   secondary storage, 282, 283
Adt (*see* Abstract data type)
Advanced Instructor's Problem, 21, 84, 281, 298–306, 309
Advanced Registrar's Problem, 281, 309
Aho, Alfred, 338
AI (*see* Artificial intelligence)
ALLOCATE (*see* NEW)
Analysis (*see* Complexity)
Ancestor, 221
Architecture, 321
   (*see also* Computer organization)
Arithmetic expression, 370
   tree, 223, 240, 265

Artificial intelligence, 92, 111, 272, 333
ASCII, 30, 37, 366
Assertion, 16
Assign operator, 183, 189
Association for Computing Machinery (*see* ACM)
Average case, 72, 124, 203

Backtracking, 222, 248, 249
Backus-Naur Form (*see* BNF)
Balance operator, 222, 237, 253, 258
Balanced (*see* Binary search tree)
Best case, 72, 124
Binary search, 66, 110, 222, 234, 251
Binary search tree, 223–225
   balanced, 224, 226, 254
Binary tree, 217, 222
Binomial coefficients, 101
Bit-mapped graphics, 326
BITSET type, 38, 39, 348
Block, 283
Blocksize (*see* file)
BNF, 112, 113, 261, 264, 367
Booch, Grady, 339
Bottom-up design (*see* Design)
Branch, 218
Breadth-first (*see* Traversal)

395

Bubble sort (*see* Sort)
Buffer (*see* File)
Buffer pool, 323
Byte, 30

C (*see* Programming languages)
Case, 347
Child, 220
Chomsky, Noam, 112
Church, Alonzo, 26
Church's thesis, 26, 92
Circular linked implementation of lists, 90
ClassifyLex operator, 163, 188, 195
Closed form (*see* Function definition)
Closing a file (*see* File, Close operator)
Clustering, 308
COBOL (*see* Programming languages)
CODASYL model, 292
Code generation, compiler, 260, 262, 263
Coercion, 8
Cognitive science, 333
Collision, 294, 295, 302, 308
Combinatorial explosion, 274, 333
Comment, 16
Communications of the ACM, 335
Compile step, 11
Compiler, 260, 329
Complexity, 20
  classes, 320
  of list operator implementations, 71, 83
  of priority queue operator implementations, 176
  of queue operator implementations, 171
  of stack operator implementations, 155
  of string operator implementations, 203
  of tree operator implementations, 260
Computer magazine, 335
Computer organization, 32, 156
Computer science, 1, 311–318, 334
Concurrency, 322
  producer-consumer model, 323
Contiguous implementation of lists, 61
Control, 25, 27
Correctness, 18
  (*see also* Verification)
Counting change, 105
Create operator, 54, 57, 62, 75, 150, 167, 183, 222, 231, 241
Current node
  binary tree, 228, 230
  linear list, 74
Curriculum standards, 311–313
Cycle, 44

Data processing, 327
Database, 291
Database design, 309
Database management system, 208, 281, 291
  hierarchical, 291
  network, 291
  query, 291, 330
  relational, 291
DBMS (*see* Database management system)
DEALLOCATE (*see* DISPOSE)
Declarations, 371
DEFINITION MODULE, 10, 368
Delete operator, 55, 57, 187, 199, 222, 233, 244, 247
Denning, Peter, 312
Depth operator, 222, 238
Depth-first (*see* Traversal)
Descendent, 221
Design (*see* Software life cycle)
  bottom-up, 271
  object-oriented, 271, 272
  top-down, 271
Destroy operator, 89, 222, 231, 241
Deterministic, 320
Digital VAX computer, 29, 31
Dining Philosophers' Problem, 337
Display operator, 55, 57, 64, 81, 151, 167, 189, 222, 238
DISPOSE, 59
Divide and conquer, 66, 105, 106, 121, 135
Double-linked implementation of lists, 90
Driver, 19, 33, 45, 68

Dump operator, 55, 57, 64, 81, 151, 167, 189, 222, 238
Dynamically linked structures, 51, 73, 74

EBCDIC, 30
Edge, 218
Efficiency (see Complexity)
English, 328
Enter operator, 167, 169, 175
EQ operator, 185
Error
  analysis, 331
  global variable, 53, 150, 166, 182, 222
  propagated, 331
  representation, 331
EvaluatePolish module, 164–165
Execution step, 11
Expert systems, 274

Family tree, 220
Fibonacci, Leonardo, 98, 117
Fibonacci numbers, 98
File, 280, 281, 284
  abstract data type, 281
  blocksize, 287
  buffer, 282
  close operator, 282, 285
  create operator, 285
  flat, 291
  GetPos operator, 287
  lookup operator, 285
  Modula-2, 348, 362
  open operator, 282
  Pascal, 348, 360
  random access, 281, 282, 293
  seek operator, 282
  sequential access, 282, 287
  SetModify operator, 296
  SetPos operator, 296
  SetRead operator, 296
  SetWrite operator, 296
FileSystem module, 283, 377
Flat (see File)
Floating point register, 27, 28, 31
FORTRAN (see Programming languages)

Function definition
  closed form, 97, 102, 104, 116
  iterative, 97, 100, 104
  Pascal, 355
  recursive, 104 (see also Recursive functions)
Functional programming, 275

GapSort (see Sort)
Gaussian elimination, 332
GCD (see Greatest common divisor)
General purpose register, 27, 28, 31
Generics, 58, 86, 212, 270
GetPos operator (see File)
Ghezzi, Carlo, 339
Gibbs, Norman, 312
Go to statement, 341, 344, 353
Golden ratio, 99, 103, 117
Graft operator, 222, 236, 252
Graph, 319, 336
  operators, 336
Greatest common divisor, 103
Grep (see Regular expression)
Gries, David, 16, 339

Halting problem, 321
Hashing, 281, 283, 293, 294
Heap, 139
Heapsort (see Sort)
Height, 220
  operator, 222, 238
Hexadecimal, 30
High level language, 260
Hoare, C.A.R., 135
Hofstadter, Douglas, 339
Horowitz, Ellis, 320
Human interface, 326, 328

IBM 3081 computer, 29, 31
Identifier, 206, 369
IEEE Computer Society, 311, 335
Implementation (see Software life cycle)
IMPLEMENTATION MODULE, 10
Implementation of lists (see contiguous, linked, double linked, circular linked)

Import, 8
IMPORT statement, 343
Import-export trees (*see* trees)
IMS, 291
Induction, 98, 115
Information retrieval, 309
Information systems, 207
INGRES, 292, 330
Inorder (*see* Traversal)
InOut module, 283, 374
Input tape, 25, 27
Input-output
  Modula-2, 359
  Pascal, 359
  redirection of, 362
Insert operator, 54, 57, 63, 78, 187, 197, 222, 232, 243, 245
Insertion sort (*see* Sort)
Installation and testing (*see* Software life cycle)
Institute for Electrical and Electronic Engineers (*see* IEEE)
Instruction register, 27, 28, 31
Intel 8088 computer, 29, 31
Interpolation, 332
Interpreter, 329, 330
IntStr operator, 187
Invariant, 17, 18
IR (*see* Instruction register)
Iterative (*see* Function definition)

Jazayeri, Mehdi, 339
Job queue, 178
Job scheduling, 178, 180

Key, 293
Knowledge
  acquisition, 333
  representation, 333
Knuth, Donald, 42, 43, 103, 121, 128, 293, 308, 339
Korth, Henry, 339

LE operator, 185
Leaf, 218
Leave operator, 167, 170, 175
Lehman, D.H., 43
Length operator, 188, 193
Less Naive Instructor's Problem, 84, 91
Lewis, Harry, 339
LexClass, 163
Lexical analysis, compiler, 260, 261
Lexical class (*see* LexClass)
Library information retrieval systems, 207, 208–210
Library module, 34, 62
Linear congruential method, 43
Linear list, 52, 57
Link step, 11, 12
Linked implementation of lists, 74
LISP (*see* Programming languages)
List (*see* Linear list)
ListDriver module, 68
Lists module, 384
LONGCARD type, 40, 44
Loop
  Modula-2, 354
  Pascal, 354
Lotus 1-2-3, 328
LowLevelDriver module, 33
LT operator, 184, 193
Lukasiewicz, 159

McCorduck, Pamela, 333, 339
McGill, Michael, 339
Machine instruction, 28, 31
Machine level language, 260
MACSYMA, 274
Main program module, 368
Maintenance (*see* Software life cycle)
Management information systems, 207
MAR (*see* Memory address register)
Mathematical optimization, 333
Mathematical programming, 331, 332
MathLib0 module, 380
Maxlist, 53, 75
Maxqueue, 166, 168
Maxstack, 150, 152
Maxstring, 182
Memory, 27, 28, 281
Memory address register, 27, 28, 31
Merge sort (*see* Sort)
Middle square method, 43
MIS (*see* Management information systems)

MiscLib module, 34, 62
Modula-2 (*see* Programming languages)
Module, 8, 323, 343, 371
Monitor, 323
Mouse, 328
MYCIN, 274

Naive Instructor's Problem, 3
Naive Registrar's Problem, 22
Natural languages
   translation, 329
   understanding, 274, 329
Needs analysis (*see* Software life cycle)
Network, 292
NEW, 59
Newton's method, 332
NIL pointer value, 60
Node
   binary tree, 238
   linear list, 72, 75
   tree, 217
Nondeterministic, 320
NP, 320
Numbers, 369
Numerical linear algebra, 332

Object-oriented design (*see* Design)
Opaque type, 13
Open array parameter, 9, 356
Opening a file (*see* File, open operator)
Operand, 28
Operating systems, 171–174, 326
Operators
   Modula-2, 350
   Pascal, 350
   priority, 349
   set, 351
Optimization, compiler, 260, 262
Order of complexity, 20
Ordering, 66
   strings, 184
   tree, 218
Output tape, 25, 27

P, 320
Papadimitriou, Christos, 339

Parent, 221
Parse tree (*see* Tree)
Parsing
   arithmetic expressions, 263, 273
   compiler, 260, 261, 262
   precedence, 264
   regular expressions, 279
Pascal (*see* Programming languages)
Path, 220
   length, 220
PC (*see* Program counter)
PDP-8 computer, 27–29
Peterson, James, 339
Peterson's Guide, 335
Pointer type, 59, 73
   Modula-2, 348
   Pascal, 348
Polish expression, 159, 160, 161, 162, 228
   evaluation, 164–165
Polynomial evaluation, 100
Pop operator, 150, 154
Postcondition, 17, 18
Postfix notation (*see* Polish expression)
Postorder (*see* Traversal)
Power function, 180
Precedence parsing (*see* Parsing)
Precision, extended, 332
Precondition, 17, 18
Preorder (*see* Traversal)
Primary storage (*see* Memory)
Prime numbers, 104
Priority (*see* Operators)
Priority queue, 175
Procedure, 371
   Modula-2, 355
   parameters, 144, 147
   Pascal, 355
   type, 349
Process, 322
Processes module, 323, 381
Producer-consumer model (*see* Concurrency)
Program counter, 27, 28, 31
Programming languages
   Ada, 326
   BASIC, 329, 330
   C, 213, 326
   COBOL, 326, 328
   FORTRAN, 326

Programming languages, (continued)
   LISP, 92, 111, 275, 276, 326, 329,
      330, 333
   Modula-2, 2, 6, 341
   Pascal, 2, 341
   PROLOG, 326, 329, 330
Prune operator, 222, 237, 253
Push operator, 150, 153

Qualified names, 354
QUEL, 330
Query (see Database)
Queue, 149, 166
Queues module, 387
Quicksort (see Sort)

RAM (see Random access memory)
Random access file (see File)
Random access memory, 28
Random numbers, 43, 44, 45
RandomDriver module, 45
Read operator, 188
ReadChar, 285
ReadLex operator, 162, 163, 188, 194
ReadWord, 285
Read-write head, 25
RealInOut module, 376
RealStr operator, 187
Record, 281, 371
   Modula-2, 219, 347
   Pascal, 347
Recursion, 92
  graphical display, 96, 99, 102
  inorder traversal, 250
Recursive functions, 93, 94, 96, 97, 98,
    100, 102, 105, 107, 109, 112, 114
Recursive procedures (Modula-2), 95,
    99, 102, 103, 108, 133, 137
Register, 27, 28, 31
Regular expression, 204–205
  parsing (see Parsing)
  UNIX (grep), 206
Reserved words
  Modula-2, 345
  Pascal, 345
Retrieve operator, 54, 57, 63, 78, 222,
    231, 242

Rich, Elaine, 333, 339
Root, 217
Round-robin scheduling, 118
Run-time stack, 156

Sahni, Sartaj, 320, 339
Salton, Gerald, 339
Scientific programming, 326
Scientific Subroutine Package, 50
Search, 274
  operator, 55, 57, 65, 79, 109, 188,
    200, 222, 234, 251
Searle, John, 333
Secondary storage, 280, 281
Sedgewick, Robert, 340
Seek file operator (see File)
Selection sort (see Sort)
SEND operator, 322
Sequential access file (see File)
Serial search (see Search operator)
Set
  expressions, 370
  operators, 351
  type, Modula-2, 348
  type, Pascal, 348
SetPos operator (see File)
Shell, Donald, 126
Shell sort (see Sort)
Sibling, 220
Signal, 322
Silberschatz, Abraham, 339
Sincovec, Richard, 340
Size operator, 55, 57, 64, 80, 151, 167,
    222, 224, 238
Software engineering, 270
Software life cycle, 270
Sort operator, 121
  bubble, 146
  complexity, 124, 126, 128, 134, 138,
    142, 143
  GapSort, 128
  hcapsort, 140
  insertion, 125, 126
  merge, 129, 133
  quicksort, 135, 137
  selection, 121, 123
  Shell, 126, 128
Specifications (see Software life cycle)

Spreadsheet, 328
SSP (*see* Scientific Subroutine Package)
Stack, 149, 150
  backtrack, 248, 249
  machine, 92, 157–158
  operators, 265, 266, 269
Stacks module, 386
Standard functions
  Modula-2, 357
  Pascal, 357
State transition function, 25
Statement types, 352, 353, 372
Step operator, 222, 231, 241
Storage module, 59, 382
Store operator, 54, 57, 63, 77, 222, 231, 242
String, 162, 181, 182
  assignment operator, 351
  empty, 182
Strings module, 369, 388
StrInt operator, 163, 186, 197
StrReal operator, 186
Substring, 183
  operator, 183, 193
Subtree, 218, 222, 223
Sussman, Gerald, 338
Syntactic analysis (*see* Parsing)
Syntax of Modula-2, 367ff
SYSTEM module, 32, 286, 382
System R, 292
System 2000, 291
Systems programming, 327

Tanenbaum, Andrew, 340
TAUM-METEO, 329
Team programming, 9
Team projects, 91, 147, 180, 216, 279, 309
Text editor, 216
Top-down design (*see* Design)
TOTAL, 292
Towers of Hanoi, 106
Traversal
  backtracking, 248, 249

breadth-first, 221
depth-first, 221
inorder, 228, 229, 247, 249
postorder, 228, 229
preorder, 228, 229
Tree, 53, 217, 218
  import-export, 272, 273
  parse, 264, 265, 269
  structure of LISP programs, 276
Trees module, 389
Turing, Alan, 24
Turing machine, 24, 25, 92
Types, 371
  Modula-2, 346
  Pascal, 346

Ullman, Jeffrey, 340
Universal Turing machine, 26
UNIX 50, 330
Unsolvability, 321

Verification (informal), 15, 18
  of list operator implementation, 69, 82
  of stack operator implementation, 155
  of string operator implementation, 201
  of tree operator implementation, 259
VLSI design, 321
von Neumann, John, 24, 27, 43

WAIT operator, 322
Weiner, Richard, 340
Wilks, Yorick, 274
Williams, J.W.J., 139
Window, 328
Winograd, Terry, 274
Wirth, Niklaus, 6, 340
Word, 30
Workstation, 326
Worst case, 72, 124
WriteChar, 286
WriteWord, 286